Bridging Paradox with Interfaces

Mariyak

Contents

1. Fundamental concepts of wetting

"The force exerted on the solid surface is logarithmically infinite: not even Herakles could sink a solid if the physical model were entirely valid, which it is not." [HS71, p. 94]

This famous statement by Huh and Scriven in their seminal paper on the moving contact line problem [HS71] marks the starting point of a history of research lasting for almost 50 years. The so-called "moving contact line paradox" refers to the observation that the classical no-slip condition at solid boundaries – a cornerstone of fluid mechanics – seems to be incompatible with dynamic wetting phenomena. By the term "dynamic wetting", we usually mean the motion of a droplet in a surrounding gas or a bubble in an ambient liquid along a solid boundary.

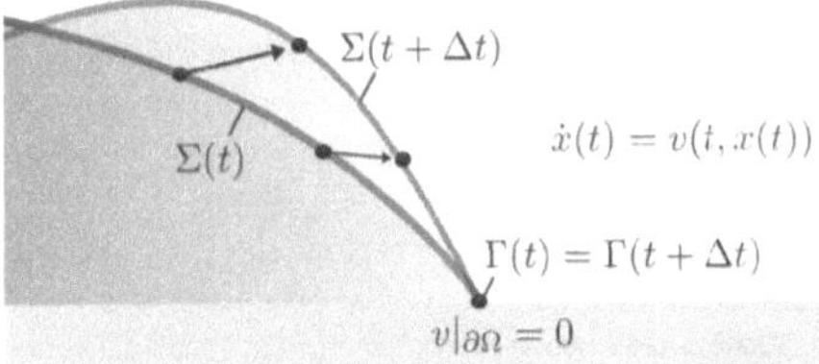

Figure 1.1.: Kinematics of wetting with no-slip.

The moving contact line paradox: The essence of the paradox can be easily described in terms of the pure *kinematics* of the flow, i.e. without considering the details of the forces acting on the fluid particles. In the class of "sharp interface" continuum mechanical models, the fluid-fluid interface is modeled as a mathematical hypersurface with zero thickness. In the simplest setting, the hypersurface is a "material surface" for the flow, i.e. it can be described by a collection of marker particles that stay on the moving interface $\Sigma(t)$ while being transported with the flow according to the ordinary differential equation

$$\dot{x}(t) = v(t, x(t)). \tag{1.1}$$

Here, v is the fluid (bulk) velocity, which is assumed to be continuous across the moving interface while its derivatives may jump at the moving interface (see Chapter 3 for the details on the mathematical modeling). Provided that v is locally Lipschitz continuous and satisfies the Dirichlet ("no-slip") boundary condition

$$v|_{\partial\Omega} = 0, \tag{1.2}$$

it is clear that (1.1) is locally well-posed[1]. Physically, the local Lipschitz continuity of the velocity field in the respective phases is related to the phenomenon of viscous dissipation of energy[2]. So, the obvious problem is that – provided that v obeys the regularity described above – a marker particle located at the "contact line" $\Gamma(t)$, i.e. the line of intersection of the free surface and the solid boundary, stays at rest and the contact line as a whole cannot move; see Figure 1.1. Since this property of the solution is clearly incompatible with experimental observations, there must be some modification to either the model or the solution concept or a combination of both. The quote above by Huh and Scriven refers to a hypothetical generalized "solution" of the problem which, however, predicts

---

[1] Note that the well-posedness of (1.1) has been proven recently in a much more general setting including mass transfer across the interface [Bot20b].

[2] In fact, the rate of viscous dissipation in the bulk is proportional to $\int_{\Omega\setminus\Sigma} D : D\,dV$, where $D = \frac{1}{2}(\nabla v + \nabla v^{T})$ is the rate-of-deformation tensor (see Section 3.2). Hence, the Lipschitz continuity of v is a sufficient (albeit not necessary) condition for a finite viscous dissipation rate.

an infinite force to move the contact line.

A generalization of the solution concept, i.e. the required regularity of the solution, leads to the study of hydrodynamic singularities of different kinds at the moving contact line. The physical implications of singularities at the moving contact line are discussed controversially in the scientific literature. Eggers and Fontelos understand singularities as "the fingerprint of a nonlinear PDE" since the structure of the singularity "is universal, i.e. independent of the initial or boundary conditions imposed over macroscopic distances" [EF15, p.4]. The latter perspective motivates to study the singularity itself in great detail to explore the physics of the process. The monograph by Eggers and Fontelos [EF15] provides an introduction to that line of research applied to various phenomena in hydrodynamics.

A contrary position raises the question about the validity of the continuum mechanical model once a singularity in one of the field variables or its derivatives is formed. In particular, Shikhmurzaev formulates the following criterion for a mathematical theory of fluid flow:

> "(B) The solution remains within the limits of applicability of the model specified via the assumptions made in its formulation. In particular, the flow parameters, that is the components of velocity and pressure, remain finite everywhere in the flow domain and on its boundaries at all times."
> [Shi06, p. 124]

The latter requirement is justified by the author by the range of validity of the modeling framework itself (see also the monograph [Shi08] for a comprehensive discussion). More specifically, he states that

> "The only element of criterion B we are interested in here is the finiteness of the flow parameters, that is regularity of the solution. This is more restrictive than just integrability and does not allow solutions with the integrably singular pressure, which causes no problems mathematically, but physically means that the pressure in a finite vicinity of the singularity can be arbitrarily high (or low) and hence the model of an incompressible fluid is no longer valid. Microscopically, this would also imply infinite energies of molecules." [Shi06, p. 124]

One of the main contributions of the present work is the development of a mathematical tool that allows to study qualitative properties of mathematical models of dynamic wetting, *provided* that the solution is sufficiently regular. The "kinematic evolution equation for the dynamic contact angle" arises from the systematic study of the kinematics of the moving contact line as sketched above. Besides its implications for different models of dynamic wetting, it has also lead to novel numerical methods which are discussed in Part II of the present work. We make no attempt to decide between the two contrary positions outlined above. This can ultimately only be done based on careful experimental observations for specific flow configurations. We rather aim at a new perspective on the field of dynamic wetting, which might lead to new insights in future research.

1.1. Capillarity

> "A liquid surface can be thought of as a stretched membrane characterized by a surface tension that opposes its distortion." [dGBWQ04, p.1]

The mathematical study of *capillarity* is an old subject originating from the work of Pierre Simon de Laplace and Thomas Young [You05] at the beginning of the 19th century, when the famous Young-Laplace equation of capillarity was derived. The main physical ingredient for capillary phenomena is the *surface tension* of liquid-liquid or liquid-gas interfaces. Microscopically, it arises from the attractive (also called "cohesive") interactions between liquid molecules. The molecules in the bulk phases are in an energetically favorable state due to the attractive interaction with all their neighbors. In contrast, a molecule at the surface misses (approximately) half its attractive interaction partners. Hence, it is energetically unfavorable for a liquid molecule to sit at the surface. As a result, there is a finite amount of energy per unit area denoted $\sigma > 0$, which is necessary to create a unit portion of the free surface. The latter concept of surface tension as *surface energy* allows for a variational approach to capillary phenomena. Note that being an energy per unit area, the surface tension σ has the SI-units

$$[\sigma] = \frac{\text{J}}{\text{m}^2} = \frac{\text{N}}{\text{m}}.$$

Usually, gravity can be neglected if the length scale of the problem is well below the capillary length

$$l_c = \sqrt{\sigma/(\rho g)}. \tag{1.3}$$

Here, $\rho = \rho_g - \rho_l$ is the density difference between the two phases and g is the gravitational acceleration. In the absence of gravitational effects, the stationary shape of the capillary surface can be found by minimizing the functional

$$\mathscr{E} = \int_\Sigma \sigma \, dA$$

subject to appropriate constraints which are typically determined by the geometry of the problem. If the surface energy σ is constant, the functional can be rewritten as

$$\mathscr{E} = \sigma \, |\Sigma|.$$

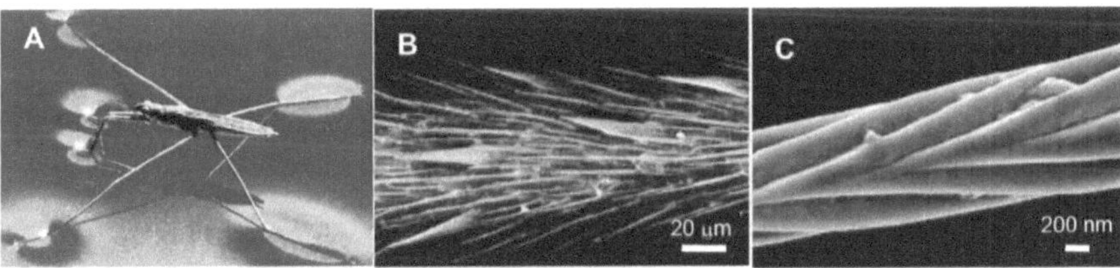

Figure 1.2.: Water strider resting on a water surface (A) and microscopic images of the animals leg (B,C). Reprinted (adapted) with permission from Feng et al., Langmuir 23(9):4892-4896, 2007. Copyright 2007 American Chemical Society.

The simplest example is that of a water drop in zero gravity, subject only to the constraint of volume conservation if incompressibility is assumed. The equilibrium shape of the drop is that of a sphere, minimizing the surface area for a given volume. A more interesting example is that of a soap film that is geometrically constrained by some kind of wireframe. In this case, the mathematical problem is to find a hypersurface with minimal area subject to a prescribed boundary curve. The latter problem, known as the "Plateau-Problem" in mathematics, fostered a lot of research in abstract differential geometry and related fields. Moreover, the effect of capillarity is present in various instances in nature and technology. An interesting example from nature is the water strider; see Figure 1.2 (A). The water strider is a small insect that is able to stand and walk easily on a water surface, while its weight is supported almost exclusively by surface tension [BH06, p.344]. Remarkably, the legs of the insect feature a specialized hierarchical structure consisting of oriented needle-shaped microsetae (i.e. tiny hairs) that themselves possess elaborate nanogrooves [FGW$^+$07, p.4892]; see Fig. 1.2 (B) and (C). As a result, the legs show superior water repellency and a single leg is able to hold a force of about 15 times the weight of the insect's body [FGW$^+$07, p.4893]. A comprehensive review of capillary and wetting phenomena in nature and technology can be found in the monograph of De Gennes et al. [dGBWQ04].

Mechanical formulation as a surface tension force: It is important to note that there is a second equivalent formulation of surface tension as a force per unit length acting along the interface. For example, consider a planar soap film that is placed between a rectangular wireframe and a movable rod of length L, as sketched in Fig. 1.3. Suppose we are able to measure the force on the rod as it is pulled outwards. The surface tension force acts *parallel* to the surface and aims to reduce the surface area of the soap film. The surface tension force acting on the rod is

$$\mathbf{f} = -2\sigma L \hat{e}_x,$$

where the factor 2 appears because two interfaces are present. Obviously, the variational and the mechanical formulation are equivalent since the work done to move the rod by an amount Δx is

$$\Delta W = 2\sigma L \Delta x = 2\sigma \Delta A.$$

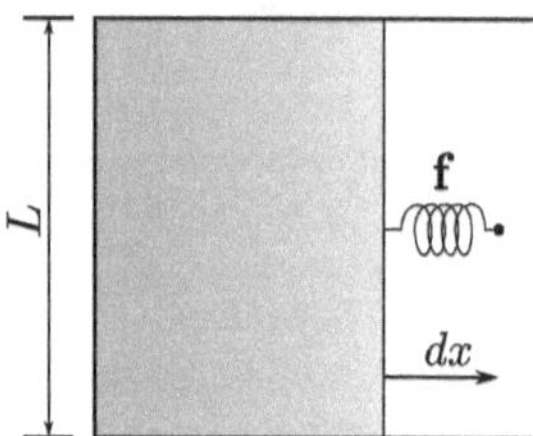

Figure 1.3.: Surface tension as a force per unit length.

1.2. Static Wetting

In the context of the present work, we mean by *wetting* a process where a two-phase flow (typically constituted by a liquid and a gas phase) interacts with a solid surface; see Fig. 1.4. We assume that the solid is rigid, i.e. we do not account for deformations of the solid resulting from the wetting process. This is expected to be a good approximation for surfaces with a sufficiently large elastic modulus. We note, however, that the deformation of the substrate can be relevant in principle, in particular in the field of "soft wetting" (see, e.g., [AS20]).

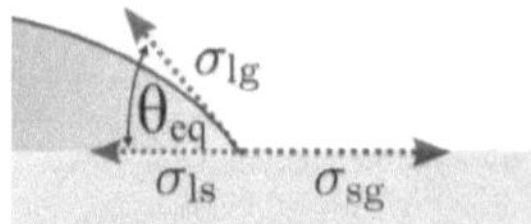

Figure 1.4.: Young diagram and equilibrium contact angle.

The Young–Dupré equation: The Young–Dupré equation was established in the early 19th century in the pioneering work of Thomas Young [You05]. It describes the equilibrium state of a wetting drop on a flat and homogeneous solid surface in terms of the local equilibrium *contact angle* θ_{eq}, i.e. the angle of intersection between the free surface and the solid boundary as depicted in Fig.1.4 according to

$$\sigma_{lg} \cos \theta_{eq} + \sigma_w = 0. \tag{1.4}$$

Here, the quantity σ_w is defined as the difference between the surface tensions σ_{ls} for the liquid-solid interface and σ_{sg} for the solid-gas interface, i.e.

$$\sigma_w := \sigma_{ls} - \sigma_{sg}.$$

Consequently, it can be understood as the specific energy of the wetted solid surface relative to the "dry surface". The latter quantity serves as a driving force for the wetting process. If the "specific wetting energy" σ_w is lower than the specific energy σ_{lg} of the liquid-gas interface, the system can gain energy by converting liquid-gas into liquid-solid interface by wetting the solid.

The usual way to read the Young equation (1.4) and the Young diagram in Fig. 1.4 is, however, based on the mechanical definition of the surface tension as a force per unit length. Then, eq. (1.4) is simply obtained from a horizontal projection of the forces depicted in Fig. 1.4. It is important to note that the interfacial tensions σ_{ls} and σ_{lg} can usually not be measured independently. Instead, eq. (1.4) may be used to *determine* σ_w from measured values of σ_{lg} and θ_{eq}. Remarkably, molecular dynamics simulations indicate that the Young equation (with the respective local values of the interfacial tensions) holds down to a length scale of a few nanometers [FTBD17]. On the other hand, there is some debate in the literature whether or not the interpretation of (1.4) as a local balance of *forces* is actually valid [Mak16, Mak18]. In particular, the interpretation of the liquid-solid and solid-gas surface tension as a force is discussed controversially.

It is, therefore, of interest to give a variational justification of (1.4) which only resorts to the concept of surface energies. An elementary derivation in two dimensions, which also serves as an introduction to some fundamental mathematical concepts, is given in Section 1.3. We note that the variational approach also allowed to extend the theory to the case of rough solid substrates; cf. [Wen36, CB44].

Static wetting model for a homogeneous substrate: In order to determine the equilibrium state, we consider the energy functional

$$\mathcal{E} = \sigma_{lg}\,|\Sigma_{lg}| + \sigma_w\,|\Sigma_{sl}| + \mathcal{E}_g, \tag{1.5}$$

where $\sigma_{lg} > 0$ is the surface tension[3] of the liquid-gas interface, $\sigma_w = \sigma_{sl} - \sigma_{sg}$ is the specific energy of the wet solid surface and $\mathcal{E}_g$ is the gravitational energy. The equilibrium state of a droplet is a minimizer of the functional (1.5) under the constraint of *volume conservation*.

Remark 1.1. From the form of the functional (1.5) one may recognize the following properties:

(i) Clearly, in the absence of gravity and without contact to a solid surface, the equilibrium states of the system are spheres with a radius determined by the volume. This is a consequence of the fact that the shape of a sphere minimizes the area enclosing a given volume.

(ii) If the specific wetting energy σ_w is larger than the liquid-gas surface tension, i.e. for

$$W_a := \sigma_{lg} - \sigma_w < 0, \tag{1.6}$$

the system does *not* gain energy by transforming a piece of liquid-gas interface into liquid-solid interface by wetting the surface. In this case, the fluid is called *non-wetting* (for the considered solid surface). Otherwise, the fluid is called *wetting*.

The quantity W_a defined above is known in the literature as the *work of adhesion*. It is "defined as the reversible thermodynamic work that is needed to separate the interface from the equilibrium state of two phases to a separation distance of infinity" [Ebn11].

(iii) If, one the other hand, the specific wetting energy σ_w is less than $-\sigma_{lg}$, i.e. if $\sigma_{lg} + \sigma_w < 0$, a simple argument shows that no local minimum with finite length L exists and the liquid forms a film: Consider a configuration of the liquid arranged in a disc of height h and radius R. Clearly, the height is a function of the radius to satisfy the volume conservation constraint, i.e.

$$h = \frac{V}{\pi R^2}.$$

If the disk is sufficiently flat, the gravitational energy can be neglected and the energy can be expressed as a function of the radius according to

$$\mathcal{E}(R) \propto \pi R^2 (\sigma_{lg} + \sigma_w) + \sigma_{lg}\,\frac{2V}{R}.$$

Consequently, the energy is not bounded from below if $\sigma_{lg} + \sigma_w < 0$ (or, equivalently, if $W_a > 2\sigma_{lg}$) and, hence, no stable configuration with a finite radius exists in this case. Fluids of this class are called *perfectly wetting* for the solid substrate.

(iv) If the work of adhesion is in between the extreme cases describe above, i.e. if the fluid is neither non-wetting nor perfectly wetting

$$0 \leq W_a \leq 2\sigma_{lg} \quad \Leftrightarrow \quad \frac{\sigma_w}{\sigma_{lg}} \in [-1, 1],$$

the fluid is said to be *partially wetting* for the solid substrate. Mathematically, there is a unique solution to the Young–Dupré equation in this case.

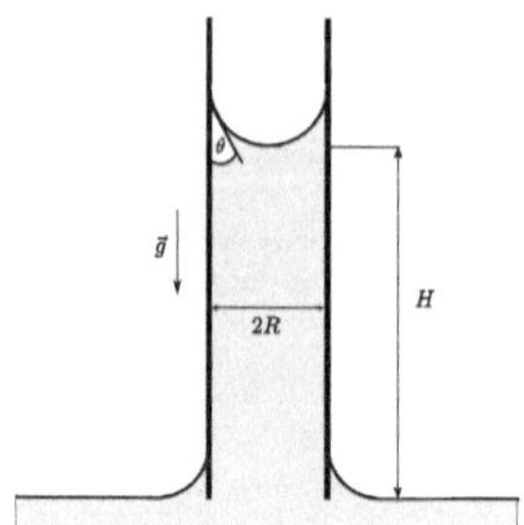

Figure 1.5.: Sketch of the capillary rise problem.

Example 1.2 (Capillary rise). One of the most prominent examples of static wetting is the rise of liquid in a capillary tube with a diameter comparable to (or smaller than) the capillary length (1.3). The rise height H of the liquid in the equilibrium state (see Fig. 1.5) can be found by means of energy considerations and is strongly dependent on the wettability of the solid. Indeed, the gain in energy due to wetting is the driving force of the process which is opposed by gravity. The height given by

$$H = \frac{2\sigma_{\mathrm{lg}} \cos \theta_{\mathrm{eq}}}{\rho g R} \tag{1.7}$$

is well-known in the literature as "Jurin's height", see, e.g., [dGBWQ04] and Chapter 11 for a more detailed discussion of the statics and dynamics of capillary rise.

Example 1.3 (Static wetting on structured surfaces). Much more complex wetting patterns arise if the model (1.5) is generalized to the case of an *inhomogeneous* solid substrate. In the latter case, the specific wetting energy may be a function of the position on the solid substrate and the energy functional generalizes to

$$\mathscr{E}_{\mathrm{i}} = \sigma_{\mathrm{lg}} \, |\Sigma_{lg}| + \int_{\Sigma_{sl}} \sigma_{\mathrm{w}} \, dA + \mathscr{E}_{g}. \tag{1.8}$$

Figure 1.6 shows an example of static and dynamic wetting on a structured surface with a stripe geometry. The surface has been prepared with photolithographic methods such that stripes with a different surface chemistry, in particular with a different wettability, are produced.

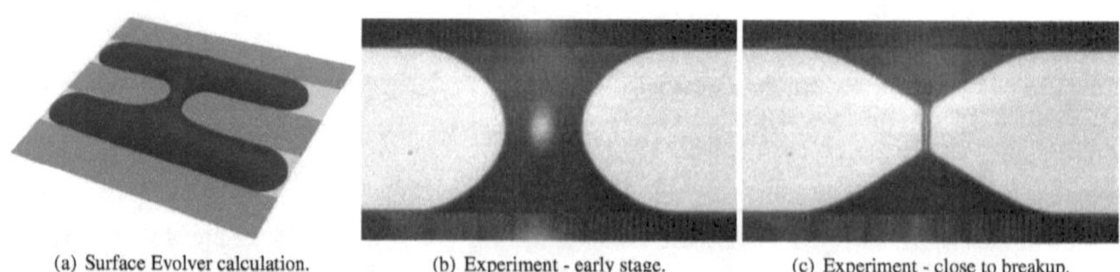

(a) Surface Evolver calculation.	(b) Experiment - early stage.	(c) Experiment - close to breakup.

Figure 1.6.: Wetting of a patterned surface with hydrophilic and hydrophobic stripes(Figures by M. Hartmann).

The geometry shown in Fig. 1.6(a) has been calculated with the Open Source tool *Surface Evolver* [Bra92, BB12], which is able to numerically minimize the functional (1.8). The droplet (blue color) prefers to wet the hydrophilic parts of the substrate (green color), leading to two elongated segments that are connected by a *capillary*

---

[3]Note that the liquid-gas surface tension is always assumed to be positive since otherwise, no stable interfaces exist.

bridge over the hydrophobic region. Note that this shape has a much larger gas-liquid interfacial area compared to a spherical cap of equal volume. However, the contact area between the liquid and the hydrophobic part of the substrate is minimized such that the overall energy is lower compared to a spherical cap of equal volume. Depending on the total volume, it can be energetically favorable for the droplet to break up into two individual droplets, wetting only the hydrophilic regions. In this case, the capillary bridge becomes unstable and a dynamic breakup process is initiated [HH19]; see Fig. 1.6(b) and 1.6(c). The dynamics of this breakup process is investigated in detail with continuum mechanical simulations in Chapter 12 (see also [HFW$^+$20]).

1.3. Variational derivation of the Young–Dupré equation in two dimensions

Let us start the discussion of the physics of wetting with a proper derivation of (1.4) based on variational principles. We consider the simplified two-dimensional case and neglect the effect of gravity. Even though this is a rather limited setting compared to real examples of static wetting, it is still useful to introduce and understand some basic mechanisms of wetting. For a more detailed mathematical discussion of equilibrium capillary surfaces see, e.g. [Fin86, Bra92, BB12].

Formulation via height functions: Suppose that the liquid-gas interface in two dimensions can be described as a graph over the solid boundary, i.e.

$$\Sigma_{lg} = \{(x, h(x)) : 0 \leq x \leq L\};$$

see Fig. 1.7. Note that this approach obviously fails for $\theta \geq \pi/2$ and another representation of the interface is necessary in this case. However, we leave this case aside for the purpose of this introduction to the topic. Moreover, we only consider the case of a single droplet and do not consider the process of breakup of a droplet into smaller droplets (see Chapter 12).

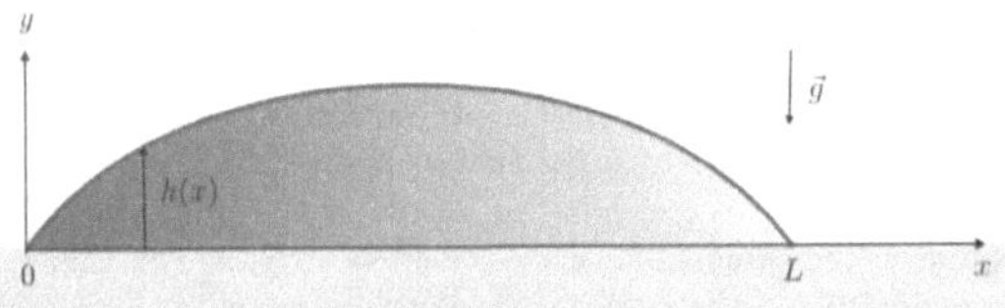

Figure 1.7.: Height function representation of a sessile wetting droplet in two dimensions.

If the interface can be represented by a height function, we may express the energy functional as

$$\mathscr{E}(L,h) = \sigma_{\mathrm{lg}} \int_0^L \sqrt{1 + h'(x)^2}\, dx + L\sigma_{\mathrm{w}} + \frac{\rho g}{2} \int_0^L h(x)^2\, dx, \tag{1.9}$$

where g is the gravitational acceleration and

$$\rho = \rho_l - \rho_g.$$

We are looking for minima of $\mathscr{E}$ in the configuration space

$$L \geq 0, \quad h \in \mathscr{C}^1(0,L) \quad \text{with} \quad h(x) \geq 0, h(0) = h(L) = 0$$

subject to the constraint

$$\int_0^L h(x)\, dx = V_0,$$

where $V_0 > 0$ is the prescribed volume of the drop.[4]

---

[4]Note that the energy of the sessile drop is invariant with respect to translations along the boundary since the solid is assumed to flat and homogeneous. We, therefore, do not need to consider translations.

Non-dimensional form of the problem: In order to proceed, it is convenient to reformulate the problem in non-dimensional form, which allows to define the height function h on a *fixed* interval. The importance of the latter approach is to allow for an *independent* variation of the length L and the height function itself. We define

$$\tilde{x} = x/L, \quad \tilde{h}(\tilde{x}) = h(\tilde{x}L)/L.$$

Hence, we have the relations

$$\tilde{h}'(\tilde{x}) = h'(\tilde{x}L), \quad \tilde{h}''(\tilde{x}) = Lh''(\tilde{x}L).$$

Then the transformed minimization problem reads as (dropping the tilde notation):

Given $V_0, \sigma_{lg}, \rho, g > 0$ and $\sigma_w \in \mathbb{R}$, minimize the functional

$$\begin{aligned}
\mathscr{E} &= L\left(\sigma_{lg}\int_0^1 \sqrt{1+h'(x)^2}\,dx + \sigma_w\right) + \frac{\rho g L^3}{2}\int_0^1 h(x)^2\,dx \\
&= L\sigma_{lg}\left(\int_0^1 \sqrt{1+h'(x)^2}\,dx + \frac{\sigma_w}{\sigma_{lg}} + \frac{\mathrm{Bo}}{2}\int_0^1 h(x)^2\,dx\right)
\end{aligned} \tag{1.10}$$

over the configuration space

$$L \geq 0, \quad h \in \mathscr{C}^1(0,1) \quad \text{with} \quad h(x) \geq 0, h(0) = h(1) = 0$$

subject to the constraint

$$\int_0^1 h(x)\,dx = \frac{V_0}{L^2}. \tag{1.11}$$

We note that the non-dimensional Bond number (also known as Eötvös number Eo), defined as[5]

$$\mathrm{Bo} = \frac{\rho g L^2}{\sigma_{lg}}, \tag{1.12}$$

measures the importance of gravitational forces compared to surface tension forces. Since in the present work we are mainly interested in capillary (i.e. surface tension dominated) flows, the Bond number will typically be small.

Euler-Lagrange Equations in the absence of gravity: We now proceed in the simplified case where gravity is negligible, i.e. we assume $\mathrm{Bo} = 0$. In order to satisfy the volume constraint, we introduce a Lagrange multiplier λ and consider the functional

$$\mathscr{E}_\lambda = L\sigma_{lg}\left(\int_0^1 \sqrt{1+h'(x)^2}\,dx + \frac{\sigma_w}{\sigma_{lg}}\right) + \lambda\left(\int_0^1 h(x)\,dx - \frac{V_0}{L^2}\right), \tag{1.13}$$

which is now to be minimized over

$$L > 0, \quad \lambda \in \mathbb{R}, \quad h \in \mathscr{C}^1(0,1) \quad \text{with} \quad h(x) \geq 0, h(0) = h(1).$$

By differentiating (1.13) with respect to L, we find the necessary condition

$$0 = \sigma_{lg}\left(\int_0^1 \sqrt{1+h'(x)^2}\,dx + \frac{\sigma_w}{\sigma_{lg}}\right) + \frac{2\lambda V_0}{L^3}. \tag{1.14}$$

We now take a smooth function $\varphi \in \mathscr{C}_c^\infty(0,1)$ with compact support in $(0,1)$ and consider the Fréchet-derivative of $\mathscr{E}_\lambda$, i.e. we consider the function

$$g_\varphi(\varepsilon) := \mathscr{E}_\lambda(h+\varepsilon\varphi) = \mathscr{E}_\lambda = L\sigma_{lg}\left(\int_0^1 \sqrt{1+(h'+\varepsilon\varphi')^2}\,dx + \frac{\sigma_w}{\sigma_{lg}}\right) + \lambda\left(\int_0^1 (h+\varepsilon\varphi)\,dx - \frac{V_0}{L^2}\right)$$

---

[5]In this case the foot-length of the droplet is chosen as the typical length scale. In a more general definition, one may define $\mathrm{Bo} := \rho g l^2/\sigma_{lg}$, where l is a characteristic length scale of the problem.

and compute its derivative at the origin

$$g'_\varphi(0) = L\,\sigma_{\text{lg}} \int_0^1 \frac{h'\varphi'}{\sqrt{1+h'^2}}\,dx + \lambda \int_0^1 \varphi\,dx.$$

Using partial integration, we obtain

$$g'_\varphi(0) = L\,\sigma_{\text{lg}} \underbrace{\frac{h'\varphi}{\sqrt{1+h'^2}}\bigg|_0^1}_{=0} + \int_0^1 \left(-L\,\sigma_{\text{lg}}\left(\frac{h'}{\sqrt{1+h'^2}}\right)' + \lambda\right)\varphi\,dx. \tag{1.15}$$

By the fundamental lemma of the calculus of variations, the necessary conditions $g'_\varphi(0) = 0$ for all $\varphi \in \mathscr{C}_c^\infty(0,1)$ only hold if the integrand in (1.15) vanishes, i.e. for a solution of

$$L\,\sigma_{\text{lg}}\left(\frac{h'}{\sqrt{1+h'^2}}\right)' = \lambda \quad \forall x \in (0,1), \quad h(0) = h(1) = 0.$$

A short calculation shows the relation

$$\left(\frac{h'}{\sqrt{1+h'^2}}\right)' = \frac{h''}{(1+h'^2)^{3/2}} = \tilde\kappa(x).$$

Here $\tilde\kappa$ is the *curvature* of the curve $(\tilde x, \tilde h(\tilde x))$, i.e. the curvature of the interface in the transformed coordinates. Note that we may rewrite $\hat\kappa$ in terms of the curvature of the original interface thanks to

$$\tilde\kappa(\tilde x) = \frac{\tilde h''(\tilde x)}{\sqrt{1+(\tilde h'(\tilde x))^2}} = \frac{Lh''(\tilde x L)}{(1+h'(\tilde x L)^2)^{3/2}} = L\,\kappa(\tilde x L)$$

Hence, we have the condition

$$\boxed{\kappa(x) = \frac{\lambda}{L^2\,\sigma_{\text{lg}}} = \text{const.}} \tag{1.16}$$

So, in fact, the Lagrange multiplier introduced to satisfy the volume constraint turns out to be the curvature of the interface. Moreover, we conclude that the minimizer of the functional is a curve with *constant* curvature, i.e. a circular cap. Combining the expression (1.16) for λ with the stationarity condition (1.14) yields

$$\begin{aligned}
0 &= \sigma_{\text{lg}} \int_0^1 \sqrt{1+\tilde h'(\tilde x)^2}\,d\tilde x + \sigma_{\text{w}} + \frac{2\,\sigma_{\text{lg}}\,\kappa V_0}{L} \\
&= \sigma_{\text{lg}}\left(\int_0^1 \sqrt{1+\tilde h'(\tilde x)^2}\,d\tilde x + \frac{2\kappa V_0}{L}\right) + \sigma_{\text{w}} \\
&= \sigma_{\text{lg}}\left(\frac{1}{L}\int_0^L \sqrt{1+h'(x)^2}\,dx + \frac{2\kappa V_0}{L}\right) + \sigma_{\text{w}} \\
&= \frac{\sigma_{\text{lg}}}{L}\left(|\Sigma_{lg}| + 2\kappa V_0\right) + \sigma_{\text{w}}.
\end{aligned} \tag{1.17}$$

Some elementary geometry shows the following relations for a circular cap

$$\kappa = -\frac{1}{R}, \quad V_0 = \theta R^2 - \frac{LR}{2}\cos\theta, \quad |\Sigma_{lg}| = 2\theta R,$$

where R is the radius of the circle and θ is the contact angle. This immediately shows that

$$|\Sigma_{lg}| + 2\kappa V_0 = L\cos\theta$$

and (1.17) is in fact equivalent to the Young–Dupré equation (1.4). In summary, we have shown that the minima of the energy functional are spherical caps with volume V_0 and a contact angle that respects (1.4). In particular, the variations in the foot-length L lead to the Young–Dupré equation (1.4) and the variations in the *rescaled* height function $\tilde h$ lead to the constant curvature condition (1.16).

1.4. Dynamic Wetting

1.4.1. Hierarchy of models

Even though the statics of wetting is well-understood for a long time, the mathematical modeling of *dynamic* wetting is still a challenge. The research efforts over the last decades lead to a lot of scientific debate and a great variety of different mathematical models. For a recent survey on the field, see, e.g., [dGBWQ04], [Bla06], [BEI$^+$09], [Shi08], [SA13] and the references therein. The purpose of this section is to give a brief (and by no means complete) overview and to put the present work into a broader context.

From the perspective of mathematical modeling, there is a whole hierarchy of models to describe dynamic wetting, ranging from microscopic descriptions via continuum mechanics to simplified/empirical descriptions of the macroscopic flow. Possible frameworks to describe dynamic wetting are:

(i) Molecular Dynamics,

(ii) Continuum Mechanics and

(iii) Simplified/Empirical descriptions.

Molecular Dynamics: The Molecular Dynamics (MD) point of view accounts for the discrete structure of matter and models the wetting problem by a large collection of point particles. Typically, the system contains two types of particles, namely fluid particles and solid particles which are arranged in some lattice structure to model the solid substrate. The physical interaction between a pair of fluid-fluid or fluid-solid particles is modeled by an effective interaction potential which is frequently chosen to be the Lennard-Jones potential leading to so-called "Lennard-Jones liquids". Once the interaction potentials are modeled, the main task is to solve Newtons equations of motion which leads to a large system of Ordinary Differential Equations (ODEs) that determines the trajectories of the particles. The advantage of the molecular dynamics approach is that it allows to study the physical processes at a moving contact line in great detail. However, the method is limited by the available computational resources. In order to be computationally feasible, MD simulations are often restricted to very small length and time scales. Moreover, the computational feasibility may also limit the range in which physical parameters (such as temperature, density, viscosity or surface tension) can be chosen in practice. Then the question arises how the MD results translate to different parameter regimes. Despite these limitations, the MD approach gives important insights into physical processes on the microscale which may lead to closure relations or boundary conditions for higher-level models such as Navier Stokes (see, e.g., [QWS03, RHE10, CWQS15]). The Molecular Kinetic Theory (MKT) of dynamic wetting by Blake and Hayes [BH69], being one of the first quantitative theories of dynamic wetting on the microscale, still leads to new insights into the physics of wetting. For example, recent work shows that key parameters of dynamic wetting can be obtained from thermal fluctuations at equilibrium [FTBDC19].

Continuum Mechanics: The continuum mechanical approach employs Partial Differential Equations (PDEs) that govern the temporal evolution of macroscopic quantities, such as the mass density and the average particle velocity. Typically, the latter is done in the framework of the Navier Stokes equations in a free-surface or sharp-interface two-phase formulation. The relevant physical effects on the microscale are modeled through constitutive equations and boundary conditions. The latter is done on a (semi-) empirical basis and/or motivated by more fundamental physical models. While the continuum mechanical models have shown their ability to describe a large number of wetting flows quite accurately, they may still be demanding in terms of computational costs. This motivates to look for simplified continuum mechanical models. A frequent choice to obtain a simplified continuum mechanical model is the *lubrication approximation*. The lubrication approximation applies in a geometry where one dimension is significantly smaller than the others. In this case, the Navier Stokes system can be simplified and the two-phase flow problem can be reduced to a PDE that only involves the free surface shape (see, e.g, [Sno06, Lea07, EF15]).

Simplified and Empirical descriptions: A substantial amount of research is dedicated to finding *empirical* correlations describing some macroscopic features of the flow with only a few parameters. The latter type of description might be useful to design systems for practical applications. A typical application example is curtain coating.

It is known that undesired air inclusions are generated if the coating speed is too high. The latter phenomenon is called "dynamic wetting failure" in the literature. The maximum speed at which the transition to the wetting failure occurs is of great practical interest. Experimental data [BBS99] can be a basis to find some empirical mathematical formula that describes the maximum coating speed. According to Weinstein and Ruschak, "genuinely predictive modeling of complex coating processes is not yet possible and coating practice remains largely empirical. Nonetheless, coating science is sufficiently advanced that physical insights and mathematical models greatly benefit design and practice." [WR04] However, recently the wetting failure in certain coating became accessible also to detailed numerical simulations [LVCK16]. Another example of a simplified model of a dynamic wetting process is the ODE model for the spreading of thin perfectly wetting drops described in [dG85]. A generalization of the latter model to partial wetting is discussed in Chapter 2.

Hybrid models: To conclude this short tour of mathematical models, we note that there are also hybrid approaches that combine some of the general frameworks listed above. For example, Diffuse Interface models employ the continuum mechanical description but model the interface as a transition region of a small but finite thickness (see [AMW98] for a review). The technical advantage of this approach is that the governing equations can be formulated on a fixed domain and discontinuities of the field variables are avoided. The physical motivation for diffuse interface models is the fact that real fluid interfaces have a small but finite thickness, determined by molecular interactions. According to Nold, diffuse interface models can be categorized as mesoscopic models "because they employ ideas from the nanoscale, and are used to compute multiphase scenarios at the macroscale." [Nol16, p.57].

1.4.2. Motion of viscous fluids: The Navier Stokes equations

The basis of the continuum mechanical description is formed by the classical Navier Stokes equations. The Navier Stokes equations are a system of PDEs that describe the conservation of mass and linear momentum for a viscous fluid. Starting from the continuity equation

$$\partial_t \rho + \nabla \cdot (\rho v) = 0,$$

one immediately arrives at the condition

$$\nabla \cdot v = 0 \tag{1.18}$$

if the flow is considered *incompressible*, i.e. if the density of fluid particles is required to be constant. The momentum balance equations, which are obtained from Newtons laws of motion and an appropriate closure relation for the stresses in the fluid, read as

$$\rho(\partial_t v + v \cdot \nabla v) - \eta \Delta v + \nabla p = \rho b. \tag{1.19}$$

The vector field b describes external forces that act on the fluid such as gravity, the scalar field p is called the pressure and η is called the dynamic viscosity of the fluid. The dynamic viscosity is a measure for the internal friction of the fluid which leads to a resistance of the medium to shear stresses. We note that (1.19) is obtained from a constitutive law that relates the shear *linearly* with the stress in the fluid. The latter assumption may be generalized to study so-called non-Newtonian fluids. We do not consider Non-Newtonian fluids in the present work, but note that the breakdown of the linear closure model is one of the suggested ways to regularize the moving contact line singularity (see, e.g., [AG02]). The system of equations (1.19) and (1.18) must be accompanied by appropriate boundary and initial conditions. The most common choice for the velocity of a viscous fluid at a solid boundary is the no-slip condition which states that the fluid particles right next to the solid boundary do not move relative to the boundary. Mathematically, the no-slip condition is a homogeneous Dirichlet boundary condition, i.e.

$$v = 0 \quad \text{at} \quad \partial\Omega. \tag{1.20}$$

1.4.3. Continuum mechanical models of dynamic wetting

In 1971, Huh and Scriven [HS71] showed that the usual *no-slip* condition for the velocity at solid boundaries is not appropriate for the modeling of moving contact lines (see also [PS82], [Sol97]). Depending on the model and the solution concept, this means that the no-slip condition either leads to the non-existence of solutions with moving contact lines or to an infinite viscous dissipation rate. Since then, many attempts have been made to solve this problem, for instance by means of numerical discretizations[6] (for an overview over numerical methods see [SDS14]) and/or by replacing the boundary conditions in the model. Essentially, some mechanism is introduced which allows for a tangential slip of the *interfacial* velocity at the solid wall.

Slip at the fluid-solid interface: The most common choice for the velocity boundary condition is the Navier slip condition, already proposed by Navier in the 19th century, which relates the tangential slip to the tangential component of normal stress at the boundary according to

$$v_\| + L(Dn_{\partial\Omega})_\| = 0, \tag{1.21}$$

where $D = \frac{1}{2}(\nabla v + \nabla v^\mathsf{T})$ is the rate-of-deformation tensor and $L > 0$ is called slip length.

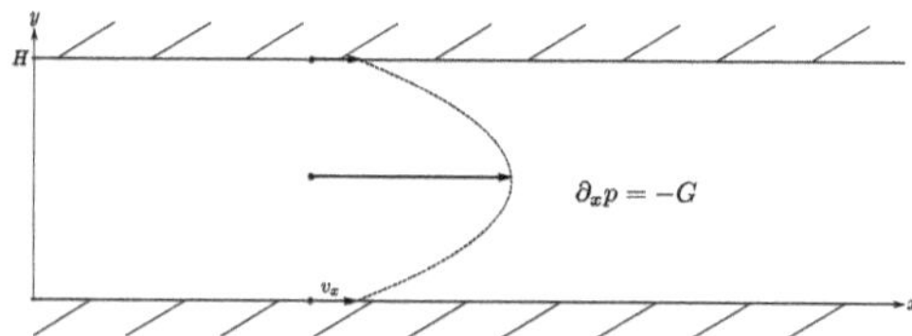

Figure 1.8.: Sketch of the channel flow problem.

Example 1.4 (Single-phase channel flow with Navier Slip). Consider the simple example of the steady flow of a Newtonian fluid described by the incompressible Navier Stokes equations through a two-dimensional channel of width H; see Fig. 1.8. The flow is driven by a prescribed, spatially constant pressure gradient $\partial_x p = -G$. The Navier slip condition is prescribed at the solid boundaries at $y = 0$ and $y = H$. So, we are looking for a solution of the Navier Stokes equations (1.19) - (1.18) with $b = 0$ of the form

$$p(x,y) = p_0 - Gx, \quad v(x,y) = (v_x(y),0)$$

subject to the boundary conditions

$$v_x - L\partial_y v_x = 0, \quad y = 0, H.$$

Substituting the ansatz for the velocity field into the Navier Stokes equations yield the ordinary differential equation

$$v_x''(y) = -\frac{G}{\eta}.$$

The two constants of integration are determined by the boundary conditions leading to the solution

$$v_x(x,y) = \frac{GH^2}{2\eta} \left(\frac{y}{H} - \left(\frac{y}{H}\right)^2 + \frac{L}{H} \right), \tag{1.22}$$

which is a modification of the well-known Hagen–Poiseuille flow. We note that the slip condition introduces a simple *additive* modification to the no-slip solution, i.e.

$$v_x(x,y) = v_x^{\text{no-slip}} + \frac{GHL}{2\eta}.$$

---

[6]A typical approach to circumvent the problem numerically is to use the so-called *numerical slip*. The main observation is (see [RRL01]) that in many cases an artificial slip is introduced by the discretization itself; see Section 7.5 for more details. Due to this numerical effect, the contact line is able to move even though the no-slip condition is used. However, the numerical slip is typically strongly dependent on the grid size. Moreover, the model which is supposed to describe the *physics* of dynamic wetting is in this case purely numerical and has no physical foundation.

In particular, the limit $L \to 0$ is regular and Navier slip with a small slip length L on a molecular length scale is practically indistinguishable from no-slip. For example, the average velocity throughout the cross-section of the channel (which is proportional to the mass transport rate) is given by

$$\langle v_x \rangle = \frac{GH^2}{12\eta} \left(1 + \frac{6L}{H} \right).$$

So, a slip length $L = 10\,\text{nm}$ gives rise to a relative increase of the mass transport in a 1 mm channel of $6 \cdot 10^{-5}$ which is irrelevant for any practical purposes. Remarkably, when we generalize this example to the case of a *two-phase* flow in a narrow channel involving a moving contact line, the influence of the slip length even on a scale as small as 10 nm on the macroscopic mass transport rate is tremendous (at least in the framework of the "standard model" of wetting). From a mathematical point of view, this is reflected in the fact that the moving contact line problem with no-slip is ill-posed in the class of physically reasonable solutions with a finite rate of viscous dissipation. A discussion of the influence of slip on the rise of liquid in a capillary is provided in Chapter 11.

Modeling the wettability: Besides the regularization of the no-slip paradox, the modeling of the *wettability* is the second main ingredient for mathematical models of dynamic wetting. In the case of sharp interface models, this is usually done (with some exceptions) by explicitly prescribing the contact angle at the solid boundary. The experimentally measured contact angle, which is always subject to a finite measurement resolution, typically shows a strong correlation to the capillary number [Hof75],

$$\text{Ca} = \frac{\eta V_\Gamma}{\sigma},$$

where η and V_Γ denote the dynamic viscosity and the contact line velocity, respectively. Motivated by this observation, many models prescribe the contact angle as some function of the capillary number and the equilibrium contact angle, i.e.

$$\theta = f(\theta_{\text{eq}}, \text{Ca}), \tag{1.23}$$

or vice versa

$$\text{Ca} = \psi(\theta; \theta_{\text{eq}}). \tag{1.24}$$

Since models of the above type are usually motivated by empirical correlations, we refer to (1.23) and (1.24) as "empirical contact angle models". Even though (1.23) and (1.24) are consistent closure relations for the entropy production if the functions f and ψ satisfy an additional thermodynamic condition (see Theorem 3.6 in Section 3.2), their validity is discussed controversially in the literature (see, e.g., [Shi20, Bot20c]). In particular, it is argued that the dynamic contact angle cannot be prescribed a priori. Instead, experimental data suggest that the dynamic contact angle depends, among others, on the details of the flow field in the vicinity of the contact line [BBS99, Shi08].

Remark 1.5 (Dynamic contact angles and regularity). It can be shown by means of an asymptotic analysis for the *stationary* Stokes equations that, for a fixed contact angle, the Navier slip condition with a finite slip length makes the viscous dissipation rate finite, while the pressure is still logarithmically singular at the moving contact line (see, e.g., [HM77], [Shi06]). This integrable type of singularity is commonly referred to as a *weak singularity*. It is an interesting question, under which circumstances even the weak singularity is removed from the description. In the publications [RE07, p.15] and [E11], Ren and E formulate the expectation that the weak singularity is removed if, instead of a fixed contact angle, a certain model for the dynamic contact angle is applied. The present work shows that this is not the case. Instead, it is shown that the dynamic behavior for sufficiently regular solutions to the simplest model is *unphysical* (if the slip length is finite); see Chapter 4.

Part I.

Mathematical Modeling
&
Qualitative Analysis

> "The challenge becomes even bigger for adaptive or responsive surfaces, that is, surfaces which change their properties with external conditions such as temperature, humidity, electric and magnetic fields or the presence of the liquid itself." [BBS+18, p.11292]

In the present chapter[1], we assess the ability of (2.1) to describe the spreading dynamics of a droplet in contact with swellable polymer brushes. In particular, different amounts of "pre-swelling" in humid air are considered. The pre-swelling influences the imbibition of fluid into the polymer brush and hence the spreading dynamics significantly. Note that a continuum mechanical model for the wetting on polymer brushes has been introduced recently in [TH20]. The present chapter aims at an empirical mathematical model to describe the process of spreading in terms of the base radius of the droplet as a function of time. Figure 2.1 shows experimental data for the spreading of a glycerol-water droplet on a silicon wafer and the spreading of a pure water droplet on a PNIPAm brush (see Section 2.3.2). Note that the timescale for the spreading dynamics on the polymer brush in Figure 2.1(b) differs by orders of magnitude from the timescale for the water-glycerol droplet in Figure 2.1(a).

Assumptions: The reasoning which has been formulated for the special case of flat drops in [dG85] is based on the following assumptions:

(I) The shape of the droplet throughout the spreading process is a spherical cap.

(II) The speed of the contact line can be expressed as a function of the contact angle[2] θ (or vice versa).

(III) The volume of the drop is known (as a function of time if it is not conserved).

The ordinary differential equation (2.13) derived in Section 2.2 is a direct consequence of (I)-(III) without further approximations or assumptions.

Remarks on assumption (I):   The first assumption (I) greatly simplifies the description since in this case, the shape is completely determined by only two parameters. Physically, the spherical cap is expected to be a good approximation in the late stage of spreading, i.e. for θ close enough to equilibrium if surface tension forces dominate over both gravity and viscous forces, i.e. if the Bond and capillary numbers defined as

$$\mathrm{Bo} = \frac{\rho g l^2}{\sigma} = \frac{\rho g}{\sigma}\left(\frac{3V}{2\pi}\right)^{2/3}, \quad \mathrm{Ca} = \frac{\eta V_\Gamma}{\sigma} \tag{2.2}$$

are sufficiently small[3]. However, in experiments, the shape of the drop is strongly influenced by the needle which is used to deposit the drop on the substrate (see Figure 2.2 for the deposition of a pure water droplet). While the contact line advances fast after the droplet gets in contact with the substrate (see Fig. 2.2 (b)-(c)), there is a complex process of detachment from the needle which is accompanied by the propagation of capillary waves and subsequent oscillations of the contact line (see Fig. 2.2 (d)-(f)). For partially wetting liquids ($\theta_{eq} > 0$) with low viscosity, the oscillations typically continue until the stationary radius is reached. Therefore, the assumption (I) is typically not applicable in this case. However, it has been reported in the literature that for highly viscous liquids such as water-glycerol mixtures, there is a viscous regime of spreading where viscous friction becomes the main source opposing capillarity [CB14]. During this final stage of wetting after detachment from the needle, the oscillations are mainly damped out by viscosity and the drop shape is quite close to a spherical cap. Moreover, the spherical cap shape is also observed for the spreading on a polymer brush since in this case, the time scale for the spreading is quite large (see Section 2.3.2).

---

[1] Please note: The results presented in the present chapter have been published as a preprint in [FFH+20].

[2] Here, by "contact angle" we mean the "macroscopic" contact angle that corresponds to the spherical cap shape.

[3] Note that the length scale for the Bond number is chosen to be the radius of a volume-equivalent drop with a contact angle of 90°, i.e. $l := \sqrt[3]{3V/2\pi}$.

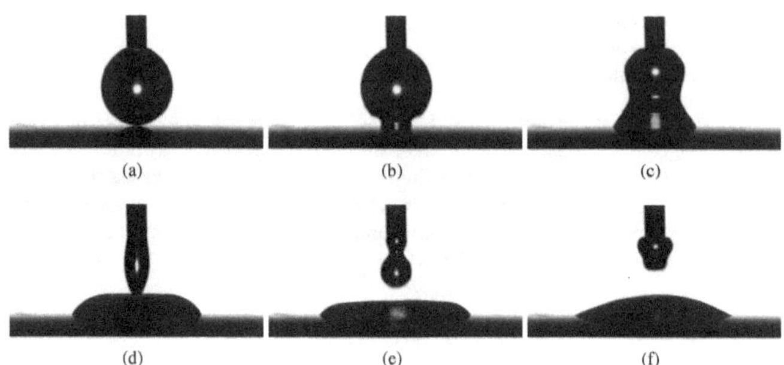

Figure 2.2.: Deposition of a pure water droplet on a silicon wafer (Figure by M. Hartmann).

Remarks on assumption (II):   Starting from the work by Hoffman [Hof75] and Jiang et al. [JSGS79], where it is suggested that there is a *universal* relationship of the form

$$\theta_{\mathrm{app}} = f(\mathrm{Ca}), \tag{2.3}$$

assumption (II) is a frequent choice to model dynamic wetting, even though its validity is discussed controversially (see, e.g., [Shi08, Shi20, Bot20c]). Here θ_{app} denotes the "apparent" (i.e. optically observable) contact angle and Ca is the capillary number proportional to the contact line speed V_Γ. Mathematically, it is more convenient to express the capillary number as a function of the contact angle, i.e.

$$\mathrm{Ca} = \psi(\theta_{\mathrm{app}}), \tag{2.4}$$

since there might be a whole interval of contact angles $[\theta_r, \theta_a]$ where the contact line does not move. This well-known effect is called contact angle hysteresis.

Example 2.1 (Cox-Voinov law). A prominent example of a relation of the type (2.4) is the Cox-Voinov law (see [BEI$^+$09] chapter III for a discussion) given by

$$\mathscr{G}(\theta_{\mathrm{app}}) = \mathscr{G}(\theta_{\mathrm{eq}}) + \mathrm{Ca}\,\ln\left(\frac{x}{L}\right). \tag{2.5}$$

Here x/L is the ratio of macroscopic to microscopic length scales, an unknown parameter that has to be found by fitting experimental data (Bonn et al. [BEI$^+$09] report $x/L = 10^4$). The function $\mathscr{G}$ defined as

$$\mathscr{G}(\theta) = \int_0^\theta \frac{x - \sin x \cos x}{2 \sin x}\, dx$$

can be well approximated by $\theta^3/9$ for $\theta < 135°$ (see [BEI$^+$09]), so that in the following we will refer to the simplified equation

$$\theta_{\mathrm{app}}^3 = \theta_{\mathrm{eq}}^3 + 9\mathrm{Ca}\,\ln\left(\frac{x}{L}\right) \tag{2.6}$$

as the "Cox-Voinov law". Equation (2.6) results from an asymptotic solution of a hydrodynamic model by Cox [Cox86], which is valid in the limit $\mathrm{Ca}, \mathrm{Re} \to 0$ for an ideal surface with no heterogeneities, if the microscopic contact angle equals the equilibrium contact angle θ_{eq}. According to [BEI$^+$09], the approximation $\theta_m \approx \theta_{\mathrm{eq}}$ is justified if viscous dissipation is large compared to local dissipation at the contact line.

Example 2.2 (Kistler's empirical function). Another commonly used example is the empirical function by Kistler [Kis93] given by the expression

$$\theta_{\mathrm{app}} = f_{\mathrm{Hoff}}(\mathrm{Ca})$$

$$= \cos^{-1}\left(1 - 2\tanh\left[5.16\left(\frac{\mathrm{Ca}}{1 + 1.31\mathrm{Ca}^{0.99}}\right)^{0.706}\right]\right). \tag{2.7}$$

The latter function has been obtained from a fit to the experimental data by Hoffman [Hof75]. In order to describe partial wetting, the function is shifted according to

$$\theta_{\mathrm{app}} = f_{\mathrm{Hoff}}[\mathrm{Ca} + f_{\mathrm{Hoff}}^{-1}(\theta_0)]. \tag{2.8}$$

A direct comparison of the empirical models (2.6) for $x/L = 10^4$ and (2.8) in the case of complete wetting shows that the two models are very similar; see Figure 2.3. Both empirical relations have been shown to be compatible with experimental data over a range of capillary numbers for different fluid/substrate combinations.

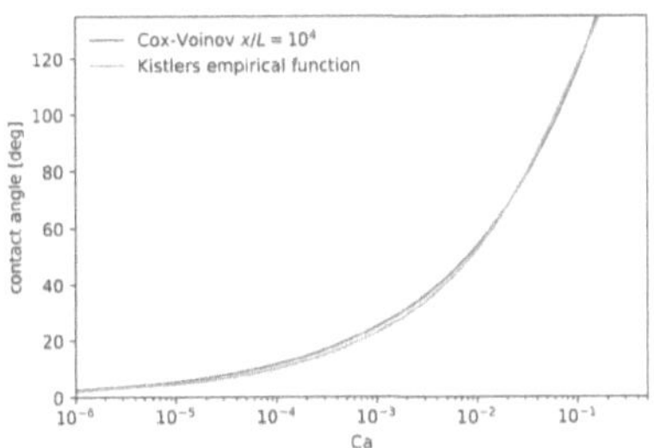

Figure 2.3.: Kistler's empirical function and the Cox-Voinov law for $\theta_{\mathrm{eq}} = 0$.

2.2. Spreading dynamics of spherical drops

Spreading dynamics in phase space: It can be advantageous to consider the spreading dynamics in phase space[4]. The idea is to express the time-derivative of the base radius $\dot{L}$ as a function of the base radius itself. Formally, we define

$$\dot{L}(L_0) := \frac{dL}{dt}\left(L^{-1}(L_0)\right). \tag{2.9}$$

Note that this is possible since $L(t)$ is a monotonically increasing function with inverse L^{-1}. The advantage of the latter approach is that it eliminates the dependence of the data on the arbitrary choice of t_0. This is helpful since the instant of contact t_0 with $L(t_0) = 0$ might, in practice, be hard to determine experimentally with sufficient precision. Mathematically, the instant of contact marks a *topological change* of the flow which is followed by a very fast initial dynamics, see [Bot20c] for a discussion.

In fact, the function $\dot{L}(L)$ eliminates the dependence on t_0 since it is invariant with respect to a shift in the time coordinate. It is easy to show that if L is given by

$$L(t) = C(t - t_0)^{\beta}$$

for some $C, \beta > 0$ and $t_0 \in \mathbb{R}$, then

$$\dot{L}(L) = (\beta C^{1/\beta}) L^{1-1/\beta}.$$

For the famous Tanner law [Tan79] ($\beta = 0.1$) this means $\dot{L}(L) \propto L^{-9}$.

A Geometry-based model for spreading drops: For a *spherical* droplet, there is a purely geometric relationship between the base-radius L, the volume V and the contact angle according to

$$\frac{L}{V^{1/3}} = g(\theta) := \sin\theta \left(\frac{\pi(1 - \cos\theta)^2(2 + \cos\theta)}{3}\right)^{-1/3}; \tag{2.10}$$

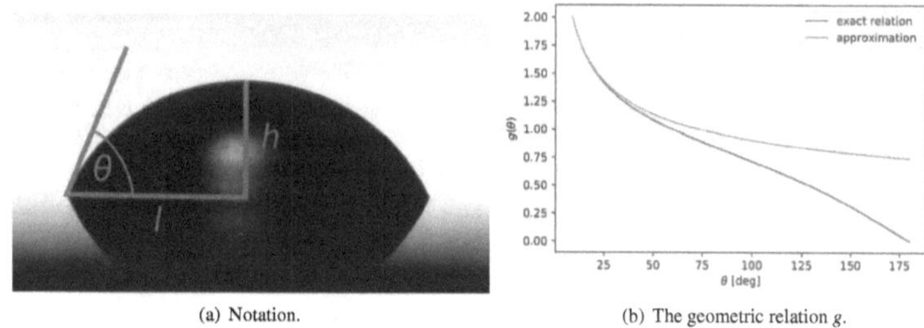

(a) Notation.

(b) The geometric relation g.

Figure 2.4.: Some basic geometry.

see Fig. 2.4(a) for notation. The function g is monotonically decreasing with θ (see Figure 2.4(b)) and hence invertible on $[0, \infty)$. For small values of θ, i.e. for flat drops, the function g can be approximated by (see [dG85])

$$g(\theta) \approx \hat{g}(\theta) = \left(\frac{4}{\pi \theta} \right)^{1/3}.$$

Inverting relation (2.10) allows to express the contact angle as a function of the base radius and the volume according to

$$\theta = g^{-1}\left(\frac{L}{V^{1/3}} \right). \tag{2.11}$$

Using the approximation for flat drops allows to simplify the above equation as

$$\theta = \frac{4}{\pi} \frac{V}{L^3}. \tag{2.12}$$

Assuming that the contact angle is related to the contact line speed V_Γ by an empirical relation of the type (2.4) allows to derive an ordinary differential equation for the spreading dynamics of spherical drops. Note that this observation has already been made by de Gennes [dG85], where (in the case of complete wetting) the approximation (2.12) for flat drops is applied. Here we generalize this idea to arbitrary contact angles.

Since $\dot{L} = V_\Gamma$, it follows from (2.11) and (2.4) that the base radius satisfies the ordinary differential equation

$$\boxed{\frac{\eta}{\sigma} \dot{L}(t) = \psi\left(g^{-1}\left(\frac{L(t)}{V(t)^{1/3}} \right) \right), \quad L(t_0) = L_0.} \tag{2.13}$$

Remark 2.3. From the form of equation (2.13) we draw the following conclusions:

(i) The problem is uniquely solvable provided that ψ is, e.g., Lipschitz continuous.

(ii) Since thermodynamics of moving contact lines implies (see, e.g., [RHE10, FKB19] and Section 3.2)

$$\psi \geq 0 \quad \text{for} \quad \theta \geq \theta_{\mathrm{eq}},$$

it follows directly that (since g^{-1} is monotonically decreasing)

$$\dot{L} \geq 0 \quad \text{if} \quad L \leq V^{1/3} g(\theta_{\mathrm{eq}}) =: L_{\mathrm{eq}}(\theta_{\mathrm{eq}}, V)$$

and vice versa for $L \geq L_{\mathrm{eq}}$.

---

[4]See Section 12.2.2 for a detailed discussion of the phase space approach applied to the breakup of a capillary bridge.

(iii) The ordinary differential equation (2.13) is autonomous if the volume is conserved. However, this is not a necessary assumption. The dynamic volume can be incorporated if the function $V = V(t)$ is known.

(iv) The dynamics of the contact angle can be inferred from a solution of (2.13), using the relation (2.11). Moreover, one can also derive an equivalent evolution equation for the contact angle, see below.

By plotting the experimental data for $\mathrm{Ca} = \frac{\eta}{\sigma}\dot{L}$ vs. $\theta(L,V) = g^{-1}(L/V^{1/3})$ one can directly read off an *empirical function* ψ, provided that the droplet is spherical and the volume V is known.

Note: The above method delivers an empirical function ψ describing the data of an individual experiment even in the case when assumption (II) does *not* hold. For example, the function ψ could depend on further variables like temperature

$$\mathrm{Ca} = \psi(\theta, T, \dots). \tag{2.14}$$

In fact, experiments in curtain coating [BBS99] suggest that ψ may also depend on the flow field near the contact line - an effect known as "hydrodynamic assist". Therefore, the proposed method should be understood as a tool to probe whether or not the data can be collapsed onto a single curve for ψ (at least for some range of parameters). It is only in the latter case, that Equation (2.13) is able to *predict* the spreading dynamics of spherical droplets (see Section 2.3).

Thin droplet approximation: Using the approximation (2.12) for small contact angles, one can approximate (2.13) by the ODE

$$\dot{L}(t) = \frac{\sigma}{\eta}\,\psi\left(\frac{4}{\pi}\frac{V(t)}{L(t)^3}\right). \tag{2.15}$$

If the volume is constant and ψ is given by a power law (corresponding to complete wetting), i.e.

$$\mathrm{Ca} = c\,\theta^m,$$

then (2.15) reads (see [dG85])

$$\dot{L} = \tilde{c}V_0^m L^{-3m}.$$

In case $L(0) = 0$, the evolution of the base radius obeys the power law

$$L \propto V_0^{\frac{m}{3m+1}}\, t^{\frac{1}{3m+1}}.$$

Hence the Tanner law $L \propto t^{1/10}$ is obtained for $m = 3$.

Contact angle dynamics: Differentiating the geometrical relation (2.10) with respect to time yields

$$\dot{L} = V^{1/3}g'(\theta)\,\dot{\theta} + g(\theta)\frac{d}{dt}V^{1/3}. \tag{2.16}$$

where $V_\Gamma = \dot{L}$ denotes the contact line speed. Then equation (2.16) combined with (2.4) yields the ordinary differential equation

$$\dot{\theta} = \frac{\frac{\sigma}{\eta}\psi(\theta) - g(\theta)\frac{d}{dt}V^{1/3}}{g'(\theta)V^{1/3}}, \quad \theta(t_0) = \theta_0. \tag{2.17}$$

Non-dimensional form for a constant volume: For constant volume, i.e. $V(t) \equiv V_0$, one may choose $L_{eq} = V_0^{1/3} g(\theta_{eq})$ as a length scale and

$$\tau = \frac{\eta V_0^{1/3}}{\sigma}$$

as a time scale for non-dimensionalization according to

$$\tilde{L}(\tilde{t}) = \frac{L(\tau \tilde{t})}{L_{eq}} \quad \Leftrightarrow \quad L(t) = L_{eq}\tilde{L}\left(\frac{t}{\tau}\right).$$

Then equations (2.13) becomes

$$\tilde{L}' = \frac{1}{g(\theta_{eq})}\,\psi\left(g^{-1}\left[g(\theta_{eq})\tilde{L}\right]\right). \tag{2.18}$$

Moreover, the non-dimensional form of $\theta(t)$, defined as

$$\tilde{\theta}(\tilde{t}) = \theta(\tau \tilde{t}),$$

satisfies the ordinary differential equation

$$\tilde{\theta}' = \frac{\psi(\tilde{\theta})}{g'(\tilde{\theta})}. \tag{2.19}$$

2.3. Experimental results

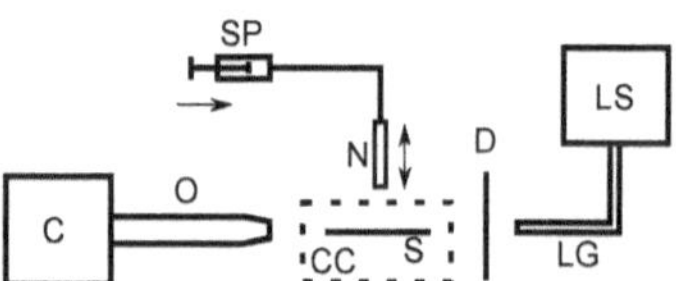

Figure 2.5.: Experimental setup: A drop is dosed with a syringe pump (SP) which is connected to a needle (N) and placed on the substrate (S) which is eventually placed inside a climate chamber (CC). The spreading process is recorded with a high-speed camera (C) connected to a long-distance microscope (O). Illumination is performed with a cold light source (LS) from which light is lead with a light guide (LG) to a diffuser (D) (Figure by Fickel and Hartmann [FFH+20]).

Experimental Methods: Experiments on the spreading dynamics of a 75 wt.% glycerol-water droplet on a bare silicon wafer and a pure water droplet on a PNIPAm coated silicon wafer have been performed and evaluated by M. Hartmann and B. Fickel. A brief description of the experimental setup is given below. For details on the experimental methods and the preparation of the PNIPAm coated substrates, the reader is referred to [FFH+20].

The droplet is deposited using a syringe pump connected to a metal needle that is mounted in a self-build construction. The construction allows to move the needle manually and independently from the rest of the experimental setup. Optical images of the spreading of the sessile droplet are taken in side-view using a high-speed camera (10,000 fps, Photron SA-X1) which is attached to long-distance microscope. A cold light source illuminates the image from the back. A sketch of the experimental setup is shown in Fig. 2.5. The whole setup can be mounted in a climate chamber to achieve a constant relative humidity in the range 15-80 %. The images taken by the high-speed camera are evaluated using the inhouse Matlab algorithm *Drop of EvolutioN: Impact, Imbibition, Propagation, evaporation (DENIISE)* developed by M. Heinz within subproject A04 of CRC 1194. The algorithm assumes an axisymmetric shape of the droplet and delivers the foot radius L, the height h, the volume V and two contact angles (left and right) for each frame.

2.3.1. Spreading of viscous droplets on a homogeneous solid substrate

As a first example, we consider the spreading of water-glycerol droplet (75% glycerol) on a bare silicon wafer. The high dynamic viscosity of $\eta = 29.96\,\mathrm{mPa \cdot s}$ of the liquid leads to a viscous stage of spreading where the droplet spreads as a spherical cap (see [CB14]). Note that the viscosity is increased with respect to pure water by a factor of more than 30. The surface tension is only slightly reduced ($\sigma = 63.5\,\mathrm{mN/m}$). Experimental data for the spreading dynamics have been recorded for 4 repetitions of the experiment. Fig. 2.6(a) shows the experimental data for the drop volume as a function of time. Note that the process of release from the needle is visible as a kink in the data. Apparently, this type of droplet application leads to a variation in the drop volume of approximately 35%. The latter also leads to different equilibrium foot lengths of the individual drops; see Fig. 2.6(b).

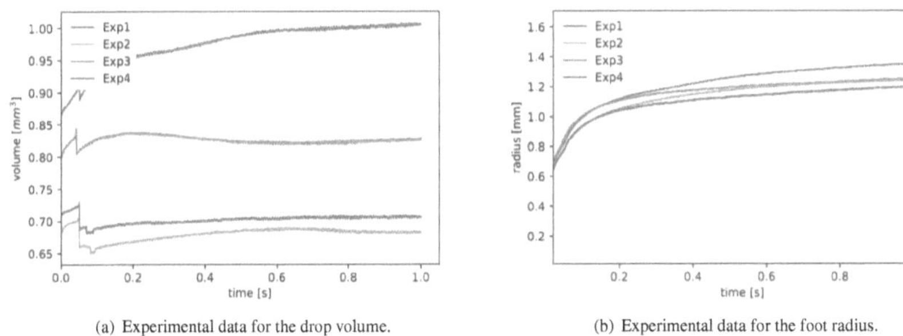

(a) Experimental data for the drop volume.   (b) Experimental data for the foot radius.

Figure 2.6.: Spreading of a 75%-glycerol droplet on a silicon wafer.

The consistency of the experimental data with respect to the spherical cap approximation can be checked in two ways, namely

(i) by comparing the experimental drop height h_exp with the expected height $h_\mathrm{cap}(L_\mathrm{exp}, V_\mathrm{exp})$ (see Appendix C for details) and

(ii) by comparing the experimental contact angle with the expected contact angle $\theta_\mathrm{cap}(L_\mathrm{exp}, V_\mathrm{exp})$.

The experimental data for the drop height for all experiments agree well with the spherical cap approximation; see Fig. 2.7. According to the results in Fig. 2.8(a), there is also a reasonable agreement of the contact angle with the theoretical values for a spherical cap for Experiments 1 and 2. However, we observe a systematic deviation in the contact angle for the Experiments 3 and 4; see Fig. 2.8(b).

The contact line velocity is obtained from the numerical differentiation of the experimental data for the base radius with respect to time. The resulting capillary number is plotted against the contact angle *computed* as a function of the measured base radius L and volume, i.e. according to eq. (2.11); see Fig. 2.9(a). Note that this method leads to a much smaller scatter in the data since the base radius and the volume can be measured with higher precision than the contact angle itself. We find that the experimental data in the θ-Ca plane are quite close for Experiments 3 and 4 while Experiments 1 and 2 show some offset. The data for Experiment 3 and 4 can be described by the common empirical function

$$\psi_\mathrm{emp}(\theta) = \max\{5 \cdot 10^{-3}(\theta - \theta_\mathrm{eq})^{2.2}, 7 \cdot 10^{-4}(\theta - \theta_\mathrm{eq})\}, \tag{2.20}$$

where $\theta_\mathrm{eq} = 26.0°$. Even though noise in the data leads to an oscillatory signal for low capillary numbers, the data show that the empirical function cannot be described by one single exponent; see Fig.2.9(b). The solution of the ODE (2.13) with ψ given by (2.20) is plotted in Fig. 2.10(a). Here, $V = V(t)$ is obtained from the experimental

21

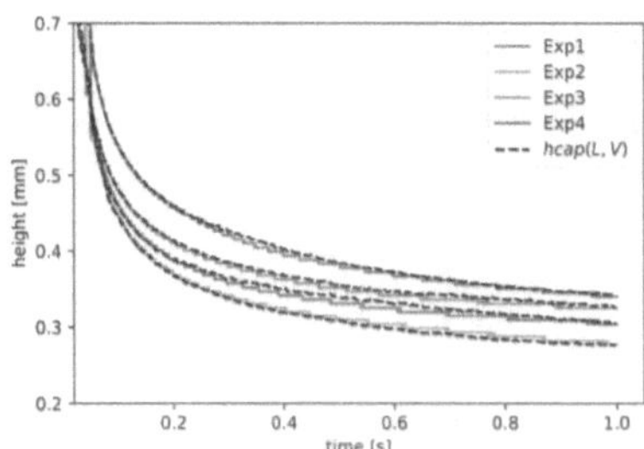

Figure 2.7.: Experimental data for the droplet height compared to $h_{\text{cap}}(L_{\text{exp}}, V_{\text{exp}})$.

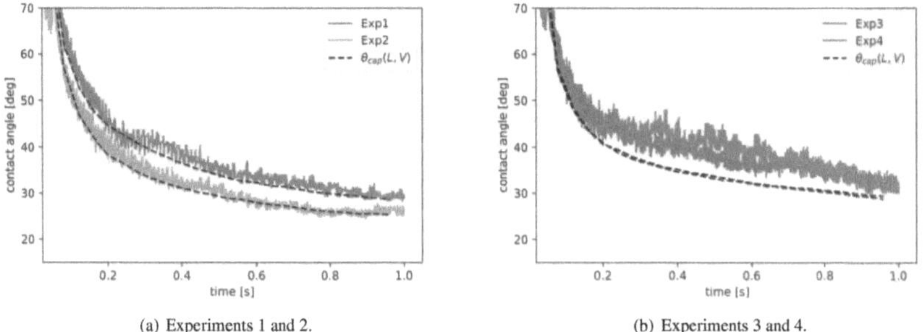

(a) Experiments 1 and 2.

(b) Experiments 3 and 4.

Figure 2.8.: Experimental data for the contact angle.

data for the volume by linear interpolation, and the initial conditions for the ODE are taken from the experimental data after detachment from the needle. It is found that the dynamics for both Experiment 3 and 4 agree very well with the ODE solution employing the common empirical function (2.20).

Comparison with literature relations: It is remarkable to note that there is a large discrepancy between the empirical function (2.20) which describes the present experiment and the well-known relations shown in Figure 2.10(b). Both the Cox-Voinov relation (2.6) with $x/L = 10^4$ as reported in [BEI$^+$09] and the Kistler function given by (2.8) are far off from the present data. Apparently, the Cox-Voinov law appears to not apply for the present case, even though viscous dissipation is large and the capillary number is small. This discrepancy might be related to the polarity of the fluid or to mixture effects; see also [HR93] where it is stated that the hydrodynamic model (2.6) is unable to produce physically reasonable values for the slip length L for polar liquids on a PET surface.

2.3.2. Spreading of water droplets on a swellable polymer brush

We consider water drops with volume $V \approx 2\,\text{mm}^3$ under standard conditions ($T = 25°\text{C}$, $p = 1$ bar) slowly spreading ($V_\Gamma \approx 10\,\mu\text{m}/s$) on a PNIPAm polymer brush (see [FFH$^+$20] for details about the polymer brush preparation). Typical values for the Bond and Capillary number are

$$\text{Bo} = \frac{\rho g}{\sigma}\left(\frac{3V}{2\pi}\right)^{2/3} \approx 0.13, \quad \text{Ca} = \frac{\eta V_\Gamma}{\sigma} \approx 1.2 \cdot 10^{-7}.$$

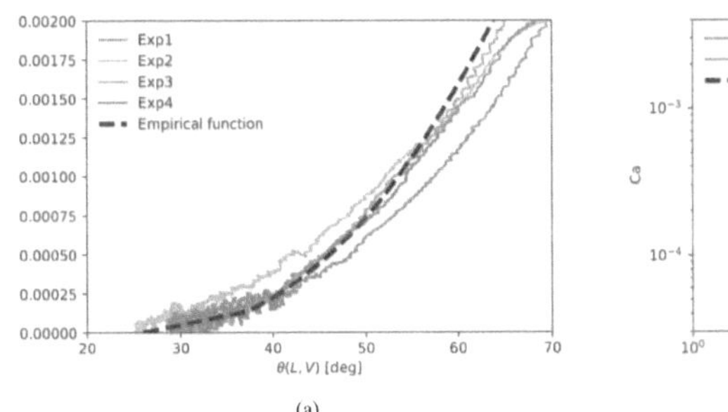

(a)

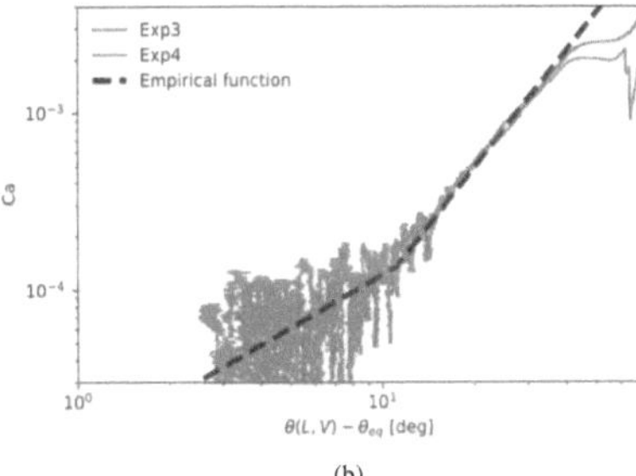

(b)

Figure 2.9.: Empirical relation for the dynamic contact angle.

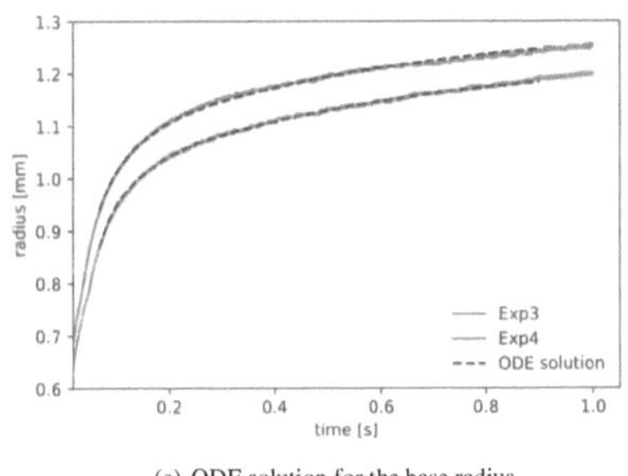

(a) ODE solution for the base radius.

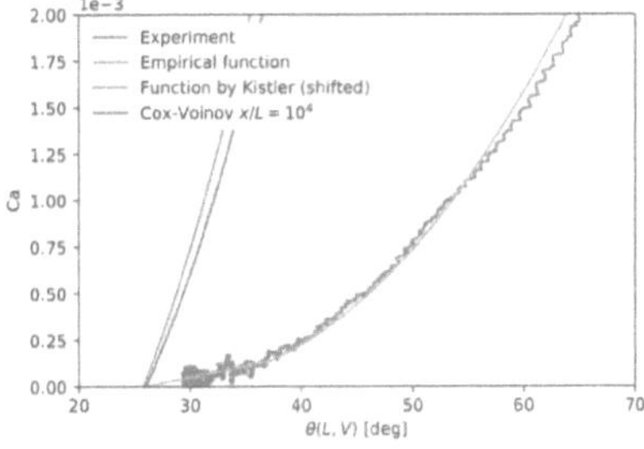

(b) Comparison with literature.

Figure 2.10.: ODE solution and literature comparison.

The shape of the droplet after detachment from the needle is close to a spherical cap. Moreover, the droplet retains a spherical shape throughout the whole process while the volume change is mainly due to evaporation. Note that a part of the drop volume is transported beyond the contact line into the thin polymer film. However, given the small heights of the swollen brush (less than 300 nm), this volume may be neglected in regard to an overall change in volume of the drop. Like in the previous experiments, the volume of the drop is extracted from the images of the high-speed camera.

Spreading in a high humidity environment: We first consider experimental data for a humidity of 80% within the climate chamber. The experimental data for the volume reported in Fig. 2.11(a) show that the droplet slowly loses volume (in this case mainly due to evaporation). Compared to the dynamics of the glycerol droplet on the silicon wafer in the previous section, the spreading on the polymer brush is extremely slow; see Fig. 2.11(b).

The experimental data for the capillary number as a function of the contact angle are shown in Figure 2.12(a). It is found that the data collapses reasonably well onto a single curve which can be described by the empirical function

$$\psi_{\mathrm{emp}}(\theta) = \max\{1.1 \cdot 10^{-6}(\theta - \theta_{\mathrm{eq}})^{2.2}, 5 \cdot 10^{-8}(\theta - \theta_{\mathrm{eq}})\}, \tag{2.21}$$

where $\theta_{\mathrm{eq}} = 65°$. This is remarkable since the physics of the interaction of the droplet with the substrate in the

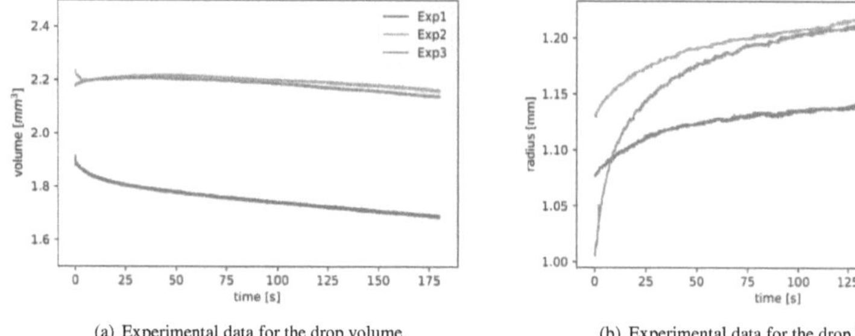

(a) Experimental data for the drop volume.

(b) Experimental data for the drop base radius.

Figure 2.11.: Spreading of a water droplet on a polymer brush (80% humidity).

spreading process is expected to be quite complex. As can be seen from Figure 2.12(b), the empirical relation (2.21) is able to describe the spreading dynamics for all considered repetitions of the experiment. Moreover, the predicted evolution of the droplet height agrees reasonably well with the experimental data; see Fig. 2.13. Moreover, we find that the data for the polymer brush can be described by the same exponents as for the water-glycerol droplet on the bare silicon wafer.

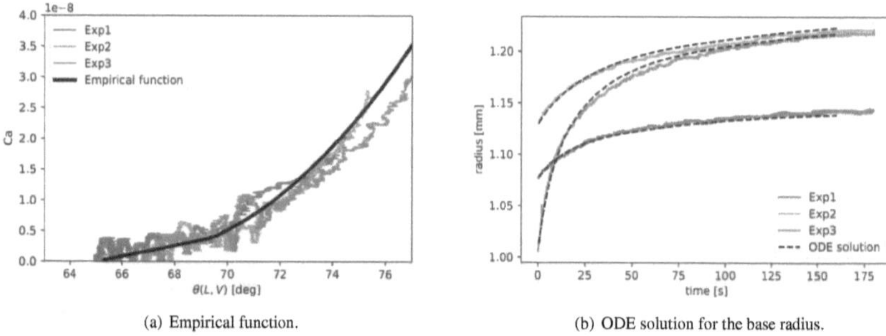

(a) Empirical function.

(b) ODE solution for the base radius.

Figure 2.12.: Empirical function and ODE solution (80% humidity).

Spreading in a low humidity environment: Finally, we consider the spreading in an environment with a reduced humidity of 50%. In this case, the evaporation rate is larger leading to a more rapid change in the drop volume; see Fig. 2.14(a). The experimental data for the drop height agree well with the assumption of a spherical cap geometry; see Fig. 2.14(c). However, the experimental data for the relation between contact angle and capillary number in Fig. 2.14(d) clearly shows that *no* universal relation of the form

$$Ca = \psi(\theta)$$

exists in this case. This is not surprising from a theoretical point of view since the presence of the droplet leads to an adaptation (i.e. swelling) of the polymer brush which in turn affects the wetting process. The latter effect can be expected to be more significant when the humidity is low since a high humidity leads to a pre-swelling of the polymer brush.

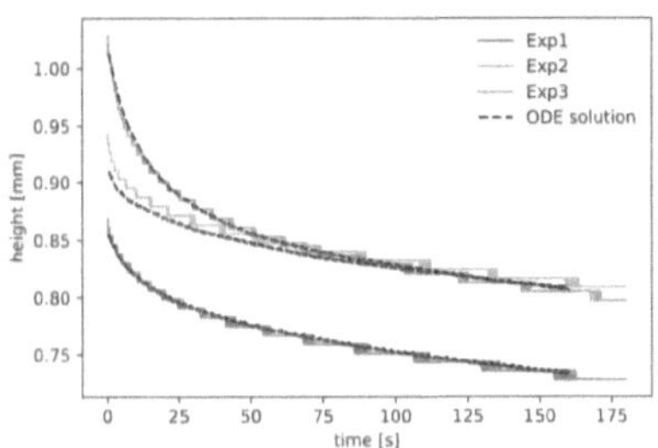

Figure 2.13.: Experimental data for the height compared to the ODE solution (80% humidity).

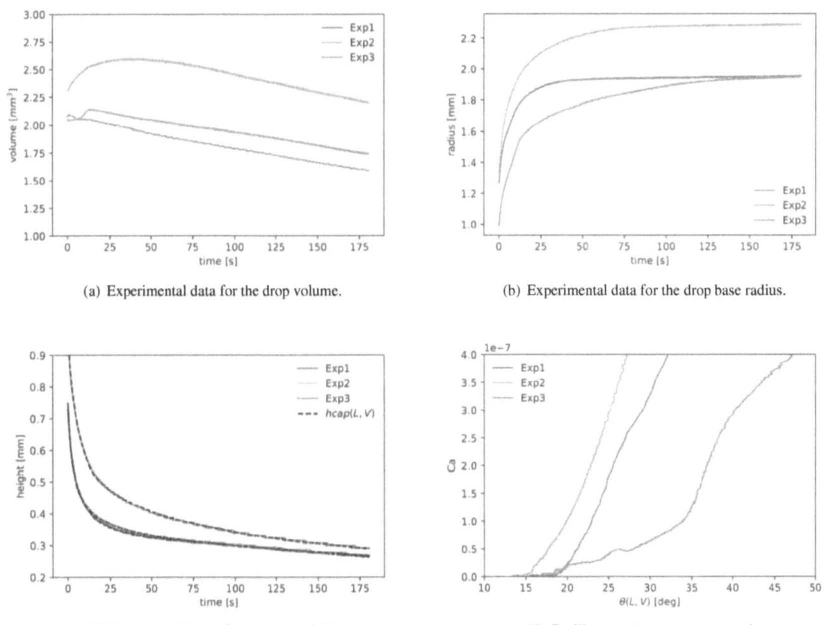

(a) Experimental data for the drop volume.

(b) Experimental data for the drop base radius.

(c) Experimental data for the drop height.

(d) Capillary number vs. contact angle.

Figure 2.14.: Spreading of a water droplet on a polymer brush (50% humidity).

2.4. Summary

A generalization of the ODE model for the spreading of thin droplets [dG85] is introduced. The main assumption for the model to be applicable is a spherical cap shape of the droplet and a functional relation between the speed of the contact line and the macroscopic contact angle. The ability of the ODE model to describe the spreading kinetics of partially wetting liquids has been demonstrated for the viscous stage of spreading of a glycerol-water droplet on a silicon wafer and the spreading of a pure water droplet on a PNIPAm-brush coated silicon wafer. It is important to note that the ODE model can only *predict* the spreading of spherical droplets in a range of parameters where a *universal* relation between macroscopic contact angle and contact line speed exists. The assumption of a spherical cap geometry allows to compute the contact angle as a function of the base radius and the volume leading to a regularization of the data compared to a direct measurement of the contact angle. The experimental data for the water-glycerol droplet show some variations in the relation between contact angle and contact line speed. It is found that the empirical relation cannot be described by a single exponent. Instead of that, there are at least two distinct stages with different exponents. Interestingly, there is a large deviation to the Cox-Voinov law and the empirical function by Kistler. The observed capillary number is one order of magnitude smaller than the prediction of the latter relations. This effect might be due to the polarity of the fluid or mixture effects and deserves further attention.

Finally, the ODE model can also describe the spreading of water droplets on a PNIPAm-brush coated silicon wafer. Interestingly, we found a reasonable collapse of the data for the experiments in a high humidity environment. The exponents in the empirical function are found to be the same as for the water-glycerol droplet on a bare silicon wafer. Conversely, there is no universal empirical relation for the experiments in a reduced humidity environment. This clearly shows the need for a more detailed continuum mechanical modeling of the complex interaction between the dynamics of drop and the polymer brush.

3. Sharp interface models

In this chapter[1], we are interested in the continuum mechanical description of a wetting process on a flat solid surface. For this purpose, we consider a two-phase system consisting of two immiscible Newtonian fluids described by the Navier-Stokes equations in the case where the fluid-fluid interface Σ has contact with a solid. Employing the sharp interface modeling approach, we describe the interfacial layer as a mathematical surface of zero thickness. The curve of intersection of the fluid-fluid interface with the solid boundary is called the *contact line*.

3.1. Notation and mathematical setting

For simplicity, let us assume that Ω is a half-space, such that the outer normal field $n_{\partial\Omega}$ is constant. This is not a real restriction for the theory since we are only interested in *local* properties. While this assumption simplifies the calculations, the results may be generalized to the case of a curved solid wall. Please note that we employ both of the notations

$$\langle a, b \rangle = \sum_i a_i b_i = a \cdot b \tag{3.1}$$

to denote the Euclidean inner product. The following definition of a $\mathscr{C}^{k,m}$-family of moving hypersurfaces can also be found in a similar form in [Gig06], [Kim08] and [PS16].

Definition 3.1. Let $I = (a,b)$ be an open interval. A family $\{\Sigma(t)\}_{t \in I}$ with $\Sigma(t) \subset \mathbb{R}^3$ is called a $\mathscr{C}^{k,m}$-*family of moving hypersurfaces* if the following holds.

(i) Each $\Sigma(t)$ is an orientable $\mathscr{C}^m$-hypersurface in $\mathbb{R}^3$ with unit normal field denoted as $n_\Sigma(t, \cdot)$.

(ii) The graph of Σ, given as

$$\mathscr{M} := \mathrm{gr}\,\Sigma = \bigcup_{t \in I} \{t\} \times \Sigma(t) \subset \mathbb{R} \times \mathbb{R}^3, \tag{3.2}$$

    is a $\mathscr{C}^k$-hypersurface in $\mathbb{R} \times \mathbb{R}^3$.

(iii) The unit normal field is k-times continuously differentiable on $\mathscr{M}$, i.e.

$$n_\Sigma \in \mathscr{C}^k(\mathscr{M}).$$

A family $\{\overline{\Sigma}(t)\}_{t \in I}$ is called a $\mathscr{C}^{k,m}$-*family of moving hypersurfaces with boundary* $\partial\Sigma(t)$ if the following holds.

(i) Each $\overline{\Sigma}(t)$ is an orientable $\mathscr{C}^m$-hypersurface in $\mathbb{R}^3$ with interior $\Sigma(t)$ and non-empty boundary $\partial\Sigma(t)$, where the unit normal field is denoted by $n_\Sigma(t, \cdot)$.

(ii) The graph of $\overline{\Sigma}$, i.e.

$$\mathrm{gr}\,\overline{\Sigma} = \bigcup_{t \in I} \{t\} \times \overline{\Sigma}(t) \subset \mathbb{R} \times \mathbb{R}^3,$$

    is a $\mathscr{C}^k$-hypersurface with boundary $\mathrm{gr}(\partial\Sigma)$ in $\mathbb{R} \times \mathbb{R}^3$.

(iii) The unit normal field is k-times continuously differentiable on $\mathrm{gr}\,\overline{\Sigma}$, i.e.

$$n_\Sigma \in \mathscr{C}^k(\mathrm{gr}\,\overline{\Sigma}).$$

---

[1] Please note that the Chapters 3 and 4 are an extended version of the work published in [FKB19].

Note that, being the boundary of a submanifold with boundary, the set $\mathrm{gr}(\partial\Sigma)$ is itself a submanifold (without boundary).

Unless stated otherwise, we consider the following geometrical situation and regularity: Let $\Omega \subset \mathbb{R}^3$ be a half-space and let the "fluid-fluid interface" $\{\Sigma(t)\}_{t\in I}$ be a $\mathscr{C}^{1,2}$-family of moving hypersurfaces with boundary $\partial\Sigma$ such that

$$\Sigma(t) \subset \Omega, \quad \partial\Sigma(t) \subset \partial\Omega \quad \forall t \in I,$$

i.e. the boundary of Σ is contained in the domain boundary. The moving fluid-fluid interface decomposes Ω into two bulk-phases, i.e

$$\Omega = \Omega^+(t) \cup \Omega^-(t) \cup \Sigma(t),$$

where the unit normal field n_Σ is pointing from $\Omega^-(t)$ to $\Omega^+(t)$. The *contact line* $\Gamma(t) \subset \partial\Omega$ is the subset of the solid boundary which is in contact with the interface $\Sigma(t)$, i.e.

$$\Gamma(t) := \partial\Sigma(t) = \partial\Omega \cap \overline{\Omega^+}(t) \cap \overline{\Omega^-}(t) \neq \emptyset.$$

We assume that $\Gamma(t)$ is non-empty and therefore do not consider the process of formation or disappearance of the contact line as a whole. Given a point $x \in \Gamma(t)$, the *contact angle* θ is defined by the relation

$$\cos\theta(t,x) := -\langle n_\Sigma(t,x), n_{\partial\Omega}(t,x)\rangle. \tag{3.3}$$

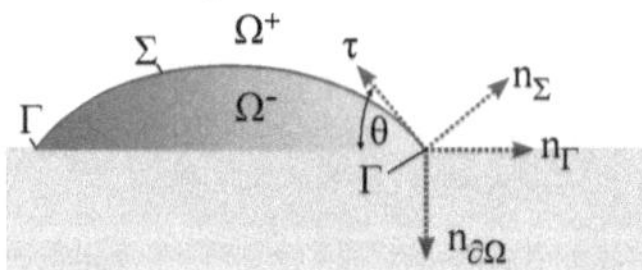

Figure 3.1.: Notation, local coordinate system.

Local coordinate system: For simplicity of notation, we choose the reference frame where the wall is at rest. Given a point $x \in \Gamma(t)$ at the contact line, we set up a local coordinate system to describe the evolution of the system. A possible choice is to use n_Σ and $n_{\partial\Omega}$ together with a third linear independent direction. However, the vectors n_Σ and $n_{\partial\Omega}$ are, in general, not orthogonal and it is more convenient to introduce a contact line normal vector.

Definition 3.2. For $0 < \theta < \pi$ the *contact line normal vector* n_Γ is defined via projection[2] (see Figure 3.1) as

$$n_\Gamma = \frac{\mathscr{P}_{\partial\Omega}\, n_\Sigma}{\|\mathscr{P}_{\partial\Omega}\, n_\Sigma\|}. \tag{3.4}$$

To complete the local basis, we define

$$t_\Gamma = n_\Gamma \times n_{\partial\Omega}.$$

Obviously, $\{n_\Gamma, n_{\partial\Omega}, t_\Gamma\}$ form a right-handed orthonormal basis of $\mathbb{R}^3$. The vector t_Γ is tangential to the interface Σ and tangential to the contact line curve Γ.

Moreover, it is useful to define an interface tangent vector τ in the plane spanned by n_Γ and $n_{\partial\Omega}$. The expansions of n_Σ and τ are given by

$$\tau = -\cos\theta\, n_\Gamma - \sin\theta\, n_{\partial\Omega}, \quad n_\Sigma = \sin\theta\, n_\Gamma - \cos\theta\, n_{\partial\Omega}. \tag{3.5}$$

Note that τ is normalized, orthogonal to n_Σ and it is pointing into the domain Ω, since

$$\langle \tau, n_{\partial\Omega}\rangle = -\sin\theta \leq 0.$$

---

[2]The orthogonal projection operator onto $\partial\Omega$ is given as $\mathscr{P}_{\partial\Omega} := \mathbb{1} - \langle n_{\partial\Omega}, \cdot\rangle\, n_{\partial\Omega}$.

Definition 3.3 (Normal and contact line velocity). To formulate the kinematic boundary condition, we need the notion of normal and contact line velocities.

(i) Let $x^\Sigma : I \to \mathbb{R}^3$ be a $\mathscr{C}^1$-curve on $\mathrm{gr}\,\overline{\Sigma}$, i.e. $(t, x^\Sigma(t)) \in \mathrm{gr}\,\overline{\Sigma}\ \forall t \in I$. Then, for $t_0 \in I$ and $x_0 = x^\Sigma(t_0) \in \overline{\Sigma}(t_0)$, the *normal velocity* is defined as[3]

$$V_\Sigma(t_0, x_0) := \left\langle \dot{x}^\Sigma(t_0), n_\Sigma(t_0, x_0) \right\rangle. \tag{3.6}$$

(ii) Let $x^\Gamma : I \to \mathbb{R}^3$ be a $\mathscr{C}^1$-curve on $\mathrm{gr}\,\Gamma$, i.e. $(t, x^\Gamma(t)) \in \mathrm{gr}\,\Gamma\ \forall t \in I$. Then, for $t_0 \in I$ and $x_0 = x^\Gamma(t_0) \in \Gamma(t_0)$, the *contact line velocity* is defined as

$$V_\Gamma(t_0, x_0) := \left\langle \dot{x}^\Gamma(t_0), n_\Gamma(t_0, x_0) \right\rangle. \tag{3.7}$$

If $V_\Gamma > 0$ ($V_\Gamma < 0$), the contact line is said to be advancing (receding).

Note that $(t, x^\Gamma(t)) \in \mathrm{gr}\,\Gamma \subset I \times \partial\Omega$ implies $\left\langle \dot{x}^\Gamma, n_{\partial\Omega} \right\rangle = 0$ and, hence,

$$V_\Sigma(t_0, x_0) = \left\langle \dot{x}^\Gamma(t_0), n_\Sigma(t_0, x_0) \right\rangle = \left\langle \dot{x}^\Gamma(t_0), \sin\theta\, n_\Gamma(t_0, x_0) - \cos\theta\, n_{\partial\Omega}(t_0, x_0) \right\rangle$$
$$= \sin\theta \left\langle \dot{x}^\Gamma(t_0), n_\Gamma(t_0, x_0) \right\rangle = \sin\theta\, V_\Gamma(t_0, x_0).$$

Therefore, we obtain the important relation

$$V_\Sigma = \sin\theta\, V_\Gamma \quad \text{on } \mathrm{gr}\,\Gamma. \tag{3.8}$$

To formulate the two-phase flow model, we need the notion of the *jump* of a quantity across the interface Σ.

Definition 3.4 (Jump across Σ). Fixing an interface configuration Σ, we define the space $\mathscr{J}(\Omega, \Sigma)$ of continuous functions on $\Omega^\pm$, admitting continuous extensions to $\overline{\Omega^\pm}$, i.e.

$$\mathscr{J}(\Omega, \Sigma) := \{ \psi \in \mathscr{C}(\Omega \setminus \Sigma),\ \exists \psi^\pm \in \mathscr{C}(\overline{\Omega^\pm})\ \text{s.t. } \psi_{|\Omega^\pm} = \psi^\pm \}.$$

The jump of ψ across the interface Σ at $x \in \overline{\Sigma}$ is defined as

$$[\![\psi]\!](x) := \lim_{n \to \infty} (\psi^+(x_n) - \psi^-(y_n)),$$

where $(x_n)_{n \in \mathbb{N}} \subset \overline{\Omega^+}$ and $(y_n)_{n \in \mathbb{N}} \subset \overline{\Omega^-}$ are sequences with

$$\lim_{n \to \infty} x_n = \lim_{n \to \infty} y_n = x.$$

By definition of $\mathscr{J}$, the jump of ψ does not depend on the choice of sequences. Note that, away from the boundary $\partial\Omega$, the jump of a quantity ψ may equivalently be expressed as

$$[\![\psi]\!](x) = \lim_{h \to 0^+} (\psi(x + h n_\Sigma) - \psi(x - h n_\Sigma)).$$

For $\psi \in \mathscr{J}(\Omega, \Sigma)$ it follows directly from the definition that $[\![\psi]\!]$ is a continuous function on $\overline{\Sigma}$.

---

[3]Note that such curves can always be constructed with the help of a local $\mathscr{C}^1$-parametrization. In the case of a hypersurface with boundary, such a parametrization is defined over the upper half ball

$$B_\varepsilon^{n,+}(0) := \{ x \in \mathbb{R}^n : \|x\| < \varepsilon,\ x_n \geq 0 \}.$$

Moreover, it can be shown that the normal velocity is well-defined, i.e. its value is independent of the choice of the curve (see, e.g., [PS16], chapter 5.2).

3.2. Entropy production

We recall the basic modeling assumptions leading to the "standard model" in the framework of the sharp interface two-phase Navier Stokes equations (for the modeling see [IH11], [Sla99], [EBW91], [PS16]). It is assumed that the system is isothermal, the flow in the bulk phases is incompressible and no mass is transferred across the fluid-fluid and the fluid-solid interface. As a further simplification, it is also assumed that the tangential component of the velocity is continuous. These assumptions lead to the formulation

$$\rho \frac{Dv}{Dt} = \nabla \cdot T, \quad \nabla \cdot v = 0 \quad \text{in } \Omega \setminus \Sigma(t), \tag{3.9}$$

$$[\![v]\!] = 0, \quad V_\Sigma = \langle v, n_\Sigma \rangle \quad \text{on } \Sigma(t), \tag{3.10}$$

$$V_\Gamma = \langle v, n_\Gamma \rangle \quad \text{on } \Gamma(t), \tag{3.11}$$

$$\langle v, n_{\partial\Omega} \rangle = 0 \quad \text{on } \partial\Omega \setminus \Gamma(t), \tag{3.12}$$

where $\frac{D}{Dt} = \partial_t + v \cdot \nabla$ is the Lagrangian time derivative and $T = T^\top$ is the Cauchy stress tensor[4].

To close the model, we consider the energy of the system.

Definition 3.5. In the simplest case, the free energy of the system is defined as (see, e.g., [RE07], [E11])

$$\mathscr{E}(t) = \int_{\Omega \setminus \Sigma(t)} \frac{\rho v^2}{2} \, dV + \int_{\Sigma(t)} \sigma \, dA + \int_{W(t)} \sigma_w \, dA, \tag{3.13}$$

where $W(t) := \overline{\Omega^-(t)} \cap \partial\Omega$ is the wetted area at time t and σ, $\sigma_w := \sigma_1 - \sigma_2$ are the specific energies of the fluid-fluid interface and the wetted surface (relative to the "dry" surface).

Assuming a *constant* liquid-gas surface energy σ and a smooth "wetting energy" $\sigma_w = \sigma_w(x)$ with $\sigma > 0$ and $|\sigma_w(x)| < \sigma$, we *define* an angle $\theta_{eq} = \theta_{eq}(x) \in (0, \pi)$ for $x \in \partial\Omega$ by the relation

$$\sigma \cos \theta_{eq}(x) + \sigma_w(x) = 0, \quad x \in \partial\Omega. \tag{3.14}$$

Note that, typically, the wetting energy σ_w will be constant. However, the wetting of *structured* surfaces in Chapter 12 requires the possibility to choose σ_w as a function of space along $\partial\Omega$.

A direct calculation shows the following result for the energy balance. A complete proof for the case of variable σ_w is given in Appendix A. See also [Sch01], [RE07] for a proof in the case of constant σ_w.

Theorem 3.6. *Let σ be constant with $\sigma > 0$ and σ_w be a smooth function on $\partial\Omega$ such that $|\sigma_w(x)| < \sigma$ for all $x \in \partial\Omega$. Let $(v, p, \mathrm{gr}\overline{\Sigma})$ be a sufficiently regular (classical) solution of the system (3.9) - (3.12). Then, the rate-of-change of the free energy is given as*

$$\frac{d\mathscr{E}}{dt} = -2 \int_{\Omega \setminus \Sigma(t)} D : T^0 \, dV + \int_{\partial\Omega} \langle v, T n_{\partial\Omega} \rangle \, dA$$
$$- \int_{\Sigma(t)} ([\![T]\!] n_\Sigma + \sigma \kappa n_\Sigma) \cdot v \, dA + \sigma \int_{\Gamma(t)} (\cos \theta - \cos \theta_{eq}) V_\Gamma \, dl, \tag{3.15}$$

where $\kappa = -\mathrm{div}_\Sigma n_\Sigma$ denotes the mean curvature of Σ, $D = \frac{1}{2}(\nabla v + \nabla v^\top)$ is the rate-of-deformation tensor and

$$T^0 = T - \frac{\mathrm{tr}(T)}{d} \mathbb{1}$$

is the traceless part of T (in dimension d).

According to the second law of thermodynamics, closure relations need to be found such that [5]

$$\frac{d\mathscr{E}}{dt} \leq 0.$$

---

[4] Here it is assumed that the fluid particles do not carry angular momentum.
[5] Note that the system is assumed to be isothermal.

3.3. The standard model for moving contact lines

Employing the standard closure for the two-phase Navier-Stokes model for a Newtonian fluid with dynamic viscosity η and constant surface tension σ, i.e.

$$T = -p\mathbb{1} + S = -p\mathbb{1} + \eta(\nabla v + (\nabla v)^{\mathsf{T}}), \quad [\![-T]\!]n_\Sigma = \sigma\kappa n_\Sigma,$$

we obtain

$$\frac{d\mathscr{E}}{dt} = -2\int_{\Omega\backslash\Sigma(t)} \eta D : D\,dV + \int_{\partial\Omega} \langle v, Sn_{\partial\Omega}\rangle \,dA + \sigma\int_{\Gamma(t)} (\cos\theta - \cos\theta_{\mathrm{eq}})\,V_\Gamma\,dl. \tag{3.16}$$

Here, the symbol

$$S = \eta(\nabla v + \nabla v^{\mathsf{T}}) = 2\eta D.$$

denotes the viscous stress tensor for a Newtonian fluid. Note that the second term in (3.16) vanishes if the usual no-slip condition is applied. However, as pointed out before, this approach does not allow for a moving contact line. Therefore, it is a frequent choice to consider the following generalization.

Remark 3.7 (Navier slip condition). Assuming that no fluid particles can move across the solid-fluid boundary one still requires $v \cdot n_{\partial\Omega} = 0$ on $\partial\Omega$. In this case, the above term can be rewritten as

$$\int_{\partial\Omega} \langle \mathscr{P}_{\partial\Omega}v, \mathscr{P}_{\partial\Omega}Sn_{\partial\Omega}\rangle \,dA.$$

Hence a possible choice to make it non-positive is given by

$$\langle v, n_{\partial\Omega}\rangle = 0, \quad \mathscr{P}_{\partial\Omega}Sn_{\partial\Omega} = -\lambda\mathscr{P}_{\partial\Omega}v \tag{3.17}$$

on $\partial\Omega$ with $\lambda \geq 0$. Note that equation (3.17) can be understood as a force balance, where λ plays the role of a friction coefficient. The no-slip condition is recovered in the limit $\lambda \to \infty$, while the case $\lambda = 0$ is known as the *free-slip condition*. The quantity

$$L = \frac{\eta}{\lambda}$$

has the dimension of a length and is called *slip length*. Note that in the two-phase case, the parameters λ and η are in general discontinuous across the interface. If L is strictly positive, it may be more convenient to use the inverse slip length

$$a = \frac{1}{L} = \frac{\lambda}{\eta}.$$

With the inverse slip length, the Navier condition can be expressed as

$$a\mathscr{P}_{\partial\Omega}v + 2\mathscr{P}_{\partial\Omega}Dn_{\partial\Omega} = 0. \tag{3.18}$$

Note that the slip length may depend on various physical parameters of the system including the wettability of the solid and the local shear-rate (see [NEB$^+$05], [LBS07] for a discussion of boundary slip). Here, we only assume that the slip length is a positive function admitting one-sided limits at the contact line, i.e.

$$a \in \mathscr{C}(\mathrm{gr}\,\overline{\Omega^+};[0,\infty)) \cap \mathscr{C}(\mathrm{gr}\,\overline{\Omega^-};[0,\infty)).$$

Remark 3.8 (Contact angle boundary condition). It remains to find a closure relation for the dissipation at the contact line. In the simplest case, we assume σ_{w} to be a constant with $|\sigma_{\mathrm{w}}| < \sigma$. Then the equilibrium contact angle θ_{eq} is a constant defined by (3.14). The more general case of structured surfaces, where σ_{w} is a function of space, is discussed in Chapter 12. A *sufficient* condition to ensure energy dissipation is to require that

$$V_\Gamma(\theta - \theta_{\mathrm{eq}}) \geq 0. \tag{3.19}$$

This may be achieved by setting[6]

$$\theta = f(V_\Gamma) \tag{3.20}$$

with some function f satisfying

$$f(0) = \theta_{\mathrm{eq}}, \quad V_\Gamma\left(f(V_\Gamma) - \theta_{\mathrm{eq}}\right) \geq 0. \tag{3.21}$$

So, in the absence of external forces, the contact line should only advance if the contact angle is above or equal to the equilibrium value defined by the Young equation (1.4) (and vice versa). This is reasonable if we think of the example of a spreading droplet with an initial contact angle larger than the equilibrium value (see Figure 3.2). We expect the contact line to advance *in order to* lower the contact angle and to drive the system towards equilibrium.

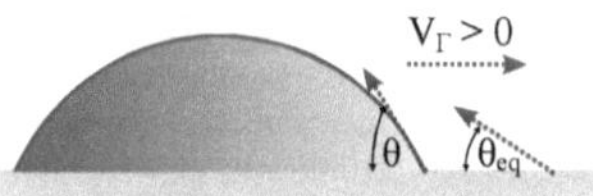

Figure 3.2.: Spreading droplet with an advancing contact line.

Standard model for moving contact lines: To summarize, we obtained the isothermal *"standard model for moving contact lines"* for incompressible two-phase flows with surface tension in the simplest possible case. This is a purely hydrodynamic model without any transfer processes of heat or mass.

$$
\begin{aligned}
\rho\frac{Dv}{Dt} - \eta\Delta v + \nabla p = 0, \ \nabla \cdot v = 0 &\quad \text{in } \Omega \setminus \Sigma(t), \\
[\![v]\!] = 0, \quad [\![p\mathbf{1} - S]\!]\, n_\Sigma = \sigma\kappa n_\Sigma &\quad \text{on } \Sigma(t), \\
\langle v, n_{\partial\Omega}\rangle = 0, \ a\mathscr{P}_{\partial\Omega}v + 2\mathscr{P}_{\partial\Omega}Dn_{\partial\Omega} = 0 &\quad \text{on } \partial\Omega \setminus \Gamma(t), \\
V_\Sigma = \langle v, n_\Sigma\rangle &\quad \text{on } \Sigma(t), \\
V_\Gamma = \langle v, n_\Gamma\rangle, \quad \theta = f(V_\Gamma) &\quad \text{on } \Gamma(t).
\end{aligned}
\tag{3.22}
$$

To ensure energy dissipation, we further require

$$\eta \geq 0,\ a \geq 0,\ \sigma \geq 0,\ V_\Gamma\left(f(V_\Gamma) - \theta_{\mathrm{eq}}\right) \geq 0, \tag{3.23}$$

where $\theta_{\mathrm{eq}} \in (0, \pi)$ is a constant characterizing the wettability of the solid.

Standard model for moving contact lines - free surface formulation: A commonly used simplification of the above model is the free surface formulation. It assumes that the outer phase is dynamically passive with a constant pressure p_0. The resulting model equations read as

$$
\begin{aligned}
\rho\frac{Dv}{Dt} - \eta\Delta v + \nabla p = 0, \ \nabla \cdot v = 0 &\quad \text{in } \Omega(t), \\
(p_0 - p + S)\, n_\Sigma = \sigma\kappa n_\Sigma &\quad \text{on } \Sigma(t), \\
\langle v, n_{\partial\Omega}\rangle = 0, \ a\mathscr{P}_{\partial\Omega}v + 2\mathscr{P}_{\partial\Omega}Dn_{\partial\Omega} = 0 &\quad \text{on } \partial\Omega \setminus \Gamma(t), \\
V_\Sigma = \langle v, n_\Sigma\rangle &\quad \text{on } \Sigma(t), \\
V_\Gamma = \langle v, n_\Gamma\rangle, \quad \theta = f(V_\Gamma) &\quad \text{on } \Gamma(t).
\end{aligned}
\tag{3.24}
$$

---

[6]Or by setting $V_\Gamma = g(\theta)$ with $g(\theta_{\mathrm{eq}}) = 0$, $g(\theta)(\theta - \theta_{\mathrm{eq}}) \geq 0$, which is more convenient if contact angle hysteresis is present.

3.4. A note on the generalized Navier boundary condition

The idea of the Generalized Navier boundary condition (GNBC) [QWS03, QWS06] is to allow for a deviation of the dynamic contact angle from the equilibrium value defined by the Young equation. This leads to a so-called *uncompensated Young stress* which "arises from the deviation of the fluid–fluid interface from its static configuration" [QWS06, p.335]. It is important to note that the GNBC is properly formulated in a *diffuse* interface framework (see [QWS06]). However, the GNBC can be formally understood in the sharp interface model as a combined closure for the terms in the entropy production (3.16) which arise from the contact line motion and from slip at the solid-liquid boundary, i.e.

$$\mathcal{T} = \int_{\partial\Omega} \langle v, Sn_{\partial\Omega} \rangle \, dA + \sigma \int_{\Gamma(t)} (\cos\theta - \cos\theta_{\text{eq}}) V_\Gamma \, dl.$$

By introducing the contact line delta function δ_Γ, one can rewrite $\mathcal{T}$ as a single integral over $\partial\Omega$ according to

$$\mathcal{T} = \int_{\partial\Omega} \left(\langle v, Sn_{\partial\Omega} \rangle + \sigma(\cos\theta - \cos\theta_{\text{eq}}) \langle v, n_\Gamma \rangle \delta_\Gamma \right) dA$$

$$= \int_{\partial\Omega} \left(Sn_{\partial\Omega} + \sigma(\cos\theta - \cos\theta_{\text{eq}}) n_\Gamma \delta_\Gamma \right) \cdot v \, dA$$

In order to ensure mass conservation, we still require $v \cdot n_{\partial\Omega} = 0$ at $\partial\Omega$ leading to

$$\mathcal{T} = \int_{\partial\Omega} \left((Sn_{\partial\Omega})_\| + \sigma(\cos\theta - \cos\theta_{\text{eq}}) n_\Gamma \delta_\Gamma \right) \cdot v_\| \, dA \tag{3.25}$$

So, formally, a quadratic form is obtained if we require

$$\lambda v_\| + (Sn_{\partial\Omega})_\| + \sigma(\cos\theta - \cos\theta_{\text{eq}}) n_\Gamma \delta_\Gamma = 0 \quad \text{on} \quad \partial\Omega \tag{3.26}$$

with a friction constant $\lambda > 0$. However, since δ_Γ is a delta distribution concentrated at the contact line, the only way to satisfy (3.26) is with

$$0 = \lambda v_\| + (Sn_{\partial\Omega})_\| \quad \text{at } \partial\Omega \quad \text{and} \quad \theta = \theta_{\text{eq}} \quad \text{on} \quad \Gamma(t). \tag{3.27}$$

The intuitive idea of the GNBC, which can be made precise in a diffuse interface model, is to smear out the contact line delta function in (3.26) over a small transition region. Note that this approach also requires to make sense of the contact angle θ and the contact line normal n_Γ away from the sharp contact line. Then, the deviation of the contact angle from the equilibrium value appears in the velocity boundary condition leading to a balance between sliding friction forces due to slip along the solid boundary, the tangential component of the viscous stress at the boundary and the uncompensated Young force. If extensions of θ *and* n_Γ on a local neighborhood of the contact line are available, one may approximate (3.26) by

$$-v_\|(x) = 2L(Dn_{\partial\Omega})_\|(x) + \frac{\sigma}{\lambda}[(\cos\theta - \cos\theta_{\text{eq}}) n_\Gamma \hat{\delta}_\Gamma](x), \tag{3.28}$$

where $\hat{\delta}_\Gamma$ is a smooth approximation of δ_Γ. However, it is not clear how a condition like (3.28) can be formulated rigorously in a sharp interface model such that the thermodynamic consistency of the model is guaranteed.

In practice, the smearing of the delta distribution can be achieved simply by the numerical discretization itself. The implementation of the condition (3.26) in a variational Arbitrary-Lagrangian-Eulerian (ALE) formulation is discussed in [GL09]. For a further qualitative analysis of the boundary condition (3.28) see Section 4.3.4. In particular, it is shown that for (3.28) the contact angle is a function of the contact line speed for quasi-stationary states.

3.5. Interface Formation Model

Another well-established approach to describe dynamic wetting is based on the idea to balance the mass contained in an interfacial layer separately from the mass in the bulk phases. A framework for this kind of modeling is provided by the non-equilibrium thermodynamics of surfaces [Bed86]. Mathematically, the mass within the interfacial layer is expressed as a density per unit *area* ρ^Σ associated with a sharp interface in the continuum limit. The resulting model, known as the Interface Formation Model (IFM) [Shi93, Shi08], adds another level of complexity to the description since it requires to solve additional balance equations on moving interfaces. We only review some core features of the model and refer to the literature for more details (see, e.g., [Shi93, Bed04, Bil06, Shi08, SSK12, BP16]).

Mass balance: The generic mass balance equation within an interfacial layer Σ reads as [BP16, p.40]

$$\partial_t^\Sigma \rho^\Sigma + \mathrm{div}_\Sigma(\rho^\Sigma v^\Sigma) + [\![\dot{m}]\!] = 0, \tag{3.29}$$

where ρ^Σ denotes the surface mass density and v^Σ denotes the velocity of liquid particles within the surface phase. Here, the one-sided *mass transfer fluxes* from the bulk to the surface are defined as

$$\dot{m}^\pm = \rho^\pm(v^\pm \cdot n_\Sigma - V_\Sigma) \quad \text{on } \Sigma.$$

If the interface is *not* able to store mass, the mass transfer flux has to be continuous, i.e. $[\![\dot{m}]\!] = 0$ leading to the condition

$$[\![v]\!] \cdot n_\Sigma = 0 \quad \text{on } \Sigma \tag{3.30}$$

in the standard model (3.22). However, this is not necessarily the case for the IFM where $[\![\dot{m}]\!]$ appears as a source term in the mass balance equation (3.29). In the usual formulation of the IFM, mass can be stored on both the liquid-solid and the liquid-gas interface. An important consequence is, that the impermeability condition $v \cdot n_{\partial\Omega} = 0$ is no longer valid along the solid boundary. Instead, the mass flux to the liquid-solid phase depends (in the simplest form of the IFM) on the deviation of the interfacial mass density ρ^{sl} from its equilibrium value $\rho^{\mathrm{sl}}_{\mathrm{eq}}$ according to [Shi08, p.201]

$$\rho\, v \cdot n_{\partial\Omega} = \frac{\rho^{\mathrm{sl}}_{\mathrm{eq}} - \rho^{\mathrm{sl}}}{\tau_r}. \tag{3.31}$$

Here τ_r is a relaxation time [Shi08, p.196] and ρ and v denote the density and the velocity in the bulk, respectively. It is important to note that (3.31) leads to a fundamental change of the flow kinematics close to the contact line compared to the standard impermeability condition. In particular, fluid particles located at the liquid-gas interface or the bulk phases are able to reach the solid wall in finite time. The latter is not possible if the standard impermeability condition holds, provided that the solution is regular; see Remark 4.16 in Chapter 4 for more details. This type of flow kinematics is called "rolling motion" in the literature (see, e.g., [Shi93]).

Contact angle boundary condition: Another major difference to the standard model (3.22) affects the contact angle boundary condition. Physically, the idea of the IFM is that the formation or disappearance of a piece of interface is a dynamic process with a characteristic relaxation timescale that leads to dynamic surface tensions. Therefore, the model *predicts* a dynamic contact angle (rather than prescribing it a priori) which is governed by a dynamic version of the Youngs equation, i.e.

$$\sigma_{\mathrm{lg}} \cos \theta_d + \sigma_{\mathrm{sl}} - \sigma_{\mathrm{sg}} = 0,$$

where the surface tensions σ_i for the respective surface layers depend on the local state of the interface through the surface mass densities ρ^i.

Notably, it is stated that the IFM completely regularizes the moving contact line singularity. In particular, the pressure and curvature at the moving contact line is claimed to be regular (see [Shi08] for a detailed discussion). The IFM has been implemented into a finite element framework in [Spr10, SS13] and successfully applied to various flow configurations including capillary rise [SS13], wetting of structured surfaces [SS12b] and coalescence of liquid drops [SS14] where it removes the singularity inherent in the standard model. On the other hand, a major criticisms of the IFM is that it introduces a large number of additional parameters with associated uncertainties in their values which makes predictions difficult [SSK12, p.33]. Recently, Lukyanov and Pryer [LP17] introduced a quasi-stationary model which can be understood as an adaptation and simplification of the full IFM. The latter model is analyzed in Chapter 5 with respect to the compatibility of the boundary conditions at the contact line.

4. Kinematics of moving contact lines

The goal of this chapter[1] is to analyze some mathematical properties of the discussed models, in particular the combination of boundary conditions at the contact line, by means of a *kinematic* approach. The key idea is to understand how the flow field transports the contact angle. Note that here we consider the most simple case of a flat, perfectly clean solid wall and ideal Newtonian fluids, a situation never met in a real-world experiment. A real surface always has some geometrical and chemical structure (see Chapter 12) leading to additional effects like contact angle hysteresis and pinning. Moreover, it might be interesting to consider more complex liquids and substrates to enhance certain properties for applications. However, it seems meaningful to first study the mathematics of the problem in the simplest setting.

Remark 4.1 (Motivation). Consider a bounded domain Ω (in $\mathbb{R}^2$ or $\mathbb{R}^3$) with a smooth boundary $\partial\Omega$. Define a passively advected interface $\Sigma(t)$ as the zero contour of some *level set* function ϕ, i.e.

$$\Sigma(t) = \{x \in \Omega : \phi(t,x) = 0\},$$

where ϕ satisfies the transport equation

$$\partial_t \phi + v \cdot \nabla \phi = 0, \quad t > 0, x \in \Omega,$$
$$\phi(0,x) = \phi_0(x), \quad x \in \Omega \tag{4.1}$$

with a given velocity field v and smooth initial data ϕ_0. The initial value problem (4.1) is well-posed if v is sufficiently regular and tangential to the boundary $\partial\Omega$, i.e.

$$v \cdot n_{\partial\Omega} = 0 \quad \text{on} \quad \partial\Omega.$$

This can be shown by the method of characteristics (see [Eva10]). In particular, there is no boundary condition for ϕ, i.e. no contact angle can be prescribed. Indeed, it is well-known from the theory of hyperbolic PDEs that boundary conditions for (4.1) are only required at *inflow* boundaries, see, e.g, [LeV02, Section 3.11]. Hence, there must be a relation that expresses the rate-of-change of the contact angle in terms of the current geometry and the transporting velocity field only.

4.1. Kinematic transport of the contact angle

Let us now derive the contact angle evolution equation. It is a purely kinematic result which, under certain regularity assumptions, follows directly from the kinematic boundary conditions on $\mathrm{gr}\Sigma$ and $\mathrm{gr}\Gamma$. Note that, in the general case, the interface velocity is only defined on the interface itself, hence trajectories need to fulfill the time-dependent constraint $x(t) \in \bar{\Sigma}(t)$ on I, or, equivalently, $(t,x(t)) \in \mathrm{gr}\bar{\Sigma}$ on I. This allows to apply the result to models where the interface is not a material interface but moves with its *own* velocity v_Σ different from the fluid velocity v. This is the case if phase change phenomena or interfacial mass densities are present.

4.1.1. Preliminaries: Solutions in closed sets

There is a well-established theory for solutions of ODEs in closed subsets of $\mathbb{R}^d$ (see, e.g., [Dei77, Dei92, Aub09, Bot96, Bot03, Nag42, Bre70, Ama90]). We use this theory for (local) existence and uniqueness of trajectories on the moving hypersurface with boundary. A key definition of the theory is the following:

---

[1] Please note that the Chapters 3 and 4 are an extended version of the work published in [FKB19].

Let K a closed subset of $\mathbb{R}^d$. Then for $y \in K$ the *Bouligand contingent cone* is the set[2]

$$T_K(y) := \{z \in \mathbb{R}^d : \liminf_{h \to 0^+} \frac{1}{h}\,\mathrm{dist}(y + hz, K) = 0\}. \tag{4.2}$$

An element of $T_K(y)$ is said to be *subtangential* to K at y. If K is a $\mathscr{C}^1$-submanifold the contingent cone coincides with the tangent space of the submanifold. For a boundary point of a submanifold with boundary, it provides a proper generalization. Note that if $\tilde{K} \subseteq K$ is a closed subset of K then[3]

$$T_{\tilde{K}}(y) \subseteq T_K(y) \quad \forall\, y \in \tilde{K}. \tag{4.3}$$

The following result is a special case of Theorem 4.2 in [Dei77] and states that a subtangential and Lipschitz continuous map induces a local semiflow on K. If, in addition, we have that both $f(y)$ and $-f(y)$ are subtangential, we obtain a local *flow* on K (in forward and backward direction).

In the following, $B_r^d(x) := \{y \in \mathbb{R}^d : \|x - y\| < r\}$ denotes the open ball in $\mathbb{R}^d$ with radius r.

Theorem 4.2 (see [Dei77]). *Let $K \subset \mathbb{R}^d$ be closed, $y_0 \in K$, $K_r := K \cap \overline{B_r^d(y_0)}$ and $f : K_r \to \mathbb{R}^d$ be Lipschitz continuous with $|f(y)| \leq c$ and*

$$f(y) \in T_K(y) \quad \forall\, y \in K_r. \tag{4.4}$$

Then the initial value problem

$$y'(s) = f(y(s)), \quad y(0) = y_0$$

has a unique solution on $[0, r/c]$ with values in K_r.

4.1.2. Trajectories on the moving hypersurface

To formulate the kinematic evolution equation, we need the notion of a surface Lagrangian derivative on the moving hypersurface with boundary. We, therefore, consider the flow on $\mathrm{gr}\overline{\Sigma}$ generated by a consistent interfacial velocity field v_Σ.

Lemma 4.3 (Trajectories on $\mathrm{gr}\overline{\Sigma}$). *Let $\mathrm{gr}\overline{\Sigma}$ be a $\mathscr{C}^{1,2}$-family of moving hypersurfaces with boundary and $v_\Sigma \in \mathscr{C}^1(\mathrm{gr}\overline{\Sigma})$ be a velocity field with*

$$V_\Sigma = \langle v_\Sigma, n_\Sigma \rangle \text{ on } \mathrm{gr}\Sigma, \quad \langle v_\Sigma, n_{\partial\Omega} = 0 \rangle \text{ on } \mathrm{gr}\Gamma. \tag{4.5}$$

Then the initial value problem

$$\frac{d}{dt}\Phi(t; t_0, x_0) = (1, v_\Sigma(\Phi(t; t_0, x_0))), \quad \Phi(t_0; t_0, x_0) = (t_0, x_0). \tag{4.6}$$

is locally uniquely solvable on $\mathrm{gr}\overline{\Sigma}$. The solution of (4.6) depends continuously on the initial data (t_0, x_0) and the manifolds $\mathrm{gr}\Sigma$ and $\mathrm{gr}\Gamma$ are invariant subsets for the flow Φ.

We call a solution $\Phi(t; t_0, x_0)$ a *trajectory* on the moving hypersurface. Note that due to the structure of $\mathrm{gr}\overline{\Sigma}$, any solution can be written in the form

$$\Phi(t; t_0, x_0) = (t, \Phi_x(t; t_0, x_0))$$

with $\Phi_x(t; t_0, x_0) \in \overline{\Sigma(t)}$.

---

[2] The *distance* of a point $x \in \mathbb{R}^d$ to a subset $A \subseteq \mathbb{R}^d$ is defined as $\mathrm{dist}(x, A) := \inf\{\|x - a\| : a \in A\}$.

[3] This follows from the fact that

$\mathrm{dist}(y + hz, K) \leq \mathrm{dist}(y + hz, \tilde{K}).$

Definition 4.4. The *Lagrangian time-derivative* of a quantity $\psi \in \mathscr{C}^1(\mathrm{gr}\overline{\Sigma})$ is defined as

$$\frac{D^{\Sigma}\psi}{Dt}(t_0, x_0) := \frac{d}{dt}\,\psi(\Phi(t; t_0, x_0))\Big|_{t=t_0}. \tag{4.7}$$

For an inner point[4] $(t_0, x_0) \in \mathrm{gr}\Sigma$, one may consider the choice

$$v_{\Sigma} := V_{\Sigma}\, n_{\Sigma}$$

and write ∂_t^{Σ} for the corresponding Lagrangian derivative (also called *Thomas derivative* [Tho57]).

For the proof of Lemma 4.3, it is useful to give the following characterization of the tangent spaces of the submanifolds $\mathrm{gr}\Sigma$ and $\mathrm{gr}\Gamma$. The proof is given in the Appendix B.

Lemma 4.5 (Tangent spaces). *The tangent space of* $\mathrm{gr}\Sigma$ *at the point* (t, x) *is given by*

$$T_{\mathrm{gr}\Sigma}(t, x) = \{\lambda\,(1, V_{\Sigma}n_{\Sigma}(t, x)) + (0, \tau) : \lambda \in \mathbb{R},\ \tau \in T_{\Sigma(t)}(x)\}.$$

Likewise, the tangent space of $\mathrm{gr}\Gamma$ *at the point* (t, x) *is given by*

$$T_{\mathrm{gr}\Gamma}(t, x) = \{\lambda\,(1, V_{\Gamma}n_{\Gamma}(t, x)) + (0, \tau) : \lambda \in \mathbb{R},\ \tau \in T_{\Gamma(t)}(t, x)\}.$$

Moreover, we observe that the conditions (4.5) also guarantee consistency with $\mathrm{gr}\Gamma$.

Lemma 4.6 (Kinematic conditions). *Let* $\mathrm{gr}\overline{\Sigma}$ *be a* $\mathscr{C}^{1,2}$*-family of moving hypersurfaces with boundary,* $\theta \in (0, \pi)$ *on* $\mathrm{gr}\Gamma$ *and the interfacial velocity field* $v_{\Sigma} \in \mathscr{C}(\mathrm{gr}\overline{\Sigma})$ *satisfies*

$$V_{\Sigma} = \langle v_{\Sigma}, n_{\Sigma} \rangle \quad on \quad \mathrm{gr}\Sigma, \quad \langle v_{\Sigma}, n_{\partial\Omega} \rangle = 0 \quad on \quad \mathrm{gr}\Gamma.$$

Then v_{Σ} *fulfills the kinematic condition*

$$V_{\Gamma} = \langle v_{\Sigma}, n_{\Gamma} \rangle \quad on \quad \mathrm{gr}\Gamma. \tag{4.8}$$

Proof. From the relation (3.8) it follows that

$$\sin\theta\, V_{\Gamma} = \langle v_{\Sigma}, n_{\Sigma} \rangle = \sin\theta\,\langle v_{\Sigma}, n_{\Gamma} \rangle - \cos\theta\,\langle v_{\Sigma}, n_{\partial\Omega} \rangle = \sin\theta\,\langle v_{\Sigma}, n_{\Gamma} \rangle \quad on \quad \mathrm{gr}\Gamma.$$

This proves the claim since $\theta \in (0, \pi)$ by assumption. $\qquad\square$

Proof of Lemma 4.3. It follows directly from (4.5) that

$$v_{\Sigma}(t, x) = V_{\Sigma}n_{\Sigma}(t, x) + \mathscr{P}_{\Sigma(t)}v_{\Sigma}(t, x) \tag{4.9}$$

if $(t, x) \in \mathrm{gr}\Sigma$. Similarly, it follows from Lemma 4.6 that

$$v_{\Sigma}(t, x) = V_{\Gamma}n_{\Gamma}(t, x) + ((\langle v_{\Sigma}, t_{\Gamma} \rangle\, t_{\Gamma})(t, x) \tag{4.10}$$

if $(t, x) \in \mathrm{gr}\Gamma$. Hence, the field $f \in \mathscr{C}^1(\mathrm{gr}\overline{\Sigma}; \mathbb{R}^4)$ defined by

$$f(t, x) := (1, v_{\Sigma}(t, x))$$

is an element of the tangent space $T_{\mathrm{gr}\Sigma}(t, x)$ or $T_{\mathrm{gr}\Gamma}(t, x)$, respectively (cf. Lemma 4.5). In order to apply Theorem 4.2, we set $X := \mathbb{R} \times \mathbb{R}^3$, fix a point $(t_0, x_0) \in \mathrm{gr}\overline{\Sigma}$ and consider the closed subsets

$$K^{\delta}(\overline{\Sigma}) := \bigcup_{t \in [t_0 - \delta, t_0 + \delta]} \{t\} \times \overline{\Sigma}(t) \subset \mathrm{gr}\overline{\Sigma},$$

$$K_r^{\delta}(\overline{\Sigma}) := K^{\delta}(\overline{\Sigma}) \cap \overline{B_r^4}(t_0, x_0),$$

$$K^{\delta}(\Gamma) := \bigcup_{t \in [t_0 - \delta, t_0 + \delta]} \{t\} \times \Gamma(t) \subset K^{\delta}(\overline{\Sigma}),$$

$$K_r^{\delta}(\Gamma) := K^{\delta}(\Gamma) \cap \overline{B_r^4}(t_0, x_0)$$

for $\delta > 0$ sufficiently small.

---

[4] Here and in the following, we mean by "inner point" an inner point of the *manifold with boundary* $\mathrm{gr}\overline{\Sigma}$. Clearly, the set $\mathrm{gr}\overline{\Sigma}$ has no inner points as a subset of $\mathbb{R}^4$ in the standard topology.

Lemma 4.7. *Under the above assumptions there is $r > 0$ such that*

$$\pm(1, v_\Sigma(t,x)) \in T_{K^\delta(\overline{\Sigma})}(t,x) \quad \forall (t,x) \in K_r^\delta(\overline{\Sigma}) \cap \mathrm{gr}\Sigma,$$
$$\pm(1, v_\Sigma(t,x)) \in T_{K^\delta(\Gamma)}(t,x) \quad \forall (t,x) \in K_r^\delta(\overline{\Sigma}) \cap \mathrm{gr}\Gamma.$$

Since $T_{K^\delta(\Gamma)} \subset T_{K^\delta(\overline{\Sigma})}(t,x)$, it also holds that

$$\pm(1, v_\Sigma(t,x)) \in T_{K^\delta(\overline{\Sigma})}(t,x) \tag{4.11}$$

for all $(t,x) \in K_r^\delta(\overline{\Sigma})$.

Proof. We choose $r > 0$ such that $K_r^\delta(\overline{\Sigma}) \subseteq K^{\delta/2}(\overline{\Sigma}) \subset K^\delta(\overline{\Sigma})$. Therefore, we do not have to consider the boundary cases $t = t_0 \pm \delta$.

Let $(t,x) \in K_r^\delta(\overline{\Sigma}) \cap \mathrm{gr}\Sigma$. In this case, the vector $(1, v_\Sigma(t,x))$ is an element of the tangent space of the manifold $\mathrm{gr}\Sigma$. This follows from (4.9) and Lemma 4.5. By definition, this means that there is an open interval $I \ni 0$ and a $\mathscr{C}^1$-curve $\gamma : I \to \mathrm{gr}\Sigma$ such that

$$\gamma(0) = (t,x), \quad \gamma'(0) = (1, v_\Sigma(t,x)).$$

Clearly, by restriction to a smaller open interval, one can always achieve $\gamma \in \mathscr{C}^1(\tilde{I}; K^\delta(\overline{\Sigma}))$. Therefore, we have

$$\begin{aligned}
&\mathrm{dist}[(t,x) + s(1, v_\Sigma(t,x)), K^\delta(\overline{\Sigma})] \\
&\leq |(t,x) + s(1, v_\Sigma(t,x)) - \gamma(s)| \\
&\leq |(t,x) + s(1, v_\Sigma(t,x)) - \gamma(0) - \gamma'(0)s + o(|s|)| \\
&= |o(|s|)| \quad \text{as } s \to 0.
\end{aligned}$$

Note that this also means that

$$\mathrm{dist}[(t,x) - s(1, v_\Sigma(t,x)), K^\delta(\overline{\Sigma})] = |o(|s|)|$$

as $s \to 0$. Hence it follows that $\pm(1, v_\Sigma) \in T_{K^\delta(\overline{\Sigma})}$.

Let $(t,x) \in K_r^\delta(\Gamma) = K_r^\delta(\overline{\Sigma}) \cap \mathrm{gr}\Gamma$. Since $(1, v_\Sigma(t,x))$ is an element of the tangent space of the manifold $\mathrm{gr}\Gamma$, there is an open interval $I \ni 0$ and a $\mathscr{C}^1$-curve $\gamma : I \to K^\delta(\Gamma)$ such that

$$\gamma(0) = (t,x), \quad \gamma'(0) = (1, v_\Sigma(t,x)).$$

With the same argument as above, we obtain

$$\mathrm{dist}[(t,x) \pm s(1, v_\Sigma(t,x)), K^\delta(\Gamma)] = |o(|s|)|$$

as $s \to 0$. $\qquad\square$

Since we have that

$$\pm(1, v_\Sigma(t,x)) \in T_{K^\delta(\Gamma)} \quad \forall (t,x) \in K_r^\delta(\Gamma),$$

Theorem 4.2 also implies that the boundary $\mathrm{gr}\Gamma$ is an *invariant subset*, i.e. any trajectory starting in the subset $\mathrm{gr}\Gamma$ stays in this subset (in both forward and backward direction). Since Φ is a *flow* on $\mathrm{gr}\overline{\Sigma}$, it follows that also the *interior* $\mathrm{gr}\Sigma$ is an invariant subset (see [Ama90]). Since we assume $v_\Sigma \in \mathscr{C}^1(\mathrm{gr}\overline{\Sigma})$, standard arguments show that the solution of (4.6) depends continuously on the initial data (t_0, x_0). $\qquad\square$

4.1.3. Contact angle evolution equation

Theorem 4.8 (Evolution of the contact angle)**.** *Consider a $\mathscr{C}^{1,2}$-family of moving hypersurfaces with boundary and a consistent velocity field $v_\Sigma \in \mathscr{C}^1(\mathrm{gr}\overline{\Sigma})$ with*

$$V_\Sigma = \langle v_\Sigma, n_\Sigma \rangle \ \text{on } \mathrm{gr}\Sigma, \quad \langle v_\Sigma, n_{\partial\Omega} \rangle = 0 \ \text{on } \mathrm{gr}\Gamma.$$

Let Ω be a half-space such that $n_{\partial\Omega}$ is constant on the boundary and let $\theta \in (0,\pi)$. Then the time derivative of the contact angle on $\mathrm{gr}\,\Gamma$ obeys the evolution equation

$$\boxed{\frac{D^\Sigma \theta}{Dt} = \langle \partial_\tau v_\Sigma, n_\Sigma \rangle,} \tag{4.12}$$

where $\tau = -\cos\theta\, n_\Gamma - \sin\theta\, n_{\partial\Omega}$.

Remark 4.9. (i) There is a short way to (formally) derive the kinematic evolution equation (4.14) using the level set formulation. For details see [FKB18].

(ii) Since $v_\Sigma \cdot n_{\partial\Omega} = 0$ on $\partial\Omega$, equation (4.12) may be reformulated as

$$\frac{D^\Sigma \theta}{Dt} = \partial_\tau V_\Sigma + \cos\theta\, V_\Gamma \langle \tau, \partial_\tau n_\Sigma \rangle - \langle v_\Sigma, t_\Gamma \rangle \langle t_\Gamma, \partial_\tau n_\Sigma \rangle.$$

In particular, for the two-dimensional case, we obtain

$$\frac{D^\Sigma \theta}{Dt} = \partial_\tau V_\Sigma - \kappa \cos\theta\, V_\Gamma.$$

In a frame of reference, where the contact line is at rest (i.e. $V_\Gamma = 0$), the latter formula reduces to

$$\frac{D^\Sigma \theta}{Dt} = \partial_\tau V_\Sigma.$$

(iii) Note that for $\theta \to 0$ or $\theta \to \pi$, the interface tangent vector τ becomes tangential to $\partial\Omega$ and $n_\Sigma \to \pm n_{\partial\Omega}$. Therefore, we obtain in the limit

$$\frac{D^\Sigma \theta}{Dt}\Big|_{\theta=0} = \frac{D^\Sigma \theta}{Dt}\Big|_{\theta=\pi} = 0.$$

In the following, we restrict ourselves to the case of *partial wetting*, i.e.

$$0 < \theta < \pi.$$

To prove Theorem 4.8, it is useful to first consider the evolution of the normal vector.

Theorem 4.10 (Evolution of the normal vector). *Consider a $\mathscr{C}^{1,2}$-family of moving hypersurfaces and a consistent velocity field $v_\Sigma \in \mathscr{C}^1(\mathrm{gr}\,\Sigma)$ satisfying*

$$V_\Sigma = \langle v_\Sigma, n_\Sigma \rangle \ \text{ on } \mathrm{gr}\,\Sigma. \tag{4.13}$$

Then the evolution of the interface normal vector on $\mathrm{gr}\,\Sigma$ obeys the evolution equation

$$\frac{D^\Sigma n_\Sigma}{Dt} = -\sum_{k=1}^{2} \langle \partial_{\tau_k} v_\Sigma, n_\Sigma \rangle \tau_k, \tag{4.14}$$

where $\{\tau_1, \tau_2\}$ is an orthonormal basis of $T_{\Sigma(t_0)}(x_0)$.

Remark 4.11. Since $V_\Sigma(t,\cdot) = \langle v_\Sigma(t,\cdot), n_\Sigma(t,\cdot) \rangle \in \mathscr{C}^1(\Sigma(t))$, equation (4.14) can be written as

$$\frac{D^\Sigma}{Dt} n_\Sigma = \sum_{k=1}^{2} \left(-\tau_k \partial_{\tau_k} V_\Sigma + \langle (v_\Sigma)_\|, \partial_{\tau_k} n_\Sigma \rangle \tau_k \right) = -\nabla_\Sigma V_\Sigma + \sum_{k=1}^{2} \langle (v_\Sigma)_\|, \partial_{\tau_k} n_\Sigma \rangle \tau_k.$$

In particular, for $v_\Sigma(t,x) := V_\Sigma(t,x)\, n_\Sigma(t,x)$ we obtain (in agreement with [Kim08], Theorem 5.15)

$$\partial_t^\Sigma n_\Sigma = -\nabla_\Sigma V_\Sigma. \tag{4.15}$$

With this notation, we may express (4.14) as

$$\frac{D^\Sigma}{Dt} n_\Sigma = \partial_t^\Sigma n_\Sigma + (\nabla_\Sigma n_\Sigma)(v_\Sigma)_\| = -\nabla_\Sigma V_\Sigma + \|(v_\Sigma)_\|\| \partial_w n_\Sigma,$$

where $w := (v_\Sigma)_\| / \|(v_\Sigma)_\|\|$ (for $(v_\Sigma)_\| \neq 0$).

Preliminaries for the proof: In order to prove Theorem 4.10, we need a *continuously differentiable* dependence of the trajectories $\Phi(\cdot, t_0, x_0)$ on the initial position $x_0 \in \Sigma(t_0)$. To this end, we construct a $\mathscr{C}^1$-extension of the velocity field v_Σ to an open neighborhood of (t_0, x_0) in $\mathbb{R}^4$, which still leaves $\mathrm{gr}\Sigma$ invariant. This construction allows to obtain the $\mathscr{C}^1$-dependence on the initial position from standard ODE theory. To show the following Lemma, it is helpful to use a special type of local parametrization for $\mathrm{gr}\Sigma$ which is constructed in the Appendix B.

Lemma 4.12 (Signed distance function). *Let $\{\Sigma(t)\}_{t \in I}$ be a $\mathscr{C}^{1,2}$-family of moving hypersurfaces and (t_0, x_0) be an inner point of $\mathscr{M} = \mathrm{gr}\Sigma$. Then there exists an open neighborhood $U \subset \mathbb{R}^4$ of (t_0, x_0) and $\varepsilon > 0$ such that the map*

$$X : (\mathscr{M} \cap U) \times (-\varepsilon, \varepsilon) \to \mathbb{R}^4,$$
$$X(t, x, h) := (t, x + h n_\Sigma(t, x))$$

is a diffeomorphism onto its image

$$\mathscr{N}^\varepsilon := X((\mathscr{M} \cap U) \times (-\varepsilon \times \varepsilon)) \subset \mathbb{R}^4,$$

i.e. X is invertible there and both X and X^{-1} are $\mathscr{C}^1$. The inverse function has the form

$$X^{-1}(t, x) = (\pi(t, x), d(t, x))$$

with $\mathscr{C}^1$-functions π and d on $\mathscr{N}^\varepsilon$.

The set $\mathscr{N}^\varepsilon$ is called "tubular neighborhood" for $\mathscr{M}$ at the point (t_0, x_0). The function d is the *signed distance* to $\mathscr{M}$ and π is the associated *projection operator*. For a fixed hypersurface Σ, this result is well-known (see, e.g., [GT01], [PS16]). The above time-dependent result is already stated without details of the proof in [Kim08], Lemma 5.12. For completeness, we include a short proof in the Appendix B.

We now employ Lemma 4.12 and set
$$v(t, x) := v_\Sigma(\pi(t, x))$$
in the tubular neighborhood $\mathscr{N}^\varepsilon$ to construct a local $\mathscr{C}^1$-continuation of v_Σ. Note that v generates a local flow map $\tilde{\Phi}$ in an open neighborhood of $(t_0, x_0) \in \mathbb{R}^4$ by means of (4.6). The moving hypersurface $\mathrm{gr}\Sigma$ is *invariant* with respect to $\tilde{\Phi}$ because of the consistency conditions (4.5). Hence we drop the tilde notation in the following. It is well-known from classical ODE theory that a $\mathscr{C}^1$-right hand side yields a *continuously differentiable* dependence on the initial data (see, e.g., [PW10, p.75]). Therefore, we have the following result.

Lemma 4.13 (Regularity of the flow map). *Let $x_0 \in \Sigma(t_0)$ and $v \in \mathscr{C}^1(U)$ for an open neighborhood U of $(t_0, x_0) \in \mathbb{R}^4$. Then $\Phi(\cdot; t_0, \cdot)$ is $\mathscr{C}^1$ on an open neighborhood of $(t_0, x_0) \in \mathbb{R}^4$.*

Lemma 4.14 (Tangent transport). *Under the assumptions of Theorem 4.10, consider an inner point $(t_0, x_0) \in \mathrm{gr}\Sigma$ and a normalized tangent vector $\tau \in T_{\Sigma(t_0)}(x_0)$. Choose a curve $\gamma^0((-\delta, \delta); \Sigma(t_0))$ such that*

$$\gamma^0(0) = x_0, \quad (\gamma^0)'(0) = \tau.$$

For simplicity let $\|(\gamma^0)'\| = 1$ on $(-\delta, \delta)$. Then the curve is transported by the flow-map according to[5]

$$\gamma(s, t) := \Phi_x(t; t_0, \gamma^0(s)). \tag{4.16}$$

Likewise, a time evolution for the (not necessarily normalized) tangent vector is defined by

$$\tau(t) := \frac{\partial}{\partial s} \gamma(s, t) \Big|_{s=0}. \tag{4.17}$$

The vector $\tau(t)$ is tangent to $\Sigma(t)$ at the point $\Phi_x(t; t_0, x_0)$ since $\gamma^0(\cdot, t) \subset \Sigma(t)$. Moreover, its time derivative is given as

$$\tau'(t_0) = \frac{\partial v_\Sigma}{\partial \tau(t_0)}(t_0, x_0). \tag{4.18}$$

---

[5]Recall that Φ has the structure

$$\Phi(t; t_0, x_0) = (t, \Phi_x(t; t_0, x_0)).$$

Proof. By definition, we have

$$\tau'(t_0) = \frac{\partial}{\partial t}\left(\frac{\partial}{\partial s}\Phi_x(t;t_0,\gamma^0(s))\Big|_{s=0}\right)\Big|_{t=t_0}.$$

Since $\gamma \in \mathscr{C}^1$ and the second partial derivative

$$\begin{aligned}
\frac{\partial}{\partial s}\frac{\partial}{\partial t}\gamma(s,t) &= \frac{\partial}{\partial s}\frac{\partial}{\partial t}\Phi_x(t;t_0,\gamma^0(s))\\
&= \frac{\partial}{\partial s}v_\Sigma(t,\Phi_x(t;t_0,\gamma^0(s)))\\
&= \nabla_\Sigma v_\Sigma(t,\Phi_x(t;t_0,\gamma^0(s)))\cdot\frac{\partial}{\partial s}\Phi_x(t;t_0,\gamma^0(s))
\end{aligned}$$

is continuous at $(0,t_0)$, it follows from the Theorem of Schwarz that we can interchange the order of differentiation to obtain

$$\tau'(t_0) = \frac{\partial}{\partial s}\left(\frac{\partial}{\partial t}\Phi_x(t;t_0,\gamma^0(s))\Big|_{t=t_0}\right)\Big|_{s=0} = \frac{\partial}{\partial s}v_\Sigma(t_0,\gamma^0(s))\Big|_{s=0} = \frac{\partial v_\Sigma}{\partial\tau(t_0)}(t_0,x_0). \qquad\square$$

Proof of Theorem 4.10. We choose *two* curves

$$\gamma_1^0,\gamma_2^0 \in \mathscr{C}^1((-\delta,\delta);\Sigma(t_0))$$

such that

$$\gamma_1^0(0) = \gamma_2^0(0) = x_0, \quad (\gamma_1^0)'(0) = \tau_1, \quad (\gamma_2^0)'(0) = \tau_2$$

with $|\tau_1| = |\tau_2| = 1$ and $n_\Sigma(t_0,x_0) = \tau_1 \times \tau_2$. The flow map Φ defines a time-evolution of γ_i and of the tangent vectors τ_i according to (4.16) and (4.17). As long as τ_1 and τ_2 are linearly independent (i.e., if $\tau_1 \times \tau_2 \neq 0$), it follows that

$$n_\Sigma(\Phi(t;t_0,x_0)) = \frac{\tau_1(t) \times \tau_2(t)}{|\tau_1(t) \times \tau_2(t)|}$$

and, in particular,

$$\frac{D^\Sigma n_\Sigma}{Dt}\Big|_{t=t_0} = \frac{d}{dt}\frac{\tau_1(t) \times \tau_2(t)}{|\tau_1(t) \times \tau_2(t)|}\Big|_{t=t_0}. \tag{4.19}$$

Note that the linear independence of $\tau_1(t)$ and $\tau_2(t)$ for t sufficiently close to t_0 follows from the initial condition, i.e.

$$|\tau_1(t_0) \times \tau_2(t_0)| = 1,$$

since $\tau_1(t)$ and $\tau_2(t)$ are continuous. From (4.19) it follows that

$$\frac{D^\Sigma}{Dt}n_\Sigma = \frac{\tau_1'(t_0) \times \tau_2(t_0) + \tau_1(t_0) \times \tau_2'(t_0)}{|\tau_1(t_0) \times \tau_2(t_0)|} - \frac{\tau_1(t_0) \times \tau_2(t_0)}{|\tau_1(t_0) \times \tau_2(t_0)|^2}\frac{d}{dt}|\tau_1(t) \times \tau_2(t)|_{t=t_0}.$$

From $\tau_1(t_0) \times \tau_2(t_0) = n_\Sigma$ and $|n_\Sigma| = 1$ we infer

$$\begin{aligned}
\frac{D^\Sigma}{Dt}n_\Sigma &= \tau_1'(t_0) \times \tau_2(t_0) + \tau_1(t_0) \times \tau_2'(t_0) - n_\Sigma\frac{d}{dt}|\tau_1(t) \times \tau_2(t)|\Big|_{t=t_0}\\
&= \tau_1'(t_0) \times \tau_2(t_0) + \tau_1(t_0) \times \tau_2'(t_0) - n_\Sigma\left\langle\frac{\tau_1(t) \times \tau_2(t)}{|\tau_1(t) \times \tau_2(t)|},\frac{d}{dt}(\tau_1(t) \times \tau_2(t))\right\rangle\Big/_{t=t_0}\\
&= \mathscr{P}_\Sigma(\tau_1'(t_0) \times \tau_2(t_0) + \tau_1(t_0) \times \tau_2'(t_0)),
\end{aligned}$$

where $\mathscr{P}_\Sigma := 1 - \langle n_\Sigma,\cdot\rangle n_\Sigma$ denotes the orthogonal projection onto T_Σ. Using (4.18), we conclude

$$\frac{D^\Sigma}{Dt}n_\Sigma = \mathscr{P}_\Sigma[(\partial_{\tau_1}v_\Sigma) \times \tau_2 + \tau_1 \times (\partial_{\tau_2}v_\Sigma)].$$

The claim follows by expanding $\partial_{\tau_1}v_\Sigma$ and $\partial_{\tau_2}v_\Sigma$ in the basis $\{\tau_1,\tau_2,n_\Sigma\}$. $\qquad\square$

Proof of Theorem 4.8. We first show that equation (4.14) also holds at the contact line. As a result, we obtain the evolution of the contact angle.

For $(t_0, x_0) \in \mathrm{gr}\,\Gamma$ we choose a sequence of points $(x_0^k)_k \subset \Sigma(t_0)$ such that x_0^k converges to x_0 and consider the trajectories $x^k(t)$ defined by

$$\frac{d}{dt} x^k(t) = v_\Sigma(t, x^k(t)), \quad x^k(t_0) = x_0^k. \tag{4.20}$$

Moreover, we define the limiting trajectory $x(\cdot)$ starting from x_0 and running on $\mathrm{gr}\,\Gamma$. Since $\mathrm{gr}\,\Sigma$ is invariant under the flow, the evolution equation (4.14) holds along x^k for every k. Since $n_\Sigma \in \mathscr{C}^1(\mathrm{gr}\,\overline{\Sigma})$, one can choose fields $\tau_1, \tau_2 \in \mathscr{C}^1(\mathrm{gr}\,\overline{\Sigma})$ such that $\{\tau_1(t,x), \tau_2(t,x)\}$ is an orthonormal basis to the tangent space of $\Sigma(t)$ at the point x such that

$$n_\Sigma(t,x) = \tau_1(t,x) \times \tau_2(t,x) \quad \text{on } \mathrm{gr}\,\overline{\Sigma}.$$

Hence we obtain by integration

$$n_\Sigma(t, x^k(t)) = n_\Sigma(t_0, x_0^k) - \sum_{j=1}^{2} \int_{t_0}^{t} [\langle (\nabla_\Sigma v_\Sigma)\, \tau_j, n_\Sigma \rangle\, \tau_j](s, x^k(s))\, ds.$$

It follows from the continuous dependence on the initial data that the trajectories converge pointwise to the limiting trajectory, i.e.

$$\lim_{k \to \infty} x^k(t) = x(t) \quad \text{on } \Gamma(t).$$

Now we pass to the limit and obtain

$$n_\Sigma(t, x(t)) = n_\Sigma(t_0, x_0) - \sum_{j=1}^{2} \int_{t_0}^{t} [\langle (\nabla_\Sigma v_\Sigma)\, \tau_j, n_\Sigma \rangle\, \tau_j](s, x(s))\, ds.$$

Differentiation with respect to t proves that (4.14) also holds at the contact line. It follows from the definition of θ that

$$\frac{D^\Sigma}{Dt} \cos\theta = -\frac{D^\Sigma}{Dt} \langle n_\Sigma, n_{\partial\Omega} \rangle.$$

Since $n_{\partial\Omega}$ is constant, we obtain

$$-\sin\theta \frac{D^\Sigma \theta}{Dt} = -\left\langle \frac{D^\Sigma n_\Sigma}{Dt}, n_{\partial\Omega} \right\rangle.$$

We choose

$$\tau_1 = \tau = -\cos\theta\, n_\Gamma - \sin\theta\, n_{\partial\Omega}, \quad \tau_2 = t_\Gamma$$

and proceed using equation (4.14) to arrive at

$$\sin\theta \frac{D^\Sigma \theta}{Dt} = -\langle \partial_\tau v_\Sigma, n_\Sigma \rangle \langle \tau, n_{\partial\Omega} \rangle - \langle \partial_{t_\Gamma} v_\Sigma, n_\Sigma \rangle \langle t_\Gamma, n_{\partial\Omega} \rangle = \sin\theta\, \langle \partial_\tau v_\Sigma, n_\Sigma \rangle.$$

This proves the claim since $\theta \in (0, \pi)$. $\qquad\qquad\square$

4.2. Contact angle evolution in the standard model

4.2.1. Preliminaries

Definition 4.15 (Regularity). In the following, we consider an open interval I and the space of functions

$$\mathscr{V} := \mathscr{C}(I \times \overline{\Omega}) \cap \mathscr{C}^1(\mathrm{gr}\,\overline{\Omega^+}) \cap \mathscr{C}^1(\mathrm{gr}\,\overline{\Omega^-}). \tag{4.21}$$

Note that we assume in particular that the fluid velocities $v^\pm$ are *differentiable* at the contact line and the viscous stress is locally *bounded*. This is a rather strong assumption in contrast to weak solution concepts which allow an *integrable singularity* in the viscous stress as long as the corresponding dissipation rate is finite.

Remark 4.16 (Flow kinematics and the impermeability condition). We note that the impermeability conditions for the free

$$\langle v^{\pm}, n_{\Sigma} \rangle = V_{\Sigma} \quad \text{on gr} \Sigma \tag{4.22}$$

and the solid surface

$$\langle v^{\pm}, n_{\partial \Omega} \rangle = 0 \quad \text{on } \partial \Omega, \tag{4.23}$$

which both hold for the bulk velocities in the standard model, have an important and immediate consequence for the flow kinematics for regular solutions of the standard model. Since (4.22) and (4.23) imply (see Lemma 4.6 above)

$$\langle v^{\pm}, n_{\Gamma} \rangle = V_{\Gamma} \quad \text{on gr} \Gamma,$$

it follows that both grΣ and grΓ are invariant subsets for the flow-maps induced by the bulk velocities (see Lemma 4.3). Hence, a fluid particle located in the bulk phases can never reach the solid surface in finite time for a regular solution. Conversely, fluid particles may reach the solid surface in finite time if the impermeability condition on the solid surface is dropped since grΣ and grΓ are not necessarily invariant with respect to the bulk flow. This kind of flow kinematics is called "rolling motion". It is discussed in the literature as one of the main qualitative feature of the Interface Formation Model (see [Shi06, Shi08]).

The Continuity Lemma: The following Lemma shows an *additional* continuity property for the velocity gradient, which *only* holds at the contact line. Typically, the gradient of the velocity field has a jump, which is controlled by the interfacial transmission conditions.

Note that we define the gradient of a vector w in Cartesian coordinates as

$$(\nabla w)_{i,j} = \frac{\partial w_i}{\partial x_j}.$$

Lemma 4.17. *Let* $\Omega \subset \mathbb{R}^3$, $0 < \theta < \pi$, $v \in \mathscr{C}(\overline{\Omega})$, $\nabla v \in \mathscr{J}(\Omega, \Sigma)$ *and*

$$\langle v, n_{\partial \Omega} \rangle = 0 \quad on \ \partial \Omega, \quad \nabla \cdot v = 0 \quad in \ \Omega \setminus \Sigma(t),$$

where $\partial \Omega$ *is the smooth boundary of* Ω. *Then* ∇v *has the following continuity property at the contact line:*

$$[\![\langle \nabla v \, \alpha, \beta \rangle]\!] = 0 \quad on \ \Gamma,$$

where α, β *are arbitrary vectors in the plane spanned by* n_{Γ} *and* $n_{\partial \Omega}$.

Proof. We consider an arbitrary point on Γ and show $[\![\nabla v \, \tau]\!] = 0$ as well as $[\![\langle \nabla v n_{\Gamma}, n_{\partial \Omega} \rangle]\!] = [\![\langle \nabla v n_{\Gamma}, n_{\Gamma} \rangle]\!] = 0$. This is already sufficient since τ and n_{Γ} are linearly independent. Since v is assumed to be continuous across Σ, the tangential derivatives of v are continuous

$$[\![\nabla v \, \tau]\!] = [\![\nabla v t_{\Gamma}]\!] = 0.$$

Since v is tangential to $\partial \Omega$, it follows that

$$\langle \nabla v n_{\Gamma}, n_{\partial \Omega} \rangle = 0 \quad \Rightarrow \quad [\![\langle \nabla v n_{\Gamma}, n_{\partial \Omega} \rangle]\!] = 0.$$

It remains to show that $[\![\langle \nabla v n_{\Gamma}, n_{\Gamma} \rangle]\!] = 0$. Since v is solenoidal, we have

$$0 = \nabla \cdot v = \langle \nabla v n_{\Gamma}, n_{\Gamma} \rangle + \langle \nabla v n_{\partial \Omega}, n_{\partial \Omega} \rangle + \langle \nabla v t_{\Gamma}, t_{\Gamma} \rangle.$$

Therefore, we can write

$$[\![\langle \nabla v n_{\Gamma}, n_{\Gamma} \rangle]\!] = -([\![\langle \nabla v n_{\partial \Omega}, n_{\partial \Omega} \rangle]\!] + [\![\langle \nabla v t_{\Gamma}, t_{\Gamma} \rangle]\!]) = -[\![\langle \nabla v n_{\partial \Omega}, n_{\partial \Omega} \rangle]\!].$$

From $\tau = -\cos\theta\, n_\Gamma - \sin\theta\, n_{\partial\Omega}$ we infer (since $0 < \theta < \pi$)

$$n_{\partial\Omega} = -\frac{1}{\sin\theta}\left(\cos\theta\, n_\Gamma + \tau\right).$$

This yields

$$\begin{aligned}
[\![\langle \nabla v\, n_\Gamma, n_\Gamma\rangle]\!] &= \frac{1}{\sin\theta}\left(\cos\theta\,[\![\langle \nabla v\, n_\Gamma, n_{\partial\Omega}\rangle]\!] + [\![\langle \nabla v\, \tau, n_{\partial\Omega}\rangle]\!]\right)\\
&= \frac{[\![\langle \nabla v\, \tau, n_{\partial\Omega}\rangle]\!]}{\sin\theta} = \frac{\langle [\![\nabla v\, \tau]\!], n_{\partial\Omega}\rangle}{\sin\theta} = 0.
\end{aligned}$$

$\square$

Note that in the 2D case the *full* gradient of v is continuous across Γ.

On the Navier boundary condition: We reconsider the Navier condition (3.18). By taking the projection onto n_Γ we have

$$a^\pm \langle v^\pm, n_\Gamma\rangle + 2\langle D^\pm n_{\partial\Omega}, n_\Gamma\rangle = 0.$$

If v satisfies the kinematic conditions $v^\pm \cdot n_\Gamma = V_\Gamma$, we obtain the jump condition

$$\langle [\![D]\!]\, n_{\partial\Omega}, n_\Gamma\rangle_{|\Gamma} = -\frac{[\![a]\!]\, V_\Gamma}{2}. \tag{4.24}$$

Under the assumptions of Lemma 4.17, we have $\langle [\![D]\!]\, n_{\partial\Omega}, n_\Gamma\rangle_{|\Gamma} = 0$ and hence

$$[\![a]\!]\, V_\Gamma = 0. \tag{4.25}$$

Hence, to allow for a regular solution with $V_\Gamma \neq 0$, one has to choose the inverse slip length a as a continuous function across the contact line, i.e.

$$\frac{\lambda^+}{\eta^+}\Big|_\Gamma = \frac{\lambda^-}{\eta^-}\Big|_\Gamma = a_{|\Gamma}.$$

In this case, we have the relations

$$[\![\lambda]\!] = a\,[\![\eta]\!] \tag{4.26}$$

and

$$2\langle Dn_{\partial\Omega}, n_\Gamma\rangle_{|\Gamma} = \langle \nabla v\, n_{\partial\Omega}, n_\Gamma\rangle_{|\Gamma} = -aV_\Gamma. \tag{4.27}$$

4.2.2. Contact angle evolution

The following Theorem shows that, for sufficiently regular solutions, $\dot\theta$ has a quite simple form for a large class of models. Note that the equations (4.28)-(4.32) say nothing about external forces, do not specify the contact angle and the slip length may be a function of space and time. Moreover, we only need the *tangential part* of the transmission condition for the stress. In this sense, the system (4.28)-(4.32) is not closed but describes a *class* of models.

The main idea for the proof is the observation that both the Navier and the interfacial transmission condition are valid at the contact line. A regular classical solution has to satisfy both of them. Hence the conditions have to be *compatible*[6].

Theorem 4.18. *Let $\Omega \subset \mathbb{R}^3$ (or $\Omega \subset \mathbb{R}^2$) be a half-space with boundary $\partial\Omega$, $\sigma \equiv$ const, $\eta^\pm > 0$, $[\![\eta]\!] \neq 0$, $a \in \mathscr{C}(\mathrm{gr}\,\partial\Omega)$ and $(v, \mathrm{gr}\,\overline{\Sigma})$ with $v \in \mathscr{V}$, $\mathrm{gr}\,\overline{\Sigma}$ a $\mathscr{C}^{1,2}$-family of moving hypersurfaces with boundary, be a classical*

---

[6]See Chapter 5 for a detailed discussion on compatibility conditions in mathematical models of dynamic wetting.

solution of the PDE-system

$$\nabla \cdot v = 0 \quad in \ \Omega \setminus \Sigma(t), \tag{4.28}$$

$$[\![v]\!] = 0, \quad \mathscr{P}_\Sigma [\![S]\!]\, n_\Sigma = 0 \quad on \ \Sigma(t), \tag{4.29}$$

$$\langle v, n_{\partial\Omega} \rangle = 0 \quad on \ \partial\Omega \setminus \Gamma(t), \tag{4.30}$$

$$a\,\mathscr{P}_{\partial\Omega} v + 2\mathscr{P}_{\partial\Omega} D n_{\partial\Omega} = 0 \quad on \ \partial\Omega \setminus \Gamma(t), \tag{4.31}$$

$$V_\Sigma = \langle v, n_\Sigma \rangle \quad on \ \Sigma(t) \tag{4.32}$$

with $\theta \in (0,\pi)$ on $\mathrm{gr}\,\Gamma$. Then the evolution of the contact angle is given by

$$\frac{D\theta}{Dt} = \frac{aV_\Gamma}{2} = \frac{V_\Gamma}{2L}. \tag{4.33}$$

Moreover, in the case $\theta = \pi/2$ it holds that

$$(aV_\Gamma)_{|\theta=\pi/2} = 0, \tag{4.34}$$

which also means that

$$\frac{D\theta}{Dt}_{|\theta=\pi/2} = 0.$$

Proof. Since v is continuous and $v^\pm \in \mathscr{C}^1(\overline{\mathrm{gr}\,\Omega^\pm})$, we can choose $v_\Sigma := v^+_{|\mathrm{gr}\,\overline{\Sigma}} = v^-_{|\mathrm{gr}\,\overline{\Sigma}} \in \mathscr{C}^1(\mathrm{gr}\,\overline{\Sigma})$ and apply Theorem 4.8 to obtain

$$\frac{D\theta}{Dt} = \left\langle (\nabla v)^\pm \tau, n_\Sigma \right\rangle. \tag{4.35}$$

Recall that the vectors τ and n_Σ can be expressed as

$$\tau = -n_\Gamma \cos\theta - n_{\partial\Omega} \sin\theta, \quad n_\Sigma = n_\Gamma \sin\theta - n_{\partial\Omega} \cos\theta. \tag{4.36}$$

Inserting (4.36) into equation (4.35) yields

$$\frac{D\theta}{Dt} = \cos^2\theta \left\langle (\nabla v)^\pm n_\Gamma, n_{\partial\Omega} \right\rangle - \sin^2\theta \left\langle (\nabla v)^\pm n_{\partial\Omega}, n_\Gamma \right\rangle + \sin\theta \cos\theta \left(\left\langle (\nabla v)^\pm n_{\partial\Omega}, n_{\partial\Omega} \right\rangle - \left\langle (\nabla v)^\pm n_\Gamma, n_\Gamma \right\rangle \right). \tag{4.37}$$

Notice that the impermeability condition implies that

$$\left\langle (\nabla v)^\pm n_\Gamma, n_{\partial\Omega} \right\rangle = 0.$$

Moreover, Lemma 4.17 allows to drop the $\pm$-notation. We now exploit that both the jump condition and the Navier condition are active at the contact line. Using the relation (4.27), it follows from the Navier condition

$$\frac{D\theta}{Dt} = \sin(\theta)^2\, aV_\Gamma + \sin\theta \cos\theta \left(\langle \nabla v\, n_{\partial\Omega}, n_{\partial\Omega} \rangle - \langle \nabla v\, n_\Gamma, n_\Gamma \rangle \right). \tag{4.38}$$

Since τ is tangential to Σ, it follows from the continuity of the tangential stress component (4.29) that

$$\left\langle [\![S]\!]\, n_\Sigma, \tau \right\rangle = 0.$$

Using Lemma 4.17, we can exploit the continuity property of ∇v at the contact line to obtain

$$0 = 2[\![\eta]\!] \langle D n_\Sigma, \tau \rangle \quad \Leftrightarrow \quad 0 = \langle D n_\Sigma, \tau \rangle.$$

Together with the expansions (4.36) for n_Σ and τ we obtain

$$0 = \sin\theta \cos\theta \left(-\langle D n_\Gamma, n_\Gamma \rangle + \langle D n_{\partial\Omega}, n_{\partial\Omega} \rangle \right) + (\cos^2\theta - \sin^2\theta)\, \langle D n_{\partial\Omega}, n_\Gamma \rangle. \tag{4.39}$$

Using the Navier condition, we can replace the last term to find

$$0 = \sin\theta\cos\theta\left(-\langle\nabla v\, n_\Gamma, n_\Gamma\rangle + \langle\nabla v\, n_{\partial\Omega}, n_{\partial\Omega}\rangle\right) + (\sin^2\theta - \cos^2\theta)\frac{aV_\Gamma}{2}\quad\text{on }\Gamma. \tag{4.40}$$

Note that for $\theta = \pi/2$ this reduces to

$$aV_\Gamma = 0.$$

The claim follows by inserting equation (4.40) into the contact angle evolution equation (4.38):

$$\begin{aligned}\frac{D\theta}{Dt} &= \sin^2(\theta)\,aV_\Gamma + \sin\theta\cos\theta(\langle\nabla v\, n_{\partial\Omega}, n_{\partial\Omega}\rangle - \langle\nabla v\, n_\Gamma, n_\Gamma\rangle)\\ &= aV_\Gamma\left(\sin^2\theta - \frac{1}{2}(\sin^2\theta - \cos^2\theta)\right) = \frac{aV_\Gamma}{2}.\end{aligned}\qquad\square$$

Note that the incompressibility condition (4.28) can be dropped leading to (see Theorem 4.29)

$$\frac{D\theta}{Dt} = \frac{[\![\lambda]\!]}{[\![\eta]\!]}\frac{V_\Gamma}{2}.$$

Remark 4.19 (Free Boundary Problem). Following the proof of Theorem 4.18, it is easy to show that (4.33) also holds for a *free boundary formulation*, where the Navier-Stokes equations are only solved in the liquid domain; see (3.24). The outer phase is represented just by a constant pressure field p_0 and the jump conditions (4.29) are replaced by

$$(p_0 - p + S)\,n_\Sigma = \sigma\kappa n_\Sigma\quad\text{on}\quad\Sigma(t).$$

In particular, the viscous stress component $\langle Sn_\Sigma, \tau\rangle$ vanishes and Lemma 4.17 is not required for the proof.

Corollary 4.20. Under the assumptions of Theorem 4.18, a quasi-stationary solution, i.e. a solution with constant contact angle, satisfies

$$aV_\Gamma = 0\quad\text{on}\quad\Gamma, \tag{4.41}$$

which means that either the contact line is at rest or $a = 0$.

Consequently, a regular, non-trivial, quasi-stationary solution only exists if a vanishes at the contact line, i.e. in the free-slip case. On the other hand free-slip at the contact line implies that the contact angle is fixed for all regular solutions. This result confirms the observation from [Sch01], where it is stated that for a regular solution with $a \in (0,\infty)$ and $\theta \equiv \pi/2$ "the point of contact does not move".

Corollary 4.21. Let $a \geq 0$ and $(v, \mathrm{gr}\,\overline{\Sigma})$ be a regular solution in the setting of Theorem 4.18 that satisfies the thermodynamic condition (3.19). Then (4.33) implies

$$\dot\theta \geq 0\quad\text{for}\quad\theta \geq \theta_{\mathrm{eq}}\quad\text{and}\quad\dot\theta \leq 0\quad\text{for}\quad\theta \leq \theta_{\mathrm{eq}}.$$

From this result, it follows that the system cannot evolve towards equilibrium with a regular solution in the setting of Theorem 4.18.

Corollary 4.22. Let $a \geq 0$ and $\{v, \mathrm{gr}\,\overline{\Sigma}\}$ be a regular classical solution of the PDE-system (4.28)-(4.32) in the setting of Theorem 4.18 that satisfies (3.19). Let the initial condition be such that

$$\theta(0,x) > \theta_{\mathrm{eq}}\quad\forall\,x \in \Gamma(0),$$

where $\Gamma(0) = \partial\Sigma(0)$ is assumed to be bounded. Then it follows that

$$\theta(t,x) \geq \min_{x'\in\Gamma(0)}\theta(0,x') > \theta_{\mathrm{eq}}$$

for all $t \in I \cap [0,\infty)$ and $x \in \Gamma(t)$. That means that the system cannot relax to the equilibrium contact angle.

Proof. Consider $t \in I \cap [0, \infty)$ and $x_t \in \Gamma(t)$ arbitrary. Then there exists an $x_0 \in \Gamma(0)$ such that the unique solution $x(s)$ of the initial value problem

$$x'(s) = v(s, x(s)), \; x(0) = x_0 \in \Gamma(0) \tag{4.42}$$

satisfies $x(t) = x_t$. The point x_0 can be found by solving (4.42) backwards in time. By integration of (4.33), we conclude

$$\begin{aligned}
\theta(t, x(t)) = \theta(t, x_t) &= \theta(0, x(0)) + \int_0^t \frac{d}{ds}\, \theta(s, x(s))\, ds \\
&= \theta(0, x_0) + \int_0^t \underbrace{\frac{aV_\Gamma}{2}}_{\geq 0} (s, x(s))\, ds \\
&\geq \theta(0, x_0) \geq \min_{x' \in \Gamma(0)} \theta(0, x') > \theta_{\mathrm{eq}}.
\end{aligned}$$

$\qquad\square$

4.2.3. Empirical contact angle models

As discussed in detail in Chapter 2, the literature contains a large variety of empirical contact angle models that prescribe the dynamic contact angle. For the simplest class of these models, it is assumed that θ can be described by a relation of the type

$$\theta = f(\mathrm{Ca}, \theta_{\mathrm{eq}}), \tag{4.43}$$

where θ_{eq} is the *equilibrium* contact angle given by the Young equation (1.4). Hence for a given system, f is a function of the contact line velocity V_Γ, i.e.

$$\theta = f(V_\Gamma). \tag{4.44}$$

If this relation is invertible, one can also write ($g := f^{-1}$)

$$V_\Gamma = g(\theta). \tag{4.45}$$

The following corollary is an immediate consequence of this modeling.

Corollary 4.23. Consider the model described in Theorem 4.18 together with the dynamic contact angle model (4.44). Let $f \in \mathscr{C}^1(\mathbb{R})$. Then, for regular solutions in the sense of Theorem 4.18, the contact line velocity obeys the evolution equation

$$f'(V_\Gamma) \frac{D}{Dt} V_\Gamma = \frac{aV_\Gamma}{2}. \tag{4.46}$$

If the model from Theorem 4.18 is equipped with the contact angle model (4.45) with $g \in \mathscr{C}^1(0, \pi)$, the contact angle for regular solutions in the sense of Theorem 4.18 follows the evolution equation

$$\frac{D\theta}{Dt} = \frac{a g(\theta)}{2}. \tag{4.47}$$

Remark 4.24. From Corollary 4.23 we draw the following conclusions.

(i) By adding on of the empirical models (4.44) or (4.45) to the model from Theorem 4.18 with a fixed slip length, the time evolution of θ and V_Γ is, for regular solutions, already completely determined by the *ordinary* differential equation (4.46) or (4.47), respectively. But note that neither the momentum equation nor the normal part of the transmission condition involving the surface tension is used for its derivation. This means that, for regular solutions, neither external forces like gravity nor surface tension forces can influence the motion of the contact line.

(ii) If the empirical function satisfies the thermodynamic condition (3.21), i.e.

$$V_\Gamma(f(V_\Gamma) - \theta_{eq}) \geq 0 \quad \text{or} \quad g(\theta)(\theta - \theta_{eq}) \geq 0,$$

respectively, there are only constant or *monotonically increasing/decreasing* solutions for $\theta(t)$ (in Lagrangian coordinates).

(iii) Moreover, we have the additional requirement that $D_t\theta = 0$ for $\theta = \pi/2$, which dictates $g(\pi/2) = 0 = g(\theta_{eq})$ (or $a = 0$ which means that θ is fixed).

4.3. Remarks on more general models

4.3.1. Marangoni effect

An obvious generalization of the model described in Theorem 4.18 is to include the effect of non-constant fluid-fluid surface tension. In this case, the interfacial transmission condition for the stress reads as

$$[\![p\mathbf{1} - S]\!]\, n_\Sigma = \sigma\kappa n_\Sigma + \nabla_\Sigma \sigma.$$

Theorem 4.25. *Let $\Omega \subset \mathbb{R}^3$ (or $\Omega \subset \mathbb{R}^2$) be a half-space with boundary $\partial\Omega$, $\eta^\pm > 0$, $[\![\eta]\!] \neq 0$, $a \in \mathscr{C}(\mathrm{gr}\,\partial\Omega)$ and $(v, \mathrm{gr}\,\overline{\Sigma})$ with $v \in \mathscr{V}$, $\mathrm{gr}\,\overline{\Sigma}$ a $\mathscr{C}^{1,2}$-family of moving hypersurfaces with boundary, be a classical solution of the PDE-system*

$$\begin{aligned} \nabla \cdot v &= 0 && in\ \Omega \setminus \Sigma(t), \\ [\![v]\!] = 0, \quad \mathscr{P}_\Sigma\,[\![-S]\!]\,n_\Sigma &= \nabla_\Sigma\sigma && on\ \Sigma(t), \\ \langle v, n_{\partial\Omega}\rangle = 0,\ a\mathscr{P}_{\partial\Omega}v + 2\mathscr{P}_{\partial\Omega}Dn_{\partial\Omega} &= 0 && on\ \partial\Omega \setminus \Gamma(t), \\ V_\Sigma &= \langle v, n_\Sigma\rangle && on\ \Sigma(t) \end{aligned}$$

with $\theta \in (0, \pi)$ on $\mathrm{gr}\,\Gamma$. Then the evolution of the contact angle is given by

$$\frac{D\theta}{Dt} = \frac{1}{2}\left(aV_\Gamma - \frac{\partial_\tau\sigma}{[\![\eta]\!]}\right). \tag{4.48}$$

Proof. The proof is analogous to the proof of Theorem 4.18. We proceed as follows: While (4.38) is still valid, the jump condition for the viscous is replaced by

$$\langle [\![S]\!]\, n_\Sigma, \tau\rangle = -\partial_\tau\sigma.$$

Using again Lemma 4.17 we find

$$-\frac{\partial_\tau\sigma}{2[\![\eta]\!]} = \sin\theta\cos\theta\left(-\langle\nabla v n_\Gamma, n_\Gamma\rangle + \langle\nabla v n_{\partial\Omega}, n_{\partial\Omega}\rangle\right) + (\sin^2\theta - \cos^2\theta)\frac{aV_\Gamma}{2} \quad \text{on } \Gamma. \tag{4.49}$$

The claim follows by inserting (4.49) into the contact angle evolution equation (4.38). $\qquad\square$

Remark 4.26. This result shows that in this case, a regular solution with an advancing contact line and $\dot\theta < 0$ is possible. To obtain a non-trivial quasi-stationary state, a surface tension gradient

$$\partial_\tau\sigma = [\![\eta]\!]aV_\Gamma \tag{4.50}$$

has to be present at the contact line.

Remark 4.27. Figure 4.1(a) shows an example of a linear velocity field in two spatial dimensions with $\theta = \pi/4$ and a gradient in surface tension corresponding to (4.50). The field satisfies Navier slip with $L > 0$ and is plotted in a *co-moving* reference frame. The streamlines are tangent to the interface and the contact angle does not change.

This situation is not possible for the case of *constant* surface tension, visualized in Figure 4.1(b). In the case $\theta = \pi/4$ and $\partial_\tau \sigma = 0$ equation (4.49) together with the incompressibility condition

$$0 = \langle \nabla v\, n_\Gamma, n_\Gamma \rangle + \langle \nabla v\, n_{\partial\Omega}, n_{\partial\Omega} \rangle$$

implies

$$\langle \nabla v\, n_\Gamma, n_\Gamma \rangle = \langle \nabla v\, n_{\partial\Omega}, n_{\partial\Omega} \rangle = 0.$$

Therefore, the linear part of the velocity field has a quite simple form. In the reference frame of the solid wall, it is given as

$$(u,v)(x,y) = V_\Gamma \left(1 + \frac{y}{L}, 0 \right).$$

Figure 4.1(b) shows the field in a co-moving reference frame. Clearly, the field geometry leads to an *increase* in the contact angle (clockwise rotation in this example).

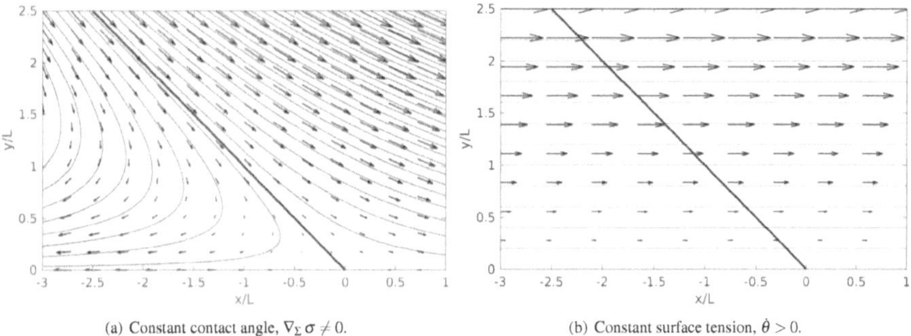

(a) Constant contact angle, $\nabla_\Sigma \sigma \neq 0$.   (b) Constant surface tension, $\theta > 0$.

Figure 4.1.: Linear velocity fields satisfying Navier slip with $L > 0$ in a co-moving reference frame.

4.3.2. Interfacial slip

Another possible generalization of the model is to allow for slip at the fluid-fluid interface. In this case, one only requires continuity of the *normal* component of the fluid velocity, i.e.

$$\langle [\![v]\!], n_\Sigma \rangle = 0 \quad \text{on } \Sigma(t),$$

which means that there is no mass flux from one phase to the other. To describe the evolution of the interface, one can use both of the fluid velocities $v^\pm$ in the kinematic conditions

$$V_\Sigma = \langle v^\pm, n_\Sigma \rangle, \quad V_\Gamma = \langle v^\pm, n_\Gamma \rangle.$$

This gives rise to two distinct Lagrangian derivative operators. To formulate the following Theorem, we choose the interfacial velocity field

$$v_\Sigma := \frac{\eta^+ v^+ - \eta^- v^-}{\eta^+ - \eta^-} = \frac{[\![\eta v]\!]}{[\![\eta]\!]}. \tag{4.51}$$

Clearly, v_Σ also satisfies the above mentioned kinematic conditions. Hence we can define a Lagrangian time derivative according to v_Σ.

Lemma 4.28. *The Lagrangian derivatives with respect to v^+, v^- and v_Σ satisfy the relation*

$$(\eta^+ - \eta^-) \frac{D^\Sigma}{Dt} = \eta^+ \frac{D^+}{Dt} - \eta^- \frac{D^-}{Dt}. \tag{4.52}$$

Proof. Each Lagrangian derivative along the contact line may be decomposed as

$$\frac{D^{\pm}}{Dt} = \partial_t^{\Gamma} + v_{\parallel}^{\pm} \cdot \nabla_{\Gamma},$$

where ∂_t^{Γ} is the "contact line Thomas derivative" following the normal motion of the contact line, ∇_{Γ} is the gradient along Γ and $v_{\parallel}^{\pm}$ is the component of $v^{\pm}$ tangential to the contact line. Multiplication with $\eta^{\pm}$ yields

$$\eta^{+}\frac{D^{+}}{Dt} - \eta^{-}\frac{D^{-}}{Dt} = [\![\eta]\!]\,\partial_t^{\Gamma} + (\eta^{+}v_{\parallel}^{+} - \eta^{-}v_{\parallel}^{-}) \cdot \nabla_{\Gamma}$$

$$= [\![\eta]\!]\left(\partial_t^{\Gamma} + \frac{\eta^{+}v_{\parallel}^{+} - \eta^{-}v_{\parallel}^{-}}{\eta^{+} - \eta^{-}} \cdot \nabla_{\Gamma}\right) = [\![\eta]\!]\frac{D^{\Sigma}}{Dt}. \qquad \square$$

Note that Lemma 4.17 cannot be used for the proof of Theorem 4.29 since v is no longer assumed to be continuous. Moreover, the following statement does *not* require the incompressibility of the flow.

Theorem 4.29. *Let $\Omega \subset \mathbb{R}^3$ be a half-space with boundary $\partial\Omega$, $\eta^{\pm} > 0$, $[\![\eta]\!] \neq 0$ and $(v, \mathrm{gr}\,\overline{\Sigma})$ with*

$$v \in \mathscr{C}^1(\mathrm{gr}\,\overline{\Omega^{+}}) \cap \mathscr{C}^1(\mathrm{gr}\,\overline{\Omega^{-}})$$

and $\mathrm{gr}\,\overline{\Sigma}$ a $\mathscr{C}^{1,2}$-family of moving hypersurfaces with boundary, be a classical solution of the PDE-system

$$[\![\langle v, n_{\Sigma}\rangle]\!] = 0, \quad \mathscr{P}_{\Sigma}\,[\![-S]\!]\,n_{\Sigma} = \nabla_{\Sigma}\,\sigma \quad \text{on } \Sigma(t),$$
$$\langle v, n_{\partial\Omega}\rangle = 0,\ \lambda\,\mathscr{P}_{\partial\Omega}v + \mathscr{P}_{\partial\Omega}Sn_{\partial\Omega} = 0 \quad \text{on } \partial\Omega \setminus \Gamma(t),$$
$$V_{\Sigma} = \langle v^{\pm}, n_{\Sigma}\rangle \quad \text{on } \Sigma(t).$$

Moreover, let

$$\lambda \in \mathscr{C}(\mathrm{gr}\,\overline{\partial\Omega^{+}}) \cap \mathscr{C}(\mathrm{gr}\,\overline{\partial\Omega^{-}})$$

and $\theta \in (0,\pi)$ on $\mathrm{gr}\,\Gamma$. Then the evolution of the contact angle is given by

$$\frac{D^{\Sigma}\theta}{Dt} = \frac{1}{2}\left(V_{\Gamma}\frac{[\![\lambda]\!]}{[\![\eta]\!]} - \frac{\partial_{\tau}\sigma}{[\![\eta]\!]}\right), \tag{4.53}$$

where $\frac{D^{\Sigma}}{Dt}$ is the Lagrangian time-derivative according to the surface velocity field (4.51).

Proof. We start from (4.12) and, by a change of coordinates, obtain

$$\frac{D^{\pm}\theta}{Dt} = -\sin^2\theta\,\langle\nabla v^{\pm}n_{\partial\Omega}, n_{\Gamma}\rangle + \sin\theta\cos\theta(\langle\nabla v^{\pm}n_{\partial\Omega}, n_{\partial\Omega}\rangle - \langle\nabla v^{\pm}n_{\Gamma}, n_{\Gamma}\rangle),$$

where the two time derivatives may now be different. Using the Navier condition, we can replace the first term according to

$$\frac{D^{\pm}\theta}{Dt} = \sin^2\theta\,a^{\pm}V_{\Gamma} + \sin\theta\cos\theta(\langle\nabla v^{\pm}n_{\partial\Omega}, n_{\partial\Omega}\rangle - \langle\nabla v^{\pm}n_{\Gamma}, n_{\Gamma}\rangle).$$

Note that a may now be discontinuous at Γ. The next step is to express $\dot{\theta}$ by means of the jump in normal stress. Thanks to $\eta^{\pm} > 0$ we can write

$$\langle\nabla v^{\pm}n_{\Gamma}, n_{\Gamma}\rangle = \frac{1}{2\eta^{\pm}}\langle S^{\pm}n_{\Gamma}, n_{\Gamma}\rangle,$$

$$\langle\nabla v^{\pm}n_{\partial\Omega}, n_{\partial\Omega}\rangle = \frac{1}{2\eta^{\pm}}\langle S^{\pm}n_{\partial\Omega}, n_{\partial\Omega}\rangle.$$

Plugging this into the above equation for $\dot{\theta}$ gives

$$\frac{D^{\pm}\theta}{Dt} = \sin^2\theta\,a^{\pm}V_{\Gamma} + \frac{\sin\theta\cos\theta}{2\eta^{\pm}}(\langle S^{\pm}n_{\partial\Omega}, n_{\partial\Omega}\rangle - \langle S^{\pm}n_{\Gamma}, n_{\Gamma}\rangle). \tag{4.54}$$

We introduce $[\![S]\!]$ by adding a zero term, i.e.

$$\frac{D^+\theta}{Dt} = \sin^2\theta\, a^+ V_\Gamma + \frac{\sin\theta\cos\theta}{2\eta^+}(\langle(S^+-S^-)n_{\partial\Omega},n_{\partial\Omega}\rangle$$
$$-\langle(S^+-S^-)n_\Gamma,n_\Gamma\rangle+\langle S^- n_{\partial\Omega},n_{\partial\Omega}\rangle-\langle S^- n_\Gamma,n_\Gamma\rangle). \tag{4.55}$$

Using the second version of the equation (4.54), we have

$$\eta^-\frac{D^-\theta}{Dt}-\sin^2\theta\, a^-\eta^- V_\Gamma = \frac{\sin\theta\cos\theta}{2}\left(\langle S^- n_{\partial\Omega},n_{\partial\Omega}\rangle-\langle S^- n_\Gamma,n_\Gamma\rangle\right).$$

Together with (4.55) we obtain (using $\lambda^\pm = a^\pm\eta^\pm$)

$$\eta^+\frac{D^+\theta}{Dt}-\eta^-\frac{D^-\theta}{Dt}=\sin^2\theta\,[\![\lambda]\!]V_\Gamma+\frac{\sin\theta\cos\theta}{2}(\langle[\![S]\!]n_{\partial\Omega},n_{\partial\Omega}\rangle-\langle[\![S]\!]n_\Gamma,n_\Gamma\rangle). \tag{4.56}$$

Now we exploit the validity of both the Navier and the jump condition for the stress at the contact line. From $\mathscr{P}_\Sigma[\![S]\!]n_\Sigma = -\nabla_\Sigma\sigma$ we obtain

$$-\partial_\tau\sigma = \langle[\![S]\!]n_\Sigma,\tau\rangle = (\cos^2\theta-\sin^2\theta)\,\langle[\![S]\!]n_{\partial\Omega},n_\Gamma\rangle$$
$$+\sin\theta\cos\theta(-\langle[\![S]\!]n_\Gamma,n_\Gamma\rangle+\langle[\![S]\!]n_{\partial\Omega},n_{\partial\Omega}\rangle) \tag{4.57}$$

From the Navier condition, i.e.

$$\lambda^\pm V_\Gamma+\langle S^\pm n_{\partial\Omega},n_\Gamma\rangle = 0,$$

we infer

$$\langle[\![S]\!]n_{\partial\Omega},n_\Gamma\rangle = -[\![\lambda]\!]V_\Gamma$$

by taking the trace. Combined with (4.57) we obtain

$$\sin\theta\cos\theta(\langle[\![S]\!]n_{\partial\Omega},n_{\partial\Omega}\rangle-\langle[\![S]\!]n_\Gamma,n_\Gamma\rangle) = (\cos^2\theta-\sin^2\theta)\,[\![\lambda]\!]V_\Gamma-\partial_\tau\sigma.$$

Plugging in this expression into (4.56), we arrive at

$$\eta^+\frac{D^+\theta}{Dt}-\eta^-\frac{D^-\theta}{Dt} = [\![\lambda]\!]V_\Gamma\left(\sin^2\theta+\frac{\cos^2\theta-\sin^2\theta}{2}\right)-\frac{\partial_\tau\sigma}{2} = \frac{1}{2}([\![\lambda]\!]V_\Gamma-\partial_\tau\sigma).$$

Now the claim follows from (4.52). $\qquad\square$

Remark 4.30.   (i) If the flow is incompressible and the velocity is continuous across Σ, equation (4.25) implies that the slip length has to be continuous across the contact line to allow for non-trivial regular solutions. In this case, we have $[\![\lambda]\!] = a[\![\eta]\!]$ and (4.53) reduces to (4.48).

  (ii) If the surface tension σ is constant, we obtain the evolution equation

$$\frac{D^\Sigma\theta}{Dt} = \frac{V_\Gamma}{2}\frac{[\![\lambda]\!]}{[\![\eta]\!]}$$

If both jumps have the same sign, i.e. if

$$\frac{[\![\lambda]\!]}{[\![\eta]\!]} \geq 0,$$

the qualitative behavior of regular solutions is still the same as in Theorem 4.18.

4.3.3. Systems with phase change

So far we only discussed the case, when no phase transitions occur. We now generalize the results for non-zero mass transfer across the fluid-fluid interface. Given an interface with interface normal field n_Σ and normal velocity V_Σ, the one-sided *mass transfer fluxes* are defined as

$$\dot{m}^\pm = \rho^\pm (v^\pm \cdot n_\Sigma - V_\Sigma) \quad \text{on} \quad \mathrm{gr}\overline{\Sigma}.$$

If the interface is not able to *store* mass, the mass transfer flux has to be continuous, i.e.

$$[\![\dot{m}]\!] = 0 \quad \Leftrightarrow \quad [\![\rho v]\!] \cdot n_\Sigma = [\![\rho]\!] V_\Sigma. \tag{4.58}$$

Note that models for dynamic wetting allowing for mass on the fluid-fluid interface have also been considered under the name Interface Formation Model, see [Shi93], [Shi08] and Section 3.5. In the case without interfacial mass, the interfacial normal velocity can be expressed as

$$V_\Sigma = v^\pm \cdot n_\Sigma - \frac{\dot{m}}{\rho^\pm}.$$

Since the interface is now transported by $V_\Sigma \neq v^\pm \cdot n_\Sigma$, the mass flux influences the evolution of the interface. From the above relation, it follows that the mass transfer flux is related to the jump in the normal component of v according to

$$[\![v]\!] \cdot n_\Sigma = [\![1/\rho]\!] \dot{m} \quad \text{on} \quad \mathrm{gr}\Sigma. \tag{4.59}$$

At the contact line, we can express n_Σ via n_Γ and $n_{\partial\Omega}$, i.e.

$$[\![v]\!] \cdot n_\Sigma = \sin\theta \, [\![v]\!] \cdot n_\Gamma - \cos\theta \, [\![v]\!] \cdot n_{\partial\Omega} \quad \text{on gr}\Gamma.$$

For simplicity, we consider in the following the case of two spatial dimensions[7]. If we assume $v^\pm$ to satisfy the impermeability condition, we find the following relation for the jump of v at the contact line

$$\sin\theta \, [\![v]\!]_{|\Gamma} = [\![1/\rho]\!] \dot{m} \, n_\Gamma. \tag{4.60}$$

Note that the above relation only holds in two spatial dimensions. A slip tangential to the contact line may be present in three dimensions. In this case, one can only state that

$$(1 - \langle t_\Gamma, \cdot \rangle t_\Gamma) \sin\theta \, [\![v]\!]_{|\Gamma} = [\![1/\rho]\!] \dot{m} \, n_\Gamma.$$

Theorem 4.31. *Let $\Omega \subset \mathbb{R}^2$ be a half-space with boundary $\partial\Omega$, $\eta^\pm > 0$, $[\![\eta]\!] \neq 0$ and $(v, \mathrm{gr}\overline{\Sigma})$ with*

$$v \in \mathscr{C}^1(\mathrm{gr}\overline{\Omega^+}) \cap \mathscr{C}^1(\mathrm{gr}\overline{\Omega^-})$$

and $\mathrm{gr}\overline{\Sigma}$ a $\mathscr{C}^{1,2}$-family of moving hypersurfaces with boundary, be a classical solution of the PDE-system

$$\dot{m} \, \mathscr{P}_\Sigma [\![v]\!] + \mathscr{P}_\Sigma [\![-S]\!] \, n_\Sigma = \nabla_\Sigma \sigma \quad on \; \Sigma(t),$$
$$\langle v, n_{\partial\Omega} \rangle = 0, \; \lambda \mathscr{P}_{\partial\Omega} v + \mathscr{P}_{\partial\Omega} S n_{\partial\Omega} = 0 \quad on \; \partial\Omega \setminus \Gamma(t),$$
$$V_\Sigma = \langle v^\pm, n_\Sigma \rangle - \frac{\dot{m}}{\rho^\pm} \quad on \; \Sigma(t)$$

with $\theta \in (0, \pi)$ on $\mathrm{gr}\Gamma$. Then, the interfacial velocity field $v_\Sigma \in \mathscr{C}^1(\mathrm{gr}\overline{\Sigma})$ defined as

$$v_\Sigma := \frac{[\![\rho v]\!]}{[\![\rho]\!]} = \frac{\rho^+ v^+ - \rho^- v^-}{\rho^+ - \rho^-} \quad on \; \mathrm{gr}\overline{\Sigma} \tag{4.61}$$

---

[7]Note that equation (4.58) implies that the "natural" interfacial velocity to be considered here is (4.61), i.e. the bulk velocities should be weighted with the density ρ. Recall that in the case of interfacial slip without mass transfer, the natural interfacial velocity to choose is (4.51), i.e. weighted with the viscosity η. In the present case of interfacial slip with mass transfer, it is not obvious which interfacial velocity to choose. We exclude this problem by restricting the Theorem to the 2D case, where the interfacial velocity following the contact line is unique.

satisfies the consistency conditions

$$V_\Sigma = \langle v_\Sigma, n_\Sigma \rangle \quad \textit{on } \mathrm{gr}\Sigma, \tag{4.62}$$

$$V_\Gamma = \langle v_\Sigma, n_\Gamma \rangle \quad \textit{on } \mathrm{gr}\Gamma \tag{4.63}$$

and the corresponding evolution of the contact angle is given by

$$\begin{aligned}
[\![\eta]\!] \frac{D^\Sigma \theta}{Dt} &= \frac{[\![\lambda]\!] V_\Gamma}{2} - \frac{\partial_\tau \sigma}{2} - [\![\eta/\rho]\!]\, \partial_\tau \dot{m} \\
&\quad + \dot{m}\left(-[\![\eta \partial_\tau(1/\rho)]\!] - \kappa \cot\theta \left[\!\!\left[\frac{\eta}{\rho}\right]\!\!\right] - \frac{\cot\theta}{2}\left[\!\!\left[\frac{1}{\rho}\right]\!\!\right]\dot{m} + \frac{1}{2\sin\theta}\left[\!\!\left[\frac{\lambda}{\rho}\right]\!\!\right] \right).
\end{aligned} \tag{4.64}$$

In the special case of zero mass flux at the contact line, the above equation simplifies to

$$[\![\eta]\!] \frac{D^\Sigma \theta}{Dt} = \frac{[\![\lambda]\!] V_\Gamma}{2} - \frac{\partial_\tau \sigma}{2} - [\![\eta/\rho]\!]\, \partial_\tau \dot{m}. \tag{4.65}$$

Proof. We observe that, as a consequence of (4.58), the velocity v_Σ defined by (4.61) satisfies the consistency condition (4.62). It also satisfies $v_\Sigma \cdot n_{\partial\Omega} = 0$ on $\mathrm{gr}\Gamma$ since $v^\pm$ are tangential to $\partial\Omega$. Hence, Lemma 4.6 implies that (4.63) also holds. Moreover, it is easy to check that v_Σ can be expressed in two different ways as

$$v_\Sigma = v^\pm - \frac{[\![v]\!]}{\rho^\pm [\![1/\rho]\!]} \quad \text{on} \quad \mathrm{gr}\overline{\Sigma}. \tag{4.66}$$

Applying Theorem 4.8 yields, using (4.59),

$$\begin{aligned}
\frac{D^\Sigma \theta}{Dt} &= \langle \partial_\tau v^\pm, n_\Sigma \rangle - \left\langle \frac{\partial}{\partial\tau} \frac{[\![v]\!]}{\rho^\pm [\![1/\rho]\!]}, n_\Sigma \right\rangle \\
&= \langle \partial_\tau v^\pm, n_\Sigma \rangle - \partial_\tau \left\langle \frac{[\![v]\!]}{\rho^\pm [\![1/\rho]\!]}, n_\Sigma \right\rangle - \frac{[\![v]\!]\cdot\tau}{\rho^\pm [\![1/\rho]\!]}\langle \tau, \partial_\tau n_\Sigma \rangle \\
&= \langle \nabla v^\pm \tau, n_\Sigma \rangle - \partial_\tau \frac{\dot{m}}{\rho^\pm} - \kappa \cot\theta \frac{\dot{m}}{\rho^\pm} \\
&=: \langle \nabla v^\pm \tau, n_\Sigma \rangle + \mathscr{R}.
\end{aligned} \tag{4.67}$$

Here we used the relation

$$\frac{[\![v]\!]\cdot\tau}{[\![1/\rho]\!]} = \frac{\dot{m}}{\sin\theta}\, n_\Gamma \cdot \tau = -\cot\theta\, \dot{m} \quad \text{on } \mathrm{gr}\Gamma,$$

which follows from (4.60). Multiplication of the first term in (4.67) with $\eta^\pm$ together with a change of basis vectors yields

$$\begin{aligned}
\eta^\pm \langle \nabla v^\pm \tau, n_\Sigma \rangle &= -\sin^2\theta\, \eta^\pm \langle \nabla v^\pm n_{\partial\Omega}, n_\Gamma \rangle + \sin\theta\cos\theta\, \eta^\pm(\langle \nabla v^\pm n_{\partial\Omega}, n_{\partial\Omega}\rangle - \langle \nabla v^\pm n_\Gamma, n_\Gamma \rangle) \\
&= -\sin^2\theta\, \langle S^\pm n_{\partial\Omega}, n_\Gamma \rangle + \frac{\sin\theta\cos\theta}{2}(\langle S^\pm n_{\partial\Omega}, n_{\partial\Omega}\rangle - \langle S^\pm n_\Gamma, n_\Gamma \rangle).
\end{aligned}$$

We may now multiply (4.67) by $\eta^\pm$ to find

$$[\![\eta]\!] \frac{D^\Sigma \theta}{Dt} = [\![\eta\mathscr{R}]\!] - \sin^2\theta\, \langle [\![S]\!] n_{\partial\Omega}, n_\Gamma \rangle + \frac{\sin\theta\cos\theta}{2}(\langle [\![S]\!] n_{\partial\Omega}, n_{\partial\Omega}\rangle - \langle [\![S]\!] n_\Gamma, n_\Gamma \rangle). \tag{4.68}$$

The tangential stress condition at Γ reads

$$\langle [\![S]\!] n_\Sigma, \tau \rangle = -\partial_\tau \sigma + \dot{m}[\![v]\!]\cdot\tau = -\partial_\tau \sigma - \cot\theta\, [\![1/\rho]\!]\, \dot{m}^2.$$

We rewrite the left-hand side using the expansions for n_Σ and τ, i.e.

$$\begin{aligned}
\langle [\![S]\!] n_\Sigma, \tau \rangle &= (\cos^2\theta - \sin^2\theta)\langle [\![S]\!] n_{\partial\Omega}, n_\Gamma \rangle \\
&\quad + \sin\theta\cos\theta(\langle [\![S]\!] n_{\partial\Omega}, n_{\partial\Omega}\rangle - \langle [\![S]\!] n_\Gamma, n_\Gamma \rangle) \\
&= -\partial_\tau \sigma - \cot\theta\, [\![1/\rho]\!]\, \dot{m}^2.
\end{aligned} \tag{4.69}$$

From (4.68) and (4.69) we obtain

$$[\![\eta]\!]\frac{D^\Sigma\theta}{Dt} = [\![\eta\mathscr{R}]\!] - \frac{1}{2}\langle[\![S]\!]\,n_{\partial\Omega}, n_\Gamma\rangle - \frac{\partial_\tau\sigma}{2} - \frac{\cot\theta}{2}[\![1/\rho]\!]\dot{m}^2. \tag{4.70}$$

Using (3.8) we can compute the contact line velocity

$$\sin\theta\, V_\Gamma = v^\pm\cdot n_\Sigma - \frac{[\![v]\!]\cdot n_\Sigma}{\rho^\pm[\![1/\rho]\!]} = \sin\theta\, v^\pm\cdot n_\Gamma - \frac{\dot{m}}{\rho^\pm}.$$

Hence the contact line velocity reads

$$V_\Gamma = v^\pm\cdot n_\Gamma - \frac{\dot{m}}{\sin\theta\,\rho^\pm} \quad\text{on}\quad \mathrm{gr}\,\Gamma. \tag{4.71}$$

Equation (4.60) shows that the above expression is indeed well-defined, i.e. the two representations are equal. Note that Γ is no longer a material interface. The mass transfer term can cause a motion of the contact line. Hence the Navier condition at Γ reads

$$\langle S^\pm n_{\partial\Omega}, n_\Gamma\rangle = -\lambda^\pm v^\pm\cdot n_\Gamma = -\lambda^\pm\left(V_\Gamma + \frac{\dot{m}}{\rho^\pm\sin\theta}\right).$$

We, therefore, obtain the jump condition

$$\langle[\![S]\!]\,n_{\partial\Omega}, n_\Gamma\rangle = -[\![\lambda]\!]V_\Gamma - \frac{\dot{m}}{\sin\theta}\left[\!\!\left[\frac{\lambda}{\rho}\right]\!\!\right] \tag{4.72}$$

on $\mathrm{gr}\,\Gamma$. This finally leads to

$$[\![\eta]\!]\frac{D^\Sigma\theta}{Dt} = \frac{[\![\lambda]\!]V_\Gamma}{2} - \frac{\partial_\tau\sigma}{2} - \left[\!\!\left[\eta\,\partial_\tau\left(\frac{\dot{m}}{\rho}\right)\right]\!\!\right]$$
$$-\frac{\dot{m}}{\sin\theta}\left(\kappa\cos\theta\left[\!\!\left[\frac{\eta}{\rho}\right]\!\!\right] + \frac{\cos\theta}{2}\left[\!\!\left[\frac{1}{\rho}\right]\!\!\right]\dot{m} - \frac{1}{2}\left[\!\!\left[\frac{\lambda}{\rho}\right]\!\!\right]\right).$$

The claim follows from

$$\left[\!\!\left[\eta\,\partial_\tau\left(\frac{\dot{m}}{\rho}\right)\right]\!\!\right] = [\![\eta/\rho]\!]\,\partial_\tau\dot{m} + \dot{m}\,[\![\eta\,\partial_\tau(1/\rho)]\!]. \qquad\square$$

4.3.4. Generalized Navier Slip

The idea of the Generalized Navier Boundary Condition (GNBC) described briefly in Section 3.4 is to allow for a deviation of the contact angle from the equilibrium value which is then relaxed by a transient process. Let us consider the standard model in two dimensions in the free surface form (3.24) with the Navier slip condition replaced by an approximation of the formal GNBC (3.26), i.e.

$$\lambda v_\| + (Sn_{\partial\Omega})_\| + \sigma(\cos\theta - \cos\theta_{eq})n_\Gamma\delta_\Gamma = 0 \quad\text{on}\quad \partial\Omega$$

at the contact line. The approximation reads as

$$\lambda v_\| + (Sn_{\partial\Omega})_\| + \frac{1}{\varepsilon}\sigma(\cos\theta - \cos\theta_{eq})n_\Gamma = 0 \quad\text{at }\Gamma, \tag{4.73}$$

where $\varepsilon > 0$ is a small parameter of dimension length. Leaving aside the issue of the thermodynamical consistency of the formulation, we analyze the contact angle dynamics for a regular solution. By taking the inner product with the contact line normal vector and using the impermeability condition, we obtain from (4.73) the relation

$$\frac{\lambda}{\eta}V_\Gamma + \langle n_\Gamma, \nabla v n_{\partial\Omega}\rangle + \frac{\sigma}{\varepsilon\eta}(\cos\theta - \cos\theta_{eq}) = 0. \tag{4.74}$$

Using the impermeability condition, the rate-of-change of the contact angle reads as (see (4.37))

$$\dot{\theta} = -\sin^2\theta\,\langle \nabla v\, n_{\partial\Omega}, n_\Gamma\rangle + \sin\theta\cos\theta(\langle \nabla v\, n_{\partial\Omega}, n_{\partial\Omega}\rangle - \langle \nabla v\, n_\Gamma, n_\Gamma\rangle). \tag{4.75}$$

Thanks to the zero tangential stress condition $\langle Sn_\Sigma, \tau\rangle = 0$, we have

$$0 = \frac{\sin\theta\cos\theta}{2}\left(-\langle \nabla v\, n_\Gamma, n_\Gamma\rangle + \langle \nabla v\, n_{\partial\Omega}, n_{\partial\Omega}\rangle\right) + (\cos^2\theta - \sin^2\theta)\,\langle \nabla v\, n_{\partial\Omega}, n_\Gamma\rangle. \tag{4.76}$$

Hence, we can express the time derivative of the contact angle as

$$\dot{\theta} = -\frac{1}{2}\langle n_\Gamma, \nabla v\, n_{\partial\Omega}\rangle.$$

It follows from (4.74) that the contact angle dynamics for a regular solution reads as

$$\boxed{\dot{\theta} = \frac{V_\Gamma}{2L} + \frac{1}{\varepsilon}\frac{\sigma}{2\eta}(\cos\theta - \cos\theta_{eq})).} \tag{4.77}$$

Remark 4.32.   (i) The uncompensated Young stress in the GNBC leads to an additional term in the rate-of-change in the contact angle which reads as

$$\frac{1}{\varepsilon}\frac{\sigma}{2\eta}(\cos\theta - \cos\theta_{eq})).$$

Obviously, the latter term is negative for $\theta < \theta_{eq}$ (and positive for $\theta > \theta_{eq}$) and drives the system towards equilibrium. Therefore, the GNBC may give rise to physically reasonable regular solutions. In particular, we note that the uncompensated Young stress is able to change the direction of the velocity gradient at the contact line according to

$$-\langle n_\Gamma, \nabla v\, n_{\partial\Omega}\rangle = \frac{\lambda}{\eta}V_\Gamma + \frac{\sigma}{\varepsilon\eta}(\cos\theta - \cos\theta_{eq}). \tag{4.78}$$

Hence, the kinematics of a spreading droplet with $\theta > \theta_{eq}$ is changed fundamentally. Now, the fluid particles at the solid boundary may have a larger tangential velocity than the fluid particles slightly above the boundary leading to $\langle n_\Gamma, \nabla v\, n_{\partial\Omega}\rangle > 0$. The latter effect looks like a *negative* "effective slip length". It is, however, caused by the uncompensated Young stress in the velocity boundary condition.

(ii) Moreover, the relaxation term is proportional to $1/\varepsilon$ which means that the rate-of-change becomes singular as $\varepsilon \to 0$. This observation is consistent with the fact that eq. (3.26) (without "smearing out" the delta function) implies $\theta = \theta_{eq}$.

(iii) It is important to note that the GNBC gives rise to a functional dependence between dynamic contact angle and contact line speed for *quasi-stationary* states. In fact, setting $\dot{\theta} = 0$ leads to the relation

$$\boxed{\mathrm{Ca} = \frac{\eta V_\Gamma}{\sigma} = \frac{L}{\varepsilon}(\cos\theta_{eq} - \cos\theta).} \tag{4.79}$$

Notably, the relation $V_\Gamma = g(\theta)$, with g defined by (4.79), satisfies the thermodynamic consistency conditions formulated in Section 3.3, i.e.

$$g(\theta_{eq}) = 0 \quad \text{and} \quad g(\theta)(\theta - \theta_{eq}) \geq 0.$$

4.4. Kinematic transport of the mean curvature

So far, we considered the kinematic transport of the contact line and the contact angle. The goal of the present section is to derive an evolution equation for the kinematic transport of the mean curvature at the contact line.

The kinematic transport of the mean curvature has been already studied by Kimura [Kim08] and Barrett et al. [BGN20]. In particular, Kimura computed the Thomas derivative of the mean curvature in d dimensions [Kim08, p.73]

$$\partial_t^\Sigma \kappa = V_\Sigma \sum_{i=1}^{d-1} \kappa_i^2 + \Delta_\Sigma V_\Sigma. \tag{4.80}$$

Obviously, additional regularity compared to Theorem 4.8 is required for (4.80) to hold. Kimura proved the relation (4.80) for the case of a moving $\mathscr{C}^{1,2}$-hypersurface (without boundary) with the additional regularity

$$\mathscr{W} \in \mathscr{C}^1(\mathrm{gr}\Sigma; \mathbb{R}^{d\times d}),$$

where $\mathscr{W} = -\nabla_\Sigma n_\Sigma$ denotes the Weingarten map on $\mathrm{gr}\Sigma$. The Weingarten map is real and symmetric with non-zero eigenvalues

$$\kappa_1, \dots, \kappa_{d-1}$$

called the *principal curvatures* and corresponding eigenvectors

$$w_1, \dots, w_{d-1}.$$

The eigenvectors are elements of the tangent space and are called *principals directions of curvature*. Since $\mathscr{W}$ is diagonal in the latter basis, the principal curvatures and principal directions of curvature satisfy the identity

$$\left\langle w_j, \frac{\partial}{\partial w_i} n_\Sigma \right\rangle = -\kappa_i \delta_{ij}. \tag{4.81}$$

Theorem 4.33 (Time derivative of the mean curvature). *Let* $\mathrm{gr}\overline{\Sigma} \subset \mathbb{R} \times \mathbb{R}^d$ *be a* $\mathscr{C}^{2,3}$-*moving hypersurface with boundary* $\mathrm{gr}\Gamma$. *Let* $v_\Sigma \in \mathscr{C}^2(\mathrm{gr}\overline{\Sigma})$ *be a consistent velocity field satisfying the kinematic conditions*

$$V_\Sigma = \langle v_\Sigma, n_\Sigma \rangle \quad on\ \mathrm{gr}\Sigma, \quad \langle v_\Sigma, n_{\partial\Omega} \rangle = 0 \quad on\ \mathrm{gr}\Gamma. \tag{4.82}$$

Then, the Lagrangian time-derivative of the mean curvature is given as

$$\boxed{\frac{D^\Sigma \kappa}{Dt} = V_\Sigma \sum_{i=1}^{d-1} \kappa_i^2 + \Delta_\Sigma V_\Sigma + (v_\Sigma)_\parallel \cdot \nabla_\Sigma \kappa,} \tag{4.83}$$

where $\Delta_\Sigma = \mathrm{div}_\Sigma(\nabla_\Sigma \cdot)$ *is the Laplace-Beltrami operator on* Σ *and* $\kappa_1, \dots, \kappa_{d-1}$ *are the principal curvatures, i.e. the eigenvalues of the Weingarten map* $\mathscr{W}$.

Proof. The proof of Theorem 4.33 is ongoing joint work with M. Köhne and D. Bothe. $\square$

A variant of Theorem 4.33 for the case of a moving hypersurface without boundary is given in [BGN20, p.300].

Transport of the mean curvature by a regular velocity field: We now consider the case where the interface motion is generated by a vector field $v \in \mathscr{C}^2(\mathbb{R} \times \mathbb{R}^d; \mathbb{R}^d)$ according to

$$V_\Sigma(t,x) = \langle v, n_\Sigma \rangle (t,x). \tag{4.84}$$

In what follows, we apply the following representation of the Laplace-Beltrami operator given in [KB19].

Lemma 4.34 (See [KB19]). *Let $\tilde{\phi} : U \to \mathbb{R}$ be a $\mathscr{C}^2$-extension of $\phi \in \mathscr{C}^2(\Sigma)$. Then the Laplace Beltrami of ϕ at $x \in \Sigma$ is given by the expression*

$$\Delta_\Sigma \phi(x) = \mathscr{P}_\Sigma(x) : \nabla^2 \tilde{\phi}(x) + \kappa \left\langle \nabla \tilde{\phi}(x), n_\Sigma(x) \right\rangle. \tag{4.85}$$

If $\{\tau_1, \dots, \tau_{d-1}\}$ is an orthonormal basis of the tangent space $T_\Sigma(x)$, then (4.85) can be rewritten as

$$\Delta_\Sigma \phi(x) = \sum_{i=1}^{d-1} \frac{\partial^2 \tilde{\phi}}{\partial \tau_i^2}(x) + \kappa \left\langle \nabla \tilde{\phi}(x), n_\Sigma(x) \right\rangle. \tag{4.86}$$

Here $\partial^2 / \partial \tau^2$ denotes the second directional derivative in the direction τ in $\mathbb{R}^d$.

Theorem 4.35. *Let $\mathrm{gr}\overline{\Sigma} \subset \mathbb{R} \times \mathbb{R}^d$ be a $\mathscr{C}^{2,3}$-moving hypersurface with boundary $\mathrm{gr}\Gamma$. Let $v \in \mathscr{C}^2(\mathbb{R} \times \mathbb{R}^d)$ be a consistent velocity field, i.e.*
$$V_\Sigma = \langle v, n_\Sigma \rangle \quad \text{on } \mathrm{gr}\Sigma, \quad \langle v, n_{\partial\Omega} \rangle = 0 \quad \text{on } \mathrm{gr}\Gamma.$$

Let $\{\tau_1, \dots, \tau_{d-1}\}$ be an orthonormal basis of the tangent space of $\overline{\Sigma}$. Then the Lagrangian time derivative of the mean curvature reads as

$$\boxed{\frac{D^\Sigma \kappa}{Dt} = \sum_{i=1}^{d-1} \left(\left\langle \frac{\partial^2 v}{\partial \tau_i^2}, n_\Sigma \right\rangle + 2 \sum_{j=1}^{d-1} \left\langle \tau_j, \frac{\partial v}{\partial \tau_i} \right\rangle \left\langle \tau_j, \frac{\partial n_\Sigma}{\partial \tau_i} \right\rangle \right) + \kappa \left\langle \nabla v \, n_\Sigma, n_\Sigma \right\rangle.} \tag{4.87}$$

If the τ_i are chosen to be the principal directions of curvature, i.e. $\tau_i = w_i$, then the above expression can be simplified using the identity (4.81) leading to

$$\frac{D^\Sigma \kappa}{Dt} = \sum_{i=1}^{d-1} \left(\left\langle \frac{\partial^2 v}{\partial w_i^2}, n_\Sigma \right\rangle - 2 \kappa_i \left\langle w_i, \frac{\partial v}{\partial w_i} \right\rangle \right) + \kappa \left\langle \nabla v \, n_\Sigma, n_\Sigma \right\rangle. \tag{4.88}$$

Proof. We fix a point $(t_0, x_0) \in \mathrm{gr}\overline{\Sigma}$ and compute $\frac{D^\Sigma}{Dt} \kappa(t_0, x_0)$.

(i) We first consider the special case $v(t_0, x_0) = 0$. In this case, it follows from Theorem 4.33 that

$$\frac{D^\Sigma \kappa}{Dt}(t_0, x_0) = \Delta_\Sigma V_\Sigma(t_0, x_0) = \Delta_\Sigma(v \cdot n_\Sigma)(t_0, x_0). \tag{4.89}$$

According to (4.86), we have (since $v(t_0, x_0) = 0$)

$$\begin{aligned}
\Delta_\Sigma V_\Sigma &= \sum_{i=1}^{d-1} \frac{\partial^2}{\partial \tau_i^2} \langle v, n_\Sigma \rangle + \kappa \left\langle \nabla(v \cdot n_\Sigma), n_\Sigma \right\rangle \\
&= \sum_{i=1}^{d-1} \left(\left\langle \frac{\partial^2 v}{\partial \tau_i^2}, n_\Sigma \right\rangle + 2 \left\langle \frac{\partial v}{\partial \tau_i}, \frac{\partial n_\Sigma}{\partial \tau_i} \right\rangle + \left\langle v, \frac{\partial^2 n_\Sigma}{\partial \tau_i^2} \right\rangle \right) + \kappa \left\langle (\nabla v)^\mathsf{T} n_\Sigma, n_\Sigma \right\rangle \\
&= \sum_{i=1}^{d-1} \left(\left\langle \frac{\partial^2 v}{\partial \tau_i^2}, n_\Sigma \right\rangle + 2 \left\langle \frac{\partial v}{\partial \tau_i}, \frac{\partial n_\Sigma}{\partial \tau_i} \right\rangle \right) + \kappa \left\langle (\nabla v)^\mathsf{T} n_\Sigma, n_\Sigma \right\rangle.
\end{aligned}$$

Thanks to normalization of n_Σ, we have
$$0 = \left\langle n_\Sigma, \frac{\partial n_\Sigma}{\partial \tau_i} \right\rangle$$

and hence
$$\left\langle \frac{\partial v}{\partial \tau_i}, \frac{\partial n_\Sigma}{\partial \tau_i} \right\rangle = \sum_{j=1}^{d-1} \left\langle \tau_j, \frac{\partial v}{\partial \tau_i} \right\rangle \left\langle \tau_j, \frac{\partial n_\Sigma}{\partial \tau_i} \right\rangle.$$

So (4.89) holds in the special case $v(t_0, x_0) = 0$.

(ii) Finally, we show by means of a suitable Galilean coordinate transformation, that it is sufficient to consider the special case of locally vanishing velocity. For $v(t_0,x_0) =: v_0 \neq 0$, we apply a coordinate transformation $(t,x) \leftrightarrow (t',x')$ according to

$$t'(t,x) = t, \quad x'(t,x) = x - v_0(t - t_0).$$

In fact, this is equivalent to introducing a new velocity field $\tilde{v}$ in the original variables given as

$$\tilde{v}(t,x) = v(t, x + v_0(t - t_0)) - v_0$$

and studying the motion of the hypersurface generated by $\tilde{v}$ starting from $\overline{\Sigma}(t_0)$ at time t_0. If we describe the motion of Σ via a level set function ϕ, i.e. $\overline{\Sigma}(t) = \{x \in \Omega : \phi(t,x) = 0\}$, then ϕ satisfies the advection equation

$$\partial_t \phi + v \cdot \nabla \phi = 0, \quad \phi(t_0,\cdot) = \phi_0, \tag{4.90}$$

where $\overline{\Sigma}(t_0) = \{x \in \Omega : \phi_0(x) = 0\}$. It is easy to show that if ϕ is the unique solution of (4.90) then

$$\tilde{\phi}(t,x) = \phi(t, x + v_0(t - t_0))$$

is the unique solution of the advection problem with respect to $\tilde{v}$, i.e.

$$\partial_t \tilde{\phi} + \tilde{v} \cdot \nabla \tilde{\phi} = 0, \quad \tilde{\phi}(t_0,\cdot) = \phi_0.$$

Hence, the moving hypersurface generated by $\tilde{v}$ is simply a shifted version (moving with relative velocity v_0) of the moving hypersurface generated by v. Moreover, the Lagrangian time derivatives with respect to v and $\tilde{v}$ of any geometrical quantity (encoded in the level set function ϕ or $\tilde{\phi}$, respectively) starting at (t_0,x_0) are equal. Since, moreover, all spatial derivatives of v and $\tilde{v}$ at (t_0,x_0) are equal, it follows that (4.87) also holds in the general case.

$$\square$$

Curvature Transport in Two Dimensions: Evaluating (4.87) for $n = 2$ leads to the evolution equation

$$\boxed{\frac{D^{\Sigma}\kappa}{Dt} = \frac{\partial^2 v}{\partial \tau^2} \cdot n_{\Sigma} + \kappa\,(n_{\Sigma} \cdot \partial_{n_{\Sigma}} v - 2\tau \cdot \partial_{\tau} v).} \tag{4.91}$$

For an incompressible flow in two dimensions satisfying

$$0 = \nabla \cdot v = \partial_{n_{\Sigma}} v \cdot n_{\Sigma} + \partial_{\tau} v \cdot \tau,$$

equation (4.91) may be rewritten as

$$\boxed{\frac{D^{\Sigma}\kappa}{Dt} = \frac{\partial^2 v}{\partial \tau^2} \cdot n_{\Sigma} - 3\kappa\,\tau \cdot \partial_{\tau} v.} \tag{4.92}$$

Note that the evolution of n_{Σ} and τ in (4.92) is determined by (4.12). Hence, we obtained a closed system of ODEs that describe $x(t)$, $\theta(t)$ and $\kappa(t)$ along a trajectory generated by the field v; see Section 10.1 for some examples.

Curvature Transport in Three Dimensions: Contrary to the two-dimensional case, we do not obtain a closed system of ODEs from equation (4.87) since the principal curvatures appear separately. However, equation (4.87) may still be evaluated pointwise to compute the rate of change of κ. In the case of an incompressible flow, the last term can be re-written according to

$$0 = \nabla \cdot v = \langle n_{\Sigma}, (\nabla v)n_{\Sigma} \rangle + \sum_{i=1}^{2} \langle \tau_i, (\nabla v)\tau_i \rangle.$$

Hence, the rate-of-change of the mean curvature in three dimensions reads as

$$\frac{D^{\Sigma}\kappa}{Dt} = \sum_{i=1}^{2} \left(\left\langle \frac{\partial^2 v}{\partial w_i^2}, n_{\Sigma} \right\rangle - (2\kappa_i + \kappa) \left\langle w_i, \frac{\partial v}{\partial w_i} \right\rangle \right), \tag{4.93}$$

where κ_1, κ_2 are the principal curvatures and $\{w_1, w_2\}$ are the corresponding principal directions of curvature.

Example 4.36. For a sphere (or spherical cap) in 3D with radius R it holds that $\kappa_1 = \kappa_2 = 1/R = \kappa/2$. Therefore, the *instantaneous* rate-of-change of κ reads as

$$\frac{D^\Sigma \kappa}{Dt} = \sum_{i=1}^{2} \left(\left\langle \frac{\partial^2 v}{\partial \tau_i^2}, n_\Sigma \right\rangle - 2\kappa \left\langle \tau_i, \frac{\partial v}{\partial \tau_i} \right\rangle \right).$$

Note that the above equation only holds at the instant of time when the principal curvatures are equal.

Further analytical and computational examples of the kinematic curvature transport are discussed in the Chapters 6 and 10.

5. Boundary conditions for dynamic wetting - A mathematical analysis

Starting with the work by Huh and Scriven [HS71], the scientific discussion about singularities became central for the continuum mechanical modeling of dynamic wetting (see, e.g., [dG85, Shi06, Shi08, BEI$^+$09, Vel1, SA13, EF15]). While it is generally accepted that the non-integrable singularity in the viscous dissipation introduced by the no-slip condition (see [HS71]) is unphysical for a viscous fluid, there are different approaches to relax the singularity. For the sake of brevity, we only consider two particular approaches in this chapter. Note, however, that the method of compatibility analysis is general in nature and is applicable to other modeling approaches as well.

The Navier slip law allows for tangential slip at the solid boundary according to

$$\langle v, n \rangle = 0, \tag{5.1}$$
$$-\lambda (v - w)_{\parallel} = 2\eta (Dn)_{\parallel}, \tag{5.2}$$

where $\lambda > 0$ is a friction coefficient, w is the velocity of the solid boundary, n is the unit outer normal and $D = \frac{1}{2}(\nabla v + \nabla v^{\mathsf{T}})$ is the rate-of-deformation tensor. The parameter $L = \eta / \lambda$ is called slip-length and controls the amount of tangential slip at a given shear rate (see Chapter 3).

Asymptotic methods allow to obtain information about the local structure of the solution near the contact line for the no-slip and Navier slip model (see [Mof64, Cox86]). For quasi-stationary solutions, it has been shown by asymptotic methods [HM77] that a finite and positive slip length leads to an integrable singularity with the pressure behaving like

$$p \propto \log r, \tag{5.3}$$

where r is the distance to the contact line. In this case, the force balance at the interface implies that the curvature is also infinite at the contact line to oppose the singular force due to pressure. Note that this irregular behavior of the solution might lead to problems when the model is solved numerically [SS11a]. While some authors argue that this "weak" type of singularity has little influence on the macroscopic flow [Dus76], there is also a large body of research looking for continuum mechanical models which do not even show weak singularities (see, e.g., [Shi06, Vel1, RC13, LP17]).

In the present chapter[1], we study a recently proposed model by Lukyanov and Pryer [LP17], which can be understood as a quasi-stationary adaptation/simplification of the full Interface Formation Model (IFM) [Shi93] described in Section 3.5. The basic idea is to allow for non-zero interfacial mass densities but to require that these are *constant* in space and time. This assumption allows to substantially simplify the governing equations of the IFM. In particular, there is no need to solve the mass transport equation on the surfaces. Instead, the velocity associated with transport along the surfaces can be eliminated resulting in a modified set of boundary conditions for the stationary Stokes equations. Note that the fundamental difference to a model without interfacial mass is that the impermeability condition (5.1) at the solid boundary is relaxed because mass can be transported from the bulk to the surface phase. The model is introduced and applied to nanodroplets in [LP17]. Remarkably, it is stated that there "*a small, albeit natural, change in the boundary conditions is all that is necessary to completely regularize the problem*" [LP17]. However, the authors neither prove the latter claim nor provide a numerical convergence study for the pressure and the curvature at the contact line. Before we discuss the latter model in more detail, the method of compatibility analysis is introduced and applied to the "standard Navier slip model".

---

[1]Please note that the work presented in this chapter has been published in [FB20].

5.1. Compatibility conditions for partial differential equations

So-called *compatibility conditions* appear naturally in the study of initial-boundary value problems for partial differential equations (PDEs) if one requires higher regularity of a solution, see [Tem06] and the references given therein for an introduction to the topic. A simple example is the one-dimensional convection equation:

$$\frac{\partial u}{\partial t} + \frac{\partial u}{\partial x} = f, \quad 0 < x < 1, t > 0, \tag{5.4}$$
$$u(0,t) = 0, \quad u(x,0) = u_0(x).$$

Here, we briefly recall the discussion given in [Tem06]. A first compatibility condition is obtained from taking the limit of the initial and boundary condition as $x \to 0$ and $t \to 0$, respectively. If u is continuous up to $(0,0)$ it follows that

$$u_0(0) = 0. \tag{5.5}$$

Moreover, if u is $\mathscr{C}^1$ up to $(0,0)$ we have $(\partial_t u)(0,t) = 0$ (since $u(0,t) = 0$) and hence

$$\frac{\partial u}{\partial x}(0,t) = f(0,t), \quad t > 0$$

leading (as $t \to 0$) to the second compatibility condition

$$u_0'(0) = f(0,0). \tag{5.6}$$

One can show that (5.4) is well-posed for smooth data f and u_0 [Tem06]. Moreover, the compatibility conditions (5.5) and (5.6) are necessary and sufficient for u to be $\mathscr{C}^1$; see [Tem06]. For example, in case $f = 1$ the solution[2] of (5.4) reads as

$$u(x,t) = \begin{cases} u_0(x-t)+t & \text{if } x > t, \\ x & \text{if } t > x. \end{cases}$$

Hence the conditions (5.5) and (5.6) ensure continuity and continuous differentiability of the solution, respectively.

5.2. Compatibility analysis for the standard Navier slip model

For the following calculations, we consider the geometrical configuration depicted in Figure 5.1, where for simplicity we only consider the case of two spatial dimensions. We choose Cartesian coordinates in a reference frame co-moving with the contact line, i.e. the solid boundary is moving with velocity $(V_0, 0)$ to the right, where V_0 is the speed of the contact line relative to the wall. Moreover, the interface normal and tangential vectors at the contact line have the form

$$n_1(0,0)^{\mathsf{T}} = (-\sin\theta, \cos\theta), \quad \tau_1(0,0)^{\mathsf{T}} = -(\cos\theta, \sin\theta),$$
$$n_2(0,0)^{\mathsf{T}} = (0,-1), \quad \tau_2(0,0)^{\mathsf{T}} = (1,0),$$

where θ is the contact angle. To simplify the analysis, we assume that the solid boundary is flat, i.e. $\kappa_2 = -\nabla_{\Gamma_2} \cdot n_2 = 0$.

Compatibility analysis applied to dynamic wetting: The basic idea of the compatibility analysis applied to the wetting problem is to consider a local linear expansion of the (divergence free) velocity field *at* the contact line, i.e.

$$(v_1, v_2)^{\mathsf{T}} = V_0 \left(c_1 + c_2\frac{x}{L} + c_3\frac{y}{L}, c_4 + c_5\frac{x}{L} - c_2\frac{y}{L} \right)^{\mathsf{T}} + o(|x| + |y|), \tag{5.7}$$

---

[2]The solution of the first-order PDE (5.4) can be found using the method of characteristics (see, e.g, [Eva10]).

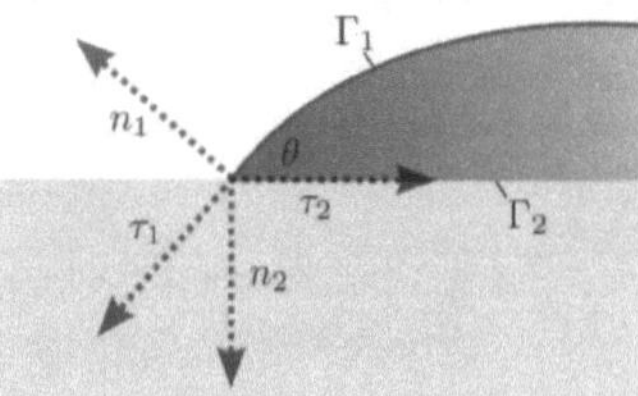

Figure 5.1.: Notation.

where $V_0 \neq 0$ is the contact line speed and $L > 0$ is the slip length. Therefore, the unknown coefficients c_i are dimensionless. The crucial property is:

If the solution is *regular*, i.e. continuously differentiable up to the contact line, it allows for a local expansion of type (5.7) and obeys all boundary conditions at the contact line, where the free surface and the solid boundary meet (see Chapter 4 and [FKB19]).

This requirement leads to a system of equations for the unknown coefficients c_i. We emphasize that the solvability of the latter system of equations is a *necessary* condition for the existence of regular solutions (in the sense defined above). To prove the existence of regular solutions is a separate task that is not addressed here. Note that the velocity itself and the velocity gradient at the contact line can be expressed as

$$v(0,0) = V_0(c_1, c_4)^{\mathsf{T}}, \quad \nabla v(0,0) = \frac{V_0}{L}\begin{pmatrix} c_2 & c_3 \\ c_5 & -c_2 \end{pmatrix}. \tag{5.8}$$

Clearly, higher order terms in (5.7) do not contribute to $\nabla v(0,0)$. As we will see below, most of the boundary conditions only involve the symmetric part of ∇v, the latter tensor being the rate-of-strain tensor D. At the contact line, it can be written in terms of the coefficients according to

$$D(0,0) = \frac{1}{2}(\nabla v + \nabla v^{\mathsf{T}})(0,0) = \frac{V_0}{2L}\begin{pmatrix} 2c_2 & c_3 + c_5 \\ c_3 + c_5 & -2c_2 \end{pmatrix}.$$

Due to the structure of $D(0,0)$, it is convenient to formally introduce a new unknown

$$c_{35} := c_3 + c_5$$

and to state the problem in terms of the unknowns $\{c_1, c_2, c_{35}, c_4\}$.

Application to the standard slip model in the free surface formulation: We consider all boundary conditions evaluated at the contact line.

(i) The kinematic boundary condition[3] at the contact line implies (in a co-moving frame)

$$0 = V_{\Gamma_1} = \langle v, n_1 \rangle = -c_1 \sin\theta + c_4 \cos\theta.$$

(ii) Due to the impermeability condition $v \cdot n_2 = 0$ on $\Gamma_2(t)$ (evaluated at the contact line) it follows that $c_4 = 0$.

(iii) The zero tangential stress condition, i.e.

$$0 = 2\eta \langle \tau_1, Dn_1 \rangle \quad \text{on} \quad \Gamma_1(t),$$

applies at the free boundary in the *absence* of surface tension gradients. Evaluating the latter condition at the contact line yields

$$0 = 2c_2 \sin 2\theta - c_{35}\cos 2\theta. \tag{5.9}$$

---

[3]Here V_{Γ_1} denotes the normal speed of the free surface.

(iv) The Navier slip condition evaluated at the contact line reads as

$$V_0 - \langle v, \tau_2 \rangle (0,0) = 2L \langle \tau_2, Dn_2 \rangle (0,0) \quad \Leftrightarrow \quad c_1 - c_{35} = 1. \tag{5.10}$$

(v) The normal stress condition (for $p_{\text{ext}} = 0$), i.e.

$$-p + 2\eta \langle n_1, Dn_1 \rangle = \sigma \kappa_1 \quad \text{on} \quad \Gamma_1(t), \tag{5.11}$$

provides the link between the two unknowns p and κ.

Hence we obtain a system of 4 linear equations for 4 unknowns (c_1, c_2, c_{35}, c_4). The linear system reads as

$$\begin{pmatrix} -\sin\theta & 0 & 0 & \cos\theta \\ 0 & -2\sin 2\theta & \cos 2\theta & 0 \\ 0 & 0 & 0 & 1 \\ 1 & 0 & -1 & 0 \end{pmatrix} \begin{pmatrix} c_1 \\ c_2 \\ c_{35} \\ c_4 \end{pmatrix} = \begin{pmatrix} 0 \\ 0 \\ 0 \\ 1 \end{pmatrix}. \tag{5.12}$$

The determinant of the system matrix is given by

$$\det A_{\text{Slip}} = 2\sin\theta \sin 2\theta.$$

For $\theta \notin \{0, \pi/2, \pi\}$ the solution reads as

$$c_1 = c_4 = 0, \; c_{35} = -1, \; c_2 = -\frac{\cot 2\theta}{2}. \tag{5.13}$$

Note that the coefficient c_2 becomes singular for $\theta \to \pi/2$. It is easy to show that no solution of the linear system exists for $\theta = \pi/2$. The latter case is distinguished mathematically since the tangential stress and Navier slip conditions produce linearly dependent equations which are incompatible (note that $c_1 = 0$). For the limiting cases $\theta \in \{0, \pi\}$, it is straightforward to show that (5.12) has a family of solutions given by

$$(c_1, c_2, c_{35}, c_4) = (1, \lambda, 0, 0), \quad \lambda \in \mathbb{R}.$$

Qualitative behavior of regular solutions: The evaluation of the boundary conditions *at* the contact line only provides information about $v(0,0)$ and $D(0,0)$. Since the impermeability condition

$$\langle v, n_2 \rangle = 0$$

applies along the whole solid boundary $\Gamma_2(t)$, it follows by differentiation with respect to τ_2 (since $\kappa_2 = 0$) that

$$\langle (\nabla v)\tau_2, n_2 \rangle = 0 \quad \text{on} \quad \Gamma_2(t).$$

The latter condition evaluated at the contact line shows

$$c_5 = 0.$$

So we found the local linear expansion of the velocity field for a regular solution (if existent) to the standard slip model. It has been shown in Section 4.1, that the rate-of-change of the contact angle can be computed from ∇v at the contact line according to

$$\dot{\theta} = -\langle (\nabla v)\tau_1, n_1 \rangle = \frac{V_0}{L} \left(-c_2 \sin 2\theta - c_3 \sin^2\theta + c_5 \cos^2\theta \right). \tag{5.14}$$

Application of (5.14) to the solution derived above yields (for $\theta \notin \{0, \pi/2, \pi\}$)

$$\dot{\theta} = \frac{V_0}{2L} (\cos 2\theta + 2\sin^2\theta) = \frac{V_0}{2L}. \tag{5.15}$$

Hence we recover the result stated in Theorem 4.18 showing that regular solution behave unphysically.

Effect of surface tension gradients: To conclude the discussion of the standard Navier slip model, we consider the case of surface tension gradients at the free surface (see Section 4.3.1). In this case, the tangential stress condition reads as

$$\frac{\partial \sigma}{\partial \tau_1} = 2\eta \, \langle \tau_1, Dn_1 \rangle \quad \text{on} \quad \Gamma_1(t).$$

Consequently, the right-hand side of equation (5.12) is generalized according to

$$A_{\text{slip}} \begin{pmatrix} c_1 \\ c_2 \\ c_{35} \\ c_4 \end{pmatrix} = \begin{pmatrix} 0 \\ -\frac{L}{V_0} \frac{\partial_{\tau_1} \sigma}{\eta} \\ 0 \\ 1 \end{pmatrix}. \tag{5.16}$$

In this case, the solution reads as ($\theta \notin \{0, \pi/2, \pi\}$)

$$c_1 = c_4 = 0, \quad c_{35} = 1, \quad c_2 = -\frac{1}{2}\left(\cot 2\theta - \frac{L}{V_0} \frac{\partial_{\tau_1} \sigma}{\eta} \csc 2\theta \right). \tag{5.17}$$

Application of the kinematic evolution equation (5.14) leads to

$$\dot\theta = \frac{1}{2}\left(\frac{V_0}{L} - \frac{\partial_{\tau_1} \sigma}{\eta} \right), \tag{5.18}$$

which is the generalization of (5.15) to the case with a non-constant surface tension. Hence, a regular quasi-stationary solution satisfying $\dot\theta = 0$ may exist if a surface tension gradient

$$\frac{\partial \sigma}{\partial \tau_1} = \frac{\eta V_0}{L} = \lambda V_0 \tag{5.19}$$

is present at the moving contact line (see also Remark 4.26 and [FKB19]). Note that for an advancing contact line ($V_0 > 0$), this means that the surface tension is locally increased at the moving contact line. Remarkably, the same formula for the surface tension gradient has been found by Sibley et al. using asymptotic methods requiring a finite pressure at the moving contact line (see [SNSK15], Appendix A). This shows that surface tension gradients at the contact line can indeed regularize the singularity.

5.3. Compatibility analysis for a model by Lukyanov and Pryer

5.3.1. The model

The model introduced in [LP17] is based on the Interface Formation Model (IFM) due to Y. Shikhmurzaev. The main simplifying assumptions are that the flow is quasi-stationary (i.e. the interface is fixed in a co-moving frame) and can be described by the stationary Stokes problem

$$\nabla \cdot v = 0, \quad \nabla p = \eta \Delta v \quad \text{in } \Omega. \tag{5.20}$$

The interfacial mass densities are assumed to be constant, i.e.

$$\rho_s^{(i)} \equiv \text{const.}$$

This allows to eliminate the interface velocity v_Σ from the model leading to a modification of the boundary conditions for the Stokes equations (see [LP17] for a derivation). In particular, the presence of interfacial mass allows for a non-zero normal component of the fluid velocity at the solid wall. In the following, we abbreviate this model with the term "CSM model" (constant surface mass model). Note that, in contrast to the IFM, the CSM model does not assume the presence of surface tension gradients at the contact line. Instead, the dynamic contact angle is an *input* parameter for the model.

The resulting boundary conditions for (5.20) are given by

$$\langle v, n_1 \rangle = \alpha_1 \nabla_{\Gamma_1} \cdot (\mathscr{P}_1 v) \quad \text{on } \Gamma_1, \tag{5.21}$$

$$\langle \tau_1, D n_1 \rangle = 0 \quad \text{on } \Gamma_1, \tag{5.22}$$

$$\langle v, n_2 \rangle = \alpha_2 \nabla_{\Gamma_2} \cdot (\mathscr{P}_2 v) \quad \text{on } \Gamma_2, \tag{5.23}$$

$$2L \langle \tau_2, D n_2 \rangle = V_0 - \langle \tau_2, v \rangle \quad \text{on } \Gamma_2, \tag{5.24}$$

$$\alpha_1 \langle v, \tau_1 \rangle = \alpha_2 (V_0 + \langle v, \tau_2 \rangle) \quad \text{at } \Gamma_1 \cap \Gamma_2, \tag{5.25}$$

$$-p + 2\eta \langle n_1, D n_1 \rangle = \sigma \kappa_1 \quad \text{on } \Gamma_1, \tag{5.26}$$

where $\mathscr{P}_i = \mathbb{1} - n_i \otimes n_i$ is an orthogonal projection operator, L is the slip length, V_0 is the velocity of the solid wall in the co-moving reference frame of the contact line and

$$\alpha_1 := \frac{\rho_s^{(1)}}{\rho}, \quad \alpha_2 := \frac{\rho_s^{(2)}}{2\rho}.$$

Note that the ratios α_i have the dimension of a length (since the liquid bulk density ρ has units of mass per volume). Therefore, it is convenient to introduce the dimensionless quantities

$$\hat{\alpha}_i := \frac{\alpha_i}{L}.$$

Note that the normal stress condition (5.26) is formulated for a constant ambient pressure $p_{\text{ext}} = 0$.

5.3.2. Compatibility analysis for regular solutions

We consider again the linear expansion of the velocity field at the contact line given by (5.7). The set of boundary conditions (5.21)-(5.26) leads to a system of algebraic equations that is discussed below.

Mass balance at the interfaces: Note that the mass balance equations (5.21) and (5.23) involving the surface divergence operator $\nabla_{\Gamma_i}\cdot$ require some clarification. A short computation shows the relation

$$\nabla_{\Gamma_i} \cdot (\mathscr{P}_i v) = \nabla_{\Gamma_i} \cdot (v - \langle n_i, v \rangle n_i)$$
$$= \nabla_{\Gamma_i} \cdot v - \langle n_i, v \rangle \nabla_{\Gamma_i} \cdot n - \underbrace{\langle n_i, \nabla_{\Gamma_i}(\langle n_i, v \rangle) \rangle}_{=0} = \nabla_{\Gamma_i} \cdot v + \langle v, n_i \rangle \kappa_i.$$

Making use of the incompressibility condition $0 = \nabla \cdot v = \nabla_{\Gamma_i} \cdot v + \langle n_i, (\nabla v) n_i \rangle$, we conclude that

$$\nabla_{\Gamma_i} \cdot (\mathscr{P}_i v) = -\langle n_i, (\nabla v) n_i \rangle + \langle v, n_i \rangle \kappa_i = -\langle n_i, D n_i \rangle + \langle v, n_i \rangle \kappa_i.$$

It follows that the mass balance equations (5.21) and (5.23) can be expressed as

$$(1 - \hat{\alpha}_i \hat{\kappa}_i) \langle v, n_i \rangle + \alpha_i \langle n_i, D n_i \rangle = 0, \tag{5.27}$$

where $\hat{\kappa}_i = \kappa_i L$ is the dimensionless curvature. We assume the solid boundary to be flat, i.e. $\hat{\kappa}_2 = 0$.

Note that (5.27) implies that the system of equations (5.21)-(5.25) does only involve the symmetric part of ∇v, i.e. the rate-of-strain tensor D. It seems that one has only 4 unknowns (c_1, c_2, c_{35}, c_4) for the 5 equations (5.21)-(5.25). But note that the curvature of the free-surface κ_1 at the contact line is introduced as an additional unknown parameter in (5.27).

Evaluating the mass balance equation (5.27) for the free surface at the contact line yields

$$(1 - \hat{\alpha}_1 \hat{\kappa}_1) \dot{m}_1 = \frac{\hat{\alpha}_1}{2} (2 c_2 \cos 2\theta + c_{35} \sin 2\theta),$$

where $\dot{m}_1 := v \cdot n_1(0,0) = -c_1 \sin\theta + c_4 \cos\theta$ is the (dimensionless) mass flux to the free surface phase at the contact line. The mass balance equation for the solid surface at the contact line reads as (since $\hat{\kappa}_2 = 0$)

$$\dot{m}_2 = \hat{\alpha}_2 c_2,$$

where $\dot{m}_2 := v \cdot n_2(0,0) = -c_4$ is the dimensionless mass flux to the solid-liquid surface phase at the contact line. Note that $\dot{m}_i = 0$ vanishes if the interface Γ_i does not carry mass, i.e. if $\hat{\alpha}_i = 0$.

Mass balance at the contact line: Equation (5.25) expresses the fact that the contact line itself cannot store mass. In terms of the unknown coefficients it translates to

$$(\hat{\alpha}_2 \cos\theta + \hat{\alpha}_1) c_1 + \hat{\alpha}_1 c_4 \sin\theta = -\hat{\alpha}_2.$$

Note that the latter equation is trivially satisfied for $\hat{\alpha}_1 = \hat{\alpha}_2 = 0$. Moreover, if the free surface does not carry mass it follows that

$$\hat{\alpha}_2 c_1 \cos\theta = -\hat{\alpha}_2. \tag{5.28}$$

Hence no regular solution exists for $\hat{\alpha}_1 = 0$, $\hat{\alpha}_2 \neq 0$ and $\theta = \pi/2$.

Zero stress condition and Navier Slip condition: Both the condition on the tangential stress (5.9) and the Navier slip condition (5.10) remain unchanged with respect to the standard model. Note, however, that in this case c_1 may be non-zero since the free surface is not a material interface.

Summary: A regular solution to the model (5.20)-(5.25) satisfies the following equations for the unknown coefficients $c_1, c_2, c_{35}, c_4, \hat{\kappa}_1$:

$$(1 - \hat{\alpha}_1 \hat{\kappa}_1)(-c_1 \sin\theta + c_4 \cos\theta) - \frac{\hat{\alpha}_1}{2}(2c_2 \cos 2\theta + c_{35} \sin 2\theta) = 0, \tag{5.29}$$

$$-2c_2 \sin 2\theta + c_{35} \cos 2\theta = 0, \tag{5.30}$$

$$\hat{\alpha}_2 c_2 + c_4 = 0, \tag{5.31}$$

$$c_1 - c_{35} = 1, \tag{5.32}$$

$$(\hat{\alpha}_1 \cos\theta + \hat{\alpha}_2) c_1 + \hat{\alpha}_1 c_4 \sin\theta = -\hat{\alpha}_2, \tag{5.33}$$

where $\hat{\alpha}_1, \hat{\alpha}_2$ and θ are given (dimensionless) data.

Note that equation (5.29), expressing the mass balance in the free surface phase, is non-linear, while equations (5.30)-(5.33) constitute a linear subsystem

$$A_{\text{CSM}} \begin{pmatrix} c_1 \\ c_2 \\ c_{35} \\ c_4 \end{pmatrix} = \begin{pmatrix} 0 \\ 0 \\ 1 \\ -\hat{\alpha}_2 \end{pmatrix}$$

with the matrix A_{CSM} given by

$$A_{\text{CSM}} = \begin{pmatrix} 0 & -2\sin(2\theta) & \cos(2\theta) & 0 \\ 0 & \hat{\alpha}_2 & 0 & 1 \\ 1 & 0 & -1 & 0 \\ \hat{\alpha}_1 \cos\theta + \hat{\alpha}_2 & 0 & 0 & \hat{\alpha}_1 \sin\theta \end{pmatrix}. \tag{5.34}$$

Note also that, in the limit of vanishing surface mass ($\hat{\alpha}_1, \hat{\alpha}_2 \to 0$), the nonlinear equation (5.29) becomes linear and the set of equations (5.29)-(5.32) reduces to (5.12) while (5.33) becomes obsolete. In this sense, the CSM model is a generalization of the standard slip model discussed in Section 5.2.

5.3.3. Solution of the non-linear system

The determinant of the system matrix A_{CSM} is given as

$$\det A_{CSM} = 2\left(\hat{\alpha}_1 \cos\theta + \hat{\alpha}_2\right)\sin 2\theta - \hat{\alpha}_1\hat{\alpha}_2 \sin\theta \cos 2\theta. \tag{5.35}$$

In the special case $\theta = \frac{\pi}{2}$ this simplifies to $\det A_{CSM} = \hat{\alpha}_1\hat{\alpha}_2$. Clearly, the linear part of the problem is uniquely solvable in case $\det A_{CSM} \neq 0$. If, moreover, the solution satisfies

$$\dot{m}_1 = c_4 \cos\theta - c_1 \sin\theta \neq 0,$$

we obtain the dimensionless curvature $\hat{\kappa}_1 = \kappa_1 L$ of the free surface at the contact line from the relation (5.29). The curvature is not determined by the compatibility conditions if there is no mass flux in the surface phase Γ_1, i.e. if $\dot{m}_1 = 0$ (see Section 5.2).

General solution: Provided that $\det A_{CSM} \neq 0$, one can uniquely solve the system of equations (5.30) - (5.33). In fact, the general solution is given by the expression

$$\begin{pmatrix} c_1 \\ c_2 \\ c_{35} \\ c_4 \end{pmatrix} = \frac{1}{\det A_{CSM}} \begin{pmatrix} -(4\cos\theta + \hat{\alpha}_1 \cos 2\theta)\hat{\alpha}_2 \sin\theta \\ -(2\hat{\alpha}_2 + \hat{\alpha}_1 \cos\theta)\cos 2\theta \\ -2(2\hat{\alpha}_2 + \hat{\alpha}_1 \cos\theta)\sin 2\theta \\ (2\hat{\alpha}_2 + \hat{\alpha}_1 \cos\theta)\hat{\alpha}_2 \cos 2\theta \end{pmatrix}. \tag{5.36}$$

Remarks:

(i) It is easy to show that the condition

$$0 < \hat{\alpha}_2 < \frac{2\hat{\alpha}_1}{2 + \hat{\alpha}_1} \tag{5.37}$$

is sufficient for $\det(A_{CSM}) \neq 0$ on $(0, \pi)$ for given $\hat{\alpha}_1 > 0$.

(ii) A short calculation using (5.36) shows that equation (5.29) can be simplified according to

$$(1 - \hat{\alpha}_1 \hat{\kappa}_1)\dot{m}_1 = -\frac{\hat{\alpha}_1}{\det A_{CSM}}(2\hat{\alpha}_2 + \hat{\alpha}_1 \cos\theta). \tag{5.38}$$

The latter equation is central for the regularity of solutions to the CSM model as we will discuss below.

(iii) Provided that $0 < \hat{\alpha}_2 \leq \frac{\hat{\alpha}_1}{2}$, there is a unique contact angle given by

$$\theta^* = \arccos\left(-\frac{2\hat{\alpha}_2}{\hat{\alpha}_1}\right) > \frac{\pi}{2}$$

which makes the right-hand side of equation (5.38) equal to zero. In this case, it follows that

$$\hat{\kappa}_1(\theta^*) = \frac{1}{\hat{\alpha}_1} \quad \text{if} \quad \dot{m}_1(\theta^*) \neq 0.$$

Otherwise (i.e. for $\theta = \theta^*$ and $\dot{m}_1(\theta^*) = 0$), the above equation (5.38) becomes obsolete. In this case the boundary conditions are compatible but the curvature at the contact line is *not* determined by the compatibility conditions.

(iv) On the other hand, if there is a set of parameters $\{\theta_s \neq \theta^*, \hat{\alpha}_1, \hat{\alpha}_2\}$ such that $\dot{m}_1(\theta_s, \hat{\alpha}_1, \hat{\alpha}_2) = 0$, then there is *no* regular solution to the model for this choice of parameters. Instead, the curvature $\hat{\kappa}_1$ becomes singular as $\theta \to \theta_s$ (see Section 5.4).

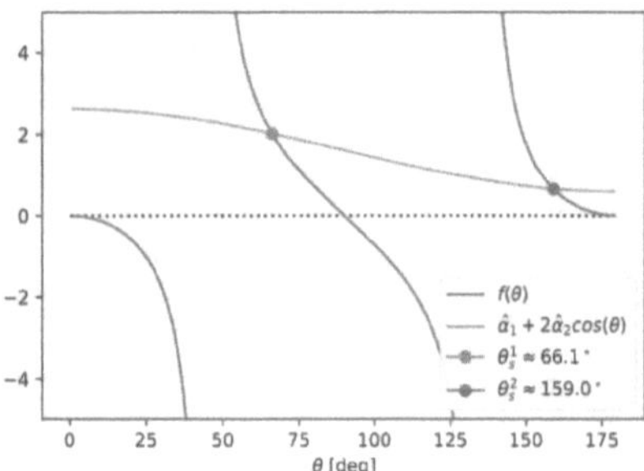

Figure 5.2.: Roots of the mass flux $\dot{m}_1$ for $\hat{\alpha}_1 = 1.6$ and $\hat{\alpha}_2 = 0.51$.

5.3.4. Singularities in the model by Lukyanov and Pryer

We will now show that for any choice of surface mass densities $\hat{\alpha}_1$, $\hat{\alpha}_2 > 0$ satisfying the invertibility condition (5.37), there is always at least one choice of the contact angle $\theta_s < \frac{\pi}{2}$ such that no regular solution exists for the parameters $\{\hat{\alpha}_1, \hat{\alpha}_2, \theta_s\}$.

The mass flux $\dot{m}_1$ can be computed from the general solution (5.36) leading to the formula

$$\dot{m}_1 = -c_1 \sin\theta + c_4 \cos\theta = \frac{\hat{\alpha}_2}{\det A_{\text{CSM}}} \left(4\cos\theta \sin^2\theta + [\hat{\alpha}_1 + 2\cos\theta\,\hat{\alpha}_2]\cos 2\theta \right).$$

Hence the roots of $\dot{m}_1$ are the solutions of

$$\hat{\alpha}_1 + 2\hat{\alpha}_2 \cos\theta = f(\theta), \tag{5.39}$$

where $f(\theta) = -(4\cos\theta \sin^2\theta)/\cos 2\theta$. Since the left-hand side of (5.39) is monotonically decreasing with $\hat{\alpha}_1 + 2\hat{\alpha}_2\cos(\frac{\pi}{2}) = \hat{\alpha}_1 > 0$, there is always a solution $\theta_s^1 < \frac{\pi}{2}$ of (5.39). Since the right-hand side of (5.38) is non-zero on $[0, \frac{\pi}{2}]$, it follows that (5.38) has no solution for $\{\hat{\alpha}_1, \hat{\alpha}_2, \theta_s^1\}$ and no regular solution exists for the latter set of parameters.

Figure 5.2 shows the example $\hat{\alpha}_1 = 1.6$ and $\hat{\alpha}_2 = 0.51$ given in [LP17]. In this case we have a singular point at

$$\theta_s^1 \approx 66.1°$$

and a second root at $\theta_s^2 \approx 159°$. Since in this case $\theta^* \neq \theta_s^2$, it follows that the second root of $\dot{m}_1$ also corresponds to a singularity of the model (see Section 5.4).

5.3.5. Pressure at the moving contact line

We can now evaluate the normal stress condition (5.26) at the free surface. If the curvature $\kappa_1(0,0)$ is uniquely determined by the compatibility conditions, we also obtain the pressure at the contact point. The non-dimensional form of equation (5.26) reads

$$\hat{p} = -\frac{\kappa_1 L}{\text{Ca}} + \frac{\langle n_1, 2Dn_1 \rangle}{V_0/L}. \tag{5.40}$$

Here we defined the non-dimensional quantities

$$\text{Ca} := \frac{\eta V_0}{\sigma}, \quad \hat{p} := \frac{p}{(\eta V_0)/L} = \frac{L}{\sigma}\frac{p}{\text{Ca}}.$$

At the contact point, we have

$$\frac{\langle n_1, 2Dn_1 \rangle}{V_0/L}(0,0) = -2c_2\cos 2\theta - 2c_{35}\sin 2\theta.$$

Therefore, the dimensionless pressure at the contact point is given by

$$\hat{p} = -\frac{\hat{\kappa}_1}{\text{Ca}} - 2(c_2\cos 2\theta + c_{35}\sin 2\theta). \tag{5.41}$$

Hence the relation for the pressure (relative to the ambient pressure) reads as

$$p = -\kappa_1\sigma - \frac{2\eta V_0}{L}(c_2\cos 2\theta + c_{35}\sin 2\theta).$$

In particular, the pressure converges to the Laplace pressure $p_L = -\kappa_1\sigma$ as $V_0 \to 0$.

5.3.6. Special case $\theta = \pi/2$

The system of equations (5.29)-(5.33) is substantially simplified in the case $\theta = \pi/2$. In this case, the nonlinear equation (5.29) reads as

$$-(1 - \hat{\alpha}_1\hat{\kappa}_1)c_1 + \hat{\alpha}_1 c_2 = 0 \tag{5.42}$$

and the matrix A_{CSM} is given by

$$A_{\text{CSM}}(\theta = \pi/2) = \begin{pmatrix} 0 & 0 & -1 & 0 \\ 0 & \hat{\alpha}_2 & 0 & 1 \\ 1 & 0 & -1 & 0 \\ \hat{\alpha}_2 & 0 & 0 & \hat{\alpha}_1 \end{pmatrix}.$$

The solution of the linear system is given by

$$\begin{pmatrix} c_1 \\ c_2 \\ c_{35} \\ c_4 \end{pmatrix} = \begin{pmatrix} 1 \\ 2/\hat{\alpha}_1 \\ 0 \\ -2\hat{\alpha}_2/\hat{\alpha}_1 \end{pmatrix}. \tag{5.43}$$

According to (5.42), it follows that the curvature at the contact line is

$$\kappa_1 L = -\frac{1}{\hat{\alpha}_1} \leq 0. \tag{5.44}$$

So the curvature is always negative, i.e. the free surface is always convex locally at the contact line for regular solutions with $\theta = \pi/2$. Moreover, the curvature becomes singular as $\hat{\alpha}_1 \to 0$, which can be understood as the transition to the standard model. Interestingly, both the curvature and pressure at the contact line do not depend on the surface mass density $\hat{\alpha}_2$ in the liquid-solid phase. Note, however, that according to (5.43) the coefficient c_4 in the expansion (5.7) still depends on $\hat{\alpha}_2$.

For the dimensionless pressure at the contact line we obtain, according to (5.41), the relation

$$\hat{p} = \frac{1}{\hat{\alpha}_1}\left(4 + \frac{1}{\text{Ca}}\right). \tag{5.45}$$

Therefore, the pressure (relative to the gas phase) is zero for $\theta = \frac{\pi}{2}$ and $\text{Ca} = -\frac{1}{4}$, independently of $\hat{\alpha}_1$ and $\hat{\alpha}_2$. For the pressure in physical units we find

$$p = \frac{\sigma\text{Ca}}{L}\hat{p} = \frac{\sigma}{L\hat{\alpha}_1}(1 + 4\text{Ca}).$$

Making use of the expression (5.44) for the mean curvature, we conclude

$$p = -\sigma\kappa_1(1 + 4\text{Ca}).$$

5.4. Comparison with results by Lukyanov and Pryer

In the following we revisit some examples given in [LP17]. The reported values for the interfacial mass densities are

$$\hat{\alpha}_1 = 1.6, \quad \hat{\alpha}_2 = 0.51.$$

The latter values are obtained from Molecular Dynamics (MD) simulations (see [LP17] for details). The matrix is invertible for all $\theta \in (0, \pi)$ since (5.37) is satisfied. Therefore, the non-dimensional mass fluxes $\dot{m}_i$ at the contact line can be computed from the general solution (5.36) (see Figure 5.3). It is observed that both $\dot{m}_1$ and $\dot{m}_2$ become singular for $\theta \to 0, \pi$. Moreover, the mass flux $\dot{m}_1$ has two roots, corresponding to (see Section 5.3.4)

$$\theta_s^1 \approx 66.1° \quad \text{and} \quad \theta_s^2 \approx 159.0°.$$

The roots of the mass flux $\dot{m}_1$ lead to singularities in the curvature according to (5.38), see Figure 5.4(a). Consequently, the singularities are also present in the pressure at the contact line (see Figure 5.4(b) for a plot with fixed Ca). In the present example, the curvature has a root at $\theta_0 \approx 102.9°$. The curvature is positive for contact angles in between θ_0 and θ_s^2, i.e. the interface is locally *concave*.

The values for the dimensionless curvature and pressure at the contact line for the examples given in [LP17] are summarized in Table 5.1. For the cases (i)-(ii) and (iv), the sign of the curvature does not agree with the macroscopic form of the interface as reported in [LP17]. Hence, the present mathematical analysis predicts a bending of the interface close to the contact line even for the nanodroplet considered in [LP17]. The absolute value of the curvature for the case (iii) is much larger than the macroscopic curvature of the interface reported in [LP17]. In fact, the contact angle $\theta = 65°$ is close to the singular point $\theta_s^1 \approx 66.1°$. This is also the reason for the extremely low dimensionless pressure of $\hat{p} \approx -711$ (measured relative to the ambient pressure). This value is about three orders of magnitude lower than the pressure reported in [LP17] (being approximately -0.9).

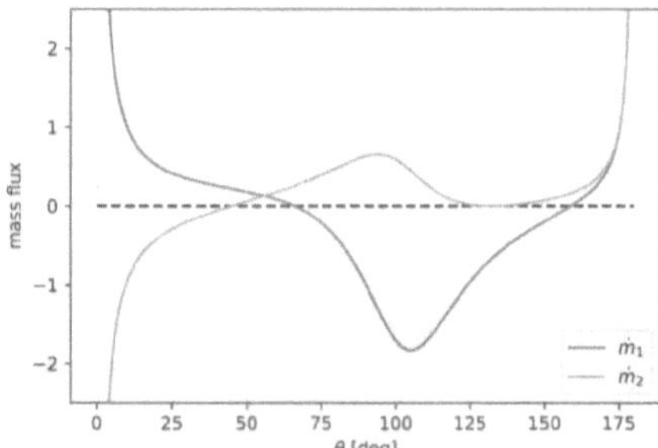

Figure 5.3.: Non-dimensional mass fluxes for $\hat{\alpha}_1 = 1.6$ and $\hat{\alpha}_2 = 0.51$.

Case	$\hat{\alpha}_1$	$\hat{\alpha}_2$	θ	Ca	$\hat{\kappa}_1$	$\hat{p}$
(i)	1.6	0.51	136°	1.14	0.81	-1.13
(ii)	1.6	0.51	114°	0.34	0.29	0.77
(iii)	1.6	0.51	65°	0.057	40.70	-711.64
(iv)	0.62	0.33	123°	0.69	1.02	12.64

Table 5.1.: Dimensionless pressure and curvature for the examples given in [LP17].

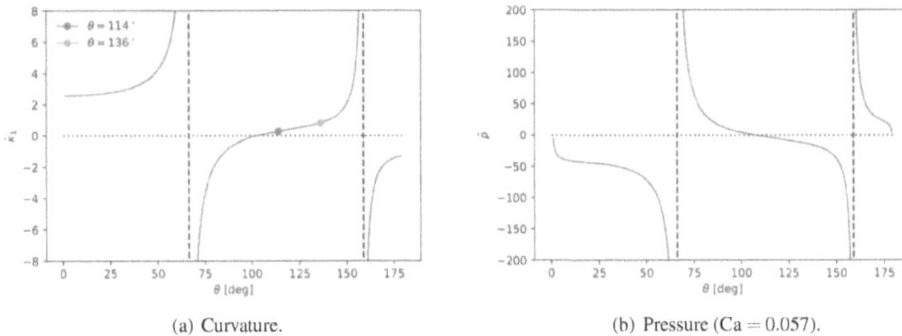

(a) Curvature.   (b) Pressure (Ca $= 0.057$).

Figure 5.4.: Dimensionless curvature and pressure at the contact line for $\hat{\alpha}_1 = 1.6$ and $\hat{\alpha}_2 = 0.51$.

5.5. Summary

The method of compatibility analysis is applied to two continuum mechanical models of dynamic wetting, namely the standard Navier slip model and the model introduced by Lukyanov and Pryer [LP17]. It is shown that no quasi-stationary regular solutions with a moving contact line exist for the standard model in the absence of surface tension gradients. Even if the contact angle is allowed to vary, we showed that regular solutions behave unphysical (see also Chapter 4 and [FKB19]). Therefore, physical solutions of the standard model with constant surface tension must be singular at the moving contact line. Moreover, it is shown that a surface tension gradient at the moving contact line may give rise to regular solutions (see also Chapter 4 and [SNSK15], [FKB19]).

The model [LP17] allows to store mass on the liquid-gas and liquid-solid interfaces (in the general framework of [Shi93]). However, the surface mass density is assumed to be constant in space and time leading to modified boundary conditions. It is shown that the standard model is recovered in the limit of vanishing surface mass densities (i.e. $\hat{\alpha}_1$, $\hat{\alpha}_2 \to 0$). The compatibility analysis for the model shows that regular solutions with finite pressure and curvature at the contact line are possible. In fact, the curvature and the pressure at the contact line can be computed from the compatibility conditions provided that the mass flux $\dot{m}_1$ to the free surface at the contact line is non-zero. On the other hand, if for certain model parameters the mass flux $\dot{m}_1$ goes to zero, then the solution becomes singular very much like in the standard model (where $\dot{m}_1$ is always zero). It is shown that such a singular point exists for every pair of interfacial mass densities $(\hat{\alpha}_1, \hat{\alpha}_2)$ satisfying (5.37). Hence the model does not always "cure" the singularity completely. Explicit expressions for the pressure and the curvature at the contact line are derived for the special case of $\theta = \pi/2$. Interestingly, the latter values for $\theta = \pi/2$ do not depend on the surface mass density $\hat{\alpha}_2$ of the liquid-solid interface.

The numerical values for the local curvature and the pressure at the contact line are compared with the continuum mechanical simulations of the model reported in [LP17] showing a quantitative and even qualitative disagreement. A possible explanation is a strong bending of the interface close to the contact line which is not resolved by the simulations in [LP17].

We emphasize that the method of compatibility analysis discussed here does only provide information *locally* *at* the contact line (or, in two dimensions at the contact point). There is no statement about the change in curvature or pressure in the vicinity of the contact line, which might explain the discrepancy to the results in [LP17]. However, the mathematical method of compatibility analysis is quite general and, therefore, applicable to a variety of models, possibly allowing for new insights into the complex problem of dynamic wetting.

Part II.

Numerical Methods

6. Numerical methods for dynamic wetting: An overview

6.1. Overview of numerical methods for multiphase flows

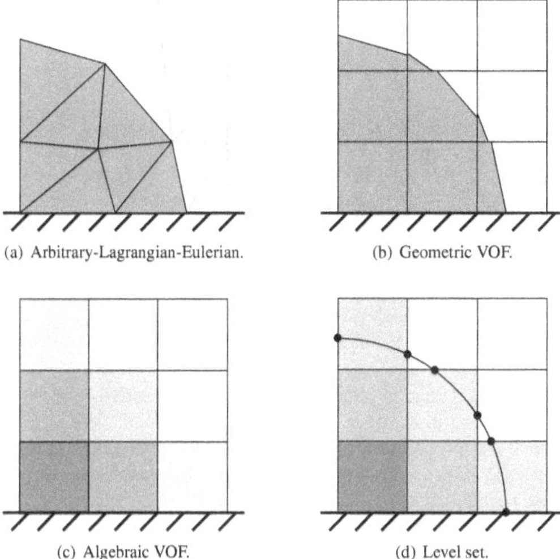

(a) Arbitrary-Lagrangian-Eulerian.

(b) Geometric VOF.

(c) Algebraic VOF.

(d) Level set.

Figure 6.1.: Different ways to represent the interface in multiphase flow simulations (Figure from [GSA$^+$20a]).

Since the beginning of computational fluid dynamics in the 1960s, the field of computational multiphase flows has developed a variety of powerful specialized methods that allow to treat rather complex multiphase flow problems numerically. For example, modern multiphase flows methods allow to simulate flows with strong deformations and topological changes such as breakup and coalescence of droplets and the atomization of liquid jets. Moreover, additional transport processes are studied such as evaporation and condensation or the transport of surface-active substances leading to local Marangoni forces. Even reactive mass transfer processes involving dissolved chemical species are accessible with numerical simulation. Clearly, there is no single method that is equally suitable for all possible flow configurations. Instead, there is a variety of numerical methods with specific advantages and disadvantages for a given multiphase flow problem. In the present section, we shall briefly review some common methods for *sharp interface* incompressible multiphase flow simulations. For more details and a more comprehensive overview of numerical methods in multiphase flows, the reader is referred to the review [SZ99] and the monographs [TSZ11, GR11] and the references given therein. The different numerical methods can be broadly classified by the mathematical representation of the moving interface. For the sake of brevity, we restrict our attention to the four approaches sketched in Fig. 6.1. At least one representative for every approach is currently in active development within CRC 1194 for the simulation of wetting flows. The four numerical methods are compared in a common numerical benchmark based on the capillary rise problem; see [GSA$^+$20a] and Chapter 11.

The (ALE) Front-Tracking method: The Arbitrary Lagrangian-Eulerian method "interTrackFoam" represents the interface as the boundary of a moving volume mesh; see Fig. 6.1(a). The latter approach allows for a quite accurate solution of the continuum mechanical problem as well as the solution of additional transport equations on the moving interface. For example, this allows to study the influence of surfactants on the wetting process [Grü20b]. However, the fact that the mesh has to follow the deformation of the interface poses the challenge to move the mesh in such a way that a sufficient quality of the mesh is maintained throughout the simulation. Moreover, the mesh motion algorithm has to guarantee volume conservation of the liquid domain which is a non-trivial constraint. In the case of interTrackFoam, an additional diffusion equation for the bulk mesh is solved. An inhomogeneous, anisotropic diffusion coefficient can be used to obtain a problem-specific mesh motion [GSA$^+$20a]. Handling the topological changes is hard within the Front-Tracking method since it requires to reconnect the whole computational mesh "by hand", i.e. by a sophisticated and computationally expensive algorithm. Therefore, other methods are better suited for multiphase flows with topological changes (see below).

The Volume-of-Fluid method: The idea of the Volume-of-Fluid (VOF) method introduced in [HW65] is to use a "marker function" defined on a fixed Eulerian grid to follow the motion of the interface. The marker function is a discrete version of the characteristic function of the liquid domain, i.e.

$$\chi(t,x) = \begin{cases} 1 & \text{if } x \in \Omega_l(t) \\ 0 & \text{if } x \notin \Omega_l(t) \end{cases}.$$

Formally, the kinematic condition for the interface motion in the absence of phase change, i.e.

$$V_\Sigma = \langle v, n_\Sigma \rangle \quad \text{on} \quad \Sigma(t), \tag{6.1}$$

translates to the hyperbolic transport equation

$$\partial_t \chi + v \cdot \nabla \chi = 0 \quad \Leftrightarrow \quad \frac{D\chi}{Dt} = 0 \tag{6.2}$$

for the (discontinuous) characteristic function χ. Note that (6.2) just states that χ is constant along the characteristics of the flow. However, equation (6.2) has to be understood in the framework of weak solutions of hyperbolic PDEs since it describes a moving discontinuity and does not admit classical solutions. It is well-known from the numerical analysis of hyperbolic PDEs (see, e.g., [LeV02]) that the numerical transport of a discontinuity is a challenging problem since it may either cause oscillations of the numerical solution or be smeared out by numerical diffusion. However, the advantage of (6.2) is that it gives rise to numerical methods that are "naturally" volume conservative. The latter property is the origin of the name of the method.

The discrete "volume fraction" α_{ijk} associated with a control volume V_{ijk} at time t is defined as the volume average of the characteristic function, i.e.

$$\alpha_{ijk}(t) = \frac{1}{|V_{ijk}|} \int_{V_{ijk}} \chi \, dV. \tag{6.3}$$

Hence, it measures the fraction of the cell volume which is occupied by liquid (or, in general, by one the phases). Integration of (6.2) over a control volume leads to the transport equation

$$\frac{d}{dt} \alpha_{ijk}(t) = -\frac{1}{|V_{ijk}|} \int_{\partial V_{ijk}} \chi \, v \cdot n \, dA + \frac{1}{|V_{ijk}|} \int_{V_{ijk}} \chi (\nabla \cdot v) \, dV, \tag{6.4}$$

where n denotes the unit outer normal field to ∂V_{ijk}. Even though the second term on the right-hand side of (6.4) vanishes for incompressible flows, it is kept in the discretization of many numerical schemes to enhance volume conservation properties (see Section 7.2 for more details). In any case, equation (6.4) forms the basis of any VOF method where the task is to approximate the numerical flux on the right-hand side. As already mentioned above, the main advantage is that any consistent numerical flux conserves the total mass of the liquid (encoded in the volume fractions) since

$$|\Omega_l| = \sum_{ijk} |V_{ijk}| \, \alpha_{ijk}$$

is conserved also in the discrete case. Another major advantage of the VOF method is the ability to handle topological changes like breakup (see Chapter 12) or coalescence events natively since no re-meshing is necessary.

In general, there are two main approaches to the numerical discretization of the flux integral on the right-hand side of (6.4). *Geometrical* VOF methods employ geometrical methods to reconstruct the local interface (see Fig. 6.1(b) for a sketch) which are then used to approximate the flux integral; see Chapter 7 for details. The second class of methods called "algebraic VOF methods" do not reconstruct the interface. Instead, an algebraic method is employed to approximate the flux integral (see Fig. 6.1(c) for a sketch). A widely used algebraic VOF method is the "interFoam" solver implemented in the OpenFoam software library. The algebraic method allows to handle complex geometries more easily. However, an additional compression method has to be applied in order to counteract the numerical diffusion of the interface. Further examples for algebraic VOF methods that study moving contact lines are [ŠWR$^+$05, KS09, DL10, RBB12, SHGL19].

Geometrical VOF methods on unstructured grids, that allow for the handling of complex geometries, are currently under active development; see, e.g, [MMB13, Mar17, MMB18, MKB20].

The Level Set method: The basic idea of the level set method is to describe the moving interface as the zero-contour of a smooth function ϕ called the "level set function", i.e.

$$\Sigma(t) = \{x \in \Omega : \ \phi(t,x) = 0\}. \tag{6.5}$$

Then the different phases can be identified by the sign of the level set function. Like for the VOF method, the kinematic condition (6.1) translates to the hyperbolic advection equation

$$\partial_t \phi + v \cdot \nabla \phi = 0 \quad \Leftrightarrow \quad \frac{D\phi}{Dt} = 0. \tag{6.6}$$

Even though the transport equation is the same as for the VOF method, the fundamental difference is that (6.6) is posed with regular initial conditions. This makes it much easier to numerically solve (6.6) compared to (6.2). For example, a simple first-order upwind discretization of the integral form of (6.6) may give quite satisfactory results for the interface advection. Section 6.2 proposes a simple level set based demonstrator code in C++ [FMVB19] which allows to study the numerical transport of the contact line, the contact angle and the curvature at the contact line. Moreover, the level set function allows to compute geometrical quantities like the normal vector or the curvature quite accurately. While the missing regularity of the volume fraction field leads to problems for VOF methods, this is not the case for the level set method where the geometrical information is encoded in a regular function. The only constraint is that the gradient must stay non-degenerate at the moving interface. In this case, the normal field can be computed from the relation

$$n_\Sigma = \frac{\nabla \phi}{|\nabla \phi|}.$$

If the gradient at the interface satisfies the additional property that it is normalized along Σ, i.e. if ϕ is locally a signed distance function, then the mean curvature can simply be computed as the Laplacian of ϕ. However, a major drawback of the level set method compared to VOF is the fact that volume conservation is not naturally ensured. Instead, the formulation leads to the conservation of the quantity

$$\int_\Omega \phi \, dV,$$

which, however, does not carry any physical information. Therefore, additional effort is necessary to achieve satisfactory volume conservation with level set methods. Obviously, there is a whole class of functions which all encode the same interface evolution through the representation (6.5). This freedom in the choice of ϕ can be facilitated to "reinitialize" to level set function by computing a new function $\tilde{\phi}$ that represents the same interface geometry. The latter may become necessary when $|\nabla \phi|$ becomes too small close to the interface.

The level-set based extended Discontinuous Galerkin (DG) method "BoSSS" [Kum12, Kum16] is the fourth method (besides interTrackFoam, FS3D and interFoam) applied to study the capillary benchmark rise problem; see Fig.6.1(d). The main advantage of the latter method is that the DG discretization allows for higher-order approximations of the solution.

Hybrid methods: Moreover, there is a large class of hybrid methods that combine several different approaches for the numerical simulation of multiphase flows. The general idea is to couple different methods and to take advantage of the specific strengths of each of them. For example, Sussman [Sus03] introduced the so-called coupled level set and volume-of-fluid (CLSVOF) method. In this method, both the volume fraction field and a level set function are transported. Then the level set function is used to compute the normal vectors for the interface reconstruction and to bound the volume fractions between 0 and 1. Conversely, the volume fractions are used to construct a "volume-preserving" distance function [Sus03, p.114]. More examples for hybrid methods for interface advection can be found in [TSZ11, Section 5.6].

6.2. Contact line advection using the level set method

We consider the problem of the advection of a contact line as discussed in detail in Chapter 4. The goal is to develop an open-source demonstrator code that allows to study the contact line advection problem numerically in three dimensions. The implementation of the level set solver in C++ was conducted by A. Vučković under the supervision of the author and is available in an open research data repository [FMB19, FMVB19].

6.2.1. Numerical Method

To solve the level set transport equation (6.6) numerically, we set up an equidistant Cartesian grid and apply an explicit Euler Finite Volume discretization. Integrating the conservative form of (6.6) over a control volume V_{ijk} yields (since $\nabla \cdot v = 0$)

$$\frac{d}{dt}\,\bar{\phi}_{ijk}(t) := \frac{d}{dt}\,\frac{1}{|V_{ijk}|}\int \phi\,dx = -\frac{1}{|V_{ijk}|}\int_{\partial V_{ijk}} \phi\, v \cdot n\, dA, \tag{6.7}$$

where n denotes the unit outer normal field to ∂V_{ijk}. Equation (6.7) is solved with an explicit Euler method in time where the numerical flux over the cell faces $F_{ijk,n}$ ($n = 1, .., 6$) is approximated with the first-order upwind method (see, e.g., [LeV02, p.72]). So let $\bar{\phi}^l_{ijk}$ denote the cell-averaged value of ϕ in cell (i, j, k) at time $t_l = l\Delta t$. Then the discrete method reads as

$$\bar{\phi}^{l+1}_{ijk} = \bar{\phi}^l_{ijk} - \frac{\Delta t}{|V_{ijk}|} \sum_{n=1}^{6} |F_{ijk,n}|\, \phi^{\text{upwind}}_{ijk,n} \left\langle v_{ijk,n}(t_l), n_{ijk,n} \right\rangle. \tag{6.8}$$

Here $v_{ijk,n}(t_l)$ is the velocity evaluated at the center of the face $F_{ijk,n}$ at time t_l, $n_{ijk,n}$ is the unit outer normal and $\phi^{\text{upwind}}_{ijk,n}$ is chosen to be the cell-centered value at time t_l in the cell adjacent to the face in the opposite direction of the flow. This choice is motivated by the direction of information propagation [LeV02, p.72] and ensures the stability of the method provided that the Courant-Friedrich-Lewy (CFL) condition

$$||v||_\infty \Delta t \le C \Delta x \tag{6.9}$$

is satisfied with $0 \le C \le 1$ [LeV02, Section 8.3]. For computational purposes, it is convenient to allow for in- and outflow to the computational domain. At inflow boundaries, we impose homogeneous Neumann boundary conditions for ϕ. This can be implemented using a constant extension of $\bar{\phi}$ to a ghost cell layer next to the boundary (see [LeV02], chapter 7). Note that no special care is necessary for cell edges at the solid boundary since we assume a zero normal component of v at solid walls. For the sake of simplicity, we do not reinitialize the level set during the simulation which is usually done in order to maintain $|\nabla \phi| \approx 1$ close to the interface.

Geometrical quantities at the boundary of the domain are evaluated using one-sided finite difference operators and linear interpolation. Since the level set function is defined on the entire computational domain, we have a natural continuation of the normal vector field away from the interface and the curvature can simply be computed as minus the full divergence of the normal vector field, i.e.

$$n_\Sigma = \frac{\nabla \phi}{|\nabla \phi|}, \quad \kappa = -\nabla \cdot n_\Sigma. \tag{6.10}$$

In order to compare the numerical result with the prediction of the kinematic evolution equations (4.12) and (4.87) in three dimensions, the contact angle and the curvature are evaluated along the trajectory defined by the flow map.

6.2.2. Results

We consider the contact line advection problem in two and three dimensions. In both cases, we chose a Cartesian coordinate system such that the solid boundary is given by $y = 0$.

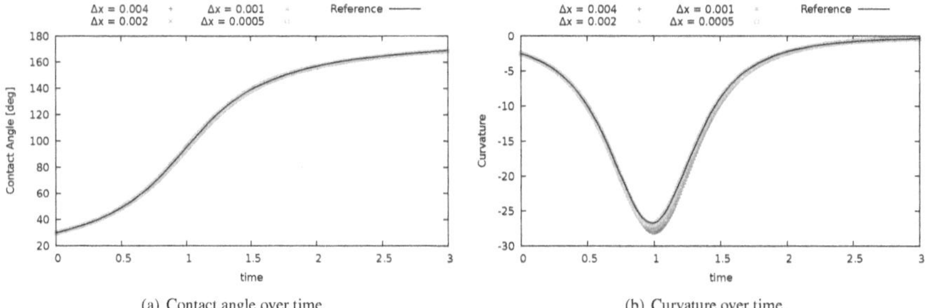

(a) Contact angle over time.　　　　(b) Curvature over time.

Figure 6.2.: Numerical results for the two-dimensional contact line advection problem.

Two-dimensional contact line advection:　As a first example, we consider the velocity field

$$v(x,y) = (-0.2 + 0.1x - 2y, -0.1y). \tag{6.11}$$

The initial shape is a spherical cap with radius $R = 0.4$ and contact angle $\theta = 30°$. The kinematic evolution equation for the contact angle and the curvature at the contact line admit an explicit solution in this case; see Sections 8.1 and 10.1 for more details. The results for the left contact point for a fixed Courant number $C = 0.1$ are shown in Figure 6.2. It is found that the evolution of both the contact angle and the curvature at the contact line can be captured quite accurately even for strong deformations. First-order convergence in the maximum norm is found for both quantities; see Fig. 6.3(a) and 6.3(b).

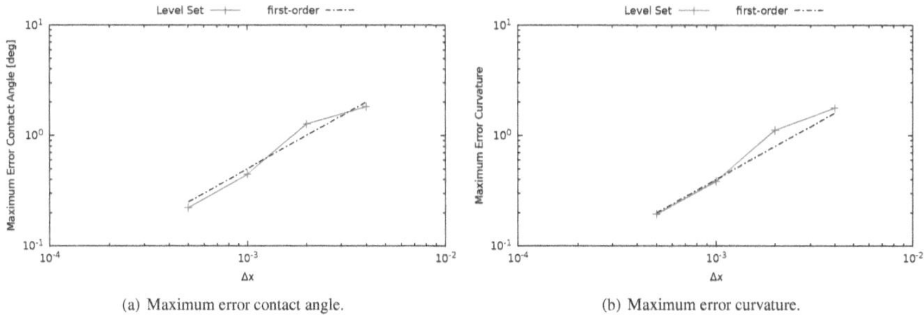

(a) Maximum error contact angle.　　　　(b) Maximum error curvature.

Figure 6.3.: Convergence analysis for the two-dimensional advection problem.

Three-dimensional contact line advection:　We take $\Omega = [0,1]^3$ and a spherical segment described by the level set function

$$\phi_0(x,y,z) = (x-1)^2 + (y-0.1)^2 + z^2 - R^2$$

with $R = 1/2$. We follow the point $\left(1 - \frac{\sqrt{3}}{5}, 0, \frac{\sqrt{3}}{5}\right) \in \Gamma(0)$ and compute the evolution of the contact angle and the mean curvature. We consider the divergence-free velocity field

$$v(x, y, z) = (-\sin(\pi x)\cos(\pi y), \cos(\pi x)\sin(\pi y), 0)$$

and solve the kinematic evolution equations numerically to obtain a reference solution for $\theta(t)$. Moreover, Equation (4.93) allows to compute a reference value for the rate-of-change of the mean curvature $\dot{\kappa}(0)$. The numerical results for a fixed Courant number $C = 0.2$ are reported in Fig. 6.4. Indeed, the initial slope of $\kappa(t)$ is correctly described by (4.93).

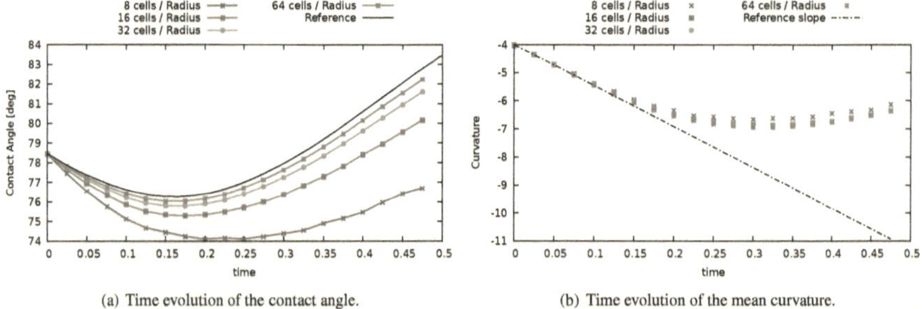

(a) Time evolution of the contact angle. (b) Time evolution of the mean curvature.

Figure 6.4.: Numerical results for the three-dimensional contact line advection problem.

A comprehensive study of the contact line advection problem in two dimensions using the geometrical VOF method is given in Chapter 8 and 10.

7. The geometrical Volume-of-Fluid method

7.1. The VOF solver FS3D: An overview

In the present work, the two-phase flow solver *Free Surface 3D* (FS3D), originally developed by Rieber and Frohn [RF99, Rie04], is employed and extended to solve the incompressible two-phase Navier Stokes equations. Since the original work by Rieber, FS3D has been further developed at the University of Stuttgart (see, e.g., [EEG$^+$16] and the references given therein) and in the *Mathematical Modeling and Analysis* (MMA) group at the Technical University of Darmstadt (see [FB15a], [ARB12, MB13, BF13, GFB16, WB17, FB15b, LB16]). It has been applied successfully to a variety of multiphase flow problems including falling films [ARB12], thermo-capillary effects [MB13], thermocapillary effects in wetting [FB15a], (reactive) mass transfer processes at fluid interfaces [BF13], [GFB16], [WB17], multi-component mass transfer at fluid interfaces [FB15b] and droplet collisions at high Weber numbers [LB16]. To allow for a time-efficient solution of the continuum mechanical model, the solver is parallelized using a domain decomposition technique implemented with the OpenMPI library.

The two-phase Navier Stokes equations in the Continuum Surface Force (CSF) formulation [BKZ92] are discretized using the finite-volume approach on a fixed Cartesian grid. Within the CSF formulation, the effect of surface tension is modeled as a singular source term in the Navier Stokes equation, i.e.

$$\rho\frac{Dv}{Dt} - \nabla \cdot (2\eta D) + \nabla p = \rho g + \sigma \kappa n_\Sigma \delta_\Sigma, \quad \nabla \cdot v = 0 \quad \text{in} \quad \Omega, \tag{7.1}$$

where δ_Σ denotes the surface delta distribution on $\Sigma(t)$; see Section 7.4 for more details. In the CSF formulation, the two-phase flow is treated as a single fluid where the density ρ is volume averaged according to

$$\rho = \alpha\rho_l + (1-\alpha)\rho_g. \tag{7.2}$$

Here α denotes the discrete volume fraction field as defined in (6.3) and the subscripts l and g refer to the liquid and gas phases, respectively. The averaging of the viscosity in interface cells is more involved (see below).

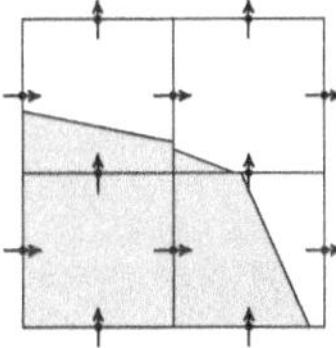

Figure 7.1.: PLIC interface and staggered grid for velocity components.

FS3D relies on structured Cartesian meshes and therefore decomposes the boundary of each cell into 4 planar faces (i.e. edges) in two dimensions with normal vectors that are collinear with coordinate axes. The grid points used for the velocity components (face/edge centroids) are shifted with respect to the grid points used for the volume fractions (volume/area centroids) as shown in Figure 7.1. Employing the Piecewise Linear Interface Calculation (PLIC) method, the interface is represented as a line in (two dimensions) or as a plane (in three dimensions) in each cell; see Figure 7.1. Unfortunately, there is currently no implementation which allows for a local adaptive refinement of the mesh.

Top-level algorithm: The time integration is based on an explicit Euler method, where the pressure-velocity coupling is realized by Chorin's projection method which leads to an elliptic equation for the pressure to perform a projection onto the space of solenoidal velocity fields. Note that the grids for velocity and pressure are staggered to enhance the stability of the method [HW65] (see Fig. 7.1). The top-level algorithm to advance the solution from t to $t + \Delta t$ in FS3D can be summarized as follows:

(Step I) Convective transport of the velocity field.

(Step II) Geometric transport of the volume fraction field, reconstruct PLIC interface (see Sections 7.2 and 7.3).

(Step III) Discretization of viscous forces.

(Step IV) Discretization of surface tension forces (see Sections 7.4 and 7.5).

(Step V) Discretization of gravitational / buoyancy forces.

(Step VI) Apply pressure projection to ensure incompressibility.

Convective transport of the velocity field: The non-linear convective term in the Navier-Stokes is discretized using a second-order Godunov method based on [BCG89, Tau94]; see Section 4.7 in [Rie04] for details.

Geometric transport of the volume fraction field: The volume fraction field is transported by solving the VOF transport equation (6.4) with an explicit discretization in time, i.e. with the prescribed velocity field v^n; see Sections 7.2 and 7.3 for details. The results is an update α^{n+1} for the volume fraction field which induces an update $\rho(\alpha^{n+1})$ for the discrete density field through volume averaging (7.2).

Discretization of viscous forces: The viscous forces are discretized using a central finite differences approximation of the Laplace operator together with a specific averaging method for the viscosity involving both arithmetic and harmonic averages as described in [TBET98] (see also [TSZ11, p.63], [FB12]). Note that the latter method originates from an early version of the monograph by Patankar [Pat18] where it has been applied to heat diffusion.

Discretization of surface tension and volume forces: The surface-tension force is discretized with the *balanced* CSF method introduced by Popinet [Pop09]. A height-function representation of the interface is constructed in order to approximate the mean curvature (see Section 7.4 for details). It has been demonstrated that this method is able to significantly reduce spurious currents at the interface away from the boundary.

Following the approach by Afkhami and Bussmann [AB08, AB09], the height function is also used to indirectly enforce the contact-angle boundary condition (see Section 7.5). The latter method has been implemented in FS3D by Lippert [Lip16]. The idea is to linearly extrapolate the height function at the contact line into a ghost cell layer, where the slope of the extrapolated interface is determined by the prescribed contact angle. As a result, the approximated value of the mean curvature is altered leading to a "numerical force" that drives the interface towards the desired contact angle. A drawback of that method is that it may create spurious currents at the contact line since the curvature in the stationary state is not estimated correctly; see Example 7.2 on page 96 for more details.

Pressure projection step: Finally, Chorin's projection method [Cho68] is applied to enforce the incompressibility constraint. Given the intermediate velocity field $\tilde{v}$ which is obtained after applying the convective transport, viscous, capillary and gravitational forces, the velocity at time step $n + 1$ is obtained from

$$v^{n+1} = \tilde{v} - \frac{\Delta t}{\rho(\alpha^{n+1})}\nabla\Pi, \quad v^{n+1} \cdot n_{\partial\Omega}\big|_{\partial\Omega} = 0. \tag{7.3}$$

where the "projector" Π is determined by the constraint that v^{n+1} is divergence-free. This leads to the elliptic equation

$$\nabla \cdot \left(\frac{1}{\rho(\alpha^{n+1})}\nabla\Pi\right) = \frac{\nabla \cdot \tilde{v}}{\Delta t}, \tag{7.4}$$

which is solved in FS3D using a multigrid solver [Rie04]. Note that, since the intermediate velocity $\tilde{v}$ satisfies the impermeability condition at a solid boundary, it follows that

$$v^{n+1} \cdot n_{\partial\Omega}\big|_{\partial\Omega} = -\frac{\Delta t}{\rho(\alpha^{n+1})} n_{\partial\Omega} \cdot \nabla\Pi\big|_{\partial\Omega}. \tag{7.5}$$

Hence, the impermeability condition for v^{n+1} implies that the projector Π must satisfy a homogeneous Neumann boundary condition at a solid boundary, i.e.

$$\frac{\partial\Pi}{\partial n_{\partial\Omega}} = 0 \quad \text{on } \partial\Omega. \tag{7.6}$$

Therefore, the scalar field Π (determined up to a constant) that solves (7.3) subject to (7.6) should not be confused with the actual pressure p in the Navier Stokes problem (7.1); see [Tem91].

Boundary conditions: The ghost cell approach (see, e.g., Chapter 7 in [LeV02]) is employed to implement boundary conditions at physical or artificial boundaries in FS3D. The ghost cells are two layers of additional control volumes outside the computational domain which (in principle) allow to apply the same discretization schemes at the boundary and in the interior of the domain. The boundary conditions are enforced by setting appropriate values for the field variables in the ghost cells. FS3D allows to apply no-slip and Navier slip conditions at solid boundaries (implemented by Fath [FB15a], see Section 7.5.1) as well as periodic and inflow/outflow boundary conditions. Moreover, the concept of ghost cells is facilitated to communicate data at processor boundaries in parallel simulations.

Stability criteria: In order to ensure the stability of the numerical method, the time step is chosen according to the stability criterion

$$\Delta t = \min\{(\Delta t)_\sigma, (\Delta t)_\eta, (\Delta t)_v\} \tag{7.7}$$

with the timescales (see [TSZ11] for a similar criterion) given by

$$(\Delta t)_\sigma = \sqrt{\frac{(\rho_l + \rho_g)(\Delta x)^3}{4\pi\sigma}}, \quad (\Delta t)_\eta = \frac{\rho_l(\Delta x)^2}{6\eta_l}, \quad (\Delta t)_v = \frac{\Delta x}{\|v\|_\infty}. \tag{7.8}$$

7.2. Interface advection

In the following[1], we describe the algorithm applied to solve the interface advection problem. For simplicity, we restrict the discussion to the two-dimensional case. Details on the extension to three dimensions can be found in [Rie04], [RK98]. As described briefly in Section 6.1, the Volume of Fluid method makes use of the phase indicator function for one of the phases $\Omega^\pm(t)$, which are separated by the interface $\Sigma(t)$, i.e.

$$\chi(t,x) = \begin{cases} 1 & \text{if} \quad x \in \Omega^-(t) \\ 0 & \text{if} \quad x \notin \Omega^-(t) \end{cases}, \tag{7.9}$$

to describe the interface. The kinematic condition for the interface motion translates to a hyperbolic transport equation for the phase-indicator function, which in its conservative forms reads as

$$\partial_t\chi + \nabla \cdot (v\chi) = \chi(\nabla \cdot v). \tag{7.10}$$

Note that the right-hand side vanishes for an incompressible flow. However, it is kept in the discretization to enhance volume conservation properties [RK98]. The latter approach is called "divergence correction". Integrating (7.10) over a control volume leads to

$$\frac{d}{dt}\alpha_{ij}(t) = -\frac{1}{|V_{ij}|}\int_{\partial V_{ij}} \chi v \cdot n \, dA + \frac{1}{|V_{ij}|}\int_{V_{ij}} \chi(\nabla \cdot v)\,dV, \tag{7.11}$$

---

[1] Please note that the Chapters 7.2, 7.3 and 8 are based on the publication [FMB20a].

where the "volume fraction" α_{ij} associated with the control volume V_{ij} at time t is defined as

$$\alpha_{ij}(t) = \frac{1}{|V_{ij}|} \int_{V_{ij}} \chi \, dV. \tag{7.12}$$

A temporal integration of (7.11) leads to the exact transport equation of the volume fraction field given as

$$\alpha_{ij}(t+\Delta t) = \alpha_{ij}(t) - \frac{1}{|V_{ij}|} \int_t^{t+\Delta t} \int_{\partial V_{ij}} \chi \, v \cdot n \, dA \, d\tau + \frac{1}{|V_{ij}|} \int_t^{t+\Delta t} \int_{V_{ij}} \chi (\nabla \cdot v) \, dV \, d\tau. \tag{7.13}$$

The conservative form of (7.13) allows for the exact conservation of the phase volume also in the discrete case. *Geometric* Volume-of-Fluid methods approximate the numerical flux, which can be decomposed in a sum over faces A_f of the control volume according to

$$\int_t^{t+\Delta t} \int_{\partial V_{ij}} \chi \, v \cdot n \, dA \, d\tau = \sum_f \int_t^{t+\Delta t} \int_{A_f} \chi \, v \cdot n \, dA \, d\tau,$$

by reconstructing a sharp geometrical approximation of the indicator function $\chi(t,\cdot)$ (see Section 7.3) and subsequently approximating the integral using geometrical methods. Within the FS3D code, equation (7.13) is solved on a structured Eulerian grid using an operator splitting method as described below (see also [RK98,Rie04,EEG$^+$16]).

Operator splitting method: The idea of the operator splitting approach [RK98, Rie04] is to decompose the full transport problem into a series of one-dimensional transport steps along the coordinate axis. Formally, this is achieved by decomposing the velocity as $v = (v_1,0) + (0,v_2) =: \tilde{v}_1 + \tilde{v}_2$. With this notation, equation (7.13) reads as

$$\alpha_{ij}(t+\Delta t) = \left(\alpha_{ij}(t) - \frac{1}{|V_{ij}|} \int_t^{t+\Delta t} \int_{\partial V_{ij}} \chi \, \tilde{v}_1 \cdot n \, dA \, d\tau + \frac{1}{|V_{ij}|} \int_t^{t+\Delta t} \int_{V_{ij}} \chi (\nabla \cdot \tilde{v}_1) \, dV \, d\tau \right)$$
$$- \frac{1}{|V_{ij}|} \int_t^{t+\Delta t} \int_{\partial V_{ij}} \chi \, \tilde{v}_2 \cdot n \, dA \, d\tau + \frac{1}{|V_{ij}|} \int_t^{t+\Delta t} \int_{V_{ij}} \chi (\nabla \cdot \tilde{v}_2) \, dV \, d\tau. \tag{7.14}$$

Note that the projected velocity fields $\tilde{v}_i$ are no longer divergence-free and it is, therefore, important to consider the divergence correction terms in the discretization of (7.14). The discrete set of equation reads as

$$(1 - \beta q_1^{i,j}) \alpha_{i,j}^* = \alpha_{i,j}^n (1 + (1-\beta) q_1^{i,j}) - \frac{\delta V_{i+1/2,j} - \delta V_{i-1/2,j}}{|V_{ij}|},$$
$$(1 - \beta q_2^{i,j}) \alpha_{i,j}^{n+1} = \alpha_{i,j}^* (1 + (1-\beta) q_2^{i,j}) - \frac{\delta V_{i,j+1/2} - \delta V_{i,j-1/2}}{|V_{ij}|}, \tag{7.15}$$

where $\delta V_{i\pm 1/2,j}$ denotes the volume flux over the edge $(i \pm 1/2, j)$ in a x-sweep, $\delta V_{i,j\pm 1/2}$ denotes the volume flux over the edge $(i, j \pm 1/2)$ in a y-sweep and

$$q_1^{i,j} := \Delta t \, \frac{v_1(i,j) - v_1(i-1,j)}{\Delta x_1}, \quad q_2^{i,j} := \Delta t \, \frac{v_2(i,j+1) - v_2(i,j)}{\Delta x_2}.$$

The choices $\beta = 0$ and $\beta = 1$ correspond to an explicit or implicit discretization of the divergence correction, respectively. In the present work, we choose $\beta = 0.5$. The order of the direction of the sweeps is exchanged after each time step to avoid numerical asymmetries [Str68]. After each directional split transport step, a heuristic volume redistribution algorithm similar to [HF00] is applied to enforce boundedness of the method, i.e. $0 \leq \alpha_{i,j}^n \leq 1$.

Approximation of the volume flux: The volume fraction field α_{ij} is used to reconstruct a planar interface in each cell which is cut by the interface $\Sigma(t)$, in effect approximating χ with the Piecewise Linear Interface Calculation (PLIC). The reconstructed PLIC indicator $\tilde{\chi}$ is then used to approximate the flux integral

$$\int_t^{t+\Delta t} \int_{A_f} \chi \, \tilde{v}_d \cdot n \, dA \, d\tau, \quad d = 1,2,$$

where A_f is a face (edge) of the cell (i,j). The geometrical interpretation of the above integral is a volume of the phase Ω^- (indicated with χ) that passes through the face A_f. The calculation of this volume is performed by sweeping the face (edge) A_f of the cell backwards along the trajectory given by $\tilde{v}_d$, and then clipping this swept volume with $\tilde{\chi}$. Note that the operator splitting simplifies the flux calculation because it simplifies the swept volume as a rectangular cuboid, whose intersection with $\tilde{\chi}$ is much simpler to calculate than for the swept volume that is traced along the Lagrangian trajectories given by the full velocity v. The simplification comes at the price of performing an additional PLIC interface intersection per splitting step. Details on the computation of the volume flux can be found in [Rie04].

Remark 7.1 (Volume flux at boundary faces). No special care is necessary to compute the flux over cell faces at an impermeable domain boundary since we assume a vanishing normal velocity leading to zero flux there.

7.3. Interface reconstruction methods

A large number of methods have been developed for the geometrical reconstruction of the interface from the volume fraction field. An overview of reconstruction algorithms can be found in [PP04, AMSZ07]. In this section, we consider two particular reconstruction algorithms, namely the classical method by Youngs [You84] and the ELVIRA method due to Pilliod and Puckett [PP04].

Moreover, we propose extensions of these two methods to reconstruct an interface close to the boundary in Chapter 8. To keep the formulas simple, assume that the mesh is equidistant in each direction with mesh sizes denoted as Δx_1 and Δx_2.

A natural measure for the interface reconstruction error is the L^1-error defined as

$$\mathscr{E}_1 := \int_\Omega |\chi(x) - \hat{\chi}(x)|\,dx, \tag{7.16}$$

where $\hat{\chi}$ is the characteristic function of the reconstructed domain.

Youngs Reconstruction Method: The idea of the Youngs method is to approximate the interface normal vector by the discrete gradient of the volume fraction field, i.e.

$$n_\Sigma \approx n_\Sigma^Y = -\frac{\nabla_h \alpha}{|\nabla_h \alpha|}. \tag{7.17}$$

Then a plane with orientation n_Σ^Y is positioned such that the volume fraction in the local cell is matched (see [SZ00] for details of the positioning algorithm). The gradient in (7.17) is approximated by weighted central finite differences on a 3×3-block of cells. For an equidistant mesh, the gradient at cell (i,j) is discretized with central finite differences as

$$\begin{aligned}
(\nabla_h \alpha)_1 &= \frac{1}{2}\frac{\alpha(i+1,j)-\alpha(i-1,j)}{2\Delta x_1} + \frac{1}{4}\frac{\alpha(i+1,j+1)-\alpha(i-1,j+1)}{2\Delta x_1} + \frac{1}{4}\frac{\alpha(i+1,j-1)-\alpha(i-1,j-1)}{2\Delta x_1}, \\
(\nabla_h \alpha)_2 &= \frac{1}{2}\frac{\alpha(i,j+1)-\alpha(i,j-1)}{2\Delta x_2} + \frac{1}{4}\frac{\alpha(i+1,j+1)-\alpha(i+1,j-1)}{2\Delta x_2} + \frac{1}{4}\frac{\alpha(i-1,j+1)-\alpha(i-1,j-1)}{2\Delta x_2}.
\end{aligned} \tag{7.18}$$

The Youngs Method is known to be one of the fastest methods for interface reconstruction from volume fractions fields. But it is only *first-order* accurate with respect to the L^1-norm since it fails to reconstruct all planar interfaces exactly, see [PP04]. This may be explained as a consequence of the lack of regularity of the volume fraction field α, which can be understood as the *evaluation* at the cell centers of the continuous function

$$F(x) = \frac{1}{|V_0|}\int_{V_0} \chi(x+x')\,dx',$$

obtained from averaging the phase indicator function over a control volume (see Appendix D). It is well-known [SZ00] that the latter function is only of class $\mathscr{C}^1$. One can, therefore, *not* expect convergence of the finite differences scheme (7.18). This underlines the need for more advanced methods.

(E)LVIRA Method: The idea of the *Least Squares VOF Interface Reconstruction Algorithm* (LVIRA) method proposed by Puckett [Puc91] is to find a planar interface reconstruction that *minimizes* the quadratic deviations of the volume fractions in a 3×3-block under the constraint that this interface exactly reproduces the volume fraction in the central cell with index (i, j). Hence, one minimizes the functional

$$\mathscr{F} = \sum_{k,l=-1}^{1} [\tilde{\alpha}_{i+k,j+l}(n) - \alpha_{i+k,j+l}]^2, \tag{7.19}$$

where $\tilde{\alpha}_{i+k,j+l}(n)$ is the volume fraction in cell $(i+k, j+l)$ which is induced by a plane with orientation n satisfying $\tilde{\alpha}_{ij}(n) = \alpha_{ij}$. Due to the nonlinear constraint, the minimization problem cannot be reformulated as a linear system of equations.

Since the minimization of (7.19) is computationally expensive compared to a direct method like the Youngs reconstruction, Pilliod and Puckett introduced the *Efficient Least Squares VOF Interface Reconstruction Algorithm* (ELVIRA) [PP04]. The computational costs are reduced by minimizing (7.19) only over a *finite* set of candidate orientations obtained in the following way:

Suppose the interface can be described in the slope-intercept form

$$x_2 = m_1 x_1 + b. \tag{7.20}$$

Then the interface normal vector is either

$$n_\Sigma = (-m_1, 1)/\sqrt{1+m_1^2} \quad \text{or} \quad n_\Sigma = (m_1, -1)/\sqrt{1+m_1^2}.$$

The slope is approximated by central-, forward- and backward-finite-differences of column sums. The candidates for the slope m_x in the cell (i, j) are

$$\pm m_1^b \quad \text{with} \quad m_1^b = \frac{\Delta x_2}{\Delta x_1} \sum_{l=-1}^{1} (\alpha_{i,j+l} - \alpha_{i-1,j+l}),$$

$$\pm m_1^c \quad \text{with} \quad m_1^c = \frac{\Delta x_2}{2\Delta x_1} \sum_{l=-1}^{1} (\alpha_{i+1,j+l} - \alpha_{i-1,j+l}), \tag{7.21}$$

$$\pm m_1^f \quad \text{with} \quad m_1^f = \frac{\Delta x_2}{\Delta x_1} \sum_{l=-1}^{1} (\alpha_{i+1,j+l} - \alpha_{i,j+l}).$$

We observe that the slope should be approximated with $+m_1^b$, $+m_1^c$ or $+m_1^f$ if the second component of n_Σ is positive and vice versa with $-m_1^b$, $-m_1^c$ or $-m_1^f$ if the second component of n_Σ is negative. This results in 6 candidates for the normal vector obtained from column sums in the x_2-direction.

Obviously, it is not always possible to represent the interface as a graph over x_1. Therefore, one also has to consider the case

$$x_1 = m_2 x_2 + b. \tag{7.22}$$

This gives rise to analogous approximations for m_2^b, m_2^c and m_2^f. This results in 12 candidates for the interface normal in two dimensions. It can be shown to be sufficient to reconstruct any straight line exactly which makes the method formally second-order accurate with respect to the L^1-error, see [PP04].

7.4. Numerical modeling of surface tension

> "Numerical models of surface tension play an increasingly important role in our capacity to understand and predict a wide range of multiphase flow problems. The accuracy and robustness of these models have improved markedly in the past 20 years, so that they are now applicable to complex, three-dimensional configurations of great theoretical and practical interest." [Pop18, p.49]

As pointed out by Popinet in his survey article [Pop18], the numerical modeling of the physical effect of surface tensions plays a key role in the understanding of a wide range of multiphase flow problems. In particular, when it comes to wetting flows, the surface tension forces are typically of great importance. The purpose of this section is to briefly summarize the height function based CSF approach to model surface tension in VOF methods as described in [Pop09]. The extension of the latter method to wetting problems is discussed in Section 7.5.2. We refer to [Pop18] for the discussion of alternative numerical models of surface tension.

In the original formulation of the two-phase flow model (3.22), the surface tension force appears in the interfacial jump condition for momentum, i.e. for the case of constant surface tension

$$[\![p\mathbf{1} - S]\!]\, n_\Sigma = \sigma \kappa n_\Sigma \quad \text{on } \Sigma(t). \tag{7.23}$$

In this formulation, the complete model is formulated as two coupled incompressible Navier Stokes problems on time-dependent domains. The surface tension affects the flow through the coupling condition (7.23) which is related to the momentum transfer from one phase to the other.

CSF formulation: The idea of the CSF formulation of the two-phase Navier Stokes equations due to Brackbill et al. [BKZ92] is to replace the model (3.22) by a system of PDEs that is valid on the entire domain. This is achieved by replacing the jump condition (7.23) by a singular source term of the form

$$f_\sigma = \sigma \kappa n_\Sigma \delta_\Sigma \tag{7.24}$$

in the momentum balance equation. Here, δ_Σ denotes the surface delta distribution on $\Sigma(t)$. The complete CSF formulation of the model (3.22) reads as

$$
\begin{aligned}
\rho \frac{Dv}{Dt} - \eta \Delta v + \nabla p &= \sigma \kappa n_\Sigma \delta_\Sigma, \ \nabla \cdot v = 0 \quad \text{on } \Omega, \\
\langle v, n_{\partial\Omega} \rangle &= 0, \ a\,\mathscr{P}_{\partial\Omega} v + 2\mathscr{P}_{\partial\Omega} D n_{\partial\Omega} = 0 \quad \text{on } \partial\Omega \setminus \Gamma(t), \\
V_\Sigma &= \langle v, n_\Sigma \rangle \quad \text{on } \Sigma(t), \\
V_\Gamma &= \langle v, n_\Gamma \rangle, \quad \theta = f(V_\Gamma) \quad \text{on } \Gamma(t).
\end{aligned}
\tag{7.25}
$$

Since the surface tension appears as a force density, the latter model is referred to as a *volumetric* formulation of surface tension in the literature (see, e.g., [Pop18]). In order to apply the source term f_σ in the discrete problem, one has to approximate both the mean curvature κ as well as the product of the interface normal vector and the surface delta distribution $n_\Sigma \delta_\Sigma$. Motivated by the identity

$$\nabla \chi = -n_\Sigma \delta_\Sigma, \tag{7.26}$$

which holds in the sense of distributions, a common choice to approximate the singular volumetric force density f_σ in VOF methods is

$$f_\sigma \approx -\sigma \hat{\kappa} \hat{\nabla} \alpha. \tag{7.27}$$

Here, $\hat{\kappa}$ denotes the discrete approximation of the mean curvature and $\hat{\nabla}\alpha$ is the discrete gradient applied to the discrete volume fraction field.

Height function method to approximate the mean curvature: The height function method is based on a representation of the interface as a graph of some $\mathscr{C}^2$-function h in a suitable coordinate system, e.g.

$$\Sigma = \{(x, h(x)) : x \in I\}$$

in two dimensions or

$$\Sigma = \{(x, y, h(x, y)) : (x, y) \in \mathscr{D}\}$$

in three dimensions. If such a representation is available, one can easily compute the mean curvature using the formulas

$$\kappa(x_0, h(x_0)) = \frac{h''(x_0)}{(1 + h'(x_0)^2)^{3/2}} \tag{7.28}$$

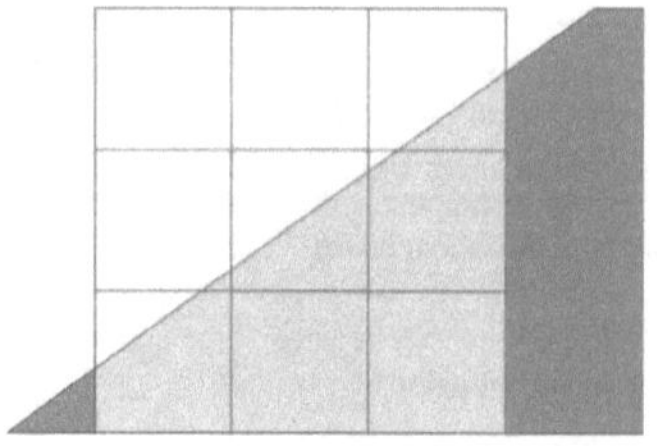

(a) Stencil to approximate κ in the central cell.

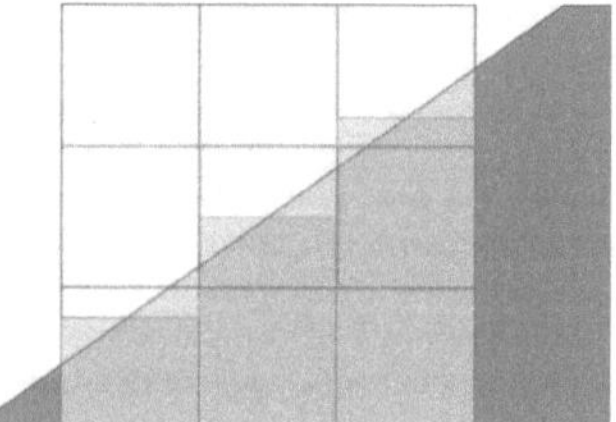

(b) Averaged height function from VOF data.

Figure 7.2.: Local height function representation of the interface.

in two dimensions and

$$\kappa(x_0, y_0, h(x_0, y_0)) = \frac{h_{xx}(1 + h_y^2) + h_{yy}(1 + h_x^2) - 2h_{xy}h_xh_y}{(1 + h_x^2 + h_y^2)^{3/2}}(x_0, y_0) \tag{7.29}$$

in three dimensions. Hence, the algorithm constructs a discrete local graph representation of the interface and employs some finite differences scheme to approximate (7.28) and (7.29), respectively. The implementation in FS3D uses a stencil of 3 columns in 2D and a stencil of 3×3 columns in 3D and central finite differences of second-order. The discrete approximation in two dimensions reads

$$\hat{\kappa}_i = \frac{\hat{h}_i''}{(1 + \hat{h}_i'^2)^{3/2}},$$

where

$$\hat{h}_i' = \frac{h_{i+1} - h_{i-1}}{2\Delta x} \quad \text{and} \quad \hat{h}_i'' = \frac{h_{i+1} - 2h_i + h_{i-1}}{(\Delta x)^2} \tag{7.30}$$

are second-order finite differences approximations of the first and second derivative.

According to Popinet [Pop18], the height function method to compute the curvature was first introduced by Poo et al. [PA89] and later described in the context of two-phase flows by Sussman [Sus03]. The height function method can be applied naturally in VOF methods on Cartesian meshes since a local height function can simply be obtained by summing up the volume fraction field in a certain direction. More precisely, if the volume fraction field α_{ij} is known exactly[2] (i.e. without computational errors), then the *averaged* height function

$$H(x) := \frac{1}{\Delta x} \int_{x - \Delta x/2}^{x + \Delta x/2} h(s)\, ds \tag{7.31}$$

can be computed from the sum of the volume fractions without a further approximation. However, it is important to note that there is a constraint that must be satisfied to get a consistently averaged height function from the sum of volume fractions; see Fig. 7.2 for an illustration. The direction for the summation and the height of the stencil must be chosen such that all cells below the considered stencil are full ($\alpha = 1$) and all cells above (in the direction of the summation) are empty ($\alpha = 0$), i.e. a common baseline must be found. For the example in Fig. 7.2 this means that the summation must be performed in the vertical direction or the stencil must be enlarged for a summation in the horizontal direction. Since this constraint cannot always be satisfied in practice, in particular when the interface curvature is locally under-resolved, there is a fall-back strategy that employs a fitting algorithm to approximate the curvature if no valid height function representation can be found.

---

[2] A rigorous error analysis for the height function method, in particular in the presence of noisy volume fractions, is given in Chapter 9.

Well-balanced methods and spurious currents: An obvious but non-trivial question is whether or not the numerical scheme is able to recover the known stationary solutions of the model. In the absence of gravity, a *stationary* solution ($v \equiv 0$) to the two-phase flow problem satisfies the equilibrium conditions

$$\nabla p = 0 \text{ in } \Omega^{\pm}, \quad \llbracket p \rrbracket = \sigma \kappa \tag{7.32}$$

or (in the CSF formulation)

$$\nabla p = \sigma \kappa n_{\Sigma} \delta_{\Sigma}. \tag{7.33}$$

Clearly, the equilibrium shapes are spheres with constant pressures inside and outside that respect the Laplace pressure jump. Numerical schemes that are able to recover the equilibrium solutions are called "well-balanced methods" in the literature [Pop18]. The velocity patterns which appear in a numerical simulation of a stationary two-phase flow problem are called "spurious currents" or "parasitic currents" (see, e.g, [TSZ11, p.177]).

If the approximation (7.27) is employed, then the discrete equilibrium condition reads as

$$\tilde{\nabla} p + \sigma \hat{\kappa} \hat{\nabla} \alpha = 0. \tag{7.34}$$

Hence, a well-balanced method is achieved if the terms in (7.34) cancel out (at least to leading order). A common choice to construct a well-balanced method is to apply the same discrete gradient operator to both the pressure and the volume fraction field [Pop09, Pop18]. Then, equation (7.34) can be rewritten for a *constant* discrete curvature $\hat{\kappa}$ according to

$$\hat{\nabla}(p + \sigma \hat{\kappa} \alpha) = 0. \tag{7.35}$$

In this case, there is an exact discrete solution

$$p = -\sigma \hat{\kappa} \alpha + \text{const}.$$

Note, however, that the requirement of exactly constant curvature is not realistic if the curvature is approximated numerically (see Chapter 9). In fact, oscillations in the numerical approximation of the curvature along the interface act as a source to generate spurious currents.

7.5. State of the art: Wetting with geometrical VOF methods

The numerical simulation of wetting flows with the Volume-of-Fluid method has a quite long history. Remarkably, already in the year 1980, Nichols, Hirt, and Hotchkiss described a VOF method called "SOLA-VOF" that was capable of modeling wall adhesion through a contact angle boundary condition [NHH80, p.22]. Later, the latter method was modified by Pasandideh-Fard et al. to simulate a droplet impact on a solid surface [PFQCM96]. In this work, the authors "incorporated the contact angle, θ, in the free surface boundary condition by using it to calculate the mean curvature of the liquid meniscus near the substrate. The technique has earlier been described in detail by Nichols, Hirt, and Hotchkiss." [PFQCM96, p. 652] In fact, the method of altering the curvature at the boundary became a common approach to numerically model wettability effects in VOF methods (see below). Josserand et al. studied droplet impact on a dry surface using a PLIC-VOF method in an axisymmetric geometry in [JLTZ05]. In the latter work, the authors considered the case of a fixed contact angle of 90 degrees. This special case allows to impose a homogeneous Neumann boundary condition for the volume fraction field to model the wettability. Renardy, Renardy, and Li extended the SURFER code by Li and Zaleksi to study wetting flows in two dimensions in [RRL01]. Their work was the first to systematically report on the phenomenon of "numerical slip":

> "Explicitly imposed slip is found to increase the speed of contact line spreading, but even in the absence of explicit slip, there is effective slip on the scale of the mesh. We find a contact line speed which is roughly inversely proportional to the logarithm of the mesh size." [RRL01, p.45]

The numerical slip is a property of the advection algorithm, which uses face-centered values to transport the volume fraction field as shown in Fig. 7.3. If the physical velocity profile has a significant gradient within the boundary cell, which is almost always the case when the slip length is not resolved, the advection method will not be able to recover the correct contact line motion. Moreover, the viscous dissipation in the contact line region is usually underestimated by the numerical method if the flow in the contact line region is not well-resolved. Both effects lead typically to an over-prediction of the contact line velocity (see Chapter 11 for an example).

In fact, the need to resolve the slip length on the scale of nanometers, which is many orders of magnitude smaller than the typical scale of the flow (say mm or cm), poses one of the major challenges in the numerical simulation of dynamic wetting. One way to solve this problem is by massive local mesh refinement (see, e.g., [SS12a]). However, doing so is computationally expensive and requires a quite sophisticated mesh that is tailor-made for the specific flow configuration at hand. Another approach, which has been introduced for a geometrical VOF method by Afkhami et al. [AZB09], is to make use of the numerical slip on a relatively coarse mesh and to apply a mesh-dependent model for the dynamic contact angle based on the analysis of Cox [Cox86] to reduce the mesh-dependence of the overall solution. Satisfactory mesh-independent results have been obtained with that method for a spreading drop and the withdrawing plate problem (see [AZB09]). We introduce a novel adaptation of the discrete Navier slip condition (7.37) called "staggered slip" in Section 11.4. The staggered slip condition shows improved convergence for the capillary rise problem for an under-resolved slip length and might open another route for a "subgrid modeling" of dynamic wetting in the future.

The contact angle boundary condition in geometrical VOF methods: There are several approaches present in the literature to incorporate the contact angle boundary condition in geometrical VOF methods. According to [SDS14], there is a common feature shared by most of the methods:

> "Recent developments in VOF methods have allowed the representation of MCLs in droplet impact (...) or spreading (...) and bubble generation in microfluidic T-junctions (...). Despite differences in the contact-line models used, the implementations commonly impose a gradient of the volume fraction at the contact line in terms of a prescribed contact angle." [SDS14, p.105]

The current implementation in FS3D (see [FB15a, Lip16]) employs the method introduced by Afkhami and Bussmann [AB08, AB09]. The method prescribes the interface orientation according to the contact angle boundary condition and modifies the surface tension force at the boundary (see Section 7.5.2 for details). It was originally implemented in an early version of the geometrical VOF solver *Gerris* developed by Popinet [Pop03] and it is still in use in recent works to study the transition to a Landau-Levich-Derjaguin film in forced dewetting [ABG$^+$18] and the dynamic wetting failure in curtain coating [FZP20]. Interestingly, recent studies compare VOF methods directly with molecular dynamics and/or phase field methods for nano-scale drops [SHGL19, LJF$^+$20].

In fact, the interface orientation is commonly determined directly by the contact angle boundary condition (with a few exceptions, including, e.g., [ŠWR$^+$05]). However, since the advection of the volume fraction field is mostly discretized explicitly in time, the contact angle boundary condition is usually not satisfied after an interface advection step. Instead, the contact angle is enforced by an explicit adjustment of the interface orientation at computational cells located at the boundary (see, e.g., [RRL01, AB08, AB09]). Enforcing the contact angle like this is, however, not consistent with the kinematics of moving contact lines as discussed in Chapter 4. We observed that it can also be a source for numerical instabilities in the vicinity of the contact line (see [RBB12] for a discussion of instabilities close to the contact line). Specialized methods to reconstruct the interface close to the boundary are developed in the present work (see Section 8.2). These methods increase the accuracy of the VOF method at the contact line and are consistent with the fundamental kinematics described in Chapter 4.

7.5.1. No-slip and Navier slip boundary conditions

To allow for a motion of the contact line, one can make use of the *numerical slip* inherent to the method or prescribe the Navier slip condition. Technically, the velocity boundary condition is indirectly enforced within the Finite Volume method using the concept of "ghost cells".

(a) In the classical approach, the no-slip boundary condition is enforced by extrapolating the tangential velocity field into the layer of ghost cells adjacent to the physical boundary, such that the velocity interpolates to zero

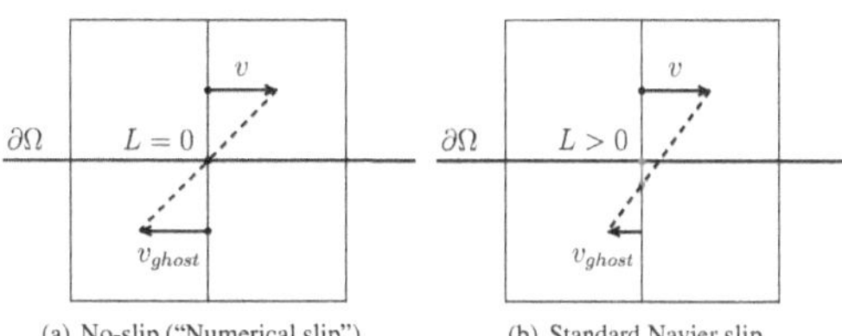

(a) No-slip ("Numerical slip").   (b) Standard Navier slip.

Figure 7.3.: Ghost-cell based numerical realization of the no-slip and Navier slip boundary conditions in FS3D.

exactly at the boundary (see FIG. 7.3(a)), i.e.

$$v_{\text{ghost}} = -v. \tag{7.36}$$

This velocity gradient is subsequently counteracted by the discrete realization of the viscous forces applied next to the boundary. This approach enforces the no-slip condition only in the limit of the mesh size going to zero. Therefore, the face-centered velocity at the boundary cell layer may be non-zero leading to a motion of the contact line. However, the extent of numerical slip decreases with increasing mesh resolution, leading to a significant mesh dependence of the solution. This numerical effect has been first described in the context of VOF methods by Renardy et al [RRL01].

(b) The Navier slip boundary condition is enforced following the same approach by setting a different velocity in the ghost-cell layer, such that the tangential velocity interpolates to zero at a fixed distance $L > 0$ from the physical boundary (see FIG. 7.3(b)), i.e.

$$v_{\text{ghost}} = v\,\frac{2L - \Delta x}{2L + \Delta x}. \tag{7.37}$$

It has been demonstrated in the literature that this may lead to mesh-convergent results if the resolution of the computational mesh is well below the slip length L (see, e.g., [SS12a, GSA$^+$20a] and Chapter 11). However, physically reasonable slip lengths are on the scale of nanometers [NEB$^+$05]. This length scale is not accessible with the present numerical method without massive computational costs. Moreover, note that for $L > 0$ the magnitude of the "counter velocity" v_{ghost} in the ghost cell is always less than or equal to $|v_{\text{ghost}}|$ in the case of no-slip. This follows from the inequality

$$\left|\frac{2L - \Delta x}{2L + \Delta x}\right| \leq 1,$$

which is valid for positive L.

7.5.2. The height function method for applying contact angles

The height function method described in Section 7.4 was adapted by Afkhami and Bussmann [AB08, AB09] to enforce the contact angle boundary condition in Volume-of-Fluid simulations.

Basic methodology: The purpose of the method is to "impose" the contact angle boundary condition required in the continuum mechanical model (7.25), i.e.

$$\langle n_\Sigma, n_{\partial\Omega}\rangle = -\cos\theta \quad \text{at} \quad \Gamma(t), \tag{7.38}$$

where θ satisfies a relation of type $\theta = f(V_\Gamma)$, to a VOF simulation. The boundary condition (7.38) has to two implications for the algorithm, namely "it defines the orientation $\vec{n}$ of the VOF reconstruction in the contact line cell, and it influences the calculation of F_{st} by affecting the calculated curvature." [AB08, p.459]

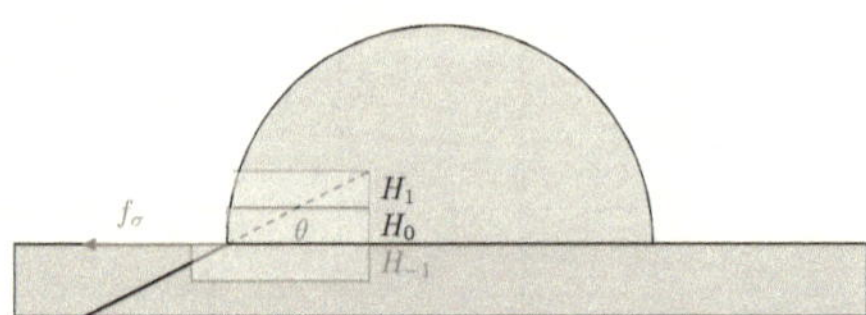

Figure 7.4.: Linear extrapolation of the height function as a numerical driving force for wetting.

(i) The implication of the first statement is that the interface orientation is prescribed at the solid boundary according to the contact angle boundary condition instead of being a result of the interface reconstruction method. As described above, this prescribed orientation might be inconsistent with the interface orientation which results from the interface kinematics.

(ii) The second ingredient in the numerical method to apply the contact angle adapts the numerical approximation of the mean curvature in a contact line cell. A sketch of the method is given in Fig. 7.4. If an interface cell is located at the domain boundary, one cannot apply the central finite differences formulas (7.30) to compute the curvature since, by definition, the height information is missing outside the computational domain (see discrete height H_{-1} in Fig. 7.4). The suggestion of the method [AB08] is to reconstruct a virtual height in the boundary cell layer using the contact angle boundary condition and to compute the curvature with the formulas (7.30) using the virtual height information. More precisely, the height function is extrapolated linearly into the ghost-cell layer with a slope that is determined by the contact angle boundary condition. For the configuration depicted in Fig. 7.4, the formula to compute H_{-1} is

$$H_{-1} = H_0 + \Delta x \cot \theta.$$

The generalization of the method to three spatial dimensions is described in [AB09]. Note that both the two- and three dimensional variant of the method have been implemented in the FS3D solver by Lippert[3].

It is clear that the linear extrapolation according to the contact angle leads to a kink in the virtual interface if the current contact angle does not coincide with the desired contact angle according to (7.38). This leads to a singularity in the curvature at the contact line in the limit as $\Delta x \to 0$, which might lead to very large numerical values of $\hat{\kappa}$ even on coarse meshes. When applied to the numerical approximation of the surface tension force, the singular curvature leads to large velocities at the contact line that drive the interface towards the desired contact angle; see Fig. 7.4 for an example. Hence, the height function method [AB08, AB09] introduces a numerical driving force to indirectly "apply" the contact angle boundary condition. In this sense, the method is similar to the Generalized Navier Boundary condition (GNBC) described in Section 3.4. However, contrary to the GNBC, the driving force is introduced directly in the numerical method with no proper counterpart on the PDE level.

Failure of the method in the equilibrium state: A fundamental drawback of the interface extrapolation method is the missing convergence in stationary state. In fact, the *linear* extrapolation of the interface beyond the solid boundary creates a height function representation of class $\mathscr{C}^1$ only (unless the curvature at the contact line vanishes). In the case of a two-dimensional spherical droplet, the curvature of the extrapolated height function $\tilde{h}$ admits a jump from $-1/R$ to zero at the contact line. As a result, the central finite differences scheme does *not* converge to the correct curvature at the contact line, even if the height function is known exactly. In fact, a much higher regularity of the height function ($h \in \mathscr{C}^5$) is needed to prove convergence of the method; see Lemma 9.4 in Chapter 9 for details. Example 7.2 illustrates the inconsistency of the method.

Example 7.2 (Height Function Extrapolation for $\theta = \pi/2$). For simplicity, we consider the case of a spherical droplet in 2D with contact angle $\theta = \pi/2$; see Fig.7.5 for the setup. A height function representation of the interface above the solid boundary $x = 0$ is given by

$$\{(x, h(x)) : 0 \leq x \leq R\}$$

---

[3]More details on the implementation in FS3D and some basic validation of the contact line dynamics in two and three dimensions can be found in [Lip16].

with $h(x) = R\sqrt{1-(x/R)^2}$. The linear extension of the height function reads

$$\tilde{h}(x) = R \begin{cases} \sqrt{1-\left(\frac{x}{R}\right)^2}, & 0 \le x \le R \\ 1 & x \le 0 \end{cases}.$$ (7.39)

Clearly, the extended height function is of class $\mathscr{C}^1((-\infty, R])$. For a finite grid size $\Delta > 0$, the discrete heights $H_{\pm 1}$

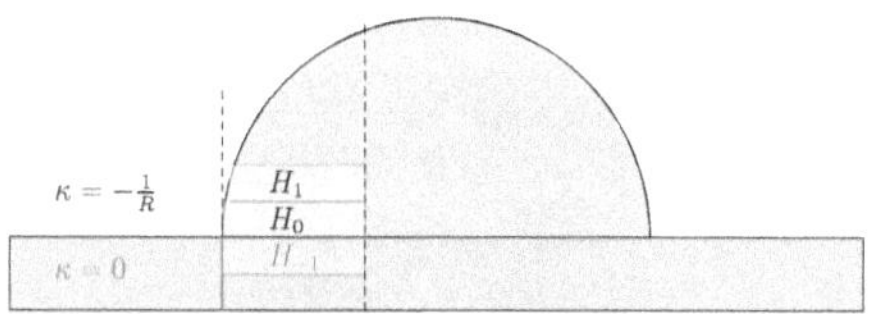

Figure 7.5.: Linear extrapolation for $\theta = \pi/2$.

and H_0 are defined by integration

$$H_0(\Delta) = \frac{1}{\Delta} \int_0^\Delta h(x)\,dx = \frac{R}{2}\left(\sqrt{1-\left(\frac{\Delta}{R}\right)^2} + \frac{R}{\Delta}\arcsin\left(\frac{\Delta}{R}\right)\right),$$

$$H_1(\Delta) = \frac{1}{\Delta} \int_\Delta^{2\Delta} h(x)\,dx = R\left(\sqrt{1-\left(\frac{2\Delta}{R}\right)^2} + \frac{R}{2\Delta}\arcsin\left(\frac{2\Delta}{R}\right)\right) - H_0.$$

$$H_{-1}(\Delta) = \frac{1}{\Delta} \int_{-\Delta}^0 h(x)\,dx = R.$$

Note that $\lim_{x\to 0^+} \frac{1}{x}\arcsin(x) = 1$ implies $\lim_{\Delta\to 0^+} H_0 = \lim_{\Delta\to 0^+} H_1 = R$. Using l'Hospital's rule one easily shows that

$$\frac{H_1(\Delta) - H_{-1}(\Delta)}{2\Delta} \to 0 \quad \text{as} \quad \Delta \to 0^+.$$

Consequently, the numerical approximation of the curvature at the contact line satisfies

$$\lim_{\Delta\to 0^+} \hat{\kappa} = \lim_{\Delta\to 0^+} \frac{H_1(\Delta) - 2H_0(\Delta) + H_{-1}(\Delta)}{\Delta^2}.$$

A short calculation shows that

$$\lim_{\Delta\to 0^+} (H_1(\Delta) - 2H_0(\Delta) + H_{-1}(\Delta))' = 0$$

and, by l'Hospital's rule, it follows that

$$\lim_{\Delta\to 0^+} \hat{\kappa} = \lim_{\Delta\to 0^+} \frac{(H_1(\Delta) - 2H_0(\Delta) + H_{-1}(\Delta))''}{2} = -\frac{5}{6R}.$$ (7.40)

So, the curvature at the contact line does *not* converge to the correct value of $-1/R$.

8. Contact line advection using the geometrical VOF method

The goal of the present chapter[1] is to develop an advection scheme for the geometrical VOF method that allows to transport the contact angle consistently with the fundamental kinematic relation derived in Chapter 4, i.e.

$$\dot{\theta} = \frac{\partial v}{\partial \tau} \cdot n_\Sigma. \tag{8.1}$$

Focusing on the *kinematics* of wetting, we treat the velocity field as *given*, while keeping in mind that it is a solution to some continuum mechanical model. The kinematics of wetting is studied analytically in Chapter 4 (see also [FKB19]) where it is shown that the contact line advection problem is a well-posed initial value problem if the velocity field is sufficiently regular and tangential to the domain boundary. Hence the full dynamics of the interface can be inferred from the (time-dependent) velocity field and the initial interface configuration. Note that this is true even though in the full continuum mechanical model the interface shape is typically strongly coupled to the flow. The reason is that the velocity field contains enough information to reconstruct the evolution of the interface from the initial configuration In particular, the motion of the contact line as well as the evolution of the contact angle, i.e. the angle of intersection between the fluid-fluid interface and the solid boundary, can be computed from the knowledge of the velocity field and the initial geometry. On the other hand, mathematical models for dynamic wetting usually *prescribe* a boundary condition for the contact angle. Note that in view of (8.1), a boundary condition for the contact angle leads to a consistency condition for the velocity field.

Problem formulation: The motion of a material interface is governed by the kinematic condition

$$V_\Sigma = \langle v, n_\Sigma \rangle \quad \text{on} \quad \mathrm{gr}\,\overline{\Sigma}, \tag{8.2}$$

where v is the transporting velocity field. Here it is assumed that $v \in \mathscr{C}^1(\overline{\Omega})$ is divergence free and tangential to the domain boundary, i.e.

$$\nabla \cdot v = 0 \quad \text{in } \Omega, \tag{8.3}$$

$$v \cdot n_{\partial\Omega} = 0 \quad \text{on } \partial\Omega. \tag{8.4}$$

For simplicity, we further assume that the solid boundary is *planar*. This assumption is not essential and may be dropped to study the contact angle evolution over curved surfaces. Note also that incompressibility of the flow is not necessary to study the contact angle evolution. However, it is assumed here since the VOF method is most commonly applied to incompressible flows.

We emphasize that the assumption of a globally continuously differentiable velocity field is *not* met in a typical multiphase flow, where the velocity gradient admits a jump which is controlled by the interfacial transmission condition for the stress. However, it has been shown in Lemma 4.17, that in the case of two spatial dimensions[2] the conditions

$$[\![v]\!] = 0 \text{ on } \mathrm{gr}\,\overline{\Sigma}, \quad \nabla \cdot v = 0 \text{ in } \Omega \setminus \Sigma(t), \quad v \cdot n_{\partial\Omega} = 0 \text{ on } \partial\Omega$$

imply continuity of ∇v *at* the contact line (under certain regularity assumptions). For simplicity, we therefore assume a globally continuously differentiable field.

---

[1] Please note that the Chapters 7.2, 7.3 and 8 are based on the publication [FMB20a].

[2] A similar statement holds in three spatial dimensions. For the that case, one can show the continuity property $\langle [\![\nabla v]\!]\,\alpha, \beta \rangle = 0$ at Γ, where $[\![\cdot]\!]$ denotes the jump over the interface and α, β are arbitrary vectors in the plane spanned by $n_{\partial\Omega}$ and n_Γ.

In this chapter, we focus on the Volume-of-Fluid method for advecting the interface, whose reconstruction algorithm must be adapted in order to achieve second-order convergence in the near-wall region. However, the contact line advection problem can be used to verify near-wall advection of any other interface advection method. For example, a brief discussion of the contact line advection problem with the Level Set Method [Set96, SFSO98] in two dimensions can be found in Section 6.2 (see also [FMB19]). An open research data record containing the full C++-implementation of the Level Set Method used in Section 6.2 together with a number of computational examples is available online, see [FMVB19].

8.1. An analytical reference solution

The kinematic evolution equation allows to compute the rate of change of the contact angle in terms of the transporting velocity field. The evolution of the contact angle is considered along the trajectories (or "characteristics") of the flow, i.e. along solutions of the ordinary differential equation

$$\dot{x}(t) = v(t, x(t)), \quad x(t_0) = x_0 \in \overline{\Sigma}(t_0). \tag{8.5}$$

The conditions (8.2), (8.3) and (8.4) imply that both $\mathrm{gr}\,\Gamma$ and $\mathrm{gr}\,\Sigma = \mathrm{gr}\,\overline{\Sigma} \setminus \mathrm{gr}\,\Gamma$ are *invariant* for the flow generated by (8.5), i.e. a solution of (8.5) starting on the contact line (the fluid-fluid interface) will stay on the contact line (the fluid-fluid interface). Given a $\mathscr{C}^1$-velocity field, the Lagrangian time-derivative of the interface normal vector is given by (see Chapter 4)

$$\dot{n}_\Sigma(t, x) = -[\mathbb{1} - n_\Sigma(t, x) \otimes n_\Sigma(t, x)] \nabla v(t, x)^{\mathsf{T}} n_\Sigma(t, x). \tag{8.6}$$

Clearly, the evolution of the contact angle can be inferred from the normal vector evolution. Moreover, it has been shown that, for a planar boundary[3], the contact angle follows the evolution equation (8.1), where the tangential direction τ is defined as (see Figure 3.1)

$$\tau(t, x) = -\cos[\theta(t, x)] n_\Gamma(t, x) - \sin[\theta(t, x)] n_{\partial\Omega}(t, x).$$

The goal of the present chapter is to verify the numerical solution delivered by the VOF method against an analytical (if available) or numerical solution of (8.1).

An analytical solution for linear velocity fields in 2D: We first consider the case of general linear divergence free velocity fields in 2D. In this case, the velocity gradient ∇v is constant in space and time and the ODE system (8.5) and (8.6) is *explicitly* solvable. Note that this also provides a local approximation for general differentiable velocity fields.

We choose a Cartesian coordinate system (x_1, x_2) such that the solid wall is represented by $x_2 = 0$. We consider a velocity field of the form

$$v(x_1, x_2) = (v_0 + c_1 x_1 + c_2 x_2, -c_1 x_2). \tag{8.7}$$

The coefficients c_1 and c_2 in this formulation have the dimension of s^{-1}. Therefore, it is more convenient to choose a length scale L and a time scale T and write

$$\frac{v(x_1, x_2)}{L/T} = (\hat{v}_0 + \hat{c}_1 \hat{x}_1 + \hat{c}_2 \hat{x}_2, -\hat{c}_1 \hat{x}_2) =: \hat{v}(\hat{x}_1, \hat{x}_2) \tag{8.8}$$

with the non-dimensional quantities $\hat{x}_i = x/L$, $\hat{c}_i = c/T$ and $\hat{v}_0 = (T v_0)/L$. In the following, we will use the formulation (8.8) while dropping the hats. For a field of this form, the (constant) gradient is given by

$$\nabla v = \begin{pmatrix} c_1 & c_2 \\ 0 & -c_1 \end{pmatrix}.$$

---

[3]Note that (8.6) also holds if $\partial\Omega$ is not planar.

Motion of the contact line: The motion of the contact line is determined by the ordinary differential equation

$$\dot{x}_1(t) = v_1(x_1(t),0) = v_0 + c_1 x_1(t), \quad x_1(0) = x_1^0.$$

The unique solution of the above initial value problem is

$$x_1(t) = x_1^0 e^{c_1 t} + \frac{v_0}{c_1}\left(e^{c_1 t} - 1\right) \quad \text{for } c_1 \neq 0 \tag{8.9}$$

and $x_1(t) = x_1^0 + v_0 t$ for $c_1 = 0$.

Contact angle evolution: Note that the constancy of ∇v decouples the system (8.5) and (8.6). Hence, the evolution of the normal vector can be solved independently of the evolution of the contact point. To find the solution, we make use of the fact that in two dimensions the normal vector n_Σ is, up to a reflection, uniquely determined by the contact angle θ. Given a contact angle θ, the two possibilities are

$$n_\Sigma^l = \begin{pmatrix} -\sin\theta \\ \cos\theta \end{pmatrix} \quad \text{and} \quad n_\Sigma^r = \begin{pmatrix} \sin\theta \\ \cos\theta \end{pmatrix}.$$

In the case of a droplet (and for $\theta < \pi$), this corresponds to the two distinct contact points (left and right). The corresponding expressions for τ are

$$\tau^l = \begin{pmatrix} \cos\theta \\ \sin\theta \end{pmatrix} \quad \text{and} \quad \tau^r = \begin{pmatrix} -\cos\theta \\ \sin\theta \end{pmatrix}.$$

This allows to infer the evolution of θ for the left and the right contact point directly from (8.1) without the need to solve the system (8.6).

Inserting the expressions for ∇v, $n_\Sigma^{l,r}$ and $\tau^{l,r}$ to (8.1) yields the nonlinear ordinary differential equation[4]

$$\dot{\theta}(t) = \pm c_2 \sin^2\theta - 2c_1 \sin\theta\cos\theta, \quad \theta(0) = \theta_0 \tag{8.10}$$

with the "+" for the evolution of the right contact point and the "−" for the evolution of the left contact point. Equation (8.10) may be solved with the following Ansatz: We look for solutions of the form

$$\theta(t) = \frac{\pi}{2} + \arctan(f(t)). \tag{8.11}$$

It is an easy exercise to show that this yields the following ordinary differential equation for f:

$$\dot{f} = \pm c_2 + 2c_1 f. \tag{8.12}$$

The initial condition for θ translates to

$$f(0) = -\cot\theta_0. \tag{8.13}$$

For $c_1 \neq 0$, the initial-value problem (8.12)-(8.13) has the unique solution

$$f(t) = -\cot\theta_0\, e^{2c_1 t} \pm c_2 \frac{e^{2c_1 t} - 1}{2c_1}. \tag{8.14}$$

Hence, we obtain the desired solution

$$\theta(t) = \frac{\pi}{2} + \arctan\left(-\cot\theta_0\, e^{2c_1 t} \pm c_2 \frac{e^{2c_1 t} - 1}{2c_1}\right). \tag{8.14}$$

---

[4]Note that we now use the Lagrangian formulation and write $\theta(t)$ for the contact angle at $x(t) \in \Gamma(t)$ where $x(t)$ is a trajectory of the flow, i.e. a solution of (8.5).

Remark: Obviously, the solution is independent of the parameter v_0. This is to be expected since the two differential equations (8.5) and (8.6) decouple and the parameter v_0 can be eliminated by a change of the frame of reference. Moreover, the evolution of the left and the right contact point is identical if $\theta_0^r = \theta_0^l$ and $c_2 = 0$. Finally, we note that (8.14) has a well-defined limit for $c_1 \to 0$ since

$$\lim_{c_1 \to 0} \left(-\cot \theta_0 \, e^{2c_1 t} \pm c_2 \frac{e^{2c_1 t} - 1}{2c_1} \right) = -\cot \theta_0 \pm c_2 t.$$

8.2. Interface reconstruction close to the boundary in two dimensions

We propose an adaptation of well-known methods for interface reconstruction in Volume-of-Fluid methods, aiming for accurate reconstruction of the interface close to the domain boundary. The FORTRAN implementations of the developed interface reconstruction methods are available online in an open research data repository, see [FMB20b].

For simplicity of notation, we consider in the following the domain boundary at $x_2 = 0$, i.e. we consider an interface cell with index $(i, j = 1)$.

Boundary Youngs Method:

We consider a 3×3-block of cells and aim at reconstructing the interface in the lower middle cell. We propose to discretize the gradient of the volume fraction field in two space dimensions in the following way (see Figure 8.1):

(a) Tangential to the domain boundary central finite differences are used.

(b) In normal direction to the domain boundary, weighted *forward* finite differences are employed.

From Taylor's formula, one can show that for a $\mathscr{C}^3$-function f, the first derivative $f'(x)$ can be approximated with second-order accuracy according to

$$f'(x) = \frac{-f(x + 2\Delta x) + 4f(x + \Delta x) - 3f(x)}{2\Delta x} + \mathcal{O}(\Delta x^2).$$

This formula is applied to approximate the derivative of the volume fraction normal to the boundary. Note, however, that the volume fraction α is only $\mathscr{C}^1$ (see Section 7.3). One can, therefore, *not* expect a convergence of the orientation with that method. But we still consider it here since it is a straightforward extension of the widely used Youngs method to the boundary case.

For an equidistant grid in two space dimensions, the Boundary Youngs gradient in a cell with index $(i, 1)$ is discretized as

$$\begin{aligned}
(\nabla_h \alpha)_1 &= \frac{\alpha(i+1, 1) - \alpha(i-1, 1)}{2\Delta x_1}, \\
(\nabla_h \alpha)_2 &= \frac{-\alpha(i, 3) + 4\alpha(i, 2) - 3\alpha(i, 1)}{4\Delta x_2} \\
&\quad + \frac{-\alpha(i+1, 3) + 4\alpha(i+1, 2) - 3\alpha(i+1, 1)}{8\Delta x_2} \\
&\quad + \frac{-\alpha(i-1, 3) + 4\alpha(i-1, 2) - 3\alpha(i-1, 1)}{8\Delta x_2}.
\end{aligned} \tag{8.15}$$

Boundary ELVIRA Method:

In order to allow for mesh convergent results for the contact angle evolution, one needs a reconstruction method which is second-order accurate at the boundary. Therefore, we propose the following adaptation of the ELVIRA method due to Pilliod and Puckett [PP04]: For a boundary cell with index $(i, 1)$, minimize the functional

$$\mathscr{F}_b = \sum_{k=-2}^{2} \sum_{l=0}^{2} [\tilde{\alpha}_{i+k, 1+l}(n) - \alpha_{i+k, 1+l}]^2, \tag{8.16}$$

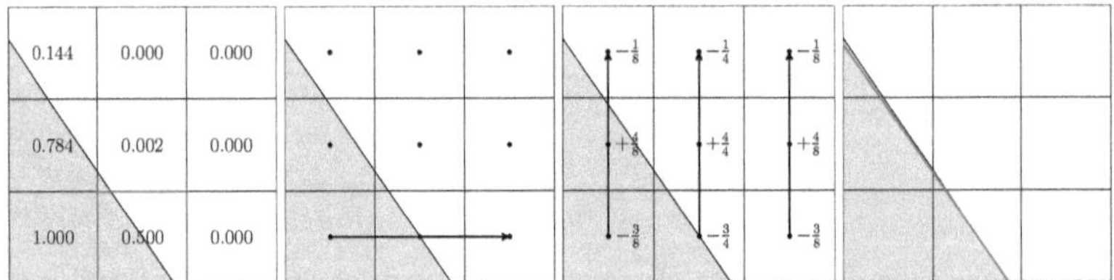

Figure 8.1.: Boundary Youngs reconstruction method for an equidistant mesh.

where $\tilde{\alpha}_{i+k,1+l}(n)$ is the volume fraction in cell $(i+k,1+l)$ which is induced by a plane with orientation n satisfying $\tilde{\alpha}_{i,1}(n) = \alpha_{i,1}$. Here the minimization is performed over a *larger* stencil of 5×3 cells. This turns out to be necessary to reconstruct every straight line at the boundary exactly. Following the idea of the *Efficient Least Squares VOF Interface Reconstruction Algorithm* [PP04], the functional (8.16) is minimized over a finite set of candidate orientations obtained from finite differences of column sums (see Figure 8.2, where the column sums in horizontal direction are visualized in red).

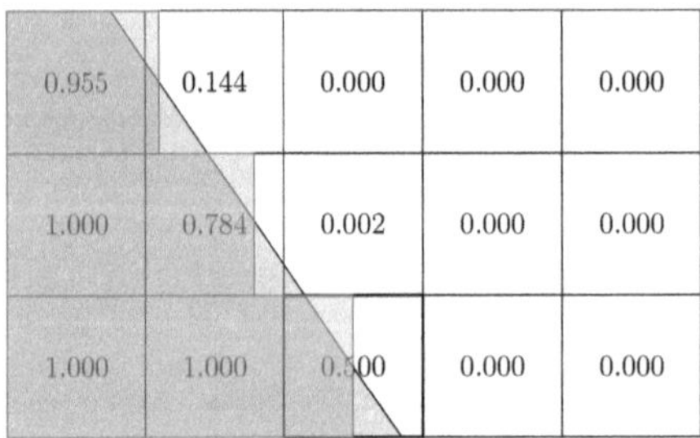

Figure 8.2.: Boundary ELVIRA method on a 5×3-stencil in 2D.

The following candidate slopes are computed in the cell $(i, 1)$ in normal direction to the boundary

$$m_1^c = \frac{\Delta x_2}{2\Delta x_1} \sum_{l=0}^{2} (\alpha_{i+1,1+l} - \alpha_{i-1,1+l}),$$

$$m_1^b = \frac{\Delta x_2}{\Delta x_1} \sum_{l=0}^{2} (\alpha_{i,1+l} - \alpha_{i-1,1+l}),$$

$$m_1^{b^*} = \frac{\Delta x_2}{\Delta x_1} \sum_{l=0}^{2} (\alpha_{i-1,1+l} - \alpha_{i-2,1+l}),$$

$$m_1^f = \frac{\Delta x_2}{\Delta x_1} \sum_{l=0}^{2} (\alpha_{i+1,1+l} - \alpha_{i,1+l}),$$

$$m_1^{f^*} = \frac{\Delta x_2}{\Delta x_1} \sum_{l=0}^{2} (\alpha_{i+2,1+l} - \alpha_{i+1,1+l}).$$

$$(8.17)$$

The following candidate slope is computed from sums tangentially to the boundary

$$m_2^f = \frac{\Delta x_1}{\Delta x_2} \sum_{l=-2}^{2} (\alpha_{i+l,2} - \alpha_{i+l,1}),$$

$$m_2^{f*} = \frac{\Delta x_1}{2\Delta x_2} \sum_{l=-2}^{2} (\alpha_{i+l,3} - \alpha_{i+l,1}), \tag{8.18}$$

$$m_2^{f**} = \frac{\Delta x_1}{\Delta x_2} \sum_{l=-2}^{2} (\alpha_{i+l,3} - \alpha_{i+l,2}).$$

This yields 16 candidates for the interface normal. We can demonstrate by numerical experiments that this is sufficient to reconstruct any straight line at the boundary up to machine precision, see [FMB20b]. Details on the implementation of the (Boundary) ELVIRA method in FS3D are provided in Appendix D.

Numerical errors:

It is well-known from the literature that the standard Youngs method (7.18) fails to reconstruct arbitrary straight lines, while the error is typically of the order of a few degrees. As a numerical test, a straight line is moved with a fixed inclination angle on an equidistant grid with $\Delta x_1 = \Delta x_2$. This motion produces volume fractions ranging from 0 to 1 for the considered computational cell away from the boundary. The reconstructed orientation with the standard Youngs and ELVIRA methods are shown in Figure 8.3(a). While the ELVIRA method always delivers the correct angle, the Youngs method shows an error of about $1° - 2°$ in the considered example. The situation is much different for the same translation test for a *boundary* cell, see Figure 8.3(b). While the Boundary ELVIRA method is still able to deliver the correct orientation, the Boundary Youngs method shows a large error of up to $\pm 20°$ that is also highly dependent on the position of the interface. Therefore, one can only expect a very rough estimate of the contact angle from the Boundary Youngs method which cannot converge with mesh refinement.

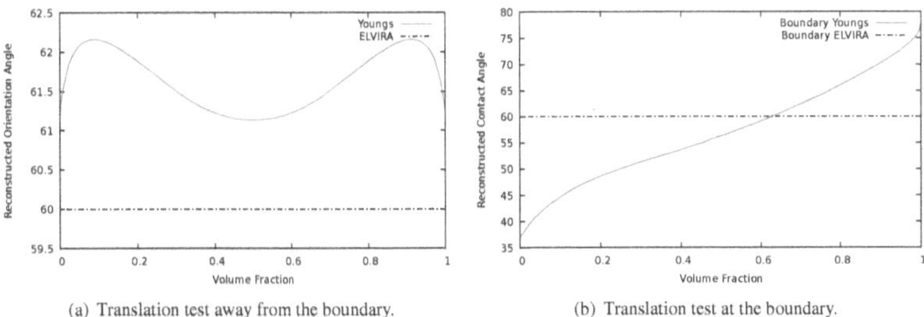

(a) Translation test away from the boundary.   (b) Translation test at the boundary.

Figure 8.3.: Translation of a straight line with a fixed orientation angle of $\theta = 60°$.

8.3. Numerical results

To verify the advective transport of the contact angle, a spherical cap sitting at the boundary is initialized and transported using different velocity fields. To study the convergence in space and time, the time step Δt is linked to the grid spacing Δx by fixing the Courant number

$$\mathrm{CFL} = \frac{\Delta t \, \|v\|_{L^\infty(\Omega)}}{\Delta x}.$$

The influence of the choice of the Courant number is discussed below (see Figures 8.14 and 8.17). The following computational examples are carried out with (unless stated otherwise)

$$\mathrm{CFL} = 0.2.$$

Fixing the Courant number defines a temporal grid $\mathscr{T}$ (equidistant if v does not depend on time). We report the error for both the contact line position and the contact angle in the maximum norm over all time steps, i.e.

$$\mathscr{E}_\theta^\infty([0,T]) := \max_{t_i \in \mathscr{T} \cap [0,T]} |\,\theta_{\mathrm{num}}(t_i) - \theta_{\mathrm{ref}}(t_i)| \quad \text{and} \quad \mathscr{E}_{\mathrm{cl}}^\infty([0,T]) := \max_{t_i \in \mathscr{T} \cap [0,T]} |(x_{\mathrm{cl,num}}(t_i) - x_{\mathrm{cl,ref}}(t_i))/R_0|,$$

as a function of $\Delta x / R_0$. Note that the error in the contact line position is normalized by the initial radius R_0. The reference values $x_{\mathrm{cl,ref}}(t)$ and $\theta_{\mathrm{ref}}(t)$ come either from an exact or from a numerical solution of the ordinary differential equations (8.5) and (8.1). The numerical values for the contact line position $x_{\mathrm{cl,num}}$ and the contact angle θ_{num} are evaluated directly from the reconstructed PLIC element intersecting the domain boundary (see Figure 8.4). To this end, the point of intersection of the local interface with the domain boundary is computed. If this point lies within the cell, the cell is recognized as a contact line cell and the contact angle and the contact line position are computed. Note that, due to the finite reconstruction tolerance of the VOF method (in this case 10^{-6}) , irregular cases where no contact point is found may occur. An example is sketched in Figure 8.4(b), where the point of intersection lies slightly outside the current cell but the volume fraction of the neighbor cell is below the reconstruction tolerance so that it is not recognized as an interface cell. These irregular cases are excluded from the following error analysis.

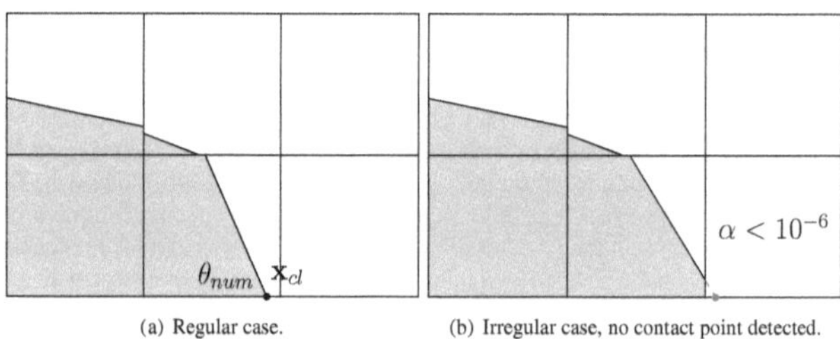

(a) Regular case.   (b) Irregular case, no contact point detected.

Figure 8.4.: Contact angle and contact line position from PLIC reconstruction.

Computational setup: For the subsequent examples, we choose the following common setup. The computational domain $\Omega = [0,1] \times [0,0.25]$ is covered by an equidistant Cartesian grid of $N \times N/4$ cells, where N varies from 128 to 2048. A spherical cap with dimensionless radius $R_0 = 0.2$ is initialized at the "solid boundary"

$$\partial\Omega_s = \{(x_1,0) : 0 \le x_1 \le 1\},$$

where the flow is assumed to be tangential. The center of the sphere is placed at $(0.4, -0.1)$ yielding an initial contact angle of

$$\theta_0 = \arccos\left(\frac{0.1}{0.2}\right) = \frac{\pi}{3}.$$

Since we are only interested in the *local* transport of the interface, we can allow for an artificial inflow boundary to the computational domain away from the contact line. Inflow boundaries are characterized by $v \cdot n_{\partial\Omega} < 0$ (see Figure 8.5). At inflow boundaries we formally apply a homogeneous Neumann boundary condition for the phase indicator function, i.e.

$$\frac{\partial \chi}{\partial n_{\partial\Omega}} = 0 \quad \text{on} \quad \partial\Omega_{in}(t) = \{x \in \partial\Omega : v(t,x) \cdot n_{\partial\Omega}(x) < 0\}. \tag{8.19}$$

This condition is straightforward to implement using a simple constant continuation of the volume fraction field into a layer of "ghost cells" (see, e.g., [LeV02]). Here we only consider the case where the interface does not meet the artificial boundary such that (8.19) simply states that no additional volume is transported into the computational domain. In particular, the boundary condition does not affect the dynamics of the interface and (8.1) still holds.

Three examples for the transporting velocity field are studied with the Youngs and ELVIRA methods, where these methods are combined with their newly developed boundary versions to treat the contact line advection.

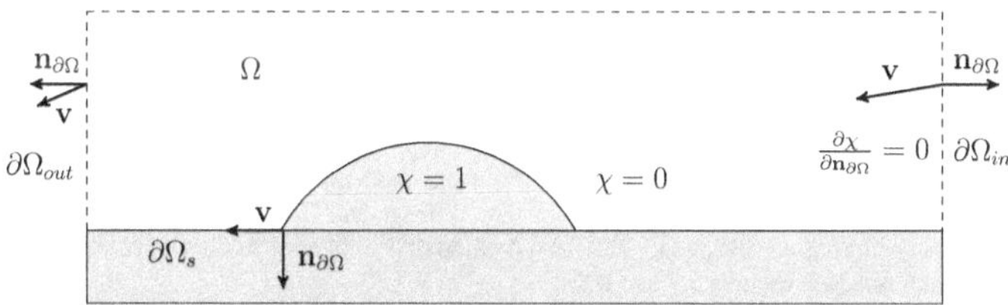

Figure 8.5.: Computational setup.

8.3.1. Vortex-in-a-box test

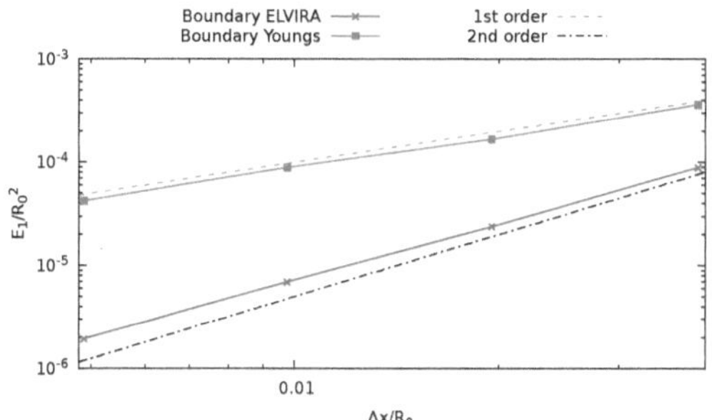

Figure 8.6.: Convergence with respect to the discrete L^1-norm for the field (8.20) comparing initial and final shapes.

We start with a classical test for interface advection methods given by

$$v(x_1, x_2) = v_0 \cos\left(\frac{\pi t}{\tau_\mathrm{p}}\right) (-\sin(\pi x_1)\cos(\pi x_2), \cos(\pi x_1)\sin(\pi x_2)). \tag{8.20}$$

This particular field called "vortex-in-a-box" has been routinely used to test numerical methods for interface advection; see [RK98], [TSZ11]. In the classical test this velocity field is used to strongly deform a sphere into a spiral. Due to the periodicity in time, it follows that the initial shape at $t = 0$ and the final shape at $t = \tau_\mathrm{p}$ would coincide if the problem is solved exactly. This allows to study aspects of the convergence behavior of the advection method even though the solution to the advection problem with the velocity field (8.20) is not known. The discrete L^1-error

$$E_1 = \sum_{ij} |\alpha_{ij}(\tau_\mathrm{p}) - \alpha_{ij}(0)| \Delta x_1 \Delta x_2 \tag{8.21}$$

is usually used to quantify the rate-of-convergence. Note, however, that this kind of test does not say anything about the intermediate *dynamics* of the numerical solution[5]. Here we revisit this classical test in the presence of a moving contact line. The results for $v_0 = 0.1$ and $\tau_\mathrm{p} = 0.2$ are reported in Figure 8.6. The simulations are carried out with a fixed Courant number of CFL $= 0.2$, where the numerical time step is chosen such that $t = \tau_\mathrm{p}$ is reached after an integer number of time steps. As expected from the case without a contact line, the Boundary Youngs method shows a first-order convergence while the Boundary ELVIRA method is nearly second-order convergent.

---

[5]Formally, a numerical method which keeps the volume fractions fixed passes this test with zero error.

Thanks to the kinematic evolution equation, it is also possible to study the *dynamics* of the advection in terms of the contact line position and the contact angle. The ordinary differential equations (8.5) and (8.1) are solved numerically to obtain reference solutions $x_{\mathrm{cl,ref}}(t)$ and $\theta_{\mathrm{ref}}(t)$.

Contact Line Motion: The numerical evolution of the left (in this case the advancing) contact point reconstructed from the PLIC interface is investigated for the Boundary Youngs and Boundary ELVIRA method. It is found that both the Boundary Youngs and Boundary ELVIRA method deliver at least first-order convergent results for the motion of the contact line, see Figures 8.7 and 8.8.

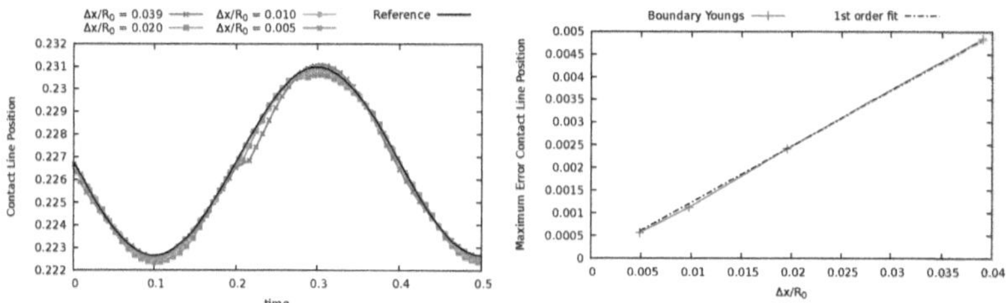

Figure 8.7.: Numerical motion of the contact line for the field (8.20) using the Boundary Youngs reconstruction.

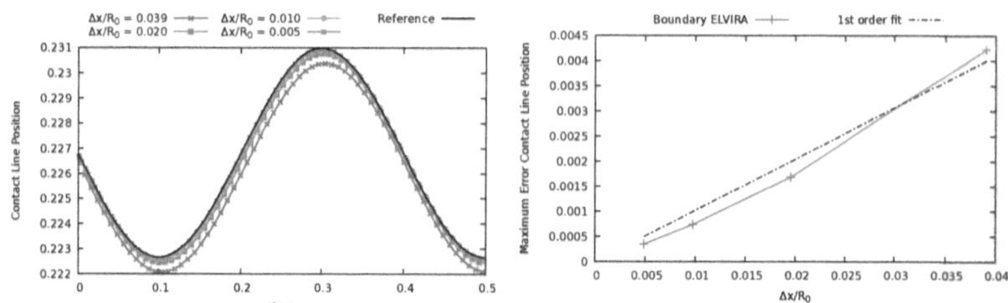

Figure 8.8.: Numerical motion of the contact line for the field (8.20) using the Boundary ELVIRA reconstruction.

Contact Angle Evolution: The results for the contact angle over time are shown in Figures 8.9 and 8.10. While the numerical solution convergences to the reference solution for the Boundary ELVIRA method, the Boundary Youngs method does, as expected, *not* deliver mesh convergent results. In fact, one observes a strong oscillation of the reconstructed contact angle with a jump discontinuity when the contact line passes from one cell to the other; see Figure 8.11, where the reconstructed contact angle is plotted along with the discrete cell index. This behavior might be due to the spatial structure of the reconstruction error as reported in Figure 8.3. Clearly, the frequency of these jumps increases with mesh refinement leading to the strongly oscillatory behavior. The error in the maximum norm may even increase with mesh refinement, see Figure 8.9. Therefore, the Boundary Youngs method does *not* allow for a meaningful evaluation of the contact angle based on the local interface orientation even though it is first-order convergent with respect to the contact line motion and the discrete L^1-error regarding the initial and final shape comparison.

Following Figures 8.10 and 8.11, the evolution of the numerical contact angle for the Boundary ELVIRA method is reasonably smooth even on coarse grids. Some small oscillations are visible which, however, disappear with mesh refinement. In fact, the method shows a *first-order* convergence with respect to $\mathscr{E}_\theta^\infty([0,0.5])$. The maximum error on the finest mesh with $\Delta x/R_0 = 5 \cdot 10^{-3}$ is about 0.5 degrees.

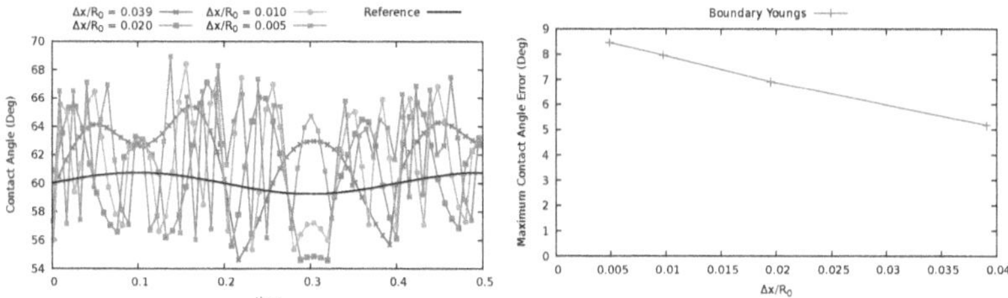

Figure 8.9.: Numerical contact angle evolution for the field (8.20) using the Boundary Youngs method.

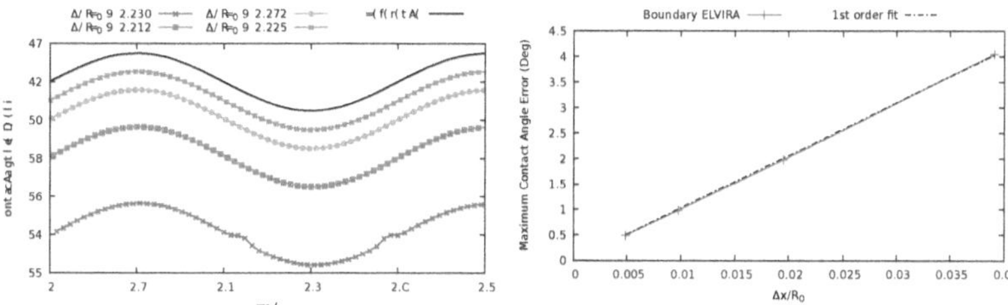

Figure 8.10.: Numerical contact angle evolution for the field (8.20) using the Boundary ELVIRA method.

8.3.2. Linear Velocity Field

We now consider linear velocity fields of the form (8.8). In this case, the explicit solution (8.14) is available for verification. We choose the example

$$v(x_1,x_2) = (-0.2 + 0.1x_1 - 2x_2, -0.1x_2). \tag{8.22}$$

The time evolution is investigated up to dimensionless time $T = 0.4$. According to (8.14), the exact solution for the left contact point is given by

$$x_1(t) = x_1^0 e^{0.1t} - 2(e^{0.1t} - 1), \quad \theta_{\text{ref}}(t) = \frac{\pi}{2} + \arctan\left(-\frac{1}{\sqrt{3}}e^{0.2t} + 10(e^{0.2t} - 1)\right),$$

where $x_1^0 = 0.4 - \sqrt{0.2^2 - 0.1^2} \approx 0.227$ is the initial coordinate of the left contact point.

Contact Line Motion: Like in the previous example, both methods show first-order convergence with respect to the maximum norm regarding the motion of the contact line, see Figure 8.12.

Contact Angle Evolution: The numerical contact angle for the Boundary Youngs method is again subject to strong oscillations ($\pm 10°$ in this case) and does not convergence with mesh refinement as visible in Figure 8.13(a). In contrast to that, the evolution of the contact angle for the Boundary ELVIRA method is first-order convergent and smooth with jumps visible only on a coarse grid, see Figure 8.13(b).

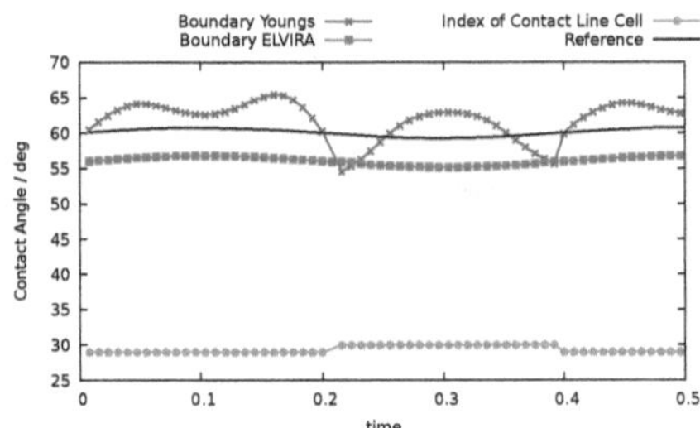

Figure 8.11.: Jump in the numerical contact angle for the field (8.20) (here for $\Delta x/R_0 = 0.039$).

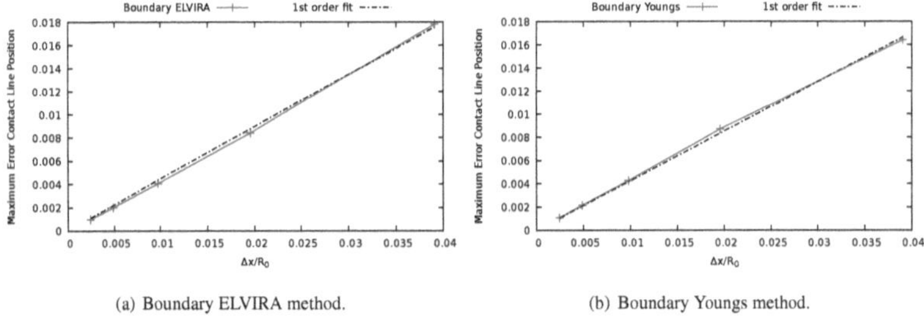

(a) Boundary ELVIRA method.

(b) Boundary Youngs method.

Figure 8.12.: Contact line evolution for the field (8.22).

Influence of the Courant number: The influence of the Courant number for the convergence of the Boundary ELVIRA method (with respect to the contact angle) and the Boundary Youngs method (with respect to the contact line position) is shown in Figure 8.14. Apparently, there is hardly any influence in the considered example. Linear convergence is achieved for all reported Courant numbers from 0.1 to 0.9.

Both numerical methods show excellent volume conservation. The relative volume error is at most of the order 10^{-10}. Thanks to the volume redistribution algorithm, the volume fraction fields are exactly bounded up to machine precision.

8.3.3. Time-dependent Linear Velocity Field

As a third example, we consider the spatially linear, time-dependent velocity field of the form

$$v(t,x_1,x_2) = \cos\left(\frac{\pi t}{\tau_p}\right)(v_0 + c_1 x_1 + c_2 x_2, -c_1 x_2). \tag{8.23}$$

As mentioned before, the time-dependent coefficient $\cos((\pi t)/\tau_p)$ is a classical choice to test advection methods by comparing the phase volumes at $t = 0$ and $t = \tau_p$. Here we consider the full dynamics of the advection by solving the kinematic evolution equation for the field (8.23) explicitly.

Using the ansatz (8.11), it is easy to show that the exact solution for the latter velocity field is given by (for $c_1 \neq 0$)

$$x_1(t) = x_0 e^{c_1 s(t)} + \frac{v_0}{c_1}\left(e^{c_1 s(t)} - 1\right), \quad \theta_{\text{ref}}(t) = \frac{\pi}{2} + \arctan\left(-\cot\theta_0 e^{2c_1 s(t)} \pm \frac{c_2}{2c_1}\left(e^{2c_1 s(t)} - 1\right)\right), \tag{8.24}$$

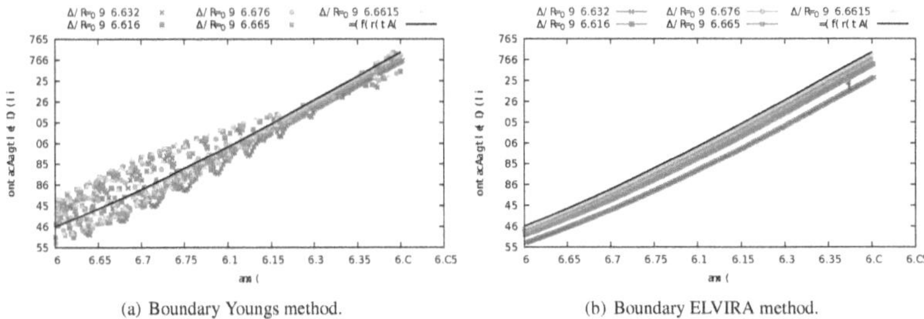

(a) Boundary Youngs method.

(b) Boundary ELVIRA method.

Figure 8.13.: Numerical contact angle evolution for the field (8.22).

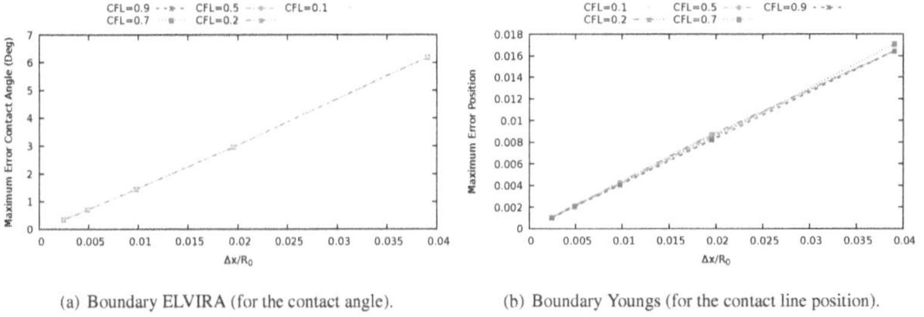

(a) Boundary ELVIRA (for the contact angle).

(b) Boundary Youngs (for the contact line position).

Figure 8.14.: Convergence behavior for the field (8.22) and different values of CFL.

where $s(t)$ is defined as

$$s(t) = \frac{\tau_p \sin(\pi t / \tau_p)}{\pi}.$$

In particular, the evolution is periodic in t with period $2\,\tau_p$. Note that the solution (8.14) is recovered in the limit $\tau_p \to \infty$ since

$$\lim_{\tau_p \to \infty} \frac{\tau_p \sin(\pi t / \tau_p)}{\pi} = \lim_{\tau_p \to \infty} \frac{\tau_p(\pi t / \tau_p)}{\pi} = t.$$

As a concrete example, we choose again $v_0 = -0.2$, $c_1 = 0.1$ and $c_2 = -2$ together with $\tau_p = 0.2$.

Contact Line Motion: The contact line motion (see Figure 8.15) is first-order convergent for both methods.

Contact Angle Evolution: Like in the previous examples, the numerical contact angle shows strong oscillations for the Boundary Youngs method, see Figure 8.16(a). The evolution of the numerical contact angle for the Boundary ELVIRA method is reported in Figure 8.16(b). While the numerical contact angle shows some deviations from the smooth reference curve on coarse grids, the period of the exact solution is still captured correctly. Like in the examples discussed before, refinement of the mesh at a fixed Courant number of CFL = 0.2 leads to smoothening of the results and first-order convergence in the maximum norm. The results show the ability of the Boundary ELVIRA method to accurately capture the dynamics of the contact angle evolution.

Influence of the Courant number: The results for the time-dependent linear field (8.23) turn out to be much more sensitive to the choice of the Courant number, see Figure 8.17.

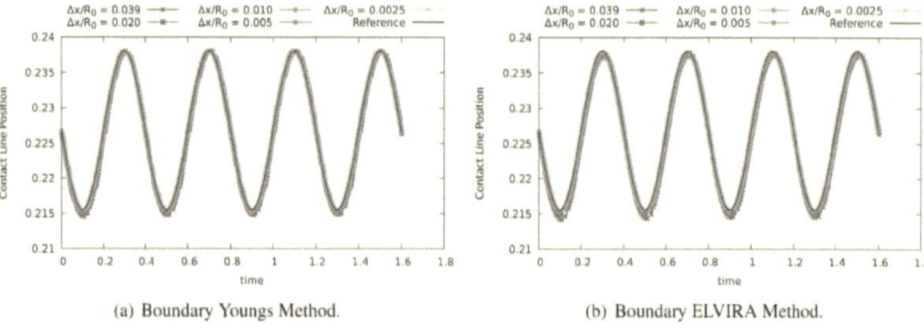

(a) Boundary Youngs Method.

(b) Boundary ELVIRA Method.

Figure 8.15.: Contact line motion for the field (8.23).

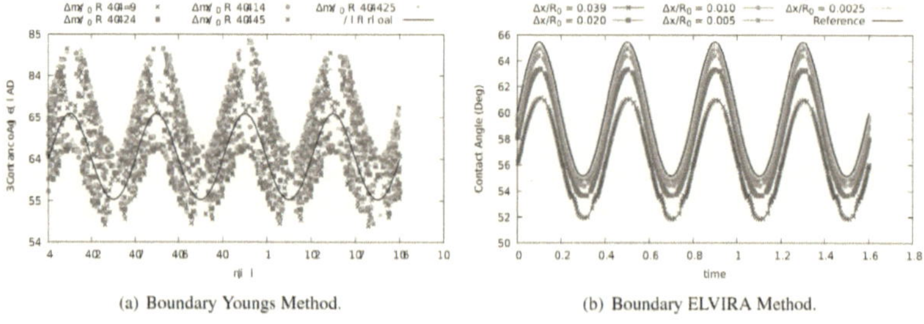

(a) Boundary Youngs Method.

(b) Boundary ELVIRA Method.

Figure 8.16.: Contact angle evolution for the field (8.23).

The Boundary Youngs reconstruction fails completely for CFL greater than 0.5 due to the appearance of interface cells with $|\nabla_h \alpha| \approx 0$. The convergence of the contact angle in the maximum norm for the Boundary ELVIRA method breaks down for CFL ≥ 0.7 (see Figure 8.17(a)). Note, however, that a Courant number as large as 0.7 is rarely achieved in multiphase flow simulations of systems governed by capillary effects (which is typically the case for wetting problems). In these systems, the numerical time step is usually limited by a stability criterion based on the propagation of capillary waves (see, e.g., [TSZ11]) and the (advective) CFL number is small.

8.4. Summary

The contact line advection problem is studied based on the geometrical Volume-of-Fluid method. Adaptations of the Youngs and ELVIRA methods to reconstruct the interface close to the boundary are introduced (see [FMB20b] for the implementations in FORTRAN). This allows to solve the transport equation for the interface without enforcing any boundary condition on the volume fraction field (except for inflow boundary conditions on artificial boundaries). Both the contact line position and the contact angle are evaluated based on the piecewise linear approximation of the interface (PLIC). The Boundary Youngs method allows to track the motion of the contact line with first-order accuracy. However, a meaningful evaluation of the contact angle in terms of the local interface orientation is not possible. Instead, the numerical contact angle shows strong oscillations resulting from a spatial dependence of the reconstruction error which is already present for a planar interface. The Boundary ELVIRA method delivers first-order convergent results for the dynamics of both the contact line motion and the contact angle evolution. The results are verified using an explicit and a numerical solution of the kinematic evolution equation (8.1).

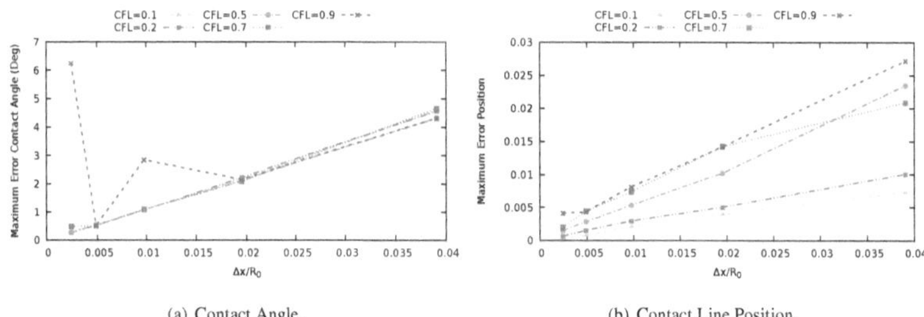

(a) Contact Angle.

(b) Contact Line Position.

Figure 8.17.: Convergence behavior for the field (8.23) with the Boundary ELVIRA method.

Based on the Boundary ELVIRA method to transport the contact angle, one may develop numerical methods of dynamic wetting, where the contact angle is not prescribed as a geometric boundary condition. Instead, a local force term depending on the interface orientation may be introduced. The latter approach, as discussed e.g. in [ŠWR⁺05] for an algebraic VOF method, avoids the necessity to manually "adjust" the contact angle after a transport step. The present method allows to evaluate the local interface orientation with high accuracy in geometrical Volume of Fluid methods and may, therefore, serve as a basis for future numerical methods in dynamic wetting.

9. Curvature from Height Functions: A mathematical error analysis

The Volume of Fluid method was introduced by Hirt and Nichols [HN81] with the motivation to present a simple and efficient method for treating free boundaries. They concluded that the method is "particularly useful because it uses a minimum of stored information, treats intersecting free boundaries automatically, and can be readily extended to three-dimensional calculations." [HN81, p.224] Since then, the method has been massively advanced in terms of accuracy and has been successfully applied to various multiphase flow problems. However, the method did not attract much attention from the mathematics community in terms of rigorous numerical analysis. An important exception from this observation is the work by Puckett [Puc10b, Puc10a, Puc13]. In particular, Puckett presented a rigorous proof for the existence of second-order accurate interface reconstruction algorithm [Puc10b] and also presented an example of such an algorithm in [Puc10a]. It turns out that the analysis is quite involved due to the complexity of the geometrical operations. Some years later, Zhang and Fogelson [ZF16] gave a convergence proof for a class of PLIC-VOF based interface advection methods.

The goal of the present chapter is to establish a rigorous error analysis for the height function method (see Section 7.4) in the presence of *data errors*. Data errors are deviations from the exact (discrete) graph representation of the interface which arise either from numerical quadrature errors in the case of initialized shapes or from accumulation of "numerical noise" in a numerical simulation.

Kromer showed that an undesired checkerboard-type pattern appears in the numerical approximation of the curvature if lower-order methods are employed to initialize the volume fraction field [Kro19]. The numerical quadrature error can, in principle, be controlled either by a "brute force"-approach or by specialized numerical methods (see, e.g., [KB19]) to achieve a high order of accuracy for the initialization. It is, however, much harder or even unfeasible in practice to achieve a similar order of accuracy for the overall two-phase flow solver. For example, the numerical method for interface advection introduces numerical errors which, in turn, can introduce significant errors in the approximation of the surface tension force as noted by [AAL15]. We will investigate the curvature errors introduced by advection in detail in Chapter 10.

Example 9.1 (Numerical differentiation). The essence of the problem is the *error amplification* which is a consequence of the double numerical differentiation of noisy data. For a perturbation $(\delta_0, \delta_1, \delta_{-1})$ of the discrete heights (H_0, H_1, H_{-1}), the numerical error amplification for the second derivative is given by

$$\mathscr{A} = \frac{(H_1 + \delta_1) - 2(H_0 + \delta_0) + (H_{-1} + \delta_{-1})}{(\Delta x)^2} - \frac{H_1 - 2H_0 + H_{-1}}{(\Delta x)^2} = \frac{\delta_1 - 2\delta_0 + \delta_{-1}}{(\Delta x)^2}. \tag{9.1}$$

As a consequence of linearity, the error amplification is simply the discrete second derivative of the perturbation itself. If $\bar{\delta} := \max\{|\delta_0|, |\delta_1|, |\delta_{-1}|\}$ is perturbation amplitude, we can estimate the numerical error amplification according to

$$|\mathscr{A}| = \frac{|\delta_1 - 2\delta_0 + \delta_{-1}|}{(\Delta x)^2} \leq \frac{4\bar{\delta}}{(\Delta x)^2}. \tag{9.2}$$

So, obviously, the perturbation amplitude has to decay faster than second-order to allow for convergence of the second derivative.

The error amplification for the height function method is similar to the above example. However, there is a modification to (9.2) which is due to the nonlinear term in the discrete curvature operator. For simplicity, we restrict the analysis to the two-dimensional case.

9.1. Analytical error estimate in two dimensions

Let $(x, f(x))$ be a local parametrization of Σ as a graph and fix a point x_0. The curvature of Σ at the point $(x_0, f(x_0))$ is defined as

$$\kappa(f) := \frac{f''(x_0)}{(1 + f'(x_0)^2)^{3/2}}. \tag{9.3}$$

It is convenient to introduce the smooth non-linear function

$$\gamma(s) := (1 + s^2)^{-3/2} \tag{9.4}$$

and write $\kappa(f) = f'' \cdot \gamma(f')$. The first and second derivative of γ read as

$$\gamma'(s) = -\frac{3s}{(1+s^2)^{5/2}} = -\frac{3s\,\gamma(s)}{1+s^2}, \quad \gamma''(s) = -3(1+s^2)^{-5/2}\left(1 - \frac{5s^2}{1+s^2}\right).$$

Note that γ, γ' and γ'' are bounded with

$$0 \le \gamma(s) \le 1, \quad |\gamma'(s)| \le |\gamma'(1/2)| =: c_\gamma \approx 0.86, \quad |\gamma''(s)| \le 3.$$

With the above definition, we may express the discrete curvature operator in two dimensions as

$$\hat{\kappa}(f) := \hat{f}''(x_0) \cdot \gamma(\hat{f}'(x_0)). \tag{9.5}$$

where

$$\hat{f}'(x_0) := \frac{f(x_0 + \Delta x) - f(x_0 - \Delta x)}{2\Delta x},$$
$$\hat{f}''(x_0) := \frac{f(x_0 + \Delta x) - 2f(x_0) + f(x_0 - \Delta x)}{(\Delta x)^2}$$

are second-order finite difference approximations of f' and f'', respectively.

Definition 9.2. Let $(x, f(x))$ be a local parametrization of Σ as a graph and $\Delta x > 0$. Then we define the averaged height function as

$$H(x) := \frac{1}{\Delta x} \int_{x-\Delta x/2}^{x+\Delta x/2} f(t)\,dt. \tag{9.6}$$

We will show below that

$$H(x) = f(x) + \frac{f''(x + \xi\Delta x/2)}{24}(\Delta x)^2, \quad \xi \in [-1, 1].$$

Hence $H(x)$ is a **second-order approximation** of $f(x)$ if $f \in \mathscr{C}^2(x - \Delta x/2, x + \Delta x/2)$.

Goal of this chapter: We are interested in estimating the total error

$$\mathscr{E} := \hat{\kappa}(H^\delta) - \kappa(f),$$

where H^δ is a *perturbation* of the height function satisfying

$$|H(x) - H^\delta(x)| \le \delta.$$

The total error can be decomposed into two parts by adding a zero term

$$\boxed{\mathscr{E} := \hat{\kappa}(H^\delta) - \kappa(f) = [\hat{\kappa}(H^\delta) - \hat{\kappa}(H)] + [\hat{\kappa}(H) - \kappa(f)].} \tag{9.7}$$

The second contribution is called *approximation error* (or discretization error) given by

$$\mathscr{D} := \hat{\kappa}(H) - \kappa(f)$$

and the first contribution in (9.7) is called *data error amplification*

$$\mathscr{A} := \hat{\kappa}(H^\delta) - \hat{\kappa}(H).$$

We will study both error contributions separately starting with the approximation error.

9.1.1. Approximation Error

The expansions of the approximation error given in Lemma 9.3 and Lemma 9.4 are well-known in the literature (see, e.g., [BCM$^+$11]). We give a proof here for completeness.

Lemma 9.3 (Approximation Error - Linear Part)**.** *Let f be of class $\mathscr{C}^4$, H be defined by (9.6) and*

$$\hat{H}'(x) := \frac{H(x+\Delta x) - H(x-\Delta x)}{2\Delta x},$$

$$\hat{H}''(x) := \frac{H(x+\Delta x) - 2H(x) + H(x-\Delta x)}{(\Delta x)^2}.$$

Then we have the expansions $(-1 \leq \xi_i \leq 1)$

$$H(x) = f(x) + \frac{f''(x+\xi_0 \Delta x/2)}{24}(\Delta x)^2, \tag{9.8}$$

$$\hat{H}'(x) = f'(x) + \frac{5}{24}f^{(3)}(x+\xi_1 3\Delta x/2)(\Delta x)^2, \tag{9.9}$$

$$\hat{H}''(x) = f''(x) + \frac{1}{8}f^{(4)}(x+\xi_2 3\Delta x/2)(\Delta x)^2 \tag{9.10}$$

and the bounds

$$|H(x) - f(x)| \leq \frac{1}{24}|f''||_\infty (\Delta x)^2, \tag{9.11}$$

$$|\hat{H}'(x) - f'(x)| \leq \frac{5}{24}||f^{(3)}||_\infty (\Delta x)^2, \tag{9.12}$$

$$|\hat{H}''(x) - f''(x)| \leq \frac{1}{8}||f^{(4)}||_\infty (\Delta x)^2, \tag{9.13}$$

where

$$||f^{(n)}||_\infty := \max_{|s| \leq 3\Delta x/2} |f^{(n)}(x+s)|.$$

Proof. By definition of the height function we have

$$H(x) = \frac{F(x+\Delta x/2) - F(x-\Delta x/2)}{\Delta x}, \tag{9.14}$$

where

$$F(x) = \int_{x_0}^{x} f(t)\,dt$$

for any fixed $x_0 \in \mathbb{R}$. Hence the derivatives of H are given by

$$H^{(n)}(x) = \frac{f^{(n-1)}(x+\Delta x/2) - f^{(n-1)}(x-\Delta x/2)}{\Delta x} = f^{(n)}(x+\xi\Delta x/2) \tag{9.15}$$

for some $\xi \in [-1,1]$ and $n \geq 1$. If g is of class $\mathscr{C}^3$, there are $\zeta_1, \zeta_2 \in [0,1]$ such that

$$\frac{g(x+\Delta x/2) - g(x-\Delta x/2)}{\Delta x} = g'(x) + \frac{(\Delta x)^2}{24}\frac{g^{(3)}(x+\zeta_1 \Delta x/2) + g^{(3)}(x-\zeta_2 \Delta x/2)}{2}$$

$$= g'(x) + \frac{(\Delta x)^2}{24}g^{(3)}(x+\xi\Delta x/2) \tag{9.16}$$

for some $\xi \in [-1,1]$. Application of (9.16) to (9.14) immediately leads to (9.8). Moreover, (9.16) applied to (9.15) shows that $(-1 \leq \xi \leq 1)$

$$H^{(n)}(x) = f^{(n)}(x) + \frac{(\Delta x)^2}{24}f^{(n+2)}(x+\xi\Delta x/2). \tag{9.17}$$

Clearly, relation (9.16) with $\Delta x = 2\Delta \tilde{x}$ implies

$$\hat{H}'(x) = \frac{H(x+\Delta x) - H(x-\Delta x)}{2\Delta x} = H'(x) + \frac{(\Delta x)^2}{6} H^{(3)}(x+\xi\Delta x)$$

for some $\xi \in [-1,1]$. Thanks to (9.15) and (9.17) for $n = 1$ we conclude that ($|\xi_i| \leq 1$)

$$\hat{H}'(x) = f'(x) + \frac{5(\Delta x)^2}{24}\left(\frac{1}{5}f^{(3)}(x+\xi_1\Delta x/2) + \frac{4}{5}f^{(3)}(x+\xi_2 3\Delta x/2)\right)$$

$$= f'(x) + \frac{5}{24}f^{(3)}(x+\xi 3\Delta x/2)$$

for some $-1 \leq \xi \leq 1$. Finally, we consider the approximation of the second derivative. Thanks to Taylors Theorem, we have ($0 \leq \zeta_1, \zeta_2 \leq 1$)

$$(\Delta x)^2 \hat{H}''(x) = [H(x+\Delta x) - H(x)] - [H(x) - H(x-\Delta x)]$$

$$= H''(x)(\Delta x)^2 + \frac{(\Delta x)^4}{12}\frac{H^{(4)}(x+\zeta_1\Delta x) + H^{(4)}(x-\zeta_2\Delta x)}{2}$$

$$= H''(x)(\Delta x)^2 + \frac{(\Delta x)^4}{12}H^{(4)}(x+\xi\Delta x)$$

for some $-1 \leq \xi \leq 1$. The relations (9.15) and (9.17) for $n = 2$ imply that there are $\xi_1, \xi_2 \in [-1,1]$ such that

$$\hat{H}''(x) = f''(x) + \frac{(\Delta x)^2}{24}f^{(4)}(x+\xi_1\Delta x/2) + \frac{(\Delta x)^2}{12}f^{(4)}(x+3\xi_2\Delta x/2)$$

$$= f''(x) + \frac{(\Delta x)^2}{8}\left(\frac{1}{3}f^{(4)}(x+\xi_1\Delta x/2) + \frac{2}{3}f^{(4)}(x+\xi_2 3\Delta x/2)\right)$$

$$= f''(x) + \frac{(\Delta x)^2}{8}f^{(4)}(x+\xi 3\Delta x/2), \quad -1 \leq \xi \leq 1.$$

$$\square$$

Lemma 9.4 (Approximation Error). *Let* $\Sigma = \{x, f(x)\}$ *be a* $\mathscr{C}^5$-*hypersurface in* $\mathbb{R}^2$. *Then, the approximation error for the curvature in two dimensions can be expressed as*

$$\boxed{\hat{\kappa}(H) - \kappa(f) = \psi(x)(\Delta x)^2 + \mathscr{R}(x)} \tag{9.18}$$

with the leading-order term

$$\psi(x) := \frac{\gamma(f'(x))}{24}\left(3f^{(4)}(x) - 15\frac{(f'f''f^{(3)})(x)}{1+f'(x)^2}\right) \tag{9.19}$$

and the remainder $\mathscr{R}(x)$ *satisfying*

$$|\mathscr{R}(x)| \leq \frac{3}{16}\gamma[f'(x)]\|f^{(5)}\|_\infty (\Delta x)^3 + (\Delta x)^3\left(|f''(x)| + \frac{(\Delta x)^2}{8}\|f^{(4)}\|_\infty\right)$$

$$\cdot \left(\frac{15}{48}|\gamma'[f'(x)]|\cdot\|f^{(4)}\|_\infty + \frac{75}{1152}\|f^{(3)}\|_\infty^2\Delta x\right) \tag{9.20}$$

$$= \left(\frac{3}{16}\gamma[f'(x)]\cdot\|f^{(5)}\|_\infty + \frac{15}{48}|f''(x)|\cdot|\gamma'[f'(x)]|\cdot\|f^{(4)}\|_\infty\right)(\Delta x)^3 + \mathscr{O}((\Delta x)^5).$$

Remark 9.5. In fact, the remainder term $\mathscr{R}(x)$ can be shown to be of 4th-order if the hypersurface is sufficiently regular; see [BCM$^+$11]. However, for the sake of brevity, we only prove $\mathscr{R} \in \mathscr{O}((\Delta x)^3)$ here.

Proof. We rewrite the approximation error by inserting a zero term

$$\hat{\kappa}(H) - \kappa(f) = \hat{H}'' \cdot \gamma(\hat{H}') - f'' \cdot \gamma(f')$$
$$= (\hat{H}'' - f'')\,\gamma(f') + \hat{H}''\,(\gamma(\hat{H}') - \gamma(f'))\,.$$

Thanks to Lemma 9.3 we have with $-1 \le \xi_i \le 1$

$$\hat{\kappa}(H) - \kappa(f) = \frac{(\Delta x)^2}{8} f^{(4)}(x + \xi_2 3\Delta x/2)\,\gamma[f'(x)]$$
$$+ \left(f''(x) + \frac{(\Delta x)^2}{8} f^{(4)}(x + \xi_2 3\Delta x/2) \right) \left(\gamma[f'(x) + \frac{5}{24} f^{(3)}(x + \xi_1 3\Delta x/2)(\Delta x)^2] - \gamma[f'] \right).$$

(9.21)

By means of Taylor expansions of γ and f we obtain (with $-1 \le \xi_i \le 1$, $s \in \mathbb{R}$)

$$\gamma[f'(x) + \frac{5}{24} f^{(3)}(x + \xi_1 3\Delta x/2)(\Delta x)^2] - \gamma[f']$$
$$= \frac{5}{24} \gamma'[f'(x)]f^{(3)}(x + \xi_1 3\Delta x/2)(\Delta x)^2 + \frac{1}{2}\gamma''(s) \left(\frac{5}{24} f^{(3)}(x + \xi_1 3\Delta x/2)(\Delta x)^2 \right)^2$$
$$= \frac{5}{24} \gamma'[f'(x)](\Delta x)^2 \left(f^{(3)}(x) + f^{(4)}(x + \xi_3 3\Delta x/2)\frac{3\xi_1 \Delta x}{2} \right) + \frac{25}{1152}\gamma''(s)f^{(3)}(x + \xi_1 3\Delta x/2)^2(\Delta x)^4.$$

Moreover, a Taylor expansion of the first term in (9.21) leads to

$$\frac{(\Delta x)^2}{8} f^{(4)}(x + \xi_2 3\Delta x/2)\,\gamma[f'(x)] = \frac{(\Delta x)^2}{8} \gamma[f'(x)] \left(f^{(4)}(x) + f^{(5)}(x + \xi_4 3\Delta x/2)\frac{3\xi_2 \Delta x}{2} \right)$$

(9.22)

Hence we have

$$\hat{\kappa}(H) - \kappa(f) = \psi(x)(\Delta x)^2 + \mathscr{R}(x)$$

with the leading-order term (using $\gamma'(s) = -\frac{3s\,\gamma(s)}{1+s^2}$)

$$\psi(x) = \frac{\gamma(f'(x))}{24} \left(3f^{(4)}(x) - 15\frac{(f' f'' f^{(3)})(x)}{1 + f'(x)^2} \right)$$

(9.23)

and the remainder

$$\mathscr{R}(x) = \frac{(\Delta x)^2}{8} \gamma[f'(x)]f^{(5)}(x + \xi_4 3\Delta x/2)\frac{3\xi_2 \Delta x}{2} + \left(f''(x) + \frac{(\Delta x)^2}{8} f^{(4)}(x + \xi_2 3\Delta x/2) \right)$$
$$\cdot \left(\frac{5}{24} \gamma[f'(x)]f^{(4)}(x + \xi_3 3\Delta x/2)\frac{3\xi_1 (\Delta x)^3}{2} + \frac{25}{1152}\gamma''(s)f^{(3)}(x + \xi_1 3\Delta x/2)^2(\Delta x)^4 \right).$$

The claim follows by a term-by-term estimate of $\mathscr{R}(x)$ using that $|\xi_i| \le 1$ and $|\gamma''(s)| \le 3$. $\qquad\square$

9.1.2. Data error amplification

We now consider perturbations H^δ of the height function H with amplitude $\bar{\delta}$, i.e. $\|H - H^\delta\| \le \bar{\delta}$ in a suitable norm. The goal is to find a bound for the discrete error amplification of the type

$$|\hat{\kappa}(H) - \hat{\kappa}(H^\delta)| \le C\frac{\bar{\delta}}{(\Delta x)^2} + \dots,$$

(9.24)

where the constant C may depend on the properties of the hypersurface through f. We can immediately see from (9.24), that the perturbation has to decay *faster* than $(\Delta x)^2$ to allow for convergence! Even though the latter fact has been noted explicitly by some authors including, e.g., [CG16] and [Pop18], it is still overlooked in a considerable part of the scientific literature on the topic. The goal of the present chapter is to provide a rigorous proof for an estimate similar to (9.24).

Analysis of the discrete curvature operator in two dimensions: In order to prove an estimate like (9.24), we study the properties of the discrete curvature operator

$$\hat{\kappa}(H_0, H_1, H_{-1}) = \frac{H_1 - 2H_0 + H_{-1}}{(\Delta x)^2 \left[1 + \left(\frac{H_1 - H_{-1}}{2\Delta x}\right)^2\right]^{3/2}}. \tag{9.25}$$

We note that $\hat{\kappa}$ has the form

$$\hat{\kappa}(H_0, H_1, H_{-1}) = \beta(H_0, H_1, H_{-1}) \cdot \gamma(\eta(H_0, H_1, H_{-1})), \tag{9.26}$$

where

$$\beta(H_0, H_1, H_{-1}) = \frac{H_1 - 2H_0 + H_{-1}}{(\Delta x)^2} \quad \text{and} \quad \eta(H_0, H_1, H_{-1}) = \frac{H_1 - H_{-1}}{2\Delta x} \tag{9.27}$$

are linear functions (namely the second-order finite differences for H' and H''). The discrete error amplification is defined as

$$\begin{aligned} \mathscr{A} &= \hat{\kappa}(H_0 + \delta_0, H_1 + \delta_1, H_{-1} + \delta_{-1}) - \hat{\kappa}(H_0, H_1, H_{-1}) \\ &= \beta(H + \delta) \cdot \gamma(\eta(H + \delta)) - \beta(H) \cdot \gamma(\eta(H)), \end{aligned} \tag{9.28}$$

where $H = (H_0, H_1, H_{-1})$ and $\delta = (\delta_0, \delta_1, \delta_{-1})$. Note that the following estimate for the amplification $|\mathscr{A}|$ is based solely on the linearity of the functions β and η.

Theorem 9.6 (Discrete error amplification). *Let $\hat{\kappa}$ be defined by (9.26) with linear functions β and η and let $(H_0, H_1, H_{-1}) \in \mathbb{R}^3$ be a triple of discrete heights. Then the discrete error amplification can be estimated as*

$$\begin{aligned} |\mathscr{A}| \leq &|\beta(\delta)| \left[\gamma(f'(x) + \eta(\delta)) + |\gamma'(f'(x) + \eta(\delta))(\eta(H) - f'(x))| + \frac{3}{2}(\eta(H) - f'(x))^2\right] \\ &+ c_\gamma|\beta(H)||\eta(\delta)| \end{aligned} \tag{9.29}$$

Proof. Thanks to the linearity of β and η, we have

$$\mathscr{A} = \beta(H)\left[\gamma(\eta(H) + \eta(\delta)) - \gamma(\eta(H))\right] + \beta(\delta)\gamma(\eta(H + \delta)). \tag{9.30}$$

Since γ is smooth, we may apply Taylor's theorem to find

$$\mathscr{A} = \beta(H)\gamma'(\zeta)\eta(\delta) + \beta(\delta)\gamma(\eta(H + \delta))$$

for some $\zeta \in \mathbb{R}$. Moreover, we expand the second term in (9.30) leading to

$$\beta(\delta)\,\gamma(\eta(H) + \eta(\delta)) = \beta(\delta)\,\gamma(f'(x) + \eta(\delta) + \eta(H) - f'(x))$$

$$= \beta(\delta)[\gamma(f'(x) + \eta(\delta)) + \gamma'(f'(x) + \eta(\delta))(\eta(H) - f'(x)) + \frac{1}{2}\gamma''(\tilde{\zeta})(\eta(H) - f'(x))^2]$$

for some $\tilde{\zeta} \in \mathbb{R}$. Now the claim follows from $|\gamma'(s)| \leq c_\gamma$ and $|\gamma''(s)| \leq 3$. $\qquad\square$

Now we apply Lemma 9.3 to estimate the term $|\eta(H) - f'(x)|$.

Corollary 9.7. Let $(H_0, H_1, H_{-1}) \in \mathbb{R}^3$ be a triple of discrete heights generated by a graph representation of $\Sigma = \{(x, f(x) : x \in I)\}$ with $f \in \mathscr{C}^4$ according to

$$H_0 = \frac{1}{\Delta x}\int_{x - \Delta x/2}^{x + \Delta x/2} f(t)dt, \quad H_1 = \frac{1}{\Delta x}\int_{x + \Delta x/2}^{x + 3\Delta x/2} f(t)dt, \quad H_{-1} = \frac{1}{\Delta x}\int_{x - 3\Delta x/2}^{x - \Delta x/2} f(t)dt.$$

Then the discrete error amplification for the operator (9.26) with β, η given by (9.27) is bounded by

$$
\begin{aligned}
|\mathscr{A}| \leq & |\beta(\delta)| \left[\gamma(f'(x) + \eta(\delta)) + \frac{5}{24}|\gamma'(f'(x) + \eta(\delta))|\,||f^{(3)}||_\infty (\Delta x)^2 + \frac{25}{384}||f^{(3)}||_\infty^2 (\Delta x)^4 \right] \\
& + c_\gamma \left(|f''(x)| + \frac{1}{8}||f^{(4)}||_\infty (\Delta x)^2 \right) |\eta(\delta)|
\end{aligned}
\tag{9.31}
$$

with

$$
\beta(\delta) = \frac{\delta_1 - 2\delta_0 + \delta_{-1}}{(\Delta x)^2}, \quad \eta(\delta) = \frac{\delta_1 - \delta_{-1}}{2\Delta x}.
$$

Proof. Lemma 9.3 implies that $|\beta(H)|$ is bounded by

$$
|\beta(H)| = |\beta(H) - f''(x) + f''(x)| \leq |f''(x)| + \frac{1}{8}||f^{(4)}||_\infty (\Delta x)^2.
$$

Moreover, Lemma 9.3 states that

$$
|\eta(H) - f'(x)| \leq \frac{5}{24}||f^{(3)}||_\infty (\Delta x)^2.
$$

Now the claim follows directly from (9.29). $\qquad\square$

Remark 9.8. For practical purposes, it is convenient to derive a simpler (though weaker) version of the estimate (9.31) in terms of the perturbation amplitude only. The remaining step is to expand

$$
\begin{aligned}
\gamma(f'(x) + \eta(\delta)) &= \gamma(f'(x)) + \gamma'(\zeta)\eta(\delta), \\
\gamma'(f'(x) + \eta(\delta)) &= \gamma'(f'(x)) + \gamma''(\tilde{\zeta})\eta(\delta).
\end{aligned}
$$

Moreover, with $\bar{\delta} := \max\{|\delta_1|, |\delta_0|, |\delta_{-1}|\}$ we have

$$
|\beta(\delta)| \leq \frac{4\bar{\delta}}{(\Delta x)^2}, \quad |\eta(\delta)| \leq \frac{\bar{\delta}}{\Delta x}.
$$

Then, from $|\gamma'(s)| \leq c_\gamma$ and $|\gamma''(s)| \leq 3$ follows the estimate

$$
\begin{aligned}
|\mathscr{A}| \leq & \frac{4\bar{\delta}}{(\Delta x)^2} \left[\gamma(f'(x)) + c_\gamma \frac{\bar{\delta}}{\Delta x} + \frac{5}{24}||f^{(3)}||_\infty (\Delta x)^2 \left(|\gamma'(f'(x))| + \frac{3\bar{\delta}}{\Delta x} \right) \right. \\
& \left. + \frac{25}{384}||f^{(3)}||_\infty^2 (\Delta x)^4 \right] + c_\gamma \left(|f''(x)| + \frac{1}{8}||f^{(4)}||_\infty (\Delta x)^2 \right) \frac{\bar{\delta}}{\Delta x}.
\end{aligned}
\tag{9.32}
$$

Note that the leading-order terms in (9.32) for $\Delta x \to 0$ are

$$
|\mathscr{A}| \leq \frac{4\bar{\delta}}{(\Delta x)^2} \gamma(f'(x)) + 4c_\gamma \frac{\bar{\delta}^2}{(\Delta x)^3} + c_\gamma |f''(x)| \frac{\bar{\delta}}{\Delta x} + \dots.
$$

From (9.32) it follows that the discrete error amplification $\mathscr{A}$ converges with order $n - 2$ if the perturbation amplitude $\bar{\delta}$ converges with order $n > 2$.

9.2. Computational examples

The purpose of this section is to illustrate the theory developed in Section 9.1 with some computational examples. This is done by choosing a polynomial function $f(x)$ representing the interface on some interval

$$\Sigma = \{(x, f(x)) \ : \ a \leq x \leq b\}.$$

The advantage of choosing a polynomial function is that the continuous height function $H(x)$ defined by (9.6) can be easily computed exactly. Here we use the symbolic toolbox of *Matlab* to compute the reference data. As an (arbitrary) example function we choose

$$f(x) = 3 + \frac{x^2}{2} + 2x^3 + \frac{2x^4}{5} - \frac{x^6}{10}. \tag{9.33}$$

The exact curvature for the latter function is depicted in Fig. 9.1 along with the finite differences approximation (9.5) for *exact* heights, i.e. in the absence of any data errors. As we have shown in Section 9.1, the discrete curvature converges with second-order accuracy in this case. However, the absence of data errors is not realistic in the context of multiphase flow simulations. We, therefore, consider the convergence properties of the discrete curvature in the presence of data errors in the sequel.

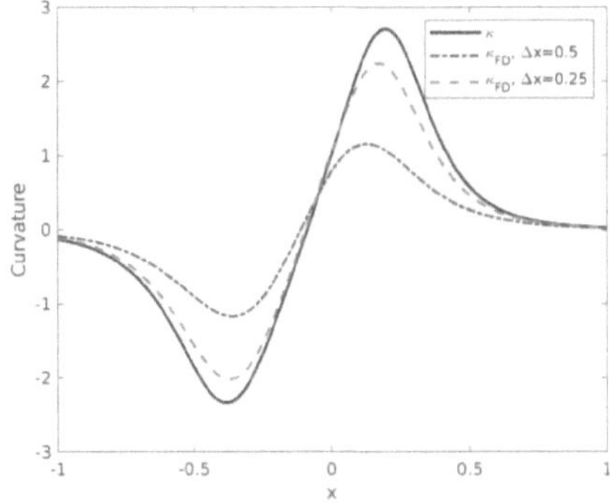

Figure 9.1.: Finite differences based curvature for symbolically computed heights.

9.2.1. Curvatures from numerical quadrature

An obvious way to test the convergence properties in a more realistic setting is to compute the discrete heights

$$H_0 = \frac{1}{\Delta x}\int_{x-\Delta x/2}^{x+\Delta x/2} f(t)dt, \quad H_1 = \frac{1}{\Delta x}\int_{x+\Delta x/2}^{x+3\Delta x/2} f(t)dt, \quad H_{-1} = \frac{1}{\Delta x}\int_{x-3\Delta x/2}^{x-\Delta x/2} f(t)dt$$

by numerical quadrature rather than symbolic quadrature. Note, however, that using the midpoint rule

$$H_0 = \frac{1}{\Delta x}\int_{x-\Delta x/2}^{x+\Delta x/2} f(t)dt \approx f(x_0)$$

is not a reasonable test since it delivers the exact height $f(x_0)$ which should be thought of as unknown. In this sense, there is no "natural" choice to test lower-order formulas. We will consider an example of a first-order convergent data error in the curvature transport problem in Chapter 10.

We fix $x_0 = 1/4$ and apply the trapezoidal rule

$$H_0 \approx \frac{1}{2} f(x_0 - \Delta x/2) + \frac{1}{2} f(x_0 + \Delta x/2) \tag{9.34}$$

and the Gauß-Legendre quadrature rule ($n = 2$)

$$H_0 \approx \frac{1}{2} f\left(x_0 - \frac{\Delta x}{2}\sqrt{1/3}\right) + \frac{1}{2} f\left(x_0 + \frac{\Delta x}{2}\sqrt{1/3}\right) \tag{9.35}$$

to compute approximate heights H_0, H_1, H_{-1} for different choices of Δx. Since the exact heights are available from symbolic integration of the polynomial f, we can explicitly evaluate the maximum data error

$$\bar{\delta} = \max\{|H_0 - \hat{H}_0|, |H_1 - \hat{H}_1|, |H_{-1} - \hat{H}_{-1}|\}$$

as well as the expressions

$$\beta(\delta) = \frac{\delta_1 - 2\delta_0 + \delta_{-1}}{(\Delta x)^2}, \quad \eta(\delta) = \frac{\delta_1 - \delta_{-1}}{2\Delta x}.$$

This allows to compare the actual errors with the following models which are motivated by the leading-order contributions in the analytical estimates in Section 9.1

$$\mathscr{E}_1(\Delta x) = |\psi(x)| (\Delta x)^2 + \frac{4\bar{\delta}}{(\Delta x)^2} \gamma(f'(x)), \tag{9.36}$$

$$\mathscr{E}_2(\Delta x) = |\psi(x)| (\Delta x)^2 + |\beta(\delta)| \gamma(f'(x) + \eta(\delta)). \tag{9.37}$$

Remark 9.9. We note that the model (9.36) only involves the perturbation amplitude while (9.37) also reflects the structure of the local perturbation vector δ. Clearly, the above expressions are only simple models for the error neglecting the higher-order contributions. For example, at positions x with $\psi(x) = 0$ one has to consider the higher-order terms to describe the approximation error reasonably.

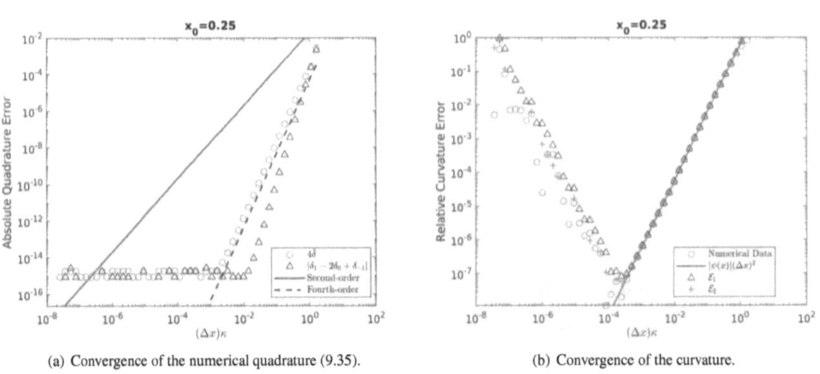

(a) Convergence of the numerical quadrature (9.35).

(b) Convergence of the curvature.

Figure 9.2.: Convergence of the curvature for the Gauß-Legendre quadrature.

Results for the Gauß-Legendre quadrature: From Fig. 9.2 we see that the maximum data error $\bar{\delta}$ is fourth-order convergent until the arithmetic precision $\varepsilon \approx 2.2 \cdot 10^{-16}$ is reached. For smaller values of Δx, the perturbation is $\mathcal{O}(1)$ leading to a second-order divergence of the curvature approximation. This phenomenon, however, becomes significant only at very fine meshes with approximately 10^4 or more cells per radius of curvature. Such a high mesh resolution is not realized in current numerical simulations of realistic multiphase flow problems. The actual error is well-described by both of the models $\mathscr{E}_1$ and $\mathscr{E}_2$.

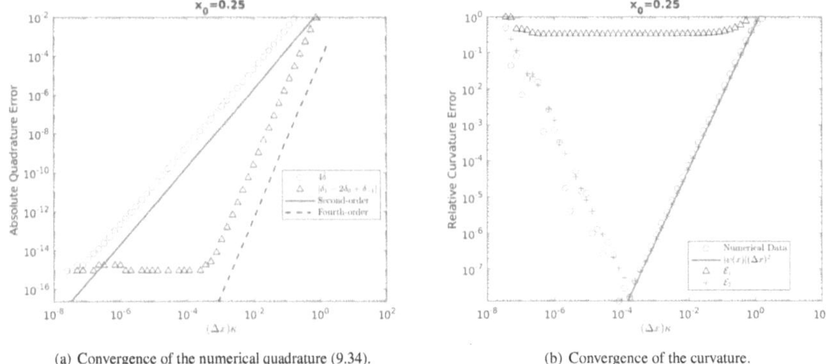

(a) Convergence of the numerical quadrature (9.34).　　　(b) Convergence of the curvature.

Figure 9.3.: Convergence of the curvature for the trapezoidal rule.

Results for the trapezoidal quadrature: Remarkably, there is large difference between $4\bar{\delta}$ and $|\beta(\delta)|$ for the trapezoidal quadrature; see Fig.9.3(a). The finite difference term $|\delta_1 - \delta_0 + \delta_{-1}|$ converges with fourth-order accuracy while the maximum perturbation $\bar{\delta}$ is only second-order convergent. As a result, the relative curvature error is over-predicted by the model $\mathscr{E}_1$ by more than six orders of magnitude. In fact, the finite difference term $|\delta_1 - \delta_0 + \delta_{-1}|$ converges with fourth-order until the arithmetic precision is reached so that the relative error behaves quite similarly to the Gauß-Legendre quadrature. Moreover, the error is well-described by the model $\mathscr{E}_2$. This example shows that, in general, it is important to consider the structure of the perturbation to obtain a realistic estimate of the error.

9.3. A note on higher-order methods

> "Accurately estimating the curvature of the fluid-fluid interface is key to correctly account for capillary effects, and to avoid the generation of parasitic flow currents" [EDvW20, p.1].

The need for highly accurate surface tension forces motivated research which aims at higher-order curvature estimates from volume fraction data; see, e.g, [SO06, BCM$^+$11, EDvW20]. We will show below that the data error amplification is particularly important when it comes to higher-order methods. For all methods which rely on the second derivative of a graph representation of the interface, it is necessary to have $(n+2)$-order convergence of the data error to retain n-th order convergence of the curvature as $\Delta x \to 0$. Hence, the higher-order convergence rate is lost immediately if the quality of the VOF data is not sufficient. Moreover, the methods tend to become more sensitive to perturbations as the approximation order increases. This is natural since the higher-order methods involve more data points to compute the curvature estimates. In practice, this means that higher-order methods may produce less accurate estimates than lower-order methods; see in particular Chapter 10. One should, therefore, be careful when applying higher-order methods.

Example 9.10 (Higher-order approximation by Sussman and Ohta [SO06]). Sussman and Ohta [SO06] introduced a systematic way to construct higher-order approximations of the curvature from volume fractions on equidistant Cartesian meshes in two and three dimensions. The idea is to construct *linear* approximation operators of the first and second derivatives of H, where it is required that the approximation is exact for polynomials up to order m. The resulting linear system for the unknown coefficients leads to the desired formula via

$$\kappa(x) \approx \frac{\hat{H}''(x)}{\sqrt{1 + \hat{H}'(x)^2}}.$$

A concrete example of a fourth-order approximation given in [SO06] is

$$\hat{H}'(x) = \frac{1}{\Delta x}\left(\frac{5}{48}(H_{-2}-H_2)+\frac{17}{24}(H_1-H_{-1})\right),\tag{9.38}$$

$$\hat{H}''(x) = \frac{1}{(\Delta x)^2}\left(-\frac{11}{4}H_0+\frac{3}{2}(H_1+H_{-1})-\frac{1}{8}(H_2+H_{-2})\right)\tag{9.39}$$

Note that Theorem 9.6 is applicable with $\eta = \eta_4(H)$ and $\beta = \beta_4(H)$ given by (9.38) and (9.39), respectively. The leading-order contribution to the error amplification can be estimated in terms of the perturbation amplitude $\bar{\delta}$ by

$$|\beta_4(\delta)| \leq \frac{1}{(\Delta x)^2}\left(\frac{11}{4}\bar{\delta}+3\bar{\delta}+\frac{1}{4}\bar{\delta}\right)=\frac{6}{(\Delta x)^2}.$$

So, from this simple calculation, we can expect that the error amplification is increased by typically 50% compared to the standard second-order approximation.

A direct comparison of the fourth-order approximations (9.38) and (9.39) with the standard second-approximations for the interface described by (9.33) at $x_0 = 1$ is shown in Fig. 9.4. As expected, the fourth-order accuracy is not reached if the trapezoidal quadrature is used; see Fig. 9.4(c). Instead, the convergence order degenerates to second-order until the arithmetic precision is reached. Note that the error is only slightly smaller compared to the standard method, even on coarse grids. Moreover, second-order convergence is achieved only because the discrete second-derivative of the error $\beta_4(\delta)$ converges with second-order; see Fig. 9.4(a). The error estimate based on the perturbation amplitude $\bar{\delta}$ guarantees only $\mathcal{O}(1)$ for the trapezoidal rule. The proficiency of the higher-order method becomes visible when the Gauß-Legendre quadrature is applied; see Fig. 9.4(d). The fourth-order convergence is reached since the discrete second derivative of the perturbation $\beta_4(\delta)$ converges with fourth-order; see Fig. 9.4(b).

Remark 9.11. The extreme cases of higher-order methods are "arbitrary order" methods for curvature estimation like the one proposed recently in [EDvW20]. Indeed, up to 10th-order convergence was demonstrated in numerical examples in [EDvW20]. However, this could only be achieved by a brute-force approach to obtain sufficiently accurate discrete heights:

> "From a computational point of view, all calculations are conducted in quadruple precision (128 bits) in order to not be limited by floating-point errors for the range of resolutions considered. The heights are integrated using the Gauss-Legendre quadrature rule with enough integration points so that no significant bias is introduced in the convergence study." [EDvW20, p.9]

Hence, the applicability of the latter method in practical applications, where data errors are unavoidable, is strongly limited.

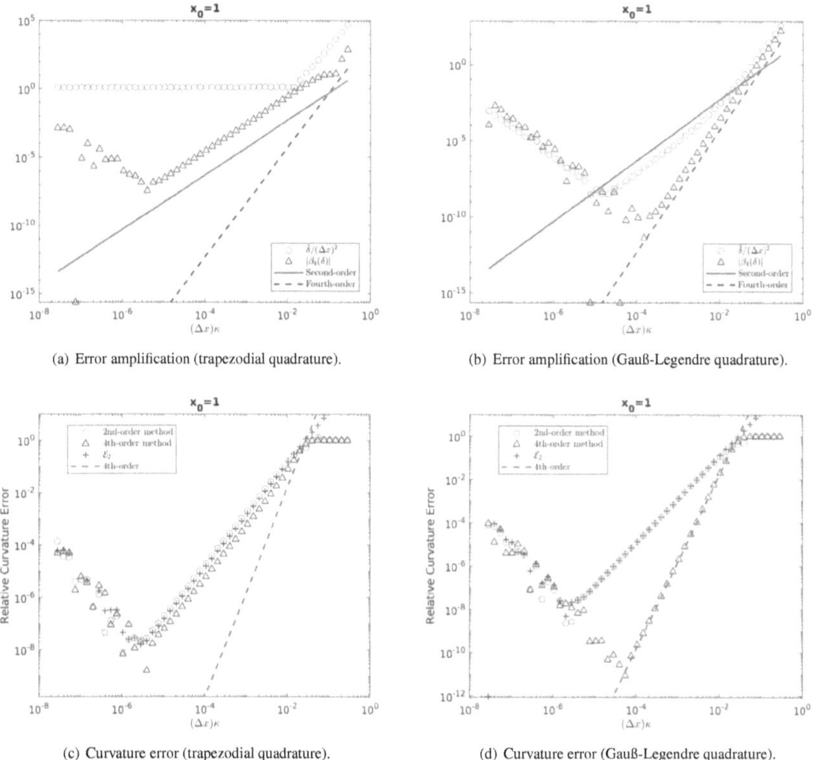

(a) Error amplification (trapezodial quadrature).

(b) Error amplification (Gauß-Legendre quadrature).

(c) Curvature error (trapezodial quadrature).

(d) Curvature error (Gauß-Legendre quadrature).

Figure 9.4.: Standard second-order finite differences vs. 4th-order method by Sussman and Ohta [SO06].

10. Numerical transport of the mean curvature

The numerical scheme to approximate the surface tension force is a central element of any method which aims for an accurate description of capillary flows; see [Pop18]. As already discussed in Section 7.4, the volumetric formulation of the surface tension force

$$f_\sigma = \sigma \kappa n_\Sigma \delta_\Sigma$$

requires an accurate estimate of the mean curvature $\kappa = -\mathrm{div}_\Sigma\, n_\Sigma$. There is a large variety of numerical methods to approximate the mean curvature in VOF methods which are usually validated for *known* (initialized) shapes such as spheres or ellipsoids; see, e.g., [CFK05, FS10] for an overview. To the best of the authors knowledge, there are only a few studies including [AAL15, CG16] and [Pop18] that pay particular attention to the errors in the curvature computation that arise from the errors produced during interface advection. As we have shown rigorously in the previous chapter, an advection method must converge faster than second-order to allow for convergence of the mean curvature in the limit $\Delta x \to 0$. Abadie et al. formulate the following conclusion in [AAL15]:

> "It can be concluded that the height function curvature calculation is very accurate and is particularly interesting for the case of static bubbles and near-static bubble or oscillating bubbles [22,19]. However, since the errors generated during the advection step are captured while they are smoothed with the convolution method, the height function method needs to be coupled with an accurate transport scheme, as it has been shown for the translating and rotating cases in this study. Otherwise, the classic CSF formulation with a smoothing of the volume fraction gives better results in terms of maximum spurious current intensity."
>
> [AAL15, p. 632]

The fundamental mathematical investigation on the kinematic transport of the mean curvature in Section 4.4 allows to study the *numerical* transport locally, based on an exact reference solution.

In the remainder of this chapter, the numerical curvature transport is studied based on the geometrical Volume-of-Fluid Code FS3D. In particular, we compare the Boundary Youngs and Boundary ELVIRA methods developed in Chapter 8. Finally, the results from the geometrical VOF method are compared with the results obtained with the first-order upwind Level Set method (see Section 6.2).

Remark 10.1 (Interface advection and error amplification). Following the error analysis discussed in Chapter 9, the error amplification due to numerical errors in the advection of the interface can be expected to have a significant influence on the overall transport error for the curvature. In particular, the dominant contributions (in the simplest form of the estimate) to the error in the curvature transport are

$$\mathscr{E}_\kappa \propto C_1^\kappa (\Delta x)^{n_\kappa} + C_2^\kappa \frac{\bar\delta}{(\Delta x)^2} + \dots, \tag{10.1}$$

where n_κ is the approximation order of the finite differences method and $\bar\delta$ is the perturbation amplitude due to transport errors. A similar argument, as outlined in detail in the previous chapter for the curvature, applies for the numerical transport of the contact angle θ and the contact line Γ. Since for the computation of the contact angle, the marker field is differentiated *once*, we expect a first-order error amplification leading to

$$\mathscr{E}_\theta \propto C_1^\theta (\Delta x)^{n_\theta} + C_2^\theta \frac{\bar\delta}{\Delta x} + \dots. \tag{10.2}$$

Finally, the error for the numerical transport of the contact line is expected to behave like

$$\mathscr{E}_\Gamma \propto C_1^\Gamma (\Delta x)^{n_\Gamma} + C_2^\Gamma \bar\delta. \tag{10.3}$$

Since the advection error $\bar{\delta}$ converges with first-order for Boundary Youngs and with second-order for Boundary ELVIRA (see Chapter 8), the expected convergence rates in the limit $\Delta x \to 0$ are

$$\mathscr{E}_\Gamma \propto \Delta x, \quad \mathscr{E}_\theta \propto \text{const}, \quad \mathscr{E}_\kappa \propto \frac{1}{\Delta x} \tag{10.4}$$

for the Boundary Youngs method and

$$\mathscr{E}_\Gamma \propto (\Delta x)^2, \quad \mathscr{E}_\theta \propto \Delta x, \quad \mathscr{E}_\kappa \propto \text{const} \tag{10.5}$$

for the Boundary ELVIRA method. In particular, the Boundary Youngs method is expected to deliver first-order *divergent* results for the curvature transport.

Before we consider the numerical curvature transport, we discuss some examples which serve as a reference for validation of the numerical methods.

10.1. Reference solutions for the curvature transport in two dimensions

We construct analytical solutions to the kinematic transport equation for the curvature in two dimensions (see Section 4.4)

$$\dot{\kappa} = \frac{\partial^2 v}{\partial \tau^2} \cdot n_\Sigma - 3\kappa\,\tau \cdot \partial_\tau v. \tag{10.6}$$

Note that the latter equation holds if the field v is divergence-free (see Section 4.4 for a more general formula).

Example 10.2. As a first example, we consider a general *linear* divergence-free velocity field. In this case, the contact angle evolution equation can be solved explicitly, see Section 8.1 and [FMB20a].

$$v(x_1, x_2) = (v_0 + c_1 x_1 + c_2 x_2, -c_1 x_2)$$

The gradient of v is given by

$$\nabla v = \begin{pmatrix} c_1 & c_2 \\ 0 & -c_1 \end{pmatrix}.$$

The choice $c_2 = 0$ simplifies the problem since ∇v is diagonal in this case. The evolution of the contact angle in the latter case is given by (see Section 8.1)

$$\theta(t) = \frac{\pi}{2} + \arctan\left(-\cot\theta_0 e^{2c_1 t}\right) \tag{10.7}$$

Hence for the left contact point, we have

$$\tau(t) = \tau^l(t) = \begin{pmatrix} \cos\theta(t) \\ \sin\theta(t) \end{pmatrix} = \frac{1}{\sqrt{1 + e^{4c_1 t}\cot^2\theta_0}} \begin{pmatrix} e^{2c_1 t}\cot\theta_0 \\ 1 \end{pmatrix}.$$

It follows that

$$(\partial_\tau v) \cdot \tau = \langle \nabla v\,\tau, \tau \rangle = c_1(\tau_1^2 - \tau_2^2) = c_1 \frac{e^{4c_1 t}\cot^2\theta_0 - 1}{e^{4c_1 t}\cot^2\theta_0 + 1}$$

$$= c_1\left(1 - \frac{2}{1 + \cot^2\theta_0\, e^{4c_1 t}}\right)$$

According to (4.92), the evolution equation for κ reads as

$$\dot{\kappa} = -3\kappa c_1\left(1 - \frac{2}{1 + \cot^2\theta_0\, e^{4c_1 t}}\right)$$

with the solution

$$\kappa(t) = \frac{\kappa_0(1+\cot^2\theta_0)^{3/2}\,e^{3c_1 t}}{(1+\cot^2\theta_0\,e^{4c_1 t})^{3/2}}.$$

(10.8)

In particular, for $\theta_0 = \frac{\pi}{2}$ the above solution simplifies to

$$\kappa(t) = \kappa_0 e^{3c_1 t}.$$

Example 10.3. As a second example, we consider a divergence-free field with a non-constant gradient such that the second-order derivative term in (10.6) is non-zero. To this end, we introduce a quadratic term according to

$$v(x_1,x_2) = (v_0 + c_1 x_1 + c_2 x_2 + c_3 x_2^2, -c_1 x_2).$$

(10.9)

Then the gradient is given by

$$\nabla v = \begin{pmatrix} c_1 & c_2 + 2c_3 x_2 \\ 0 & -c_1 \end{pmatrix}.$$

It is easy to check using the contact angle evolution equation (8.1) that the above field leaves $\theta = \frac{\pi}{2}$ invariant if $c_2 = 0$. So for $\theta_0 = \frac{\pi}{2}$ and $c_2 = 0$ we have (for the left contact point)

$$\tau(t) = \begin{pmatrix} 0 \\ 1 \end{pmatrix}, \quad n_\Sigma(t) = \begin{pmatrix} -1 \\ 0 \end{pmatrix}.$$

Therefore, the evolution equation (4.92) reads as

$$\dot{\kappa} = -2c_3 + 3c_1\kappa.$$

The solution is given by the expression

$$\kappa(t) = \kappa_0 e^{3c_1 t} + \frac{2c_3}{3c_1}\left(1 - e^{3c_1 t}\right).$$

Example 10.4. A further interesting candidate to probe the numerical curvature transport is the time-periodic field

$$v(t,x_1,x_2) = \cos\left(\frac{\pi t}{\tau_p}\right)(v_0 + c_1 x_1, -c_1 x_2), \quad \tau_p > 0,\ v_0, c_1 \in \mathbb{R}.$$

(10.10)

It is shown in Section 8.3.3 that the kinematic transport equations for the contact line and contact angle transport admit analytical solutions in this case. For the left contact point characterized by

$$\tau^l = (\cos\theta, \sin\theta)$$

the solutions are

$$x_1(t) = x_0 e^{c_1 s(t)} + \frac{v_0}{c_1}\left(e^{c_1 s(t)} - 1\right),$$

$$\theta(t) = \frac{\pi}{2} + \arctan\left(-\cot\theta_0 e^{2c_1 s(t)}\right)$$

where the periodic function $s(t)$ is given by

$$s(t) = \frac{\tau_p \sin(\pi t/\tau_p)}{\tau_p}.$$

A similar calculation as in Example 10.2 above shows that the evolution of the curvature at the contact line obeys the ordinary differential equation

$$\dot{\kappa} = -3\kappa\cos\left(\frac{\pi t}{\tau_p}\right)c_1\left(1 - \frac{2}{1+\cot^2\theta_0\,e^{4c_1 s(t)}}\right).$$

(10.11)

Unfortunately, there is no known explicit solution to (10.11).

10.2. Volume-of-Fluid-based curvature transport

We now investigate the numerical transport of the curvature for the Volume-of-Fluid method in two dimensions.

Setup: The numerical setup for FS3D is as follows: The computational domain

$$0 \leq x \leq 0.5, \quad 0 \leq y \leq 0.25$$

is decomposed into $2N \times N$ Cartesian control volumes and a circular cap with radius $R = 0.2$ is initialized with center coordinate $(0.5, -0.1)$, yielding an initial contact angle $\theta_0 = \pi/3$; see Fig. 10.1. A height function representation can now be obtained by simply summing up the volume fractions in the y-direction. To obtain a well-posed problem, we require homogeneous Neumann boundary conditions for the characteristic function χ at inflow boundaries, i.e.

$$\frac{\partial \chi}{\partial n_{\partial \Omega}}(t,x) = 0$$

for $x \in \partial \Omega$ with $v(t,x) \cdot n_{\partial \Omega} < 0$ (where $n_{\partial \Omega}$ is the outer unit normal field). In the numerical method, the above condition can easily be realized by the ghost cell approach (see 8.3 for a discussion).

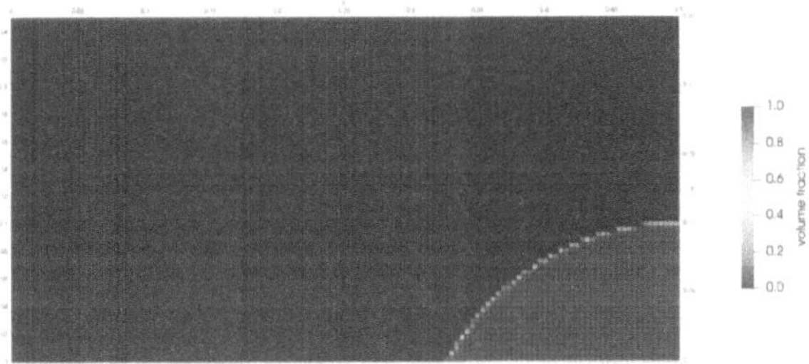

Figure 10.1.: Setup for the VOF curvature transport.

The numerical curvature transport test case proceeds in the following steps:

(i) The volume fraction field for the above geometry is initialized with fourth-order accuracy using the algorithm developed in [KB19]. A comparison with a standard second-order initialization method is also given below.

(ii) The contact line advection problem with a prescribed velocity field is solved with either the Boundary Youngs or Boundary ELVIRA method (see Chapter 8). Note that the approximation of the mean curvature is *not* part of the advection algorithm which only uses information about the local interface orientation (see Section 7.2).

(iii) The contact line position, the contact angle and the curvature at the contact line are estimated in a post-processing step using the height function method.

(iv) The results are compared with either analytical or numerical solutions of the kinematic transport equation for the contact line position, the contact angle and the curvature derived in Chapter 4.

Finite Differences Schemes: In order to estimate the contact line position, the contact angle and the curvature at the contact line from the discrete heights H_i, we need appropriate finite differences schemes. A (up to) four-point stencil at the boundary (see Fig. 10.2) allows to construct finite difference formulas of first-, second- and third-order. We follow the approach by [EDvW20] which computes a fit polynomial of order N to reproduce the $N+1$ discrete heights in the stencil. The estimates for f, f', f'' are obtained from the respective values of the fit polynomial. The resulting formulas are:

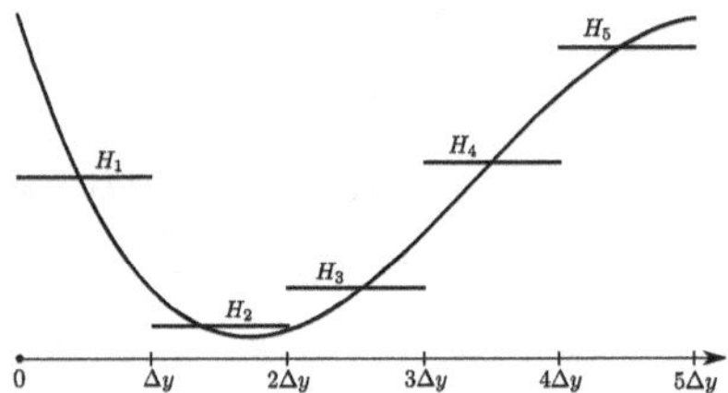

Figure 10.2.: Stencil used to approximate f, f' and f'' at the boundary coordinate $y = 0$.

N=2 (first-order approximation):

$$f(0) \approx \frac{11H_1 - 7H_2 + 2H_3}{6},$$

$$f'(0) \approx \frac{-2H_1 + 3H_2 - H_3}{\Delta y},$$

$$f''(0) \approx \frac{H_1 - 2H_2 + H_3}{(\Delta y)^2} \tag{10.12}$$

N=3 (second-order approximation):

$$f(0) \approx \frac{25H_1 - 23H_2 + 13H_3 - 3H_4}{12},$$

$$f'(0) \approx \frac{-35H_1 + 69H_2 - 45H_3 + 11H_4}{12\Delta y},$$

$$f''(0) \approx \frac{5H_1 - 13H_2 + 11H_3 - 3H_4}{(2\Delta y)^2} \tag{10.13}$$

N=4 (fourth-order approximation):

$$f(0) \approx \frac{137H_1 - 163H_2 + 137H_3 - 63H_4 + 12H_5}{60},$$

$$f'(0) \approx -\frac{45H_1 - 109H_2 + 105H_3 - 51H_4 + 10H_5}{12\Delta y},$$

$$f''(0) \approx \frac{17H_1 - 54H_2 + 64H_3 - 34H_4 + 7H_5}{4(\Delta y)^2} \tag{10.14}$$

The initial error in the contact angle and the curvature at the contact line resulting from the discretizations (10.12)-(10.14) are reported in Fig. (10.3). Indeed, a first-, second- and third-order convergence after initialization is reached for the curvature with the formulas (10.12), (10.13) and (10.14), respectively. The observed order of convergence for the contact angle is even one rank higher for each discretization. The initial error for the level set discretization converges with second-order for both the curvature and the contact angle. Note that the absolute error for the level set method is about two orders of magnitude smaller than for the second-order height function discretization.

Remark 10.5 (Initial data). In order to study the numerical curvature transport, it is important to provide highly accurate initial data for the volume fraction field. Otherwise, the discrete approximation of the curvature does not even converge for the initial shape. Instead, the initial error behaves like $\mathscr{O}(1)$ on fine grids for a second-order initialization method; see Fig. 10.4. In the present work, we employ the fourth-order initialization method for the volume fraction developed by Kromer and Bothe in [KB19].

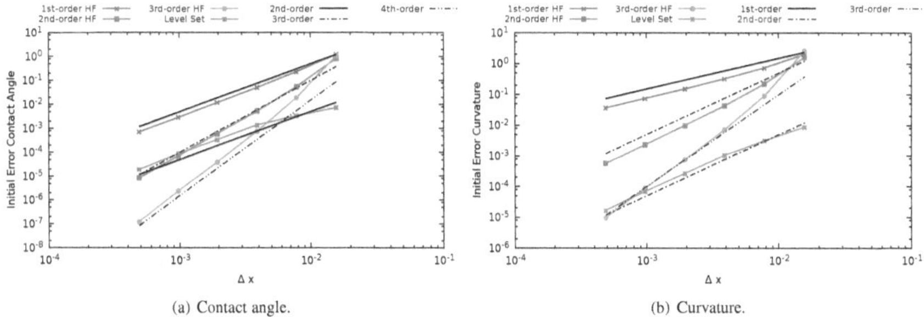

(a) Contact angle.

(b) Curvature.

Figure 10.3.: Initial errors for the contact angle and the curvature - VOF and Level Set.

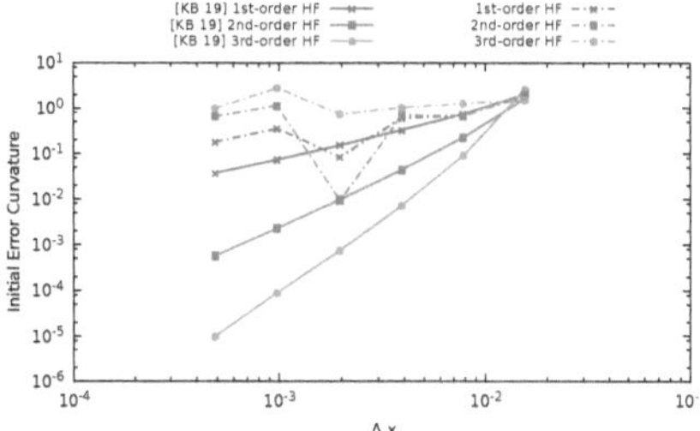

Figure 10.4.: Initial curvature error. Higher-order [KB19] vs. standard second-order initialization.

10.2.1. Linear velocity field

We consider the type of velocity field defined in Example 10.2 with $v_0 = -0.02$, $c_1 = 0.1$ and $c_2 = 0$, i.e.

$$v(x,x) = (-0.02 + 0.1x, -0.1y).\tag{10.15}$$

The results for a fixed Courant number CFL $= 0.2$ and a simulation time $T = 0.4$ are reported in Figures 10.5-10.9.

Results Boundary Youngs: The numerical results for the transport of the contact point and the contact angle based on a local height function representation are shown in Fig. 10.5. It is found that the maximum error for the contact point motion converges with second-order on coarse grids but drops to first-order on finer grids. Moreover, the maximum error in the contact angle transport behaves like $\mathcal{O}(1)$ on fine grids for all considered height function discretizations. This is to be expected since the transport error for the Boundary Youngs method behaves like $\delta \propto \Delta x$ (see Fig. 8.6) and, hence, the first-order error amplification leads to a constant error on fine grids. However, the contact angle reconstructed from a local height function representation is more robust and more accurate than the contact angle determined by the PLIC reconstruction; see Fig. 10.6(a) for a direct comparison. As expected, comparing the results for the first-order height function discretization in Fig. 10.5(a) with the second-order height function discretization in Fig. 10.5(b) shows that the evolution of the contact angle is more oscillatory for the second-order discretization.

The numerical results for the curvature transport with the Boundary Youngs method are reported in Fig. 10.7. As expected from the theoretical considerations in Chapter 9, the maximum error in the curvature transport is first-order *divergent* on fine grids for the Boundary Youngs method; see Fig. 10.7(c). Hence, the discrete error

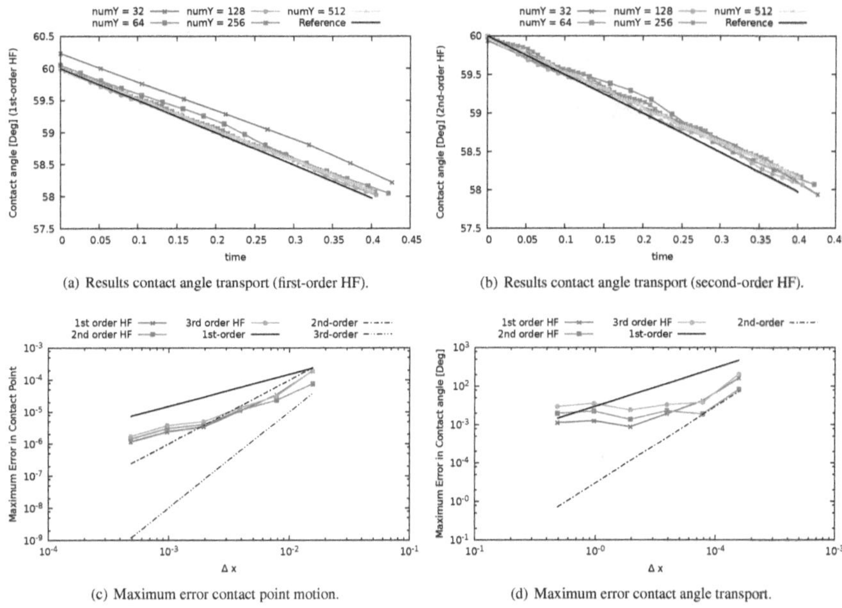

(a) Results contact angle transport (first-order HF).

(b) Results contact angle transport (second-order HF).

(c) Maximum error contact point motion.

(d) Maximum error contact angle transport.

Figure 10.5.: Numerical transport of the contact point and contact angle for the field (10.15) with Boundary Youngs.

amplification is dominant in this case. The temporal evolution of the error for the first-order height function discretization is shown in detail in Fig. 10.7(d). Obviously, the finest grid (numY=512) gives the worst results, even though the initial error is minimal on the finest grid. Note that Fig. 10.7(d) reports *all* computational steps in the simulation. A close inspection shows that it only takes four transport steps for the error on the finest grid to reach the error of the coarser grids numY = 256 and numY = 128. Moreover, it is observed that the first-order discretization (10.12) leads to the smallest error in the diverging region, followed by the second- and third-order discretizations (10.13) and (10.14). In fact, the relative magnitude of the errors in the diverging region can be roughly estimated by the (worst-case) error amplification of the discretizations for the second derivative, i.e.

$$f''(0) \approx \frac{H_1 - 2H_2 + H_3}{(\Delta x)^2} \quad \Rightarrow \quad \mathscr{A} \propto \frac{1+2+1}{(\Delta x)^2} = \frac{4}{(\Delta x)^2}, \tag{10.16}$$

$$f''(0) \approx \frac{5H_1 - 13H_2 + 11H_3 - 3H_4}{(2\Delta x)^2} \quad \Rightarrow \quad \mathscr{A} \propto \frac{5+13+11+3}{(4\Delta x)^2} = \frac{8}{(\Delta x)^2}, \tag{10.17}$$

$$f''(0) \approx \frac{17H_1 - 54H_2 + 64H_3 - 34H_4 + 7H_5}{4(\Delta x)^2} \quad \Rightarrow \quad \mathscr{A} \propto \frac{44}{(\Delta x)^2}. \tag{10.18}$$

In summary, the observed convergence rates for the Boundary Youngs methods for the contact line motion, contact angle and curvature transport match the expected rates (10.4) that are due to the numerical amplification of the transport error.

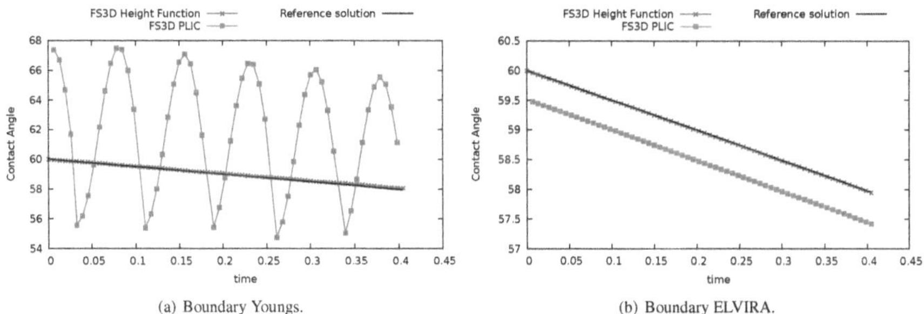

(a) Boundary Youngs.

(b) Boundary ELVIRA.

Figure 10.6.: Contact angle determined from PLIC and from a local height function (numY = 256).

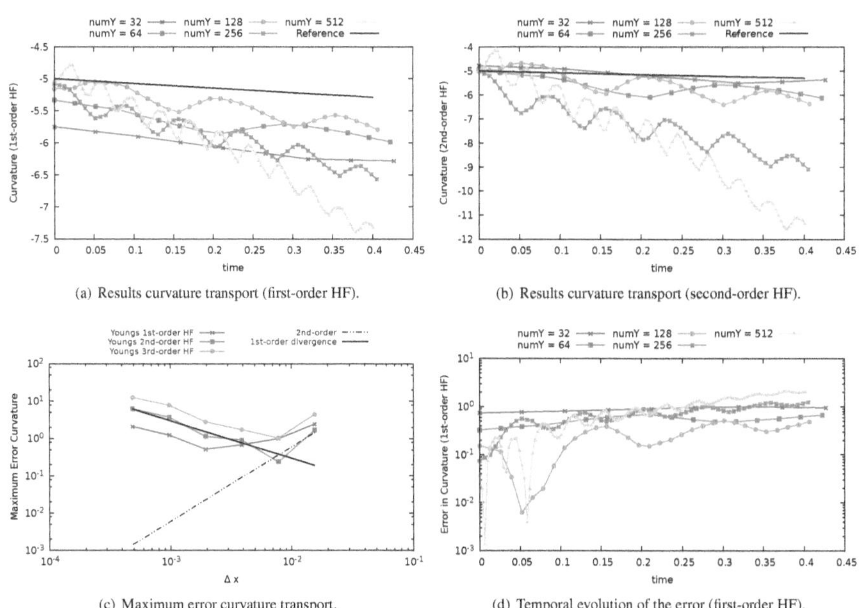

(a) Results curvature transport (first-order HF).

(b) Results curvature transport (second-order HF).

(c) Maximum error curvature transport.

(d) Temporal evolution of the error (first-order HF).

Figure 10.7.: Numerical transport of the curvature for the field (10.15) with Boundary Youngs.

Results Boundary ELVIRA: The results for the contact point and contact angle transport for the Boundary ELVIRA method are reported in Fig. 10.8. In fact, the observed order of convergence for the motion of the contact point is close to three and second-order convergence is found for the contact angle transport for each of the height function methods to evaluate the contact angle.

The numerical curvature transport with Boundary ELVIRA is shown in Fig. 10.9. For any of the considered discretization schemes (10.12)-(10.14), we observe a first-order convergence of the curvature transport. The lowest errors in the maximum norm are found for the second-order discretization (10.13) while the third-order discretization (10.14) gives errors comparable to those of the first-order discretization on fine grids. This effect can be attributed to an increased discrete error amplification. In fact, a direct comparison of the first-order discretization in Fig. 10.9(a) with the second-order discretization in Fig. 10.9(b) shows that the first-order discretization gives more stable results with fewer oscillations even though the maximum error (for the considered simulation time) is larger. Note that the expected $\mathscr{O}(1)$-behavior of the error for the Boundary ELVIRA is not observed for the chosen set of parameters (in particular for the chosen simulation time). In fact, the observed convergence rates for the contact point motion, the contact angle and the curvature transport are one rank higher than expected in the limit $\Delta x \to 0$; see Eq. 10.5. From this, we conclude that the discrete error amplification is not the dominant contribution to the overall error for the considered set of parameters. In summary, the results clearly show the superiority of the Boundary ELVIRA method over the Boundary Youngs method in the numerical curvature transport which leads to a more accurate estimate of surface tension forces.

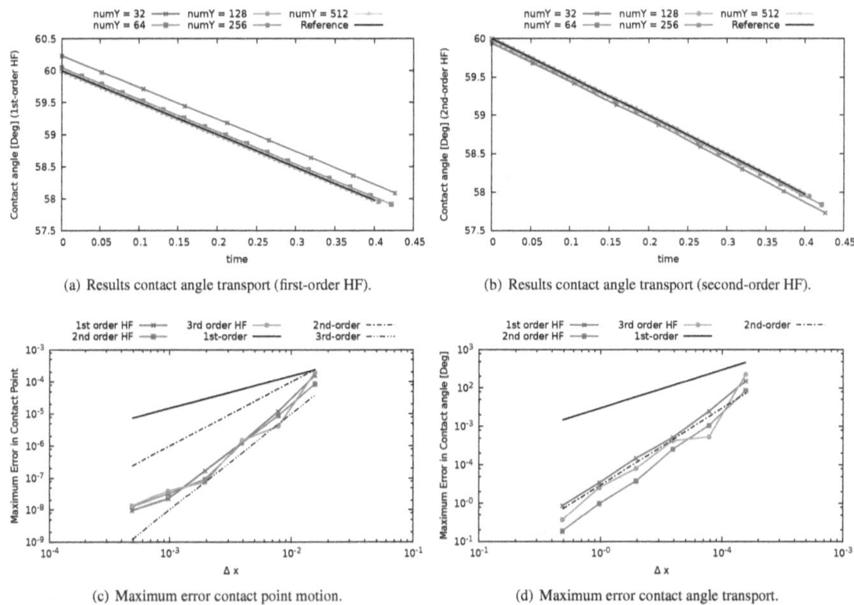

(a) Results contact angle transport (first-order HF).

(b) Results contact angle transport (second-order HF).

(c) Maximum error contact point motion.

(d) Maximum error contact angle transport.

Figure 10.8.: Numerical transport of the contact point and contact angle for the field (10.15) with Boundary ELVIRA.

Remark 10.6 (Influence of the simulation time). It is important to note that the observed convergence behavior of the numerical curvature transport depends on the simulation time ($T = 0.4$ in the above examples). This reflects

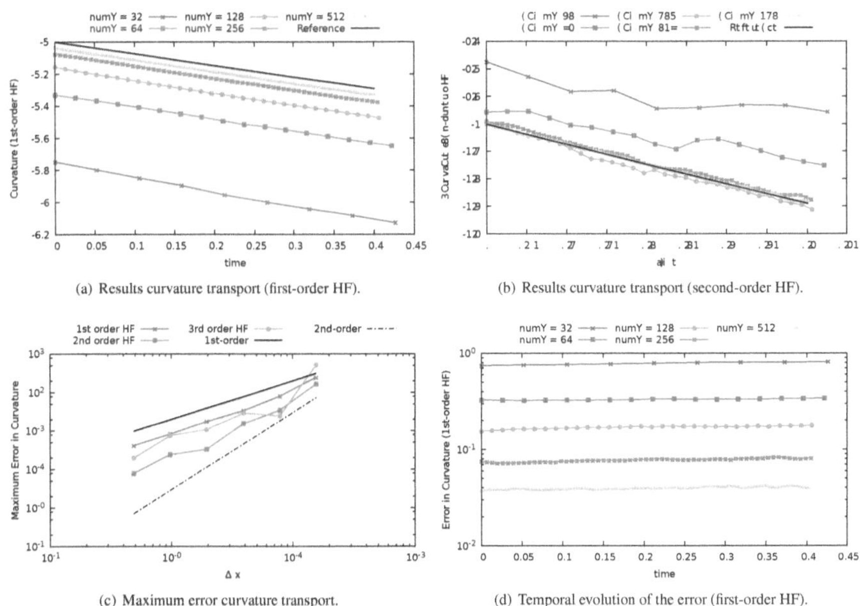

(a) Results curvature transport (first-order HF).

(b) Results curvature transport (second-order HF).

(c) Maximum error curvature transport.

(d) Temporal evolution of the error (first-order HF).

Figure 10.9.: Numerical transport of the curvature for the field (10.15) with Boundary ELVIRA.

the fact that the constant C in the advection error

$$\delta \propto C(\Delta x)^m$$

is an increasing function of the simulation time T. Hence we expect for larger values of T, that the transition from a dominant approximation error to a dominant error amplification happens on coarser meshes, i.e. for larger values of Δx. Figure 10.10 shows a comparison of the maximum error in the curvature transport for simulation times $T = 0.4$, $T = 1.2$ and $T = 2.4$. As expected, the local minimum of the error for Boundary Youngs shifts towards coarser grids for longer simulation times. In contrast to that, there is only a minor difference in the error for the Boundary ELVIRA method.

10.2.2. Time-dependent linear velocity field

We finally consider a time-dependent variant of the linear velocity field (10.15) given as

$$v(t,x_1,x_2) = \cos\left(\frac{\pi t}{0.2}\right)(-0.02 + 0.1x, -0.1y). \tag{10.19}$$

Analytical reference solutions for the contact point and the contact angle evolution are available in this case; see Example 10.4. To obtain a reference for the curvature evolution, we solve the ordinary differential equation (10.11) numerically. This example can be expected to be more challenging for a numerical method than (10.15) since the geometric quantities are changing more rapidly (in fact periodically) in time. Indeed, the results reported in Fig. 10.11 show that the maximum error in the curvature transport for the Boundary ELVIRA behaves like $\mathcal{O}(1)$ on fine grids; see Fig. 10.11(d). Moreover, it is found that the convergence rate for the numerical transport of the contact angle drops from second- to first-order on fine grids; see Fig. 10.11(b). Hence, in this case the numerical

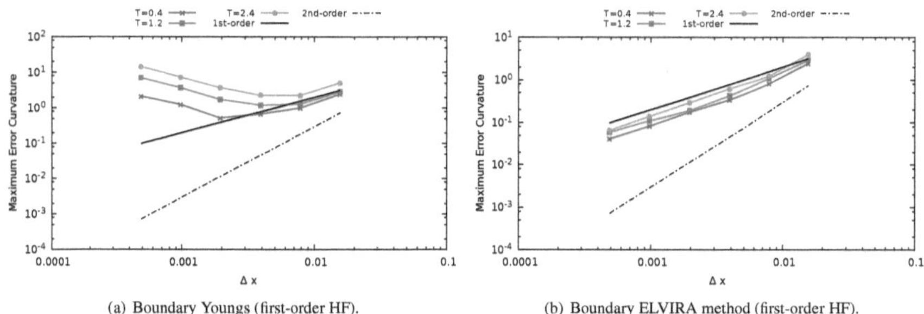

(a) Boundary Youngs (first-order HF).   (b) Boundary ELVIRA method (first-order HF).

Figure 10.10.: Maximum error curvature transport $T \in \{0.4, 1.2, 2.4\}$.

error amplification becomes dominant on fine grids and the expected asymptotic convergence rates (10.5) are observed.

Numerical curvature transport - VOF vs. Level Set: The numerical curvature transport for the field (10.19) with Boundary ELVIRA and the simple level set method described in Section 6.2 is compared in Figure 10.12. While the observed order of convergence is similar for the first-order height function evaluation of the curvature and the level set method, the absolute error is approximately three orders of magnitude larger for the VOF method. For the first-order height function discretization, this huge difference in absolute accuracy is present already for the initialized shape (see also Fig. 10.3). Even though the third-order height function method (10.14) employed to evaluate the curvature delivers comparable errors to the level set method after initialization, the error for the curvature transport is much larger since the error-amplification is increased by orders of magnitude compared to the first-order method (10.12).

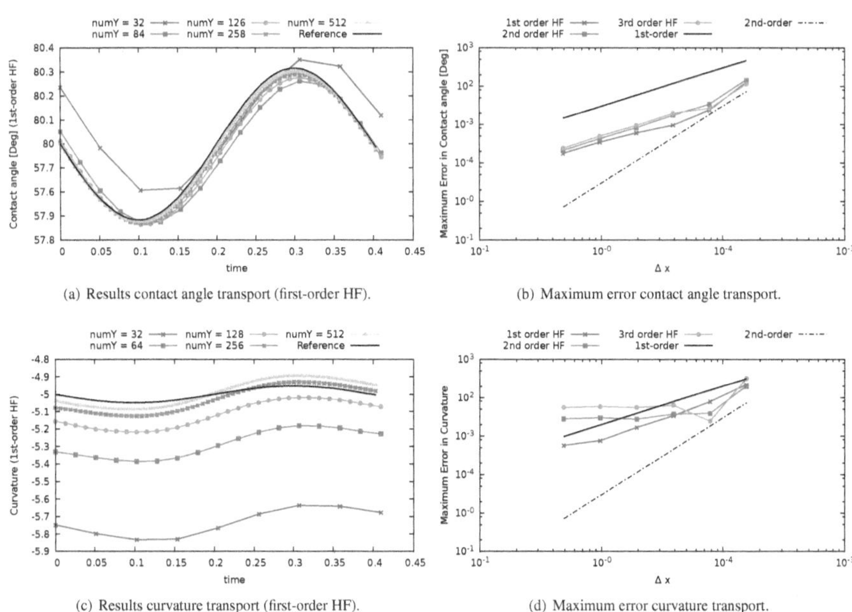

(a) Results contact angle transport (first-order HF).

(b) Maximum error contact angle transport.

(c) Results curvature transport (first-order HF).

(d) Maximum error curvature transport.

Figure 10.11.: Numerical transport of the contact angle and the curvature for the field (10.19) with Boundary ELVIRA.

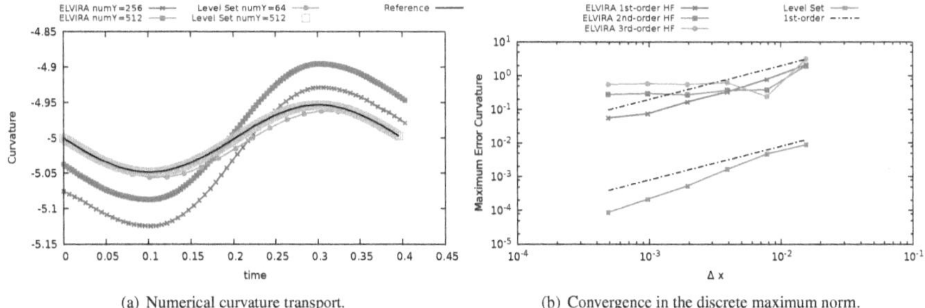

(a) Numerical curvature transport.

(b) Convergence in the discrete maximum norm.

Figure 10.12.: Direct comparison Boundary ELVIRA vs. Level Set.

Part III.

Applications

11. The capillary rise problem

The capillary rise is a prototypical example of the statics and dynamics of wetting. The surprising phenomenon of liquid rising in a narrow tube against gravity attracted the attention of scientists already more than 500 years ago. Following the monograph [dGBWQ04, p.49], which provides an interesting note about the historical background of the capillary rise problem, Leonardo da Vinci (1452-1512) was the first to observe and report on the phenomenon. His work was continued by Hauksbee, Taylor, Jurin and others leading to the well-known formula known as "Jurin's height"

$$H = \frac{2\sigma \cos\theta}{\rho g R} \tag{11.1}$$

for the equilibrium rise height of a liquid column in a cylindrical capillary of radius R; see Fig. 11.1 for a sketch of the problem. It is important to note that formula (11.1) is derived under the assumption that the radius R is small compared to the capillary length

$$l_c = \sqrt{\sigma/\rho g}. \tag{11.2}$$

In fact, equation (11.1) is valid only in the limit

$$\frac{R}{l_c} = \sqrt{\frac{\rho g R^2}{\sigma}} = \sqrt{\mathrm{Bo}} \rightarrow 0.$$

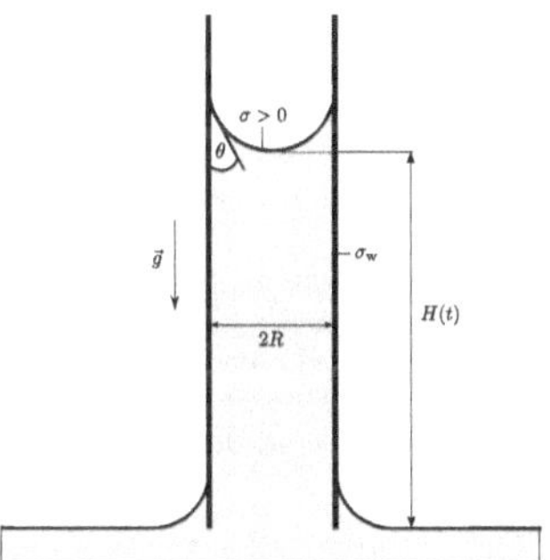

Figure 11.1.: Sketch of the capillary rise problem.

We briefly revisit the derivation of (11.1) and its two-dimensional counterpart in Section 11.1 before we discuss the dynamics of the capillary rise, which is the main focus of the present chapter. The dynamics of capillary rise has been investigated quantitatively almost 100 years ago by Lucas [Luc18], Washburn [Was21], Ridael [Rid22] and Bosanquet [Bos23]. Washburn derived an ODE model based on a simplified integral force balance considering inertial, viscous, gravitational and capillary forces. The resulting equation for the rise height in a horizontal capillary [Was21, p.280] reads as

$$\frac{dH}{dt} = \frac{R}{\eta}\frac{\sigma}{4H}\cos\theta \tag{11.3}$$

and is known in the literature as the "Lucas-Washburn equation". The solution $H(t) \propto \sqrt{t}$ of (11.3), which also describes the early rise dynamics in vertical capillaries, has been verified experimentally but it does not provide enough information to validate numerical methods for the full continuum mechanical problem. Obviously, equation (11.3) does not even predict a finite stationary rise height. Bosanquet [Bos23] improved the Washburn model by adding an additional term for inertia and obtained a finite stationary height. But also the prediction of this improved model does not agree with continuum mechanical simulations [Grü20a, Grü20b].

The latter observation by Gründing motivated the comparative study of the transient capillary using four numerical methods developed in CRC 1194 (including FS3D) [GSA$^+$20a, GSA$^+$20b]; see Sections 11.2 and 11.3 below[1]. Moreover, Gründing proposed an extended ODE model for the capillary rise [Grü20a] which takes into account slip at the solid-liquid boundary as well as the viscous dissipation in the contact line region. As a result, the agreement with the continuum mechanical simulations is substantially improved compared to the classical ODE model [Bos23].

11.1. Static capillary rise

The stationary state of the liquid column can be found by minimizing the energy functional

$$\mathscr{E} = \mathscr{E}_w + \mathscr{E}_g + \mathscr{E}_\Sigma. \tag{11.4}$$

Here $\mathscr{E}_w$ denotes the interfacial energy due to wetting given by an integral over the solid-liquid interface according to

$$\mathscr{E}_w = \int_{\Sigma_{sl}} \sigma_w \, dA \tag{11.5}$$

and

$$\mathscr{E}_\Sigma = \int_{\Sigma_{sg}} \sigma \, dA = \sigma \, |\Sigma_{sg}| \tag{11.6}$$

is the interfacial energy due to the presence of the liquid-gas interface for constant σ. The gravitational energy is denoted by $\mathscr{E}_g$. Note that the minimization of (11.4) is carried out over the liquid portion located *within* the capillary tube. The liquid bath surrounding the capillary is assumed to be infinitely large so that, essentially, the problem can be simplified by assuming the energy of the liquid pool to be constant. An important consequence of this approach is that conservation of mass is no longer assumed for the considered subsystem.[2]

In the classical derivation of the stationary rise height, the problem is simplified by ignoring the details of the liquid-gas interface shape leading to an approximation $\tilde{\mathscr{E}}$ of the energy functional defined in (11.4) in terms of the rise height as the only variable. The latter can be assumed to be a good approximation if the rise height is large compared to the radius of the capillary. In this case, the gravitational energy $\mathscr{E}_g$ and the wetting energy $\mathscr{E}_w$ are the dominant contributions to the energy functional. For a cylindrical capillary in three dimensions, the approximation reads as

$$\tilde{\mathscr{E}}(H) = 2\pi R H \, \sigma_w + \frac{\pi}{2} \rho g R^2 H^2 + \pi R^2 \sigma. \tag{11.7}$$

In particular, the interfacial energy $\mathscr{E}_\Sigma$ is assumed to be constant in this simplified model. Then, the stationarity condition $\tilde{\mathscr{E}}' = 0$ implies

$$H = -\frac{2\,\sigma_w}{\rho g R}.$$

Now eq. (11.1) directly follows if the Young–Dupré equation is substituted. In the two-dimensional situation, which corresponds to the wetting of two infinitely long parallel plates in three dimensions, the simplified energy functional reads as

$$\tilde{\mathscr{E}}(H) = 2H\,\sigma_w + \rho g R H^2 + R\sigma. \tag{11.8}$$

---

[1]Please not that the Sections 11.2 and 11.3 are a short summary of the results published in [GSA$^+$20a].

[2]This is an important difference to the variational derivation of the stationary state of a sessile drop in Section 1.3.

In this case, the stationarity condition $\tilde{\mathscr{E}}' = 0$ implies

$$H = -\frac{\sigma_{\mathrm{w}}}{\rho g R} = \frac{\sigma \cos\theta}{\rho g R}.$$
(11.9)

Non-dimensional formulation: It is convenient to rewrite eq. (11.7) to arrive at a dimensionless form of the functional, i.e.

$$\begin{aligned}
\tilde{\mathscr{E}} &= \pi R^2 \sigma \left(2\frac{H}{R}\frac{\sigma_{\mathrm{w}}}{\sigma} + \frac{\rho g R^2}{2\sigma}\left(\frac{H}{R}\right)^2 + 1 \right)\\
&= \pi R^2 \sigma \left(2\tilde{H}\tilde{\sigma}_{\mathrm{w}} + \frac{\mathrm{Bo}\,\tilde{H}^2}{2} + 1 \right).
\end{aligned}$$
(11.10)

Here $\tilde{H} = H/R$ is the dimensionless rise height, $\tilde{\sigma}_{\mathrm{w}} = \sigma_{\mathrm{w}}/\sigma$ is the dimensionless wetting energy satisfying the dimensionless form of the Young–Dupré equation

$$\cos\theta + \tilde{\sigma}_{\mathrm{w}} = 0.$$
(11.11)

Hence, the dimensionless form of equation (11.1) reads as

$$\tilde{H} = -\frac{2\tilde{\sigma}_{\mathrm{w}}}{\mathrm{Bo}} = \frac{2\cos\theta}{\mathrm{Bo}}.$$
(11.12)

In the two-dimensional case, the simplified functional reads as

$$\tilde{\mathscr{E}} = R\sigma \left(2\tilde{H}\tilde{\sigma}_{\mathrm{w}} + \mathrm{Bo}\,\tilde{H}^2 + 1 \right)$$
(11.13)

leading to the equilibrium rise height

$$\tilde{H} = -\frac{\tilde{\sigma}_{\mathrm{w}}}{\mathrm{Bo}} = \frac{\cos\theta}{\mathrm{Bo}}.$$
(11.14)

Improved stationary rise height estimate: It turns out that the approximations made in the derivation of (11.1) and (11.9) lead to systematic error which is clearly visible in the numerical simulations and which should also be measurable in an experiment. The main simplification is that the details of the interface shape are ignored approximating Σ as a flat interface in the simplified energy functionals (11.7) and (11.8). It is known that for small Bond numbers, the interface can be well approximated by a spherical section [Con68]. Hence, an improved description can be achieved by introducing an additional degree of freedom and minimizing the energy over liquid columns with a spherical interface. Note that this is also an approximation since the true liquid-gas interface must have a non-constant curvature (see [GFB19]).

The problem can be simplified further by assuming that the interface is a spherical cap with a contact angle determined by the Young-Dupré equation. Then the additional mass in the interface region can be computed and a correction to the rise height is obtained. The correction derived in [Grü20b] for the two-dimensional case reads as

$$H = \frac{\sigma \cos\theta}{\rho g R} - \Delta H \quad \text{with} \quad \Delta H = \frac{R}{2\cos\theta}\left(2 - \sin\theta - \frac{\arcsin\cos\theta}{\cos\theta} \right) > 0.$$
(11.15)

See also [LLL18], where a similar correction term is found.

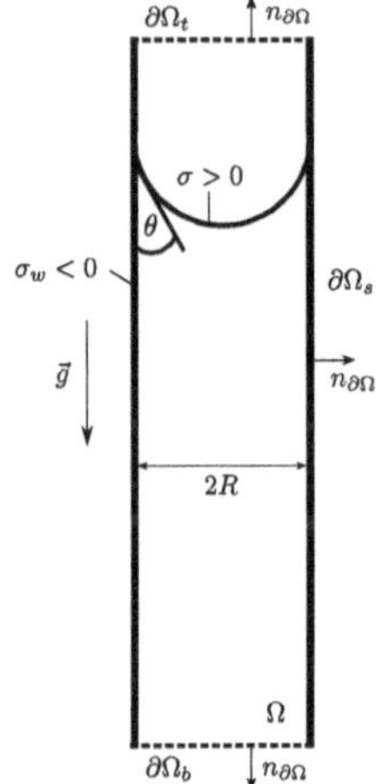

Figure 11.2.: Computational domain for the continuum mechanical model.

11.2. Continuum mechanical model

11.2.1. Governing equations and boundary conditions

We consider the standard model (3.22) with a constant slip length and a fixed contact angle, i.e.

$$\begin{aligned}
\rho\frac{Dv}{Dt} - \eta\Delta v + \nabla p &= 0, \ \nabla\cdot v = 0 &&\text{in } \Omega\setminus\Sigma(t),\\
[\![v]\!] &= 0, \quad [\![p\mathbb{1} - 2\eta D]\!]\,n_\Sigma = \sigma\kappa n_\Sigma &&\text{on } \Sigma(t),\\
\langle v, n_{\partial\Omega}\rangle &= 0, \ v_{\parallel} + 2L(Dn_{\partial\Omega})_{\parallel} = 0 &&\text{on } \partial\Omega_s\setminus\Gamma(t),\\
V_\Sigma &= \langle v, n_\Sigma\rangle &&\text{on } \Sigma(t),\\
V_\Gamma = \langle v, n_\Gamma\rangle, \quad \langle n_\Sigma, n_{\partial\Omega}\rangle &= -\cos\theta &&\text{on } \Gamma(t),
\end{aligned}$$

(11.16)

to model the dynamic capillary rise problem. In order to simplify the computational setup, we only solve for the flow inside the capillary and prescribe effective boundary conditions at the (artificial) in- and outflow boundaries $\partial\Omega_b$ and $\partial\Omega_t$ (see Fig. 11.2). Neglecting the hydrostatic pressure in the gas phase, we force the pressure to be equal at the top and bottom boundaries, i.e.

$$p = 0 \quad \text{at } \partial\Omega_t\cup\partial\Omega_b. \tag{11.17}$$

In order to allow the liquid to flow across the top and bottom boundaries, we set[3]

$$\langle(\nabla v)n_{\partial\Omega}, n_{\partial\Omega}\rangle = 0 \quad \text{at } \partial\Omega_t\cup\partial\Omega_b, \tag{11.18}$$

where $n_{\partial\Omega}$ is the unit outer normal field to

$$\partial\Omega = \partial\Omega_s\cup\partial\Omega_t\cup\partial\Omega_b.$$

---

[3]In general, the definition of appropriate inflow and outflow boundary conditions at artificial boundaries is a non-trivial subject [SG94,HRT96]. However, in the present case, the choice of the velocity boundary conditions at the artificial boundaries showed only little influence on the results since the flow profile is essentially a Poiseuille Flow (see, e.g., [Grü20b, p.70]).

Moreover, to specify the type of fluid entering at the top and bottom boundaries, we require

$$\frac{\partial \chi}{\partial n_{\partial \Omega}} = 0 \quad \text{at } \partial \Omega_t \cup \partial \Omega_b. \tag{11.19}$$

11.2.2. Choice of physical parameters

Motivated by the work by Fries and Dryer [FD09], who carried out a dimensional analysis of the ODE model [Bos23], we choose a set of physical parameters (see Table 11.1) to vary the non-dimensional group

$$\Omega = \sqrt{\frac{9 \sigma \cos \theta \eta^2}{\rho^3 g^2 R^5}} = 3\sqrt{\cos \theta}\, \frac{\text{Oh}}{\text{Bo}}, \tag{11.20}$$

where Bo and Oh denote the Bond and Ohnesorge number defined as

$$\text{Bo} = \frac{\rho g R^2}{\sigma} \quad \text{and} \quad \text{Oh} = \frac{\eta}{\sqrt{\sigma \rho R}},$$

in the range of $\Omega = 0.1, 0.5, 1, 10, 100$. Owing to the increasing influence of viscosity, varying Ω leads to different rise regimes ranging from a highly oscillatory (small Ω) to a purely monotone rise to the stationary rise height (large Ω). Note that

$$\Omega_c = 2 \tag{11.21}$$

has been shown to be the critical damping for the classical ODE model [Bos23] (see [QRO99, Grü20b, GSA$^+$20a]). It is important to note that the parameter Ω, which has been introduced for the three-dimensional case by Quéré et. al [QRO99], does not take into account the slip length. In fact, the slip length shows a strong impact on the rise dynamics in the full continuum mechanical model. We show below that the slip length does also affect the critical value Ω_c for the occurrence of oscillations in the dynamic rise.

In order to simplify the setup for the parameter study, we fix the contact angle to be $\theta = 30°$ for all cases. Moreover, the radius and the height of the capillary are fixed and the parameters are chosen such that the Jurins height is fixed as four times the radius, i.e.

$$\frac{R \cos \theta}{\text{Bo}} = 4R \quad \Leftrightarrow \quad \text{Bo} = \frac{\cos(\pi/6)}{4} \approx 0.217.$$

We choose an initial rise height $h_0 = 2R$ for all cases. The height of the complete computational domain is chosen to be $8R$ which is sufficient to capture any rise height oscillations. The density and viscosity in the gas phase is chosen small enough, i.e.

$$\frac{\rho}{\rho_g} = 1000 \quad \text{and} \quad \frac{\eta}{\eta_g} = 1000,$$

to make sure that the influence of the gas phase is negligible. This is necessary since we aim at a direct comparison with a free surface formulation of the problem, see below. The physical parameters used for the study of the dynamics in Section 11.3 and [GSA$^+$20a] are summarized in Table 11.1. The reported $\text{Ca}_{\max}$ is the maximum observed value for the capillary number. Note that the test cases serve the purpose of a *numerical* benchmark and do not necessarily correspond to the physical parameters of some real fluid-solid system in the lab. In particular, we chose the slip length *macroscopically* large such that it can be easily resolved by the computational mesh. Even though this choice is physically unrealistic, it still allows to establish a numerical reference or "numerical benchmark" which contains the wetting as a driving force.

Table 11.1.: Physical parameters for the Ω-study.

Ω	R	ρ	η	g	σ	θ_e	Ca_{max}	Eo
-	m	$\mathrm{kg\,m^{-3}}$	$\mathrm{Pa\,s}$	$\mathrm{m\,s^{-2}}$	$\mathrm{N\,m^{-1}}$	$\circ$	-	-
0.1	0.005	1663.8	0.01	1.04	0.2	30	0.003	0.217
0.5	0.005	133.0	0.01	6.51	0.1	30	0.015	0.217
1	0.005	83.1	0.01	4.17	0.04	30	0.029	0.217
10	0.005	3.3255	0.01	26.042	0.01	30	0.106	0.217
100	0.005	0.33255	0.01	26.042	0.001	30	0.110	0.217

Viscous vs. capillary timestep limit: To estimate the computational costs, we consider the numerical timestep limits already discussed in Section 7.1. The timestep limit due to surface tension is given by $(\Delta t)_\sigma = \sqrt{\rho(\Delta x)^3/(4\pi\sigma)}$. Here Δx denotes the mesh size which is assumed to be constant for the purpose of estimating the computational costs. Since the viscous terms are explicitly discretized in FS3D, there is also a viscous timestep limit for the latter method given by $(\Delta t)_\eta = \rho(\Delta x)^2/(6\eta)$. In order to identify which one is the limiting value for a given set of parameters, we take the ratio of the two quantities yielding

$$\frac{(\Delta t)_\sigma}{(\Delta t)_\eta} = \frac{3}{\sqrt{\pi}} \frac{\eta}{\sqrt{\sigma\rho R}} \left(\frac{R}{\Delta x}\right)^{1/2} = \frac{3}{\sqrt{\pi}} \mathrm{Oh}\, N_{cells}^{\frac{1}{2}}, \tag{11.22}$$

where $N_{cells} = R/\Delta x$ is the number of computational cells per radius. Hence, the two timestep limits are equal for

$$N_{cells}^* = \frac{\pi}{9\,\mathrm{Oh}^2} = \frac{\pi\cos\theta}{\Omega^2 Eo^2}.$$

The capillary timestep limit $(\Delta x)_\sigma$ is dominant for $N_{cells} \leq N_{cells}^*$, while the viscous timestep limit $(\Delta x)_\eta$ is dominant for $N_{cells} \geq N_{cells}^*$. Hence the viscous timestep limit dominates over the capillary timestep limit for large Ω.

Estimated number of timesteps: The necessary number of timesteps due to surface tension and viscosity is given by

$$N_{steps}^\sigma = \frac{T}{(\Delta t)_\sigma} = T\sqrt{\frac{4\pi\sigma}{\rho_l R^3}} N_{cells}^{3/2} \quad \text{and} \quad N_{steps}^\eta = \frac{T}{(\Delta t)_\eta} = T\frac{6\eta_l}{\rho_l R^2} N_{cells}^2,$$

respectively. Here T denotes the physical time to be simulated. The values for T are roughly estimated from Figure 11.6 in Section 11.3 to obtain an estimate for the number of timesteps, see Table 11.2. Note that the number of timesteps for FS3D is limited by the viscous timestep limit for $\Omega = 10$ and $\Omega = 100$. In particular, the latter case requires more than 10^8 timesteps if 32 cells per radius are used. Since this would lead to impractical computational costs, we used a coarser grid with 12 cells per radius for $\Omega = 100$ (reducing the number of timesteps by a factor of 7). Note the viscous timestep limit can be avoided by an implicit discretization of the viscous terms. The latter approach is not available in the current version of FS3D but will be subject of future work.

Table 11.2.: An estimate of the number of timesteps for $N_{cells} = 32$ and the physical parameters defined in Table 11.1.

Ω	N_{cells}^*	T [s]	N_{steps}^σ	N_{steps}^η
0.1	5804	10	$1.99\cdot10^5$	$1.48\cdot10^4$
0.5	232	1	$4.98\cdot10^4$	$1.85\cdot10^4$
1	58	0.5	$1.99\cdot10^4$	$1.48\cdot10^4$
10	0.58	2	$1.99\cdot10^5$	$\mathbf{1.48\cdot10^6}$
100	0.006	20	$1.99\cdot10^6$	$\mathbf{1.48\cdot10^8}$

11.3. Dynamics of capillary rise

The goal of the comparative study published in [GSA$^+$20a] and summarized below is to provide a well-founded numerical dataset[4] for the direct numerical simulation of wetting processes using the capillary rise as an example. To achieve this goal, we employ four completely different numerical methods that are currently developed further within CRC 1194 to solve the continuum mechanical problem for the parameters defined in Table 12.1. These methods are

(i) interTrackFoam [TJ12, Grü20b] - an Arbitrary Lagrangian-Eulerian method in OpenFoam,

(ii) FS3D [RF99, Rie04] - the geometrical VOF method developed further in the present work,

(iii) interFoam - an Algebraic VOF method in OpenFoam and

(iv) BoSSS [Kum12, Kum16] - a level-set based extended discontinuous Galerkin (DG) method.

See Section 6.1 for an overview of the different numerical approaches. For details on interFoam, interTrackFoam and BoSSS, we refer to [GSA$^+$20a] and the references given therein.

Numerical methods in FS3D: We employ the FS3D method described in Section 7.1 to solve (11.16)-(11.19). The Navier slip condition is applied according to the expression (7.37) for the velocity in the ghost cells. The height function method described in Section 7.5.2 is employed to enforce the contact angle boundary condition. Youngs method (7.18) is used to reconstruct the interface away from the boundary and the interface orientation at the contact line is prescribed explicitly according to the fixed contact angle condition.

Numerical setup for FS3D: We make use of the mirror symmetry of the problem and simulate only half of the domain on a uniform Cartesian grid with a symmetry plane in the center of the capillary, see Figure 11.3. The symmetry plane is realized as a second solid wall with 90-degree contact angle and free slip for the velocity, i.e. Equation (7.37) with $L \rightarrow \infty$. The volume fraction field is initialized for a spherical interface matching the contact angle boundary condition and a prescribed initial volume. The initial value for the velocity field is zero everywhere in the computational domain. The simulations in this study require between 4 and 192 cells in radial direction yielding 128 to 294912 cells in total.

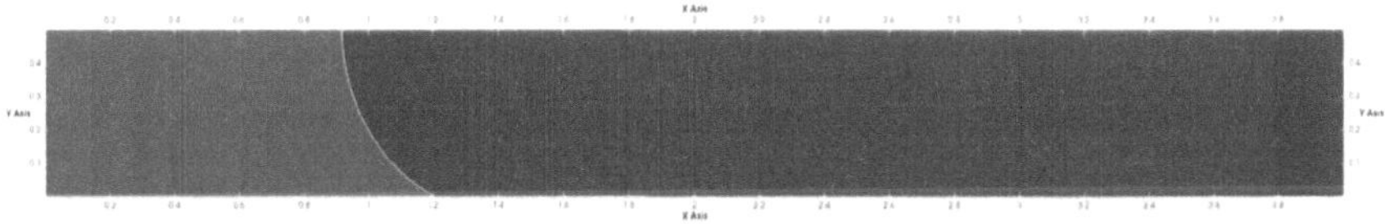

Figure 11.3.: Simulation setup for FS3D. Length in cm (Figure from [GSA$^+$20a]).

11.3.1. Numerical slip vs. Navier slip

Convergence study: The results for the dynamics of the capillary rise are highly dependent on the mesh size if *numerical slip* (7.36) is used, see Figure 11.4(a) for the results for $\Omega = 1$. This is due to the fact that the effective slip length of the method is related to the mesh size. In particular, with increasing mesh resolution the dynamics is increasingly damped. However, the final rise height is reasonably mesh-independent and agrees well with the corrected Jurins Height given by (11.15) even if numerical slip is used. On the other hand, the dynamics of the apex height becomes mesh convergent if the Navier slip condition (7.37) is applied with a macroscopic slip length $L = R/5$, which can be resolved by the computational mesh; see Figure 11.4(b). Similarly to the case of numerical slip, the numerical solution with Navier slip is more dynamic on a coarse mesh, i.e. the oscillation amplitude converges to its limiting value from *above*. This behavior is observed for FS3D with the discrete Navier slip

---

[4]The numerical reference data are available in an open research data repository see [GSA$^+$20b].

condition (7.37) as well as for interFoam and interTrackFoam (see [GSA[+]20a]). The only exception is BoSSS, where the limit is approached from *below* (see Fig. 12 and Fig. 19 in [GSA[+]20a]).

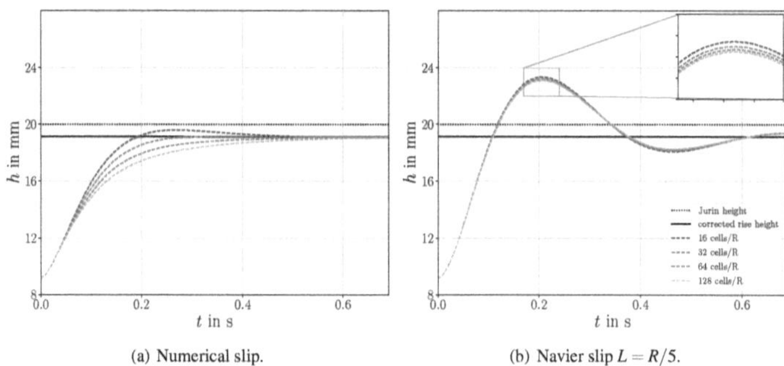

(a) Numerical slip.

(b) Navier slip $L = R/5$.

Figure 11.4.: Mesh study with FS3D using numerical slip and resolved Navier slip (Figure from [GSA[+]20a]).

11.3.2. Rise dynamics in different regimes

The comprehensive study of the rise dynamics in different regimes for the parameter Ω, as discussed in detail in [GSA[+]20a], is summarized in the following.

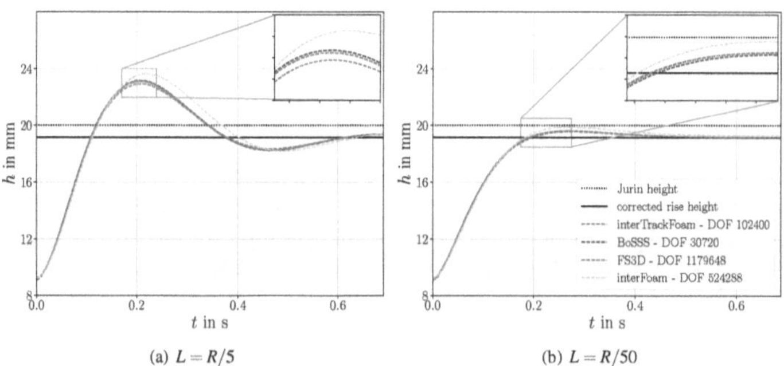

(a) $L = R/5$

(b) $L = R/50$

Figure 11.5.: Comparison of the methods for $\Omega = 1$ with different slip lengths (Figure from [GSA[+]20a]).

Convergence study and variation of the slip length: A comparison between the results of the different methods on a fine mesh for $\Omega = 1$ is shown in Figure 11.5. Strong oscillations in the dynamic rise height are visible for the large slip length $L = R/5$; see Fig. 11.5(a). The agreement between the FS3D, interTrackFoam and BoSSS solutions is very good while interFoam overestimates the maximum rise height. Note that the occurrence of rise height oscillations is consistent with the estimate for the critical Ω in (11.21) since $1 < \Omega_c = 2$. However, the results for the reduced slip length $L = R/50$ in Fig. 11.5(b) show only a small oscillation suggesting that the critical value of Ω depends on the slip length. As before, the agreement between FS3D, interTrackFoam and BoSSS is quite good with some deviations to the interFoam solution.

Ω-study: Different regimes for the capillary rise: An overview of the rise dynamics for different values of
the parameter Ω and a slip length $L = R/5$ is given in Figure 11.6. As expected, the amplitude of the oscillations
decreases with Ω. The rise to the stationary hight is monotone with no oscillations for $\Omega = 10$ and $\Omega = 100$. In
general, there is a very good agreement between the four numerical methods with some deviations for interFoam.
Figure 11.7 provides a mesh study for all cases reported in Figure 11.6 computed with FS3D.

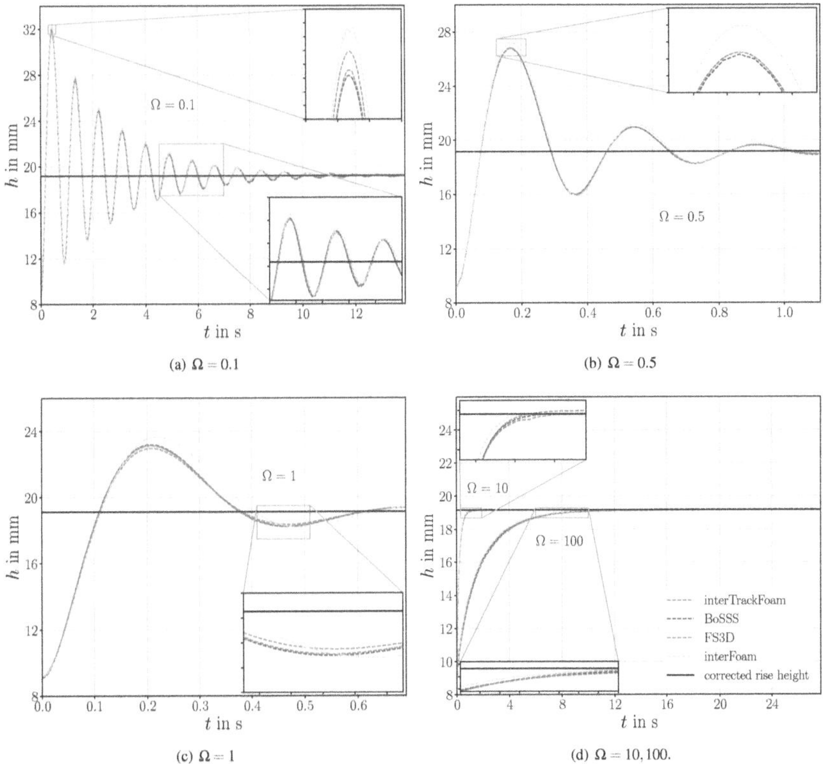

(a) $\Omega = 0.1$

(b) $\Omega = 0.5$

(c) $\Omega = 1$

(d) $\Omega = 10, 100.$

Figure 11.6.: Numerical solutions for different values of Ω (Figure from [GSA[+]20a]).

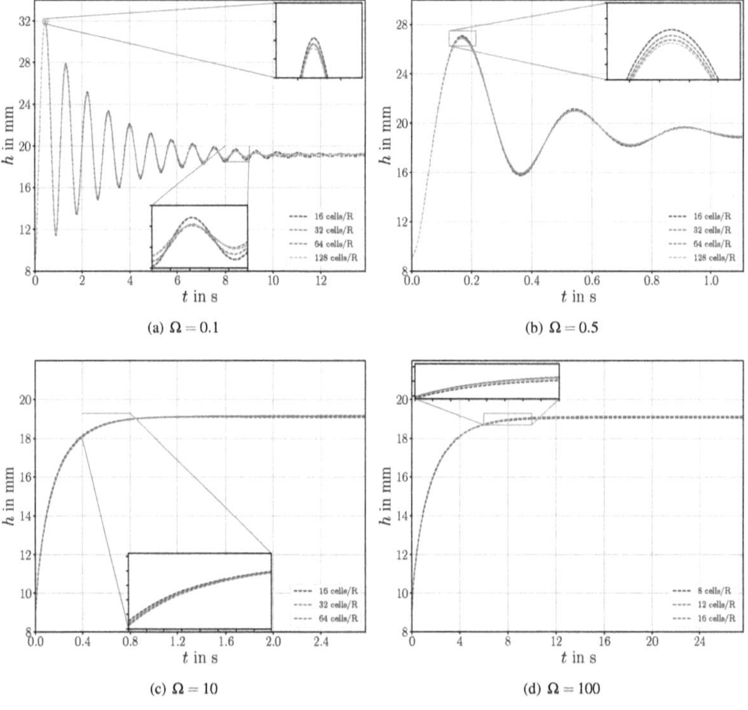

Figure 11.7.: Convergence studies with FS3D for Ω=0.1, 0.5, 10, 100 (Figure from [GSA$^+$20a]).

11.4. Staggered slip boundary condition

As discussed in Section 7.5.1, the standard way to allow for a motion of the contact line is either to use of the numerical slip inherent to the method to impose the no-slip condition, i.e.

$$v_{\text{ghost}} = -v, \tag{11.23}$$

or prescribe the discrete Navier slip condition

$$v_{\text{ghost}} = v\,\frac{2L - \Delta x}{2L + \Delta x}. \tag{11.24}$$

However, the latter condition is limited in the sense that the slip length L must be resolved by the computational mesh. If the slip length is not resolved, there is practically no difference between numerical slip (11.23) and Navier slip (11.24).

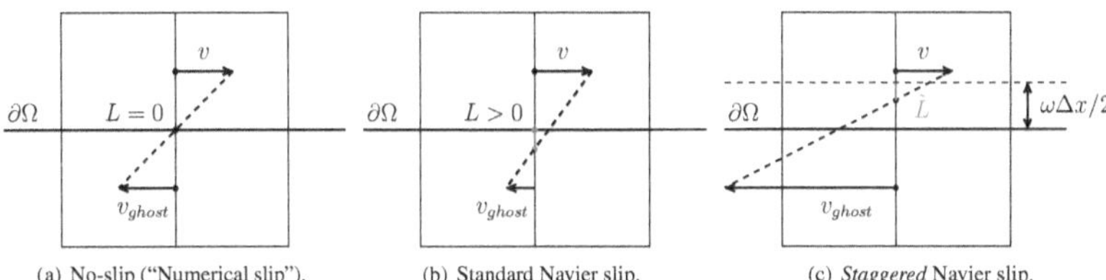

(a) No-slip ("Numerical slip").   (b) Standard Navier slip.   (c) *Staggered* Navier slip.

Figure 11.8.: Ghost-cell based numerical realization of the no-slip, Navier slip and staggered Navier slip boundary conditions in FS3D.

"Staggered" slip: The goal of the "staggered slip" boundary condition, which is introduced below, is to reduce the amount of artificial numerical slip in under-resolved cases. The idea is to apply the slip length with respect to a *virtual* "staggered" boundary located in between the physical boundary and the location of the face-centered velocity nodes (see FIG. 11.8(c)). The mathematical relation between the staggered slip length $\tilde{L}$ and the slip length with respect to the physical boundary is

$$L = \tilde{L} - \frac{\omega \Delta x}{2}, \tag{11.25}$$

where $\omega \in [0, 1]$ is an empirical parameter that allows to control the amount of viscous dissipation. Consequently, the applied ghost velocity is

$$v_{\text{ghost}} = v\,\frac{2L - \Delta x(1 + \omega)}{2L + \Delta x(1 - \omega)}, \quad \omega \in [0, 1]. \tag{11.26}$$

Note that for both conditions (11.26) and (11.24), we have $v_{\text{ghost}} \to v$ as $\Delta x \to 0$ provided that $L > 0$.

The virtual boundary allows to apply larger "counter velocities" in the ghost cell layer than the standard Navier slip or no-slip conditions. Through (discrete) viscous forces this leads to a stronger damping or numerical dissipation. In fact, for a staggered slip length $\tilde{L}$ smaller than ω times half the cell size, the staggered slip can be interpreted as standard Navier slip with a negative slip length, while $\tilde{L} = \omega \Delta x/2$ corresponds to $L = 0$ (numerical slip). Note that a small staggered slip length may lead to very small numerical timesteps since the velocity v_{ghost} in the ghost cells may become very large. Therefore, one cannot choose arbitrary small $\tilde{L}$ in practice.

In the following, we study the effect of the staggered slip boundary condition (11.26) for the capillary rise problem and a single-phase channel flow.

11.4.1. Capillary rise using the staggered slip boundary condition

We reconsider the capillary rise problem for $\Omega = 1$ to examine the effect of the staggered slip boundary condition on a dynamic wetting simulation. The numerical results for $L = R/5$ are reported in Fig. 11.9. In particular, a mesh study for the choice $\omega = 1$ shows that in this case the limiting value for the oscillation amplitude is approached from *below*; see Fig. 11.9(a). Hence in contrast to the standard Navier slip condition ($\omega = 0$), the viscous dissipation appears to be overestimated on coarse meshes for $\omega = 1$. This is a remarkable qualitative change in the behavior of the numerical solution.

In order to quantify the numerical error for different choices of the parameter ω, we investigate the discrete maximum error in the dynamic rise height defined as

$$E_\infty = \max_i |H_{\text{num}}(t_i) - H_{\text{ref}}(t_i)|, \tag{11.27}$$

where the continuous reference function H_{ref} is obtained from a linear interpolation of the numerical values for a well-resolved simulation with 192 cells per radius with the standard Navier slip condition ($\omega = 0$). A convergence study for $\omega \in \{0, \frac{1}{3}, \frac{1}{2}, \frac{2}{3}, 1\}$ is given in Fig. 11.9(b). In general, at least a first-order convergence of the solution is observed in the considered range of mesh resolutions. Following Fig. 11.9(b), the accuracy can be increased with the staggered slip condition.

The numerical results for the reduced slip length $L = R/50$ are reported in Fig. 11.10. Like in the previous example, the reference solution is obtained from a simulation with $\omega = 0$ on a very fine mesh with 192 cells per radius. As before, the numerical solutions for $\omega = 1$ approximates the oscillation amplitude from below. However, in this case, the maximum error E_∞ is similar for $\omega = 1$ and $\omega = 0$; see Fig. 11.10(a) and Fig. 11.10(b). Yet the results in Fig. 11.10(c) show that the accuracy is increased by an order of magnitude for the choice $\omega = 1/2$. The error is even smaller for $\omega = 2/3$ on coarse meshes with 8 and 16 cells per radius but a saturation of the error appears for 32 and 64 cells per radius; see Fig 11.10(d). In summary, the numerical results show that the staggered slip condition improves the accuracy for the capillary rise significantly if the slip length is not well-resolved by the mesh.

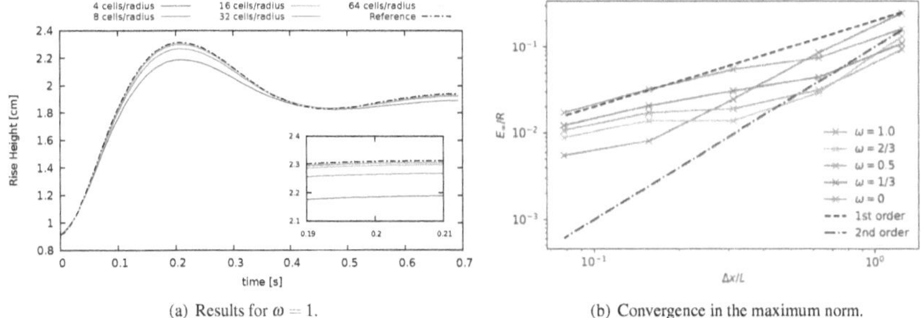

(a) Results for $\omega = 1$.

(b) Convergence in the maximum norm.

Figure 11.9.: Capillary rise with the staggered slip boundary condition, results for $L = R/5$.

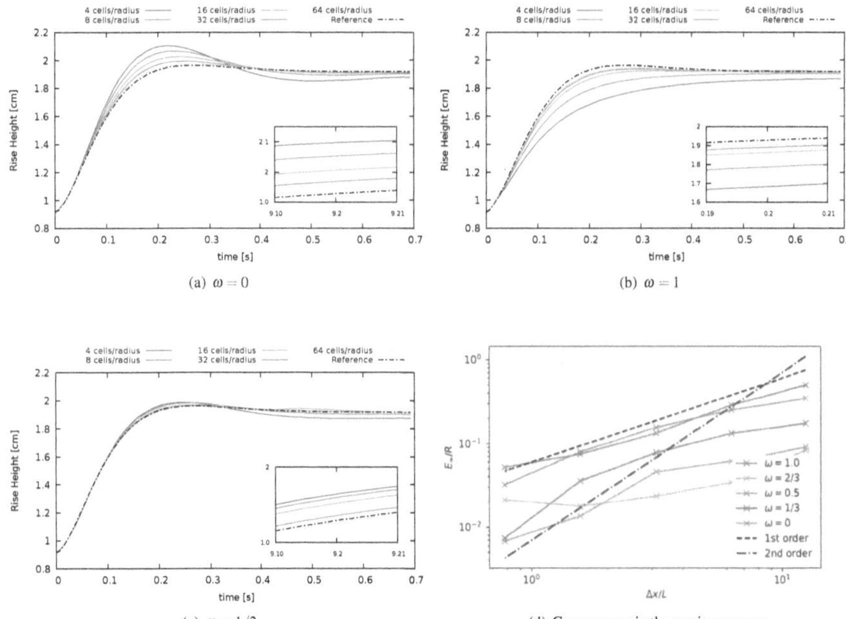

(a) $\omega = 0$

(b) $\omega = 1$

(c) $\omega = 1/2$

(d) Convergence in the maximum norm.

Figure 11.10.: Capillary rise with the staggered slip boundary condition, results for $L = R/50$.

11.4.2. Single-phase channel flow with staggered slip

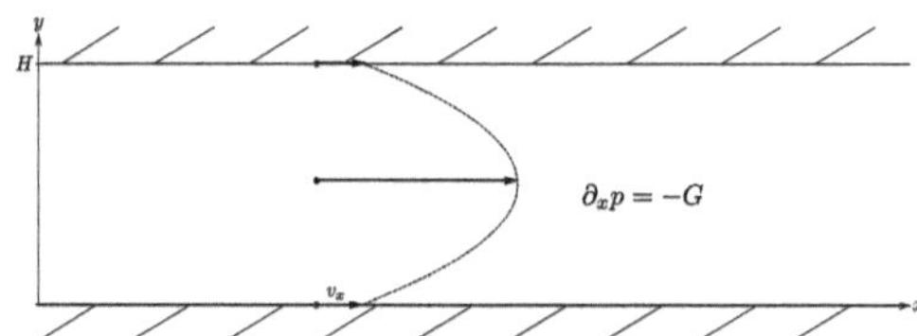

Figure 11.11.: Illustration of the single-phase channel flow problem.

In order to gain more insights into the impact of the staggered slip boundary condition, we come back to the single-phase channel flow problem in two dimensions described in Example 1.4 (see p. 12). Here we consider the flow through a channel of height H (see Fig. 11.11) which is driven by a constant pressure gradient $\nabla p = (-G,0) = \mathrm{const}$. The incompressible Navier Stokes equations are solved subject to the impermeability and Navier slip conditions at the top and bottom wall of the channel, i.e.

$$v_y = 0, \quad v_x - L\partial_y v_x = 0 \quad \text{for} \quad y = 0, H.$$

As discussed in Example 1.4, this problem can be solved explicitly with the solution

$$v(x,y) = (v_x(y),0) \quad \text{with} \quad v_x(y) = \frac{GH^2}{2\eta}\left(\frac{y}{H} - \left(\frac{y}{H}\right)^2 + \frac{L}{H}\right). \tag{11.28}$$

Note, that the solution 11.28 is physically stable only if the Reynolds number

$$\mathrm{Re} = \frac{\rho v_{\mathrm{max}} H}{\eta}$$

is small enough such that the flow is laminar. Using (11.28), the expected Reynolds number can be evaluated as

$$\mathrm{Re} = \frac{\rho H^3 G}{8\eta^2}\left(1 + \frac{4L}{H}\right).$$

We choose the following fluid parameters

$$\rho = 10^2\,\frac{\mathrm{kg}}{\mathrm{m}^3}, \quad g = 0.1\,\frac{\mathrm{m}}{\mathrm{s}^2}, \quad \eta = 10^{-2}\,\mathrm{Pa\cdot s}.$$

The channel height and the pressure gradient are chosen to be

$$H = 10^{-2}\,\mathrm{m}, \quad G = \rho g = 10\,\frac{\mathrm{kg}}{\mathrm{m}^2\,\mathrm{s}^2}.$$

With these definitions, we have

$$v_x(y) = \frac{5}{100}\left(\frac{y}{H} - \left(\frac{y}{H}\right)^2 + \frac{L}{H}\right)\frac{\mathrm{m}}{\mathrm{s}}, \quad \langle v_x\rangle = \frac{1}{120}\left(1 + \frac{6L}{H}\right)\frac{\mathrm{m}}{\mathrm{s}},$$
$$v_x^{\mathrm{max}} = \frac{5}{400}\left(1 + \frac{4L}{H}\right)\frac{\mathrm{m}}{\mathrm{s}}, \quad \mathrm{Re} = \frac{10}{8}\left(1 + \frac{4L}{H}\right). \tag{11.29}$$

Hence, the Reynolds number is small ($\mathrm{Re} \le 6.25$ for $L \le H$) and the flow is laminar.

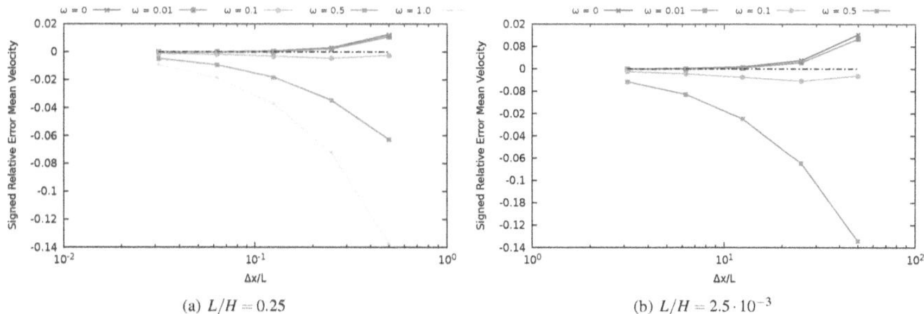

(a) $L/H = 0.25$

(b) $L/H = 2.5 \cdot 10^{-3}$

Figure 11.12.: Signed relative error for the mean velocity $\langle v_x \rangle$.

FS3D simulation results: The numerical simulations are carried out on uniform meshes with 8, 16, 32, 64 and 128 cells along the diameter of the channel. The simulation is run until steady state is reached. Then we consider the convergence of the averaged velocity (which is proportional to the mass transport rate in the channel) $\langle v_x \rangle$ for the standard discrete Navier slip condition (11.24) and compare to the staggered slip condition (11.26) for different values of the parameter ω. The analytical results (11.29) serve as a reference. The signed relative error in the mean velocity, i.e.

$$\frac{\langle v_x \rangle^{\mathrm{num}} - \langle v_x \rangle}{|\langle v_x \rangle|}$$

is reported in Fig. 11.12 for different choices of the parameter ω and a resolved ($L/H = 0.25$) as well as well as an under-resolved slip length ($L/H = 2.5 \cdot 10^{-3}$). It is found that the numerical method approximates the exact value from below for $\omega \in \{0.1, 0.5, 1\}$. In this case, the viscous dissipation is increasingly over-predicted as the mesh becomes coarser. On the other hand, the exact solution is approximated from above for the Navier slip condition ($\omega = 0$) and $\omega = 0.01$. However, a close inspection shows that the convergence for $\omega = 0.01$ is not monotone (see Fig. 11.13).

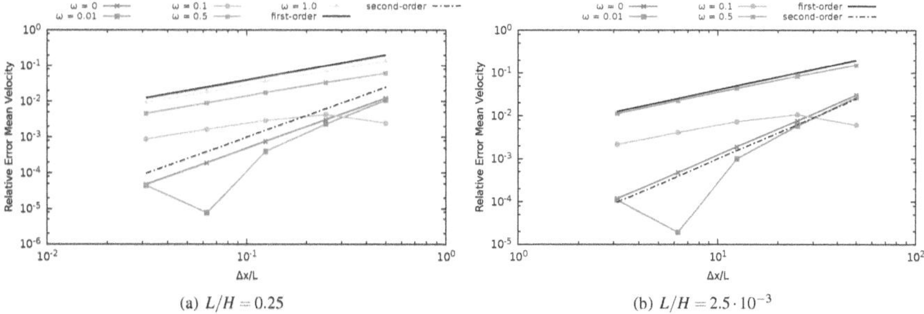

(a) $L/H = 0.25$

(b) $L/H = 2.5 \cdot 10^{-3}$

Figure 11.13.: Convergence of the mean velocity $\langle v_x \rangle$.

In order to assess the convergence of the method quantitatively, the relative error in $\langle v_x \rangle$, i.e.

$$\frac{|\langle v_x \rangle^{\mathrm{num}} - \langle v_x \rangle|}{|\langle v_x \rangle|},$$

is plotted as a function of the mesh size in units of the slip length; see Fig. 11.13. It is found that the standard Navier slip condition ($\omega = 0$) delivers second-order accuracy for the mean velocity. The order of accuracy drops to one for the staggered slip condition with $\omega \in \{0.1, 0.5, 1\}$. A local minimum appears for $\omega = 0.01$ since the convergence is not monotone in this case.

11.4.3. Summary

In summary, the staggered slip boundary condition (11.26) improves the convergence for the capillary rise problem significantly, in particular if the slip length is under-resolved; see Fig. 11.10. Depending on the choice of ω, the correct oscillation amplitude is either approximated from above or from below. On the other hand, the order of convergence for the single-phase channel flow problem drops from two to one when the staggered slip boundary condition is applied instead of the standard Navier slip condition. In the latter case, the average velocity in the channel is approximated from below except for very small values of ω.

It appears that the staggered slip condition increases the dissipation within the numerical method. This way, the staggered slip method can achieve better results than the standard slip condition if the viscous dissipation in the contact line region is not well-resolved. On the other hand, the viscous dissipation is over-estimated for the single-phase channel flow. In conclusion, the staggered slip condition is a possible approach to achieve more re-alistic results for the contact line dynamics on coarse meshes. However, further research efforts are necessary to reach a more quantitative understanding of the underlying mechanisms.

12. Wetting of structured surfaces

The wetting of structured or patterned surfaces is a widespread phenomenon in nature as well as in engineering applications. For example, the lotus leave has specialized structural and chemical modifications to achieve super-hydrophobicity. Similarly, animals like butterflies make use of specialized wetting features to adapt to the ecosystem; see [XJL12] and the references given therein for a review of the topic. Developments in engineering started to learn from biological structures and specialized materials were invented that, in many cases, employ a surface structure or pattern. For example, hierarchically structured surfaces allowed to largely increase the critical heat flux in boiling applications [CSE$^+$13].

It is, therefore, important to establish a solid understanding of wetting processes on structured surfaces. The present chapter is organized as follows: The static wetting on structured surfaces is briefly discussed in Section 12.1 where we revisit the two-dimensional energy minimization described for a homogeneous substrate discussed in Chapter 1. The breakup dynamics of a capillary bridge on a microstructured surface is studied numerically and experimentally (in cooperation with M. Hartmann and S. Hardt) in Section 12.2. Note that the results obtained in Section 12.2 are published in [HFW$^+$20]. Interestingly, dynamic surface tension effects may play a role in the breakup dynamics; see Section 12.3. Finally, the capillary rise is revisited for the case of a structured surface in Section 12.4.

12.1. Static wetting of an inhomogeneous substrate in two dimensions

The goal of this section is to extend the derivation of the Young–Dupré equation in two dimensions (see Section 1.3) to the case of an inhomogeneous solid substrate. Even though the restriction to two spatial dimensions reduces the complexity of the arising wetting patterns significantly, one can still understand some basic phenomena and mechanisms that arise from the presence of a structured surface. An interesting recent investigation of the wetting on structured surfaces in 3D can be found in [WWSN19a, WWSN19b, WWM$^+$20].

The energy functional in the presence of an inhomogeneous solid substrate reads as

$$\mathscr{E}_{\mathrm{i}} = \sigma_{\mathrm{lg}} \, |\Sigma_{lg}| + \int_{\Sigma_{sl}} \sigma_{\mathrm{w}} \, dA + \mathscr{E}_g, \tag{12.1}$$

where $\sigma_{\mathrm{lg}} > 0$ is constant. In the following, we assume that the Bond number is sufficiently small and neglect the gravitational contribution $\mathscr{E}_g$.

Energy of a single droplet: We start with the case of a single droplet. We employ the same mathematical tools as in Section 1.3, i.e. we describe the free surface by a height function. However, we have to introduce an additional parameter since the symmetry of the energy functional regarding translations of the droplet along the solid boundary is lost. Like in Section 1.3, we define the height function on a reference interval $[0, 1]$ and introduce the wetted length $L > 0$ and the coordinate $\mathsf{x}_{\min} \in \mathbb{R}$ as additional parameters describing the geometry of the drop.

Suppose the drop wets the region $\mathsf{x}_{\min} \leq x \leq \mathsf{x}_{\max} = \mathsf{x}_{\min} + L$. Then we define the dimensionless coordinate

$$\tilde{x} = \frac{x - \mathsf{x}_{\min}}{L}.$$

Hence, for a given function $\tilde{h} \in \mathscr{C}^1([0, 1])$ defined on the reference interval with $\tilde{h}(0) = \tilde{h}(1) = 0$, the height function in physical units reads as

$$h(x) = L\tilde{h}\left(\frac{x - \mathsf{x}_{\min}}{L}\right). \tag{12.2}$$

The minimization of the energy functional, which is given as

$$\mathscr{E} = \sigma_{\mathrm{lg}} L \int_0^1 \sqrt{1+\tilde{h}'^2}\, d\tilde{x} + L \int_0^1 \sigma_{\mathrm{w}}(x_{\min}+\tilde{x}L)\, d\tilde{x}, \tag{12.3}$$

has to respect the volume conservation condition

$$\int_0^1 \tilde{h}\, d\tilde{x} = \frac{V_0}{L^2},$$

where V_0 denotes the two-dimensional volume of the drop. We introduce a Lagrange parameter λ for the volume constraint and consider the functional

$$\mathscr{E}_\lambda = \sigma_{\mathrm{lg}} L \int_0^1 \sqrt{1+\tilde{h}'^2}\, d\tilde{x} + \lambda \left(\int_0^1 \tilde{h}\, d\tilde{x} - \frac{V_0}{L^2} \right) + L \int_0^1 \sigma_{\mathrm{w}}(x_{\min}+\tilde{x}L)\, d\tilde{x}. \tag{12.4}$$

Here we assume the function σ_{w} to be continuous such that the functional $\mathscr{E}_\lambda$ is $\mathscr{C}^1$. We are looking for stationary points of (12.4) in the state space

$$\tilde{h} \in \mathscr{C}^1(0,1),\ \tilde{h}(0) = \tilde{h}(1) = 0,\ L > 0,\ x_{\min} \in \mathbb{R},\ \lambda \in \mathbb{R}. \tag{12.5}$$

Lemma 12.1. *Let* $\sigma_{\mathrm{w}} \in \mathscr{C}^0(\mathbb{R})$. *A spherical cap with wetted length L, left boundary coordinate x_{min} and contact angle θ is a stationary point of the energy functional* (12.4) *if*

$$\sigma_{\mathrm{w}}(x_{min}+L) = \sigma_{\mathrm{w}}(x_{min}) \tag{12.6}$$

and the Young-Dupré equation

$$\sigma_{\mathrm{lg}} \cos\theta + \sigma_{\mathrm{w}}(x_{min}) = 0 = \sigma_{\mathrm{lg}} \cos\theta + \sigma_{\mathrm{w}}(x_{min}+L) \tag{12.7}$$

holds.

Proof. The first stationarity condition $\partial \mathscr{E}_\lambda / \partial L = 0$ yields

$$0 = \sigma_{\mathrm{lg}} \left(\int_0^1 \sqrt{1+\tilde{h}'^2}\, d\tilde{x} + \frac{\sigma_{\mathrm{w}}(x_{\min}+L)}{\sigma_{\mathrm{lg}}} \right) + \frac{2\lambda V_0}{L^3}, \tag{12.8}$$

which is a generalization of (1.14). Moreover, the variation with respect to $x_{\min}$ leads to

$$0 = \frac{\partial \mathscr{E}_\lambda}{\partial x_{\min}} = \sigma_{\mathrm{w}}(x_{\min}+L) - \sigma_{\mathrm{w}}(x_{\min}). \tag{12.9}$$

The variation of $\mathscr{E}_\lambda$ with respect to the normalized height function $\tilde{h}$ is the same as for the case of a homogeneous solid substrate discussed in Section 1.3. So, like before, the variation with respect to $\tilde{h}$ leads to the constant mean curvature condition

$$\kappa(x) = \frac{\lambda}{L^2 \sigma_{\mathrm{lg}}} = \text{const.} \tag{12.10}$$

Hence, stationary points of the energy functional $\mathscr{E}_\lambda$ in two dimensions with non-constant σ_{w} are spherical caps as well (since gravitational effects are neglected here). Combining equation (12.10) and (12.8) implies

$$0 = \sigma_{\mathrm{lg}} \left(\int_0^1 \sqrt{1+\tilde{h}'^2}\, d\tilde{x} + \frac{2\kappa V_0}{L} \right) + \sigma_{\mathrm{w}}(x_{\min}+L). \tag{12.11}$$

With some elementary geometry, one can easily show that

$$\int_0^1 \sqrt{1+\tilde{h}'^2}\, d\tilde{x} + \frac{2\kappa V_0}{L} = \cos\theta,$$

where θ is the contact angle of the spherical cap. $\qquad\square$

It is important to note that the conditions (12.6) and (12.7) are only *necessary* conditions for a local minimum of the energy functional.

Example 12.2 (Harmonic potential). As a first example, we consider the harmonic potential

$$\tilde{\sigma}_{\text{w}}(x) = \frac{\sigma_{\text{w}}(x)}{\sigma_{\text{lg}}} = \tilde{\sigma}_{\text{w},0} + \beta x^2, \tag{12.12}$$

where we assume $\tilde{\sigma}_{\text{w},0} \in (-1,1)$ such that $\theta_0 \in (0,\pi)$ exists satisfying

$$\cos \theta_0 + \tilde{\sigma}_{\text{w},0} = 0.$$

As a consequence of (12.6), the droplet in a stationary state must be centered at $x = 0$. Then, the potential at the endpoints is related to the wetted length L according to

$$\tilde{\sigma}_{\text{w}}(\pm L/2) = \tilde{\sigma}_{\text{w},0} + \frac{1}{4}\beta L^2.$$

Hence, Eq. (12.7) implies that for a stationary point of the energy functional, the contact angle is related to the wetted length via

$$\cos \theta = -\left(\tilde{\sigma}_{\text{w},0} + \frac{1}{4}\beta L^2 \right). \tag{12.13}$$

On the other hand, the contact angle is related to the wetted length for a given (two-dimensional) volume V_0 via the purely geometrical relation

$$V_0 = \frac{L^2}{4}\left(\frac{\theta}{\sin^2 \theta} - \cot \theta \right) =: \frac{L^2}{4}\zeta(\theta), \tag{12.14}$$

which is valid for a spherical cap in two dimensions. Note that the function ζ is strictly increasing with $\zeta(0) = 0$. Hence for a given volume V_0, the optimal configuration is determined by (12.13) and (12.14). Indeed, the wetted length can be eliminated in (12.13) using (12.14) leading to a non-linear equation in the contact angle

$$(\cos \theta_0 - \cos \theta)\,\zeta(\theta) = \beta V_0. \tag{12.15}$$

As expected, the standard Young-Dupré equation is recovered for $\beta = 0$.

(i) For $\beta > 0$, we define the dimensionless volume $\tilde{V}_0 = \beta V_0 > 0$. Since $\zeta \geq 0$, it directly follows that $\theta \geq \theta_0$ for positive β. Figure 12.1(a) shows the contact angle in the equilibrium state as a function of the dimensionless volume for $\theta_0 = 60°$.

(ii) In the case of negative $\beta < 0$, the energy functional is obviously unbounded from below and no global minimum exists. However, there may be (depending on $|\beta|$) one, two or no solutions to (12.15) that correspond to a stationary point of the energy. The critical value for β is given by

$$\hat{\beta} = \frac{1}{V_0} \min_{\theta \in [0,\pi]} (\cos \theta_0 - \cos \theta)\,\zeta(\theta).$$

If $\hat{\beta} < \beta < 0$, there are two solutions to (12.15). For example, the critical value for $\theta_0 = 120°$ is

$$\hat{\beta} V_0 \approx -0.8618.$$

Figure 12.1(b) shows the energy as a function of the contact angle for spherical caps centered at the origin with a fixed volume $V_0 = 1$. Indeed, for $\beta V_0 = -0.3$ (blue curve) a pronounced local maximum in the energy functional appears for $\theta \approx 17.5°$ before the energy drops towards $-\infty$ for smaller contact angles and the droplet spreads to form a film. Since the gradient in the wetting energy is relatively weak in this case, the initial gain by wetting a larger portion of the solid is overcompensated by the energy demand of the additional liquid-gas interface that is created by lowering the contact angle. Conversely, the local maximum disappears for β below the critical value (orange curve) and the energy is strictly decreasing function of the contact angle (green curve); see Fig. 12.1(b).

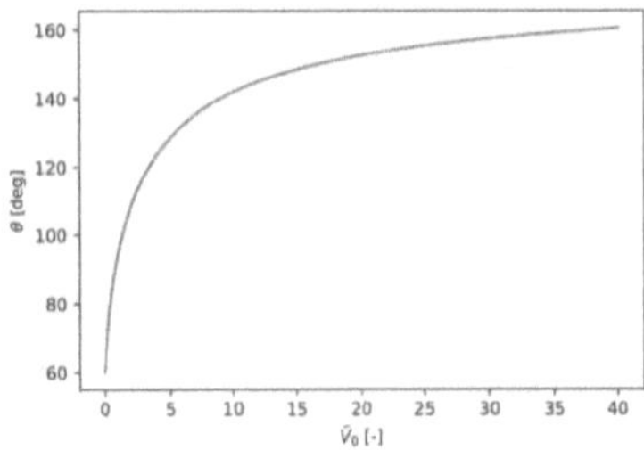

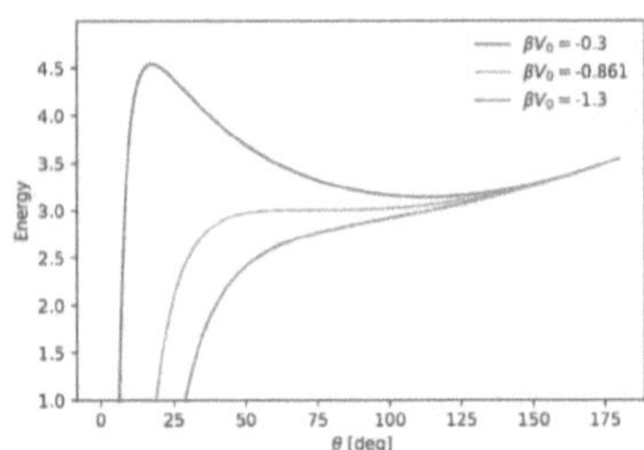

(a) Contact angle in the equilibrium state as a function of the dimensionless volume ($\theta_0 = 60°$, $\beta > 0$).

(b) Energy as function of the contact angle for spherical caps with a fixed volume.

Figure 12.1.: Wetting of a structured surface with a harmonic potential.

Remark 12.3. It is shown in Example 12.2 that, in general, the contact angle in the equilibrium configuration depends on the volume of the drop; see Equation (12.15). The latter is not the case for an ideal homogeneous solid surface where the volume only rescales the energy (as long as gravity can be neglected); see Section 1.3. We will see below that this kind of "symmetry breaking" is characteristic for the wetting of structured surfaces and leads to a variety of interesting phenomena.

Example 12.4 (Sharp wetting barriers). For the derivation of Lemma 12.1, we assumed σ_w to be continuous leading to a continuously differentiable energy functional. It is also interesting from a theoretical point of view to investigate the case of a sharp jump in σ_w. For example, let us take the example of a hydrophilic spot of length ω on a hydrophobic surface, i.e.

$$\tilde{\sigma}_w(x) = \begin{cases} \tilde{\sigma}_{w,1}, & |x| < \omega/2 \\ \tilde{\sigma}_{w,2}, & |x| > \omega/2 \end{cases} \tag{12.16}$$

where $-1 \le \tilde{\sigma}_{w,1} < \tilde{\sigma}_{w,2} \le 1$. With $\tilde{\sigma}_w$ defined as above, the functional (12.3) is still well-defined but (12.7) makes no sense at $x = \pm\omega/2$. Instead, one can show that (see [Mie02] for a proof), depending on the volume of the drop, the contact angle may take any value between

$$\theta_1 = \arccos(-\tilde{\sigma}_{w,1}) \quad \text{and} \quad \theta_2 = \arccos(-\tilde{\sigma}_{w,2})$$

if the contact line is located at $x = \pm\omega/2$. Note that the minimum energy configurations are still spherical caps even if σ_w is only $\mathscr{C}^0$ since the functional (12.4) still depends smoothly on $\tilde{h}$ and (12.10) remains valid. If the drop is sufficiently small, it simply wets the hydrophilic region only with a contact angle θ_1. In this case, the functional (12.10) is smooth in a neighborhood of the equilibrium configuration and the reasoning outlined in Lemma 12.1 applies. In fact, the latter applies for volumes smaller than (see eq. (12.14))

$$V_1 = \frac{\omega^2}{4} \left(\frac{\theta_1}{\sin^2 \theta_1} - \cot \theta_1 \right).$$

Similarly, for volumes greater than

$$V_2 = \frac{\omega^2}{4} \left(\frac{\theta_2}{\sin^2 \theta_2} - \cot \theta_2 \right),$$

the droplet wets the entire hydrophilic region and parts of the hydrophobic region while the contact angle assumes the value of the hydrophobic contact angle θ_2. So in this case, the contact angle is determined by the volume for $V_1 \le V \le V_2$.

Energy functional for two droplets and breakup: The breakup of a wetting droplet into two parts is an interesting process that can be observed for structured surfaces. Indeed, due to the non-constant wetting energy σ_w, it can be energetically favorable for a droplet to split and only wet the hydrophilic parts of the surface. Conversely, one can easily show that this is never the case for a homogeneous substrate unless other driving forces are present; see Remark 12.5 below. It is important to note that the parametrization (12.5) for the configuration space of the system does not allow to study breakup phenomena since it only encodes single droplet configurations. In order to generalize (12.5) to N droplets, further height functions $h_1, \ldots, h_N$ could be introduced together with a suitable parametrization to avoid an overlap between the droplets. Since the breakup marks a topological change of the configuration, there is no continuous way to go from N to $N+1$ droplets.

Remark 12.5 (Breakup for a homogeneous substrate). Let σ_w be constant and consider a single two-dimensional droplet with volume V_0 and energy

$$\mathscr{E}_1 = |\Sigma_{\text{lg}}| + L\tilde{\sigma}_w = \frac{\theta L}{\sin\theta} + L\tilde{\sigma}_w = L\left(\frac{\theta}{\sin\theta} + \tilde{\sigma}_w\right).$$

We can express $L = L(\theta, V_0)$ via (12.14) since the equilibrium state is a spherical cap. Hence, the minimum energy for the single droplet is

$$\hat{\mathscr{E}}_1 = \min_{\theta \in [0,\pi]} \sqrt{\frac{4V_0}{\zeta(\theta)}}\left(\frac{\theta}{\sin\theta} + \tilde{\sigma}_w\right). \tag{12.17}$$

Now we compare the single droplet energy with the energy for two spherical cap-shaped droplets with volume $V_0/2$ and contact angle θ

$$\mathscr{E}_2(\theta) = 2L(\theta, V_0/2)\left(\frac{\theta}{\sin\theta} + \tilde{\sigma}_w\right) = \sqrt{2}\sqrt{\frac{4V_0}{\zeta(\theta)}}\left(\frac{\theta}{\sin\theta} + \tilde{\sigma}_w\right) = \sqrt{2}\mathscr{E}_1(\theta). \tag{12.18}$$

Hence, the minimum energy $\hat{\mathscr{E}}_2$ in the two droplet configuration is increased by a factor of $\sqrt{2}$ compared to the single droplet.

A simplified model: Consider the following (symmetric) wetting energy function

$$\tilde{\sigma}_w(x) = \begin{cases} \sigma^+ & \text{if} \quad |x| \le \omega_{\text{phob}}/2, \\ \sigma^- & \text{if} \quad \omega_{\text{phob}}/2 < |x| < \omega_{\text{phob}}/2 + \omega_{\text{phil}}, \\ \sigma^+ & \text{if} \quad \omega_{\text{phob}}/2 + \omega_{\text{phil}} \le |x|, \end{cases} \tag{12.19}$$

where $\sigma^- < \sigma^+$. In order to simplify the reasoning, we only consider three specific types of configurations of the system:

(a) A single droplet of (two-dimensional) volume V_0 centered at the symmetry axis (see Fig. 12.2(a))

$$\mathscr{E}_1^c(\theta, V_0) = \frac{\theta L(\theta, V_0)}{\sin\theta} + \int_{-L(\theta,V_0)/2}^{L(\theta,V_0)/2} \tilde{\sigma}_w \, dA, \tag{12.20}$$

(b) a single droplet of volume V_0 located at the center point of the hydrophilic region at $x = (\omega_{\text{phob}} + \omega_{\text{phil}})/2$ (see Fig. 12.2(b))

$$\mathscr{E}_1^\star(\theta, V_0) = \frac{\theta L(\theta, V_0)}{\sin\theta} + \int_{[\omega_{\text{phob}} + \omega_{\text{phil}} - L(\theta,V_0)]/2}^{[\omega_{\text{phob}} + \omega_{\text{phil}} + L(\theta,V_0)]/2} \tilde{\sigma}_w \, dA \tag{12.21}$$

and

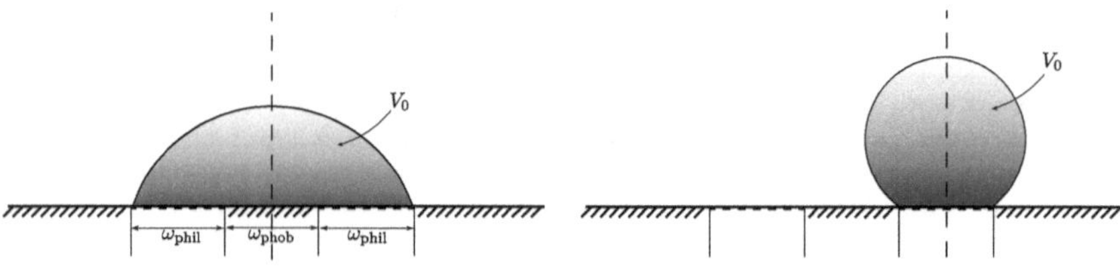

(a) Configuration with one droplet (symmetric).   (b) Configuration with one droplet at the hydrophilic stripe.

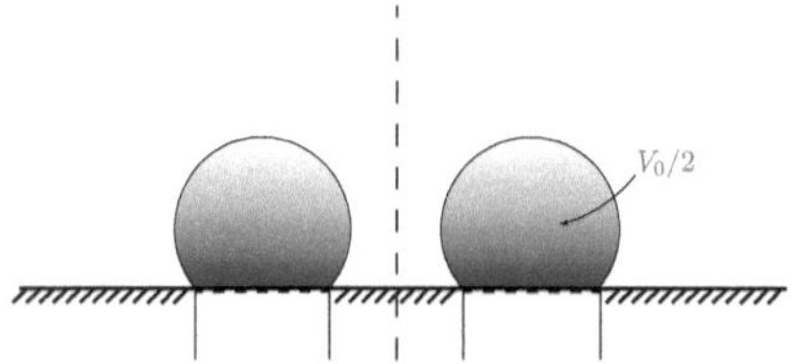

(c) Configuration with two droplets.

Figure 12.2.: Considered configurations of the system.

(c) two droplets of volume $V_0/2$ each that are located at the center points of the hydrophilic regions, i.e. at $x = \pm(\omega_{phob} + \omega_{phil})/2$

$$\mathcal{E}_2(\theta, V_0) = 2\mathcal{E}_1^\star(\theta, V_0/2), \tag{12.22}$$

see Fig. 12.2(c).

We study the dependence of the energy on the volume in the configurations (a), (b) and (c) defined above by minimizing the functionals $\mathcal{E}_1^c$, $\mathcal{E}_1^\star$ and $\mathcal{E}_2$ for a fixed volume, respectively. As an example, we choose the parameters

$$\omega_{phob} = \omega_{phil} = 1.0, \quad \sigma^+ = \frac{1}{2}, \quad \sigma^- \in \{-1/2, -2\}.$$

The results are reported in Fig. 12.3. As expected, the centered configuration (a) for a single droplet is energetically favorable for large volumes. For the partial wetting case ($\sigma^- = -0.5$) shown in Fig. 12.3(a) it is found that configuration (b) is always preferred compared to configuration (c). This is due to the fact that the energy cost for the increased liquid-gas interface is larger than the gain due to the increased wetted portion of the hydrophilic surface in configuration (c). For $V_0 \lesssim 1.53$, the energy in configuration (b) is smaller than in configuration (a). Moreover, it is found that the two droplet state is preferable compared to the centered single droplet for $V_0 \lesssim 1.00$. In contrast to the partial wetting case, the two droplet configuration is favored over configuration (b) for $V_0 \lesssim 3.1$ in the case of complete wetting on the hydrophilic stripe ($\sigma^- = -2$); see Fig. 12.3(b). For this set of parameters, the critical volume is $V^\star \approx 1.10$ below which a transition to the two droplet state is energetically favorable.

So, in summary, the simple example discussed above shows that the breakup of droplets may be energetically favorable for the wetting of structured surfaces. A detailed investigation of the dynamics of the breakup process is given in the following section.

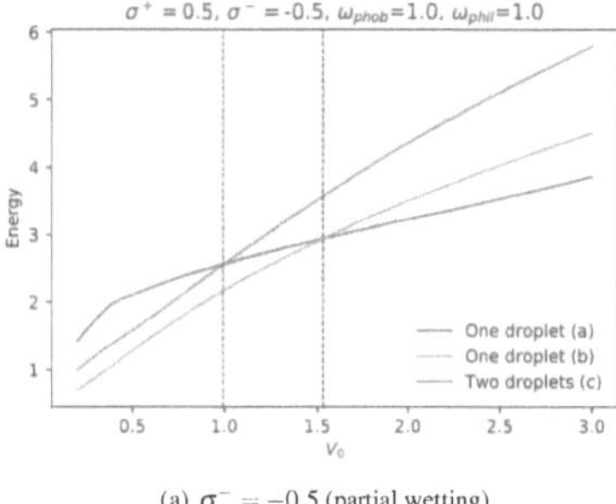
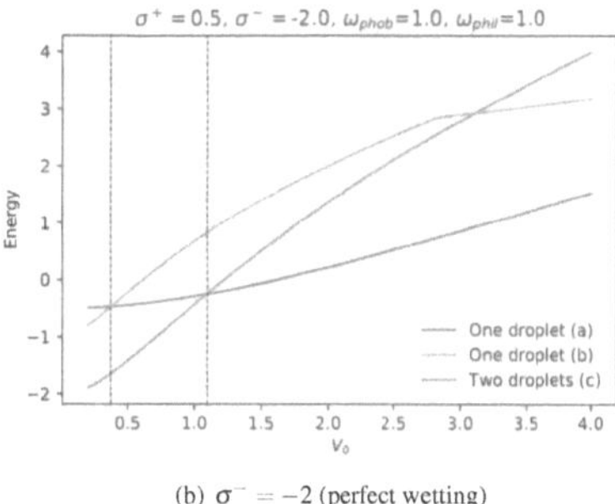

(a) $\sigma^- = -0.5$ (partial wetting)

(b) $\sigma^- = -2$ (perfect wetting)

Figure 12.3.: The energy as a function of V_0 for the configurations (a), (b) and (c) depicted in Fig. 12.2.

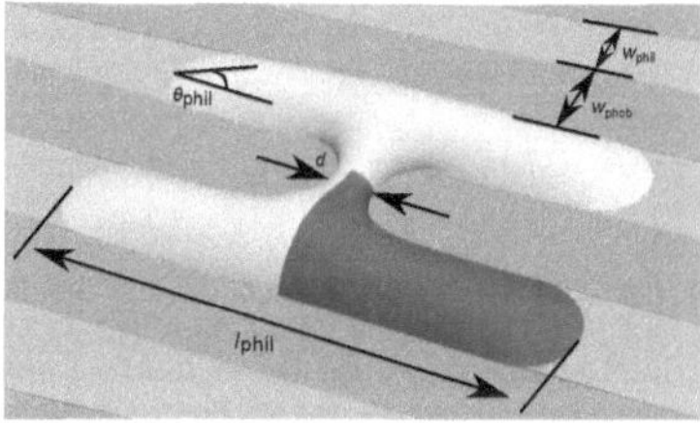

Figure 12.4.: Initial geometry from Surface Evolver (Figure by M. Hartmann [HFW+20]).

12.2. Breakup dynamics of droplets on structured surfaces

The goal of the present section[1] is to investigate the breakup dynamics of a wetting capillary bridge. The capillary bridge is formed from an evaporating water droplet in contact with a structured surface that exhibits a stripe geometry; see Fig. 12.4. The surface structure consists of alternating stripes of different wettability which are produced experimentally using photolithography (see [HH19, HFW+20] for details on the surface preparation). As the droplet evaporates, it starts to dewet the hydrophobic stripes and spreads along the hydrophilic stripes to reduce surface energy. As a result, the droplet forms a shape that looks similar to the letter "H" with a capillary bridge connecting the hydrophilic regions; see Fig. 12.5. Hartmann and Hardt studied the stability of the latter configuration in [HH19] and found that there is a critical diameter of the capillary bridge below which the bridge becomes unstable and the droplet breaks up into two smaller droplets wetting the hydrophilic regions only. Moreover, it is observed that one or more small satellite droplets remain on the hydrophobic part of the surface.

Breakup of a free capillary bridge: The breakup of a *free* capillary bridge, i.e. without contact to a solid substrate[2], is a well-understood phenomenon. Using the Buckingham Pi Theorem, one can derive a scaling law for the temporal evolution of the minimum diameter. According to [EF15], the only assumptions are that the process is controlled by inertial and capillary forces and that the minimum diameter is the only relevant length scale in the

---

[1] Please note that the results presented in this section have been published as a preprint in [HFW+20].
[2] Here we mean contact to a solid substrate along the axis of the capillary bridge.

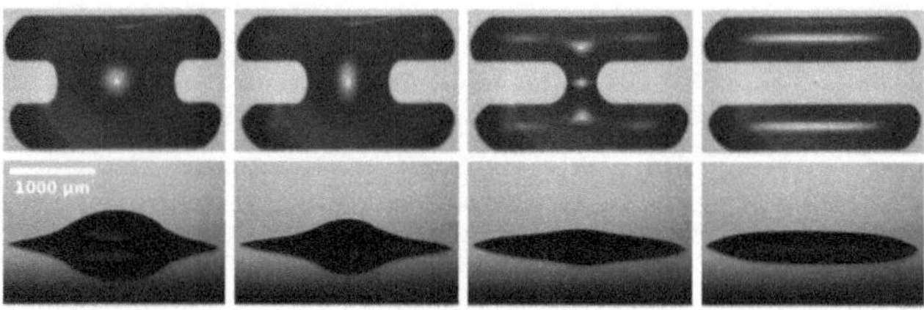

Figure 12.5.: Time series of the breakup process top and side view. Reprinted with permission from Hartmann and Hardt, Langmuir 35(14):4868-4875,2019. Copyright (2019) American Chemical Society.

process. Then, one finds[3] the relation (see, e.g., [KM83, EF15])

$$d(\tau) = C \left(\frac{\sigma \tau^2}{\rho} \right)^{1/3}, \qquad (12.23)$$

where σ is the surface tension, ρ is the fluid density and $\tau = t_0 - t$ is the time t before the bridge breaks up at t_0. In particular, the minimum diameter scales with exponent $2/3$ as a function of time before the breakup event. The prefactor C was believed to be *universal*, i.e. independent of the initial state of the system. In [EF15, p.7] it is stated that

> " Another, related, property of a singularity is the fact that its structure is insensitive to initial conditions or other aspects of the large-scale structure of the solution. This is a consequence of the fact that the singularity arises from a local balance: in drop pinch-off, the dimensionless prefactor A in (1.1) is expected to be universal since (1.1) is the solution of a nonlinear equation. "

It is important to note that the value of the prefactor C cannot be determined from dimensional analysis but has to be computed from a solution of the full Navier Stokes equations. According to [EF15], the prefactor can be found using similarity theory and its numerical value is close to 1.4. However, more recent studies show that "the correct asymptotic value of A is unobservable for all practical purposes" [DHH$^+$18]. Instead, there is a transient approach to the asymptotic law which can be quite slow. Moreover, the value of the prefactor and even the scaling exponent observed in both experimental and numerical studies is quite sensitive with respect to the breakup time t_0. This issue can, however, be solved with a method described in Section 12.2.2.

It is remarkable to note that there is a large variation of the numerical values of the prefactor in the literature. Li and Sprittles [LS16] performed numerical simulations of the breakup of a free capillary bridge in different regimes characterized by the dimensionless diameter of the capillary bridge and the Ohnesorge number. In the inviscid regime, they found C to be close to 1.2. In contrast to that, Hauner et al. [HDB$^+$17] assumed the prefactor to be universal with $C = 0.9 \pm 0.01$ and concluded from this that water exhibits a dynamic surface tension $\sigma \approx 90\,\mathrm{mN/m}$ for a freshly created piece of surface which relaxes to the equilibrium value of about $\sigma \approx 72\,\mathrm{mN/m}$ on a millisecond timescale. Remarkably, dynamic surface tension effects might be relevant for the breakup dynamics in the present case; see Section 12.3 for details. Deblais et al. [DHH$^+$18] report literature values in the range[4] from 0.9 up to 1.94.

A guiding question for the present study is to investigate if and how the presence of a moving contact line changes the breakup dynamics of the capillary bridge. To answer this question we perform VOF based direct numerical simulations of the breakup process in three dimensions. The numerical simulations are compared to experimental data by M. Hartmann and S. Hardt. Previous studies of breakup phenomena using the geometrical VOF method reported in the literature address the breakup of a liquid filament on a homogeneous substrate [DNE$^+$19] and the breakup of a free capillary bridge [DHH$^+$18].

---

[3] An accessible technical exposition of the derivation of (12.23) from dimensional analysis is given the Appendix C of the monograph [EF15].

[4] Note that the scaling law (12.23) appears in the literature in the form given here and in a formulation for the minimum *radius*. In this case, the prefactor has to be multiplied by a factor of 2 to be compatible with the present formulation for the minimum diameter.

Initial data from surface evolver: In order to simplify the mathematical model and to save computational resources, we only simulate the process starting from the onset of the instability. We, moreover, neglect the evaporation in the VOF simulation since it can be considered to be irrelevant on the timescale of the breakup process which is much smaller than the evaporation timescale (see [HFW+20] Appendix C for an estimate). A crucial requirement for a numerical simulation starting at the onset of the instability is a physically realistic initial condition in terms of the drop shape. In the present work, we make use of the drop shapes computed by M. Hartmann by minimizing the surface energy using the Open Source tool *Surface Evolver* [Bra92]. Hartmann and Hardt employed Surface Evolver to investigate the stability of evaporating droplets on a patterned surface in [HH19]. A similar approach is used here to compute surface shapes slightly below the critical volume for stability as an initial condition for the VOF method; see [HFW+20] Section 3.1 for a more detailed description.

Since Surface Evolver delivers the droplet shape as a triangulated surface mesh, the resulting geometry cannot directly be used in the VOF method. It is a non-trivial task to convert the surface mesh into a volume fraction field according to the Cartesian mesh in FS3D. This problem has been solved by D. Gründing and T. Marić using the Surface-Cell Mesh Intersection (SCMI) algorithm in OpenFoam [TMGB20] (see [HFW+20] for more details). The latter approach is quite generic and may be useful in the future to combine Surface Evolver, being a powerful tool for static capillary surfaces, with transient continuum mechanical simulations.

Experimental methods: The substrates are prepared by fabricating a stripe pattern on a borofloat33 glass wafer using photolithography. Water droplets of de-ionized Milli-Q water are placed on the substrate such that two hydrophilic stripes and one hydrophobic stripe are wetted. Then the volume of the drop decreases due to evaporation until the critical width of the capillary bridge is reached. The final time period from the onset of the instability until breakup is recorded with a high-speed camera with 75 000 frames per second in top view mode. At the same time, a second high-speed camera records the process in side-view in order to measure the wetted length and the contact angle on the hydrophilic stripe. More details on the experimental methods can be found in [HFW+20], [HH19] and [Har20].

12.2.1. Continuum mechanical model and numerical methods

We apply a continuum mechanical model based on the standard model (3.22) discussed in Chapter 3. Neglecting the evaporation of the droplet, the balance equations for momentum and mass in the bulk, the transmission conditions at the liquid-gas interface and the kinematic condition are given as

$$\rho \frac{Dv}{Dt} - \eta \Delta v + \nabla p = \rho g, \ \nabla \cdot v = 0 \quad \text{in } \Omega \setminus \Sigma(t),$$
$$[\![v]\!] = 0, \quad [\![p\mathbf{1} - S]\!]\, n_\Sigma = \sigma \kappa n_\Sigma \quad \text{on } \Sigma(t),$$
$$V_\Sigma = \langle v, n_\Sigma \rangle \quad \text{on } \Sigma(t). \tag{12.24}$$

Along the solid boundary, we apply the impermeability and Navier slip condition, i.e.

$$\langle v, n_{\partial\Omega} \rangle = 0, \ v_{\parallel} + 2L(Dn_{\partial\Omega})_{\parallel} = 0 \quad \text{on } \partial\Omega \setminus \Gamma. \tag{12.25}$$

The wettability of the solid is modeled through the contact angle boundary condition

$$n_\Sigma \cdot n_{\partial\Omega} = \begin{cases} -\cos\theta_{\text{phil}} & \text{on} \quad \Gamma(t) \cap \partial\Omega_{\text{phil}} \\ -\cos\theta_{\text{phob}} & \text{on} \quad \Gamma(t) \cap \partial\Omega_{\text{phob}}, \end{cases} \tag{12.26}$$

where $\partial\Omega_{\text{phil}}$ and $\partial\Omega_{\text{phob}}$ denote the hydrophilic and hydrophobic parts of the boundary, respectively. The stripe pattern is aligned with the y-axis such that we have

$$\partial\Omega_{\text{phil}} = \{(x, y, 0) : \frac{\alpha}{2}\, \omega_{\text{phil}} \leq |x| \leq \left(\frac{\alpha}{2} + 1\right) \omega_{\text{phil}}\}, \quad \partial\Omega_{\text{phob}} = \partial\Omega \setminus \partial\Omega_{\text{phil}}.$$

Here ω_{phil} and ω_{phob} denote the width of the hydrophobic and hydrophilic stripes, respectively. The parameter[5] α is defined as the ratio of hydrophobic and hydrophilic stripe width, i.e.

$$\alpha = \frac{\omega_{\text{phob}}}{\omega_{\text{phil}}}. \tag{12.27}$$

Remark 12.6 (On the contact angle boundary condition). It is important to note that the contact angle boundary condition (12.26) cannot hold strictly at the boundary between $\partial\Omega_{\text{phil}}$ and $\partial\Omega_{\text{phob}}$ since this would imply that n_Σ is discontinuous. This means that for a rigorous analysis of the model (12.24)-(12.26) an appropriate concept of a weak solution must be introduced or the wetting patterns must be modeled with a smooth wetting energy σ_{w} leading to a finite transition zone between hydrophilic and hydrophobic stripes. Note that the energy functional for the stripe pattern in two dimensions exhibits stationary states with any contact angle in between θ_{phil} and θ_{phob} for appropriate volumes of the drop; see Section 12.1. According to Theorem 3.6, the contact line dissipation terms for a regular solution reads as

$$\sigma \int_{\Gamma(t)} (\cos\theta - \cos\theta_{\text{eq}}) V_\Gamma \, dl,$$

where the equilibrium contact angle θ_{eq} may be a function of $x \in \partial\Omega$. So, formally, the condition (12.26) leads to vanishing contact line dissipation. However, it should be investigated further if the latter statement is still rigorously true for a sharp wetting boundary. For the present numerical simulations, we apply the contact angle boundary condition (12.26) with the Height Function-based method described in Section 7.5.2. Hence, a local force is applied in order to enforce the contact angle according to (12.26) which means that the actual contact angle may differ from θ_{phil} or θ_{phob}, respectively.

Numerical methods: We employ the FS3D solver as described in Section 7.1 to solve the continuum mechanical model (12.24)-(12.26). The contact angle is enforced with the height function approach described in Section 7.5.2 where each computational cell is assigned to either the hydrophilic or the hydrophobic part of the solid surface. The staggered slip boundary condition (11.26) with $\omega = 2/3$ is applied to damp spurious currents at the contact line. In order to increase the accuracy at the contact line, we apply a three-dimensional variant of the Boundary Youngs method described in Section 8.2.

Numerical setup for FS3D: In order to save computational resources, we make use of the symmetry of the problem and simulate only a quarter of the droplet, while applying symmetry boundary conditions at the respective symmetry boundaries. At the outer boundaries of the domain, we apply no-slip for the velocity, which turns out to be irrelevant for the breakup dynamics (compared to, e.g., fixed pressure outflow boundary conditions). The computational domain has a size of $1000\,\mu\text{m} \times 2000\,\mu\text{m} \times 500\,\mu\text{m}$ and is subdivided into an equidistant mesh of $2N \times 4N \times N$ cells, where N is varied between 48 and 128. Therefore, the maximum resolution of the mesh is $500\,\mu\text{m}/128 \approx 3.9\,\mu\text{m}$ in each direction. The physical parameters used in the numerical simulation are listed in Table 12.1.

ρ_l [kg/m^3]	ρ_g [kg/m^3]	η_l [$10^{-6}\frac{\text{kg}}{\text{m·s}}$]	η_g [$10^{-6}\frac{\text{kg}}{\text{m·s}}$]	σ [$\frac{\text{mN}}{\text{m}}$]
997.05	1.17	890.45	18.5	71.96

Table 12.1.: Physical parameters for the numerical simulations ($T = 298\,\text{K}$, $p = 100\,\text{kPa}$).

12.2.2. Phase space picture of breakup dynamics

Following the literature, the breakup dynamics of a liquid bridge is usually described via the minimum width d as a function of the time τ before the breakup event, i.e. $\tau = t_0 - t$, where t_0 is the breakup time. For the inviscid breakup of a free capillary bridge, it can be shown by means of an asymptotic analysis that this function follows the power law (12.23). However, the precise time of the breakup event is hard to determine both in experiments (due

---

[5]The geometric parameter α defined in (12.27) should not be confused with the volume fraction field which is also denoted by α throughout the present work.

to finite spatial and temporal resolution) and in the simulation. Note that the choice of t_0 can have a large effect on the effective exponent that is extracted from the data. It has been reported that the same set of data appears to be represented by power laws

$$d(\tau) \propto \tau^{\nu}$$

with an exponent ν ranging from 0.6 to 0.8 depending on the choice of t_0 [BRT07]. Both Li and Sprittles [LS16] and Deblais et al. [DHH$^+$18] eliminated the dependency on the breakup time by rewriting the power law (12.23) according to

$$d = C \left(\frac{\sigma}{\rho}\right)^{1/3} (t_0 - t)^{2/3} \quad \Leftrightarrow \quad d^{3/2} = C^{3/2} \left(\frac{\sigma}{\rho}\right)^{1/2} (t_0 - t). \tag{12.28}$$

Obviously, equation (12.28) implies that the scaling law (12.23) holds if and only if the quantity $d^{3/2}$ is linear in time and the value of C can be found from the slope of $d^{3/2}$. If, conversely, the constant C depends on time it simply means that the inviscid scaling is not valid.

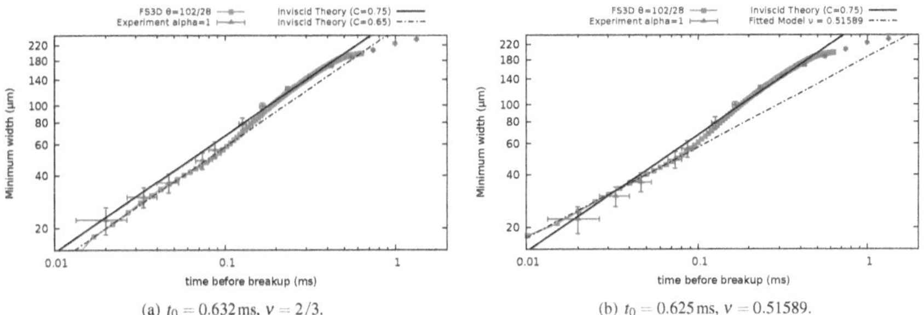

(a) $t_0 = 0.632$ ms, $\nu = 2/3$.   (b) $t_0 = 0.625$ ms, $\nu = 0.51589$.

Figure 12.6.: Breakup dynamics for different choices of the breakup time t_0 and the scaling exponent ν.

In the Volume-of-Fluid simulation, the actual breakup is usually mesh-dependent since it is ultimately performed by the interface reconstruction algorithm. Moreover, since the breakup process involves very small length scales, it cannot be fully resolved by the numerics. Therefore, the numerical results can only be considered meaningful down to a certain length scale determined by the computational mesh. In the present study, this length scale is approximately $20\,\mu$m. Consequently, the breakup time cannot be extracted from the numerics in a meaningful way without extrapolating the data.

The experimental value of the breakup time is determined from the pictures taken by the high-speed camera. The first image where the capillary bridge is pinched off defines the time $t^\star$ which is always larger than the real breakup time t_0. Clearly, the breakup must occur between $t^\star$ and the time associated with the previous image. We estimate the breakup time to be $t_0 = t^\star - \Delta t/2$, where $\Delta t = 1.33 \cdot 10^{-2}$ ms follows from the frame rate of the high-speed camera which is 75,000 fps. To account for the uncertainty in breakup time in the case of experiments, horizontal error bars with a total length of Δt are drawn. In the vertical direction, the error bar represents the standard deviation obtained from 5 experiments.

A concrete example for the sensitivity of the simulation results with respect to the choice of the breakup time is given in FIG. 12.6. Besides the experimental results, FIG. 12.6(a) shows the simulation data for the choice $t_0 = 0.632$ ms. The latter value is found by fitting the data in the final regime $d \lesssim 50\,\mu$m to the inviscid scaling exponent $\nu = 2/3$. FIG. 12.6(b) shows the same numerical data set for a slightly smaller breakup time $t_0 = 0.625$ ms. In this case, the numerical data agrees well with a power law with a smaller exponent $\nu \approx 0.52$, which has been obtained from the systematic phase space analysis described below. Note that the difference between the two choices $\Delta t_0 = 7\,\mu$s is smaller than the temporal resolution of the experiment which is approximately $\Delta t = 13\,\mu$s. This example clearly shows the need for a systematic method that does not rely on the breakup time.

Phase space analysis of the breakup dynamics: We apply a different approach to describe the breakup dynamics that is *independent* of the choice of the breakup time and allows to identify scaling regimes in a systematic way. This approach, which has been used already by Li and Sprittles [LS16], is systematically elaborated in the following.

Definition 12.7 (Phase space map). Let $I \subset \mathbb{R}$ be an open interval and $f \in \mathscr{C}^1(I;\mathbb{R})$ be a strictly monotonically increasing function. Then we define a continuous function

$$T_f : f(I) \to \mathbb{R}^+,$$

called the "phase space transformation of f", according to

$$\boxed{T_f(y) := f'(f^{-1}(y)).} \tag{12.29}$$

Obviously, the map $f \mapsto T_f$ defined by (12.29) is not invertible. In particular, it is insensitive to a shift of f with respect to the independent variable. More precisely, if f and g are $\mathscr{C}^1$ and monotonically increasing and there exists $x_0 \in \mathbb{R}$ such that

$$f(x) = g(x - x_0) \quad \text{for all} \quad x \in I$$

then it follows that

$$T_f(y) = T_g(y) \quad \text{for all} \quad y \in f(I).$$

We will show below that the remaining information encoded in f is preserved by the phase space map. In particular, the function f can be reconstructed from T_f up to a shift. The proofs of the following properties of the phase space map are based on the following simple identity:

Let $f : I \to \mathbb{R}$ be $\mathscr{C}^1$ and strictly monotonically increasing. Then the following identity holds

$$1 = \frac{d}{dy} f(f^{-1}(y)) = T_f(y)\,\frac{d}{dy} f^{-1}(y). \tag{12.30}$$

Hence, it follows by integration that there exists $x_0 \in \mathbb{R}$ and $y_0 \in f(I)$ such that

$$f^{-1}(y) = x_0 + \int_{y_0}^{y} \frac{ds}{T_f(s)}. \tag{12.31}$$

Consequently, the function f is the inverse of the right-hand side of (12.31), which is itself a strictly increasing $\mathscr{C}^1$ function. Using the latter identities, it is easy to verify the following Lemma, which allows to construct a pre-image of a given phase space function F.

Lemma 12.8 (Reverse transformation). *Let $U \subset \mathbb{R}$ be an open interval and*

$$F : U \to \mathbb{R}^+$$

be a continuous function. Let $x_0 \in \mathbb{R}$ and $y_0 \in U$. Then, the function $\mathscr{F} : U \to \mathbb{R}^+$ defined as

$$\boxed{\mathscr{F}(y) = x_0 + \int_{y_0}^{y} \frac{1}{F(s)}\,ds} \tag{12.32}$$

is invertible with $\mathscr{F}(y_0) = x_0$ and the inverse $\mathscr{F}^{-1}$ satisfies

$$T_{\mathscr{F}^{-1}} = F.$$

Moreover, we show uniqueness of the pre-image up to a shift.

Lemma 12.9 (Uniqueness up to a shift). *Let $U, I_f, I_g \subset \mathbb{R}$ be a open intervals and*

$$F : U \to \mathbb{R}^+$$

be a continuous function. Moreover, let $f : I_f \to \mathbb{R}$ and $g : I_g \to \mathbb{R}$ be $\mathscr{C}^1$ and strictly monotonically increasing functions such that

$$T_f(y) = T_g(y) \quad \text{for all} \quad y \in f(I_f) \cap g(I_g) \neq \emptyset. \tag{12.33}$$

Then, there is x_0 such that

$$f(x) = g(x - x_0).$$

Proof. Obviously, eq. (12.33) implies that

$$\frac{1}{T_f(y)} = \frac{1}{T_g(y)} \quad \text{for all} \quad y \in f(I_f) \cap g(I_g)$$

and hence using (12.30) it follows that

$$\frac{d}{dy} f^{-1}(y) = \frac{d}{dy} g^{-1}(y).$$

By integration of the latter equation, it follows that there exists $x_0 \in \mathbb{R}$ such that

$$f^{-1}(y) = x_0 + g^{-1}(y) \quad \text{for all} \quad y \in f(I_f) \cap g(I_g).$$

Hence, we have the equality of functions $f^{-1} = x_0 + g^{-1}$. By inversion, it follows that

$$f = (x_0 + g^{-1})^{-1} = g(x - x_0).$$

$$\square$$

Application to the breakup process: Given the minimum width of the capillary bridge as a function of physical time t, we consider the *breakup speed*, i.e. the time derivative

$$V = -\dot{d}$$

as a function of the *minimum width* itself, i.e. we formally define

$$V(d_0) := -\dot{d}(d^{-1}(d_0)). \tag{12.34}$$

The latter definition fits in the framework (12.29) for $f(t) = d(t_0 - t)$. As discussed above, the function $V(d)$ is invariant with respect to shifts in the time coordinate. For the power law (12.23) describing the inviscid regime, we have

$$d(t) = C \left(\frac{\sigma(t_0 - t)^2}{\rho} \right)^{1/3} \quad \Rightarrow \quad \dot{d}(t) = -\frac{2}{3} C \left(\frac{\sigma}{\rho(t_0 - t)} \right)^{1/3} = -\frac{2}{3} C^{3/2} \left(\frac{\sigma}{\rho\, d(t)} \right)^{1/2}.$$

Hence the power law (12.23) translates to

$$V(d) = \frac{2}{3} C^{3/2} \left(\frac{\sigma}{\rho d} \right)^{1/2}. \tag{12.35}$$

More generally, one can easily show the relation

$$d(t) = c(t_0 - t)^\nu \quad \Rightarrow \quad V(d) = \nu c^{1/\nu} d^{1 - 1/\nu} = \tilde{c} d^{\tilde{\nu}}, \tag{12.36}$$

which is valid for an arbitrary power law ($\nu, c > 0$). So a scaling exponent $\tilde{\nu}$ and the prefactor $\tilde{c}$ obtained from the phase space diagram can be transformed into the standard representation via

$$\nu = \frac{1}{1 - \tilde{\nu}}, \quad c = \left(\frac{\tilde{c}}{\nu} \right)^\nu = [(1 - \tilde{\nu})\tilde{c}]^{1/(1-\tilde{\nu})}. \tag{12.37}$$

For the material parameters of water in air (temperature $T = 298\,\text{K}$, pressure $p = 100\,\text{kPa}$), the relations (12.23) and (12.35) for a free liquid bridge take the form

$$d(\tau) = C \cdot 416\,\hat{t}^{2/3}\,\mu\text{m}, \quad V(d) = C^{3/2} \cdot 5657\,\hat{d}^{-1/2}\,\frac{\mu\text{m}}{\text{ms}},$$

where $\tau = \hat{t}\,\text{ms}$ and $d = \hat{d}\,\mu\text{m}$. In the present chapter, these relations will be referred to as "inviscid theory".

Note that the above method requires to differentiate potentially noisy data with respect to time. This issue has been addressed via filtering out high-frequency oscillations in the experimental values of $V(d)$ by locally fitting a straight line to the data (using six neighboring points). Despite this difficulty, the method allows studying the breakup dynamics in detail without the uncertainty in choosing t_0. In the following, we will report both $V(d)$ and $d(t_0 - t)$ for completeness.

12.2.3. Qualitative description of the breakup process

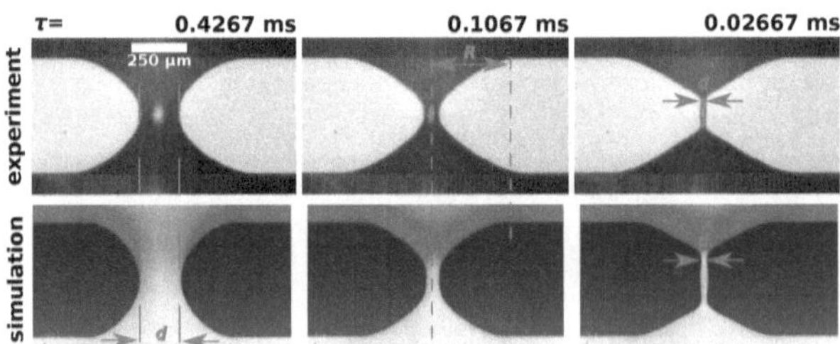

Figure 12.7.: Breakup dynamics of a capillary bridge - qualitative comparison.

Qualitatively, the considered breakup process is similar to the breakup of a free liquid bridge as described by Li and Sprittles [LS16] and the collapse of a soap film described by Chen and Steen [CS97].
The liquid bridge evolves starting from a catenoid type shape; see Fig. 12.7 (left). In both experiments and simulations, the surface evolves into a narrower shape with a cylindrical liquid thread formed in the middle of the hydrophobic area. The location of the minimum diameter is transported towards the end of the cylindrical thread in the subsequent evolution; see Fig. 12.7 (right). The qualitative agreement between the shapes in the experiment and the numerics is good. However, we note that the curvature of the free surface differs between experiment and simulation already for the initial data of the simulation; see Fig. 12.7 (left). Moreover, we note that the cylindrical liquid thread is more elongated in the simulation compared to the experiment; see Fig. 12.7 (middle) and (right). Close to the final breakup the liquid bridge develops a double cone structure which has been already observed for a free liquid bridge [LS16] and a collapsing soap film [CS97].

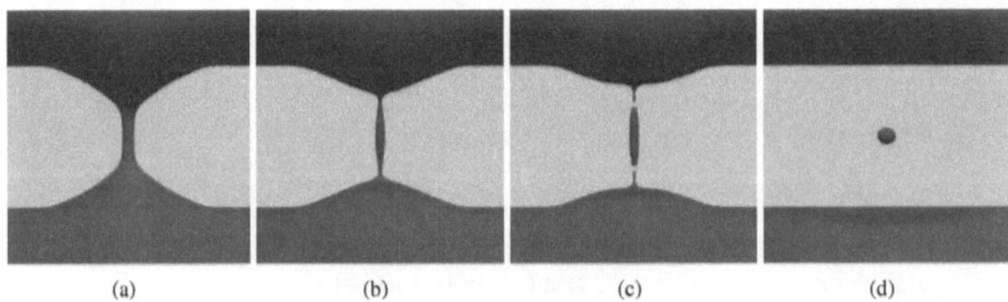

Figure 12.8.: Generation of satellite droplets in the VOF simulation.

We note that the VOF simulation is able to describe the generation of a satellite droplet as observed in the experiment; see Fig. 12.8 (d). However, we do not expect this part of the simulation to be quantitatively accurate since the interface is under-resolved close to the actual breakup; see Figure 12.8 where (b) is well-resolved while (c) is not. A careful inspection shows that even smaller *secondary* satellite droplets are produced in the experiment. These secondary satellite droplets are not visible in the simulation due to the limited spatial resolution.

12.2.4. Quantitative comparison

The case $\alpha = 1$:

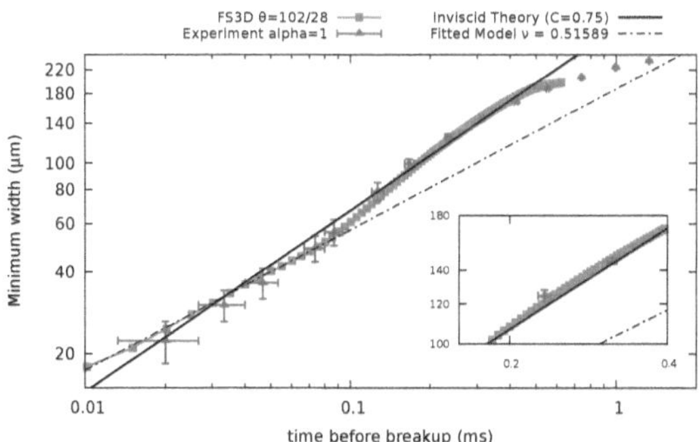

Figure 12.9.: Minimum bridge width as a function of time before breakup, experiment vs. simulation ($\alpha = 1, \tilde{L} = 500\,\mathrm{nm}$).

We first consider the case where the width of the hydrophilic and the hydrophobic stripes is equal, i.e. the case $\alpha = 1$. The evolution of the minimum bridge width as a function of the time before breakup is shown in Fig. 12.9. In general, a good agreement between the simulation results (red squares) and the experimental data (blue triangles) is found. Note that the initial bridge width computed by surface evolver ($d \approx 200\,\mu\mathrm{m}$) agrees well with the critical value observed in the experiment. At a first glance, the dynamics in the region between approximately $100\,\mu\mathrm{m}$ and $180\,\mu\mathrm{m}$ appears to be in good agreement with the inviscid theory for a free capillary bridge with constant $C = 0.75$. However, a close inspection (see inset in Fig. 12.9) shows that the data points doe *not* lie on an exactly straight line but some non-zero curvature is visible. This discrepancy becomes much more visible in the phase space diagram; see below. For values of the bridge width below approximately $100\,\mu\mathrm{m}$, there is a transition to a second dynamic region which can be characterized by a smaller exponent $\nu \approx 0.5$. The latter value is obtained mainly from the numerical data. The experimental data hardly allow to quantify the exponent for $d < 40\,\mu\mathrm{m}$ due to the limited spatial and, more importantly, temporal resolution. In this case, the numerical simulation serves as a "magnifier" to observe the process on small timescales. Obviously, there is no principal limit for the temporal resolution of the simulation while the temporal resolution in the experiment is limited by the capabilities of the optical system. However, it is important to note that the observed exponent for the simulation close to breakup is strongly dependent on the choice of the breakup time; see Fig. 12.6 above. In the present case, the breakup time has been computed from an extrapolation of the data in the phase space diagram; see below.

Phase space analysis: The phase space representation of the data in Fig. 12.9 is reported in Fig. 12.10. But instead of averaged quantities, we report the breakup speed obtained from three individual repetitions of the experiment. As a result of the noise in the experimental data, the values for the experimental values for the breakup speed are rather noisy. However, we find a good qualitative and even quantitative agreement between simulation and experiment. First of all, we notice that the slope in the region $100\,\mu\mathrm{m}$ and $180\,\mu\mathrm{m}$ does not agree with the inviscid scaling law $\nu = 2/3$ (solid black line). It only applies in an averaged sense meaning that the time it takes to go from $d \approx 180\,\mu\mathrm{m}$ down to $d \approx 100\,\mu\mathrm{m}$ is approximately equal between the actual results and the inviscid

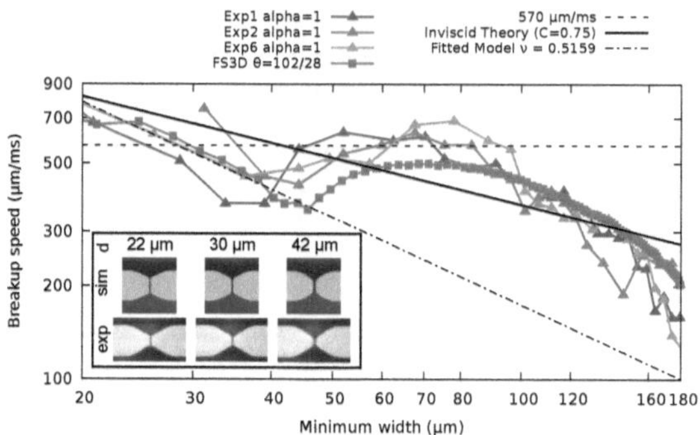

Figure 12.10.: Breakup speed ($\alpha = 1$, $\tilde{L} = 500\,\text{nm}$) as a function of the bridge width compared to three different experiments. The pictures inside of the graph show the (closest) images for simulations (sim) and experiments (exp) to the minimum bridge width indicated in the top row.

scaling law. In fact, there is a complex dynamic behavior in the evolution of the minimum bridge width. In both the experiments and the simulation, the breakup speed reaches a plateau where it is nearly constant before it decreases further towards a local minimum. The average plateau speed in the experiment ($570\,\mu\text{m}/\text{ms}$) is slightly underestimated in the simulation ($500\,\mu\text{m}/\text{ms}$).

Remarkably, the time instant of the local minimum in the breakup speed at $d \approx 45\,\mu\text{m}$ coincides with the time instant when the position of the local minimum of the bridge width starts to move from the center towards the endpoints of the liquid bridge; see Fig. 12.11. In this sense, the local minimum in the breakup speed marks the starting point of a second dynamic regime.

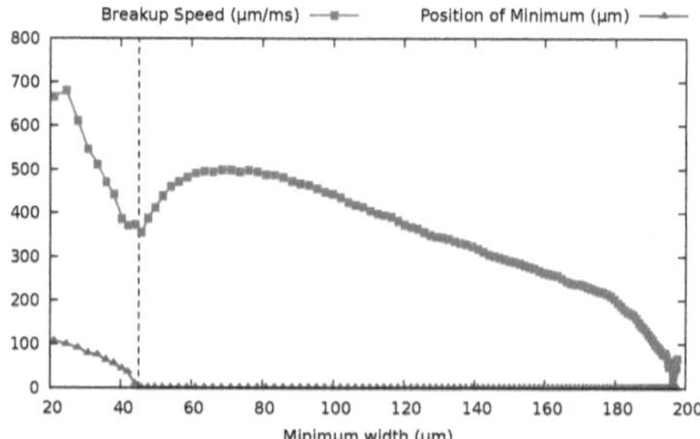

Figure 12.11.: Breakup speed and position of the local minimum relative to the center of the hydrophobic stripe (numerical simulation data).

From fitting the numerical data in the region $20\,\mu\text{m} \lesssim d \lesssim 45\,\mu\text{m}$ in the double logarithmic representation in Fig. 12.10 with a straight line, we find

$$V(d) = 13112\,\frac{\mu\text{m}}{\text{ms}} \cdot \left(\frac{d}{\mu\text{m}}\right)^{-0.9384} \tag{12.38}$$

which corresponds to

$$d(\tau) = 187.31 \,\mu\text{m} \cdot \left(\frac{\tau}{\text{ms}}\right)^{0.51589} ; \tag{12.39}$$

see the dash-dotted line in Fig. 12.9 and Fig. 12.10. In particular, the exponent ν in the standard representation $d \propto \tau^\nu$ is close to 0.5. This means that we do not observe the inviscid scaling law for a free capillary bridge characterized by $\nu = 2/3$. In fact, as it has been pointed out by Deblais et al., "the approach to asymptotic power laws can be slow and may pass through one or several transient regimes before the final universal regime is reached" [DHH$^+$18]. Hence the scaling exponent ν may change on smaller length scales below the resolution of the present experiments and simulations. This hypothesis is supported by the comparison with the numerical data for a free capillary bridge given below.

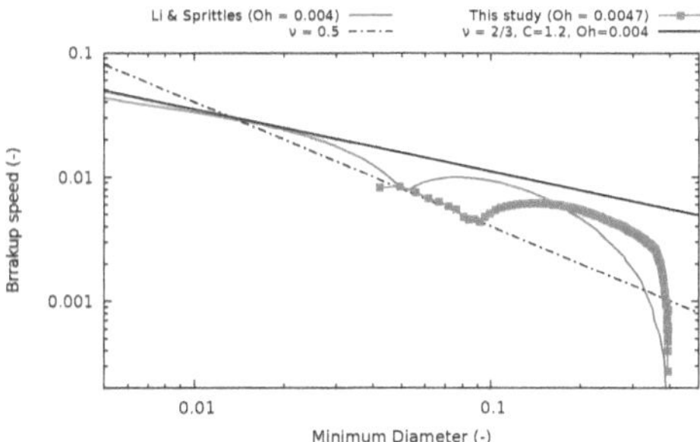

Figure 12.12.: Comparison with numerical data from Li and Sprilles [LS16] for the breakup of a free capillary bridge.

Comparison with numerical data for a free capillary bridge: The present results are compared with numerical data by Li and Sprittles [LS16] for a *free* capillary bridge in Fig. 12.12. The data are taken from Fig. 16 (a) in the work by Li and Sprittles and subsequently transformed into the representation defined in equation (12.34). The numerical data from the present study have been converted in non-dimensional form with the hydrophobic stripe width $w_{\text{phob}} = 500 \,\mu\text{m}$ as a length scale and η/σ as a velocity scale. Notably, the breakup dynamics for the free capillary bridge is qualitatively similar to the present case of a capillary bridge in contact with a substrate. In particular, there is a clear plateau and a local minimum visible in the breakup speed. However, the position of the local minimum in the phase space diagram is shifted towards smaller values of the dimensionless minimum diameter. The transition to the final inviscid scaling regime is reached for a dimensionless minimum diameter of 0.01. The latter length scale cannot be resolved in the present experiments and simulations.

Mesh study: To quantify the influence of the numerical discretization, Fig. 12.13(a) shows the breakup speed for different mesh resolutions ($8N^3$ computational cells where $N \in \{64, 96, 128\}$). Besides some oscillations in the breakup speed on the coarse mesh, the results appear to be reasonably mesh-independent for d larger than approximately $40 \,\mu\text{m}$, whereas the simulation on the coarsest mesh ($N = 48$, $\Delta x \approx 10.4 \,\mu\text{m}$) appears to be under-resolved. The finest mesh ($N = 128$, $\Delta x \approx 3.9 \,\mu\text{m}$) delivers reasonable results for $d \gtrsim 10 \,\mu\text{m}$. This corresponds to only 2.5 computational cells within the bridge width. Since mesh convergence cannot be assured on this scale, the numerical data below approximately $20 \,\mu\text{m}$ should not be used to draw a quantitative conclusion.

Influence of the slip length: As shown in Fig. 12.13(b), where $\tilde{L}$ is varied from $100 \,\text{nm}$ to $500 \,\text{nm}$, the choice of the (staggered) slip length shows only a minor influence on the breakup dynamics. This behavior is to be expected in the inviscid regime (low Oh), where viscous dissipation due to slip is irrelevant for the breakup process. A slight monotonic decrease of the breakup speed with the slip length is visible when the breakup speed approaches the local minimum at approximately $45 \,\mu\text{m}$. In all subsequent numerical simulations, we apply a staggered slip length of 500nm.

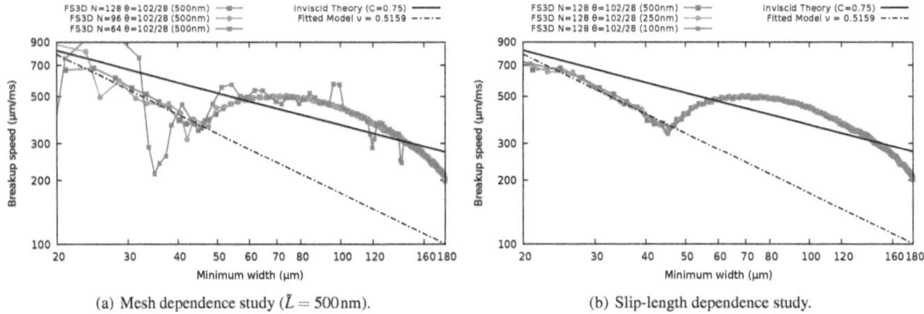

(a) Mesh dependence study ($\bar{L} = 500$ nm).

(b) Slip-length dependence study.

Figure 12.13.: Mesh and slip-length dependence study for $\alpha = 1$, $\theta_{\text{phob}} = 102°$ and $\theta_{\text{phil}} = 28°$.

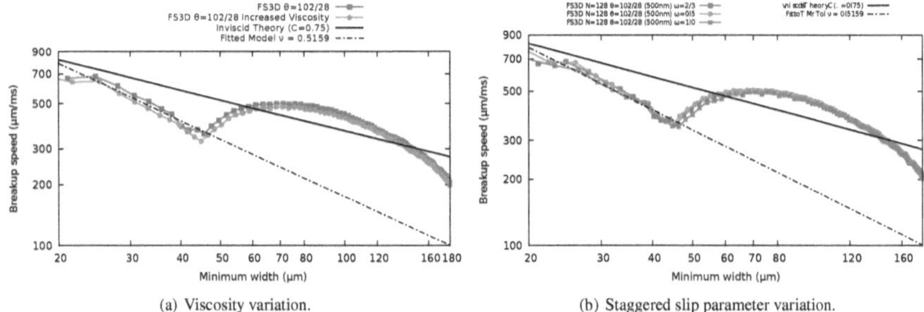

(a) Viscosity variation.

(b) Staggered slip parameter variation.

Figure 12.14.: Influence of the dynamic viscosity and the staggered slip parameter ω.

Influence of the dynamic viscosity: The influence of the dynamic viscosity on the breakup dynamics in the simulation is studied in Fig. 12.14(a). The green curve is computed with an 50% increased dynamic viscosity in both the liquid and the gas phase. Despite this large increase in the viscosity, there is only a small decrease in the breakup speed of approximately 4%. In particular, the overall shape is unchanged including the position of the local minimum and the scaling exponents. Moreover, a variation of the empirical parameter ω in the staggered slip condition (11.26) is reported in Fig. 12.14(b). The influence of the choice of ω on the breakup dynamics is weak and only visible when the local minimum in the breakup velocity is approached. From this, we conclude that viscous effects including boundary slip (see Fig. 12.13(b)) play no significant role. Instead, the process is controlled mainly by a balance of inertial and capillary forces.

Influence of the wetting conditions: The influence of the wetting conditions through the contact angle $\theta_{\text{phob}} \in \{90°, 102°, 110°\}$ on the hydrophobic stripe is studied in Fig. 12.15(a). Here we employed Surface Evolver to compute individual initial liquid surfaces for each case. The results show that the dynamics stays qualitatively similar, while the whole graph is shifted to the right with decreasing θ_{phob}. The colored lines show fits to the second dynamic regime. Note that the difference in the scaling exponents is very small so that it can be concluded that the wetting condition, i.e. the contact angle, has no major influence on the breakup dynamics in the second dynamic regime. Interestingly, the (rather complex) dynamics in the region between $20\,\mu$m and approximately $60\,\mu$m can be collapsed onto a single curve by shifting the curves in the phase space plot; see Fig. 12.15(b).

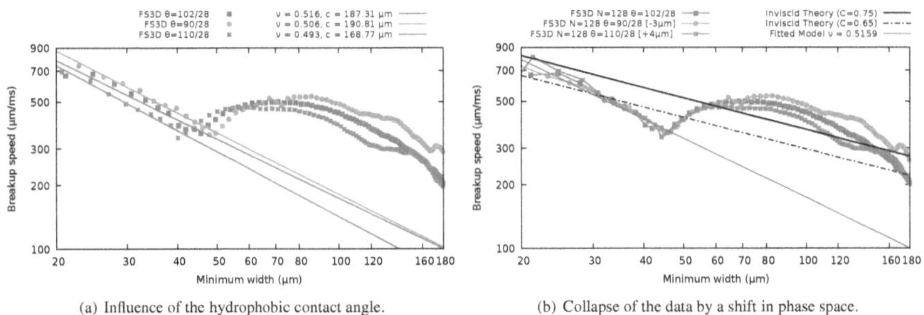

(a) Influence of the hydrophobic contact angle.　　　(b) Collapse of the data by a shift in phase space.

Figure 12.15.: Influence of the wetting conditions.

The case $\alpha = 0.5$

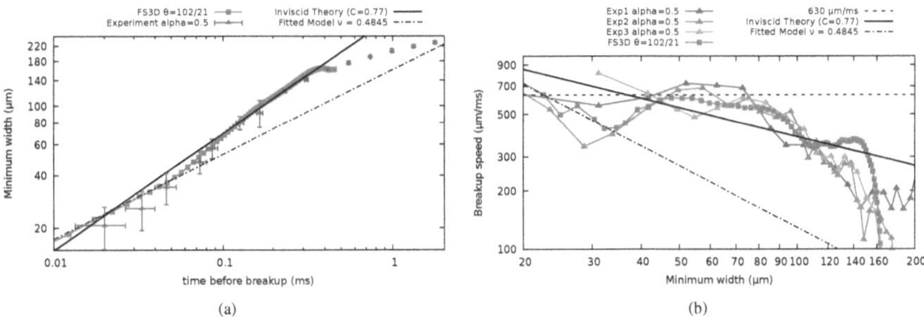

(a)　　　(b)

Figure 12.16.: Breakup dynamics for $\alpha = 0.5$. Left: Minimum bridge width as a function of time. Right: Breakup speed as a function of the bridge width.

Fig. 12.16 shows the breakup dynamics for the case $\alpha = 0.5$. Like in the previous case, we observe a complex transient behavior with a plateau in the breakup speed followed by a local minimum and a second dynamic regime. In general, the quantitative agreement between experiments and simulation is good. However, there is a short phase at the beginning of the process where the breakup speed is higher in the simulation ($d \gtrsim 100\,\mu$m). This is probably due to a deviation of the initial data computed by the surface evolver from the free surface shape in the experiment. The plateau speed in the experiment ($630\,\mu$m/ms) is well captured by the simulation. Like for the case $\alpha = 1$, the exponent in the second dynamic regime is close to $1/2$; see the dash-dotted line in Fig. 12.16(b).

The case $\alpha = 1.5$

The breakup dynamics in the case $\alpha = 1.5$ is qualitatively similar to the cases $\alpha = 0.5, 1$; see Fig. 12.17. Shortly after the onset of the instability at approximately $280\,\mu$m, the dynamics in the numerical simulation is compatible with the inviscid theory for $C \approx 0.75$ in an averaged sense; see Fig. 12.17(a). Like in the previous cases, the breakup speed reaches a plateau and a local minimum in the breakup speed is found at $d \approx 56\,\mu$m. The scaling exponent in the second dynamic regime $\nu \approx 0.55$ is slightly increased compared to the previous cases.

However, there is a large discrepancy between simulation and experiment at the onset of the instability. While

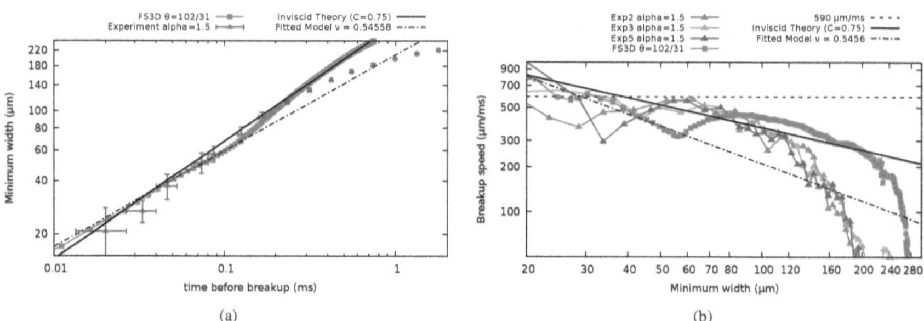

Figure 12.17.: Breakup dynamics for $\alpha = 1.5$. Left: Minimum bridge width as a function of time. Right: Breakup speed as a function of the bridge width.

the breakup starts at $d \approx 280\,\mu$m in the simulation, the onset of the instability in the experiment is observed for much smaller values of the bridge width ($d \approx 200\,\mu$m). As a result, the whole process appears to be shifted towards larger values of the bridge width in the simulation. Moreover, the plateau velocity is significantly underestimated in the simulation (445 μm/ms vs. 590 μm/ms). But still there is reasonable agreement between simulation and experiment for $d \lesssim 100\,\mu$m; see Fig. 12.17.(a). A possible explanation for the large deviation between experiment and simulation is the deviation from the initial geometry of the free surface delivered by the Surface Evolver and the observed geometry in the experiment; see bottom row of Fig. 12.18. In particular, the curvature of the free surface in the plane parallel to the substrate is notably different. So possibly the agreement could be improved with improved initial data.

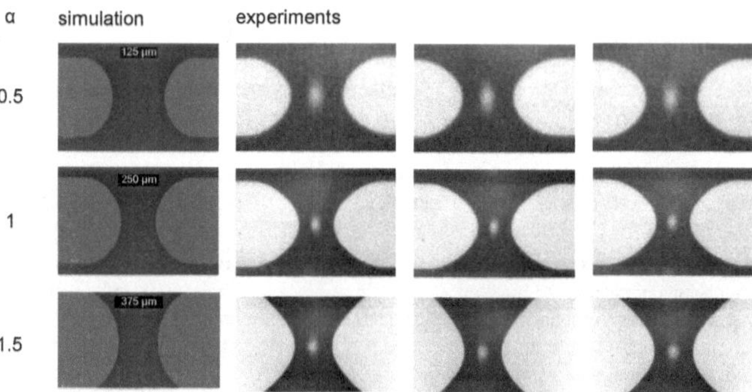

Figure 12.18.: Initial conditions from Surface Evolver compared to experimental images (Figure by M. Hartmann [HFW$^+$20]).

12.3. A note on dynamic surface tension effects

It is well-known in the literature that the breakup of a liquid thread is a process that gives rise to a high local rate of interface generation. Shihkmurzaev writes in his monograph:

> "As we can see now, the breakup phenomenon is indeed the process of the interface formation, and in this sense it is opposite to coalescence where one has the disappearance of the liquid-gas interface trapped between the coalescing bodies. Similarly to the situation we had in coalescence, where the inherent — and admissible — singularity of the free-surface curvature at $t = 0$ indicated the way to resolve the problem, the breakup is also associated with an 'additional' singularity, this time it is an emerging singularity in the rate-of-creation of the free-surface area, that gives a key to the modelling." [Shi08, p.361]

Here the author refers to the fact that the relative rate of change of the surface area tends to infinity for the stretching of a liquid cylinder which is the essential kinematics of the breakup process as also mentioned in [HDB$^+$17]. Hauner et al. studied the formation of water drops in [HDB$^+$17] and came to an interesting conclusion:

> "We therefore use the precise and universal prefactor obtained in our experiments on a series of other liquids of known surface tension. The surface tensions were verified independently on the liquids used in the snap-off experiments. Using this prefactor does not lead to the expected value of the surface tension of 72 mN/m, but rather to a surprisingly high value of 90 mN/m. This strongly suggests that the surface tension of a newly formed water surface on a time scale < 1ms is different from the equilibrium surface tension, implying that some surface relaxation must take place."
> [HDB$^+$17, p. 1600]

Note that the obtained value for the surface tension is strongly dependent on the prefactor C in (12.23). Hauner et al. determined $C = 0.9 \pm 0.01$ from their experiments even though it is expected to be close to 1.4 from similarity theory [EF15] and close to 1.2 in numerical simulations [LS16]. This discrepancy might be due to an insufficient temporal resolution of the experiments. The camera used in [HDB$^+$17] operates at 54.000 frames per second. The resulting temporal resolution of $\Delta t \approx 20\,\mu$s is probably not sufficient to capture the final regime of the breakup process. In fact, a later experimental study using 100.000 frames per second came to the conclusion that the "universality is unobservable in practice" [DHH$^+$18]. Nevertheless, using an increased surface tension in the simulation of the breakup process leads to interesting results (see below).

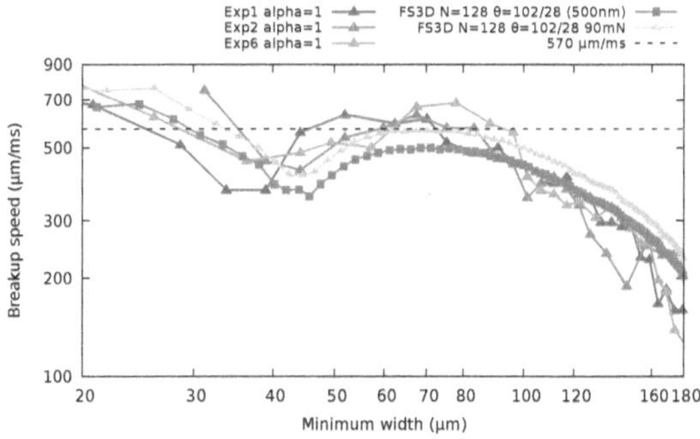

Figure 12.19.: Breakup dynamics for $\alpha = 1$, simulation with increased surface tension.

Numerical simulation with increased surface tension: Dynamic surface tension effects might be relevant also in the present case of the breakup of a wetting liquid bridge [Bot20a]. Indeed, we find a remarkable quantitative agreement between the numerical simulations and the experimental data for $d \lesssim 100\,\mu$m if the (spatially constant) surface tension of the liquid-vapor interface is set to the higher surface tension under discussion [HDB$^+$17] for a pristine water surface, namely

$$\sigma = 90\,\text{mN/m}.$$

The average experimental plateau velocity of approximately $570\,\mu\text{m/ms}$ is accurately captured by the simulation with the increased surface tension; see the yellow curve in Fig. 12.19. Conversely, the breakup speed for large diameters is overestimated. This, however, can be explained qualitatively by the fact that the dynamic surface tension effect becomes relevant when fresh liquid-vapor interface is created locally at a sufficiently high rate comparably to $1/\tau$, where τ is the surface tension relaxation timescale (according to Hauner et al. [HDB$^+$17] $\tau \propto 1\,\text{ms}$). The local interface generation rate at the onset of the breakup process is probably too small for the effect to be significant. Moreover, we emphasize that the corresponding Marangoni forces due to local gradients in the dynamic surface tension cannot be captured with the present numerical method. We, therefore, consider the Dynamic Surface Tension effect as a hypothesis that might be able to explain the quantitative deviations between experiment and simulation. Further efforts[6] in both mathematical modeling and numerical methods are necessary in order to confirm or falsify the hypothesis.

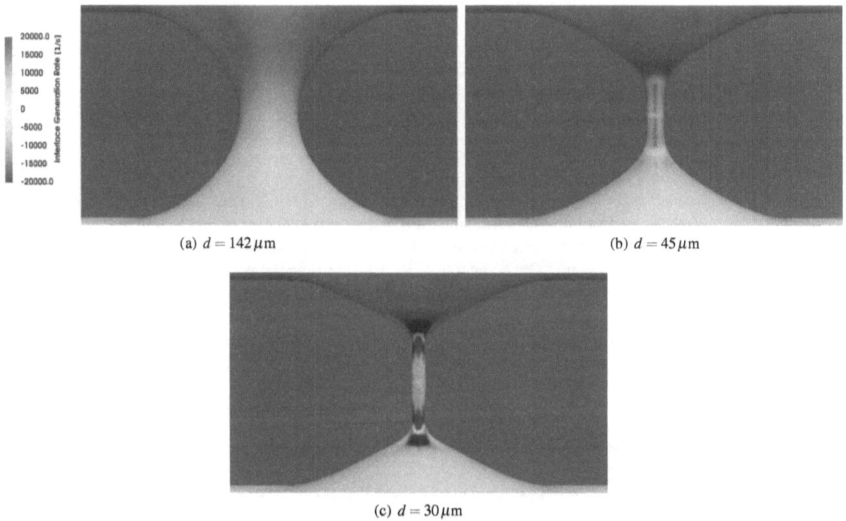

(a) $d = 142\,\mu\text{m}$

(b) $d = 45\,\mu\text{m}$

(c) $d = 30\,\mu\text{m}$

Figure 12.20.: Local interface generation rate during breakup ($\alpha = 1$, $\sigma = 72\,\text{mN/m}$).

Local free surface generation rate: In order to check whether or not the hypothesis of a dynamic surface tension influence is reasonable in the present process, we compute the local rate of interface generation for our numerical simulations with the equilibrium surface tension $\sigma = 72\,\text{mN/m}$. Mathematically, the relative rate of local interface generation can be expressed as (see Equation A.8 in Appendix A)

$$\mathcal{R}(t,x) = \frac{1}{A}\frac{dA}{dt} = \text{div}_\Sigma v_\Sigma(x), \quad x \in \Sigma(t), \tag{12.40}$$

where v_Σ is the full interface velocity. In the present model (12.24), we have a continuous bulk velocity across Σ and may, therefore, choose $v_\Sigma = v^\pm$ leading to

$$\mathcal{R} = \text{div}_\Sigma v = \nabla \cdot v^\pm - \langle n_\Sigma, (\nabla v^\pm) n_\Sigma \rangle = -\langle n_\Sigma, D^\pm n_\Sigma \rangle. \tag{12.41}$$

---

[6]This is an ongoing joined work with D. Bothe and S. Hardt.

In order to estimate the interface generation rate according to (12.41), we discretize ∇v at interface cells using the three dimensional Youngs method. Note that according to (12.24), the velocity gradient ∇v may jump at the interface. However, eq. (12.41) implies that $\langle n_\Sigma, (\nabla v^\pm) n_\Sigma \rangle$ is continuous since

$$-\langle n_\Sigma, (\nabla v^+) n_\Sigma \rangle = \mathscr{R} = -\langle n_\Sigma, (\nabla v^-) n_\Sigma \rangle \quad \text{on } \Sigma.$$

The results for the local interface generation rate at different instances of the breakup process are shown in Figure 12.20. Note that the physical unit of $\mathscr{R}$ is $1/\text{s}$. The dynamic surface tension effect can be expected to be relevant for the process if the interface generation rate is comparable to the inverse relaxation time [Shi08, HDB$^+$17], i.e.

$$\mathscr{R} \gtrsim \frac{1}{\tau}. \tag{12.42}$$

Hence, for a hypothetical relaxation time $\tau = 1\text{ms}$ as suggested by Hauner et al. [HDB$^+$17], the condition would be $\mathscr{R} \gtrsim 10^3\,1/\text{s}$. The estimates for $\mathscr{R}$ shown in Figure 12.20 show that values greater than $10^4\,1/\text{s}$ appear in the center of the liquid cylinder and later at the pinch-off points (red color) where the surface is stretched at a high rate. Moreover, the local interface generation rate is negative (blue color) where the double cone structure develops. The spatial distribution of $\mathscr{R}$ in Fig. 12.20 suggests that strong Marangoni forces would act in the regions with a high gradient of $\mathscr{R}$ if dynamic surface tension effects would be present in the system. In fact, these forces would point in the direction of the center of the capillary bridge and could explain the deviation in the free surface shape between experiment and simulation reported in Figure 12.7. In particular, the Marangoni forces could possibly explain why the liquid cylinder is shorter in the experiment. However, a quantitative study of dynamic surface tension effects is outside the scope of the present work and will be addressed in our future research.

12.4. Structured capillary rise

The combination of the capillary rise problem described in Chapter 11 with a chemically patterned surface may give rise to a rather complex and interesting dynamic behavior. In order to understand the qualitative differences to the case of a homogeneous surface, we briefly revisit and generalize the derivation of the stationary rise height given in Section 11.1. For the sake of simplicity, we only study the two-dimensional case.

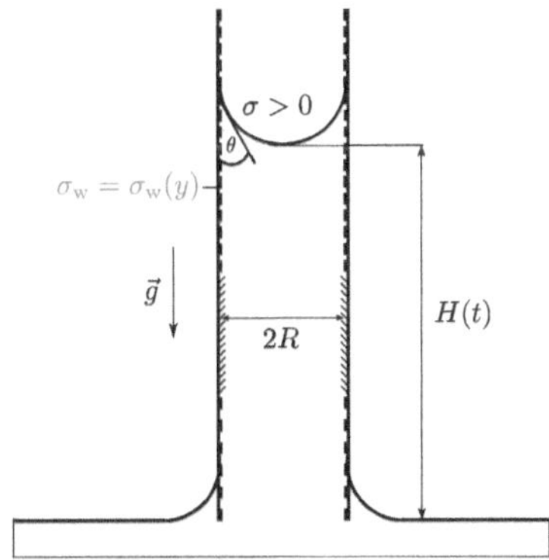

Figure 12.21.: Capillary rise problem for a structured solid surface.

We follow the simplified reasoning outlined in Section 11.1, where the details of the meniscus shape are ignored in the energy functional, i.e.

$$\frac{\mathcal{E}}{R\sigma} \approx \tilde{\mathcal{E}}(\tilde{H}) = 2\int_0^{\tilde{H}} \tilde{\sigma}_{\mathrm{w}}(\tilde{y})\,d\tilde{y} + \mathrm{Bo}\,\tilde{H}^2 + 1. \tag{12.43}$$

Here $\tilde{y} = y/R$ is the dimensionless coordinate in the vertical direction and $\tilde{H} = H/R$ denotes the dimensionless rise height. The only generalization compared to Section 11.1 is that the wetting energy $\sigma_{\mathrm{w}} = \sigma_{\mathrm{sl}} - \sigma_{\mathrm{sg}}$ may now be a function of the vertical coordinate, i.e.

$$\tilde{\sigma}_{\mathrm{w}}(\tilde{y}) = \frac{\sigma_{\mathrm{w}}(\tilde{y}R)}{\sigma}.$$

Continuous wetting energy: Provided that σ_{w} is continuous, the stationary points of the functional (12.43) are characterized by the (in general nonlinear) equation

$$\tilde{H} = -\frac{\tilde{\sigma}_{\mathrm{w}}(\tilde{H})}{\mathrm{Bo}}. \tag{12.44}$$

Note that a solution of (12.44) may be a local minimum, a local maximum, or a saddle point of the functional (12.43). In fact, we have the relation

$$\tilde{\mathcal{E}}''(\tilde{H}) = 2\left(\tilde{\sigma}_{\mathrm{w}}'(\tilde{H}) + \mathrm{Bo}\right).$$

Hence, $\tilde{H}$ is a local minimum of the simplified energy functional if (12.44) holds and (provided that $\tilde{\sigma}_{\mathrm{w}} \in \mathscr{C}^1$)

$$\tilde{\sigma}_{\mathrm{w}}'(\tilde{H}) + \mathrm{Bo} > 0.$$

Clearly, the latter condition is trivially fulfilled in the case of constant wetting energy.

Capillary rise in the presence of sharp wetting boundaries: In analogy to Section 12.2, we now investigate the effect of a stripe pattern on the capillary rise dynamics. We consider the prototypical example

$$\tilde{\sigma}_{\mathrm{w}}(\tilde{y}) = \begin{cases} \tilde{\sigma}_w^1 & \text{for} \quad \tilde{y} \leq H_0, \\ \tilde{\sigma}_w^2 & \text{for} \quad H_0 \leq \tilde{y} \leq H_0 + \Delta, \\ \tilde{\sigma}_w^3 & \text{for} \quad \tilde{y} > H_0 + \Delta. \end{cases} \tag{12.45}$$

By combining hydrophobic and hydrophilic areas, it is possible to construct an energy functional with two stable configurations and thereby introduce a bifurcation in the dynamic behavior.

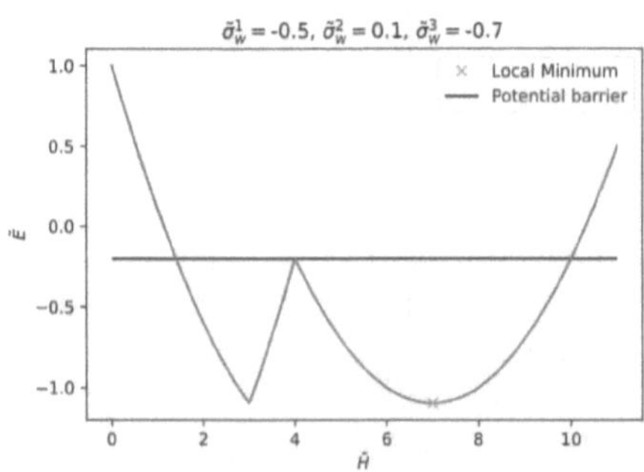

Figure 12.22.: Approximation of the energy functional (Example 12.10).

Example 12.10. As an example, we choose

$$\text{Bo} = 0.1, \; H_0 = 3, \; \Delta = 1$$

and

$$\tilde{\sigma}_w^1 = -0.5, \; \tilde{\sigma}_w^2 = 0.1, \; \tilde{\sigma}_w^3 = -0.7.$$

In this case, two hydrophilic regions are separated by a hydrophobic stripe. The simplified energy functional $\tilde{E}$ for the latter set of parameters is shown in Fig. 12.22. The hydrophobic stripe acts as a potential barrier leading to two stable configurations at $\tilde{H} = 3$ and $\tilde{H} = 7$. Note, however, that the functional $\tilde{E}$ is only an approximation to the energy such that the actual stable configurations will be slightly shifted. An interesting consequence of the form of the energy functional is that the system can, depending on the initial condition and the dissipation in the system, asymptotically reach both stable states. The critical value of the initial rise height based on the approximate energy shown in Figure 12.22 is $\tilde{H}_c \approx 1.4$. We expect, however, that the critical value of the dimensionless initial height in the continuum mechanical simulation is less than 1.4 since part of the initial potential energy is dissipated during the rise process.

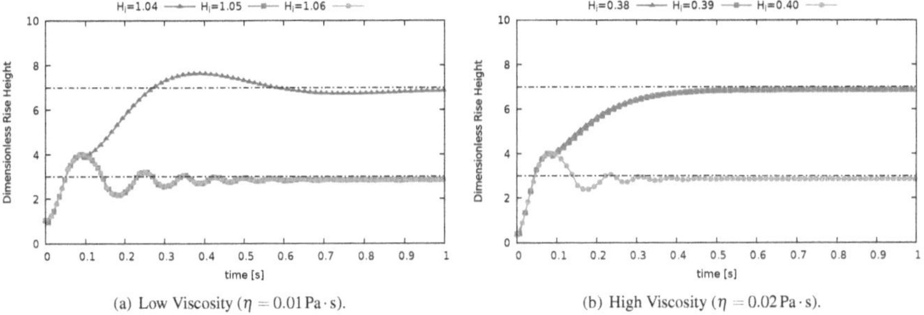

(a) Low Viscosity ($\eta = 0.01\,\text{Pa}\cdot\text{s}$).   (b) High Viscosity ($\eta = 0.02\,\text{Pa}\cdot\text{s}$).

Figure 12.23.: Dynamics of the structured capillary rise ($L/R = 1/5$).

Continuum mechanical simulation: We perform a full continuum mechanical simulation of a two-phase system that corresponds to the set of parameters defined in Example 12.10. To this end, we adapt the set of parameters for $\Omega = 1$ in Table 11.1 on p. 144 and choose

$$R = 5 \cdot 10^{-3}\,\text{m}, \; \rho = 80\,\frac{\text{kg}}{\text{m}^3}, \; g = 4\,\frac{\text{m}}{\text{s}^2}, \; \sigma = 0.08\,\frac{\text{N}}{\text{m}}. \tag{12.46}$$

This choice leads to the desired Bond number $\text{Bo} = 0.1$. The basic computational setup for FS3D is the same as in Section 11.3.

The results of the continuum mechanical simulation for a macroscopic slip length $L/R = 1/5$ are reported in Fig. 12.23. As expected from the simplified energy functional, the evolution chooses one of the two stable configurations depending on the initial potential energy. Following Figure 12.23(a), the critical initial height for a dynamic viscosity $\eta = 0.01\,\text{Pa}\cdot\text{s}$ lies within the interval

$$1.04 \leq \tilde{H}_c \leq 1.05.$$

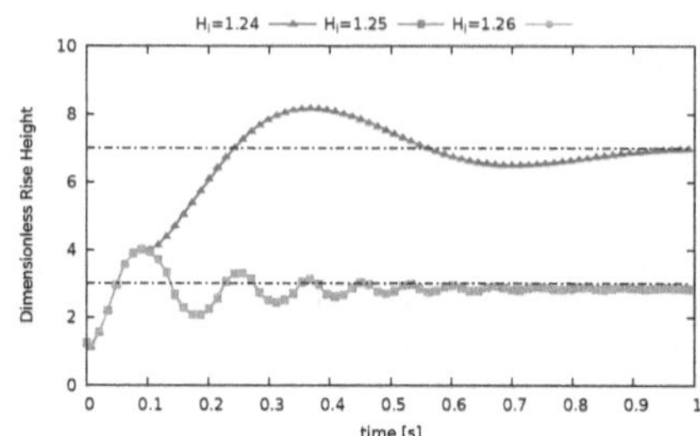

Figure 12.24.: Dynamics of the structured capillary rise with increased slip length ($L/R = 2/5$).

The latter value is significantly lower than 1.4 which corresponds to the potential barrier shown in Fig. 12.22. Clearly, this is due to the dissipative processes in the system. Obviously, the dissipation is increased when the dynamic viscosity is increased. According to the numerical results shown in Fig. 12.23(b), the critical height for a dynamic viscosity $\eta = 0.02\,\mathrm{Pa \cdot s}$ lies within the interval

$$0.39 \leq \tilde{H}_c \leq 0.40.$$

Note also that the rise height oscillations, which appear for initial heights H_i above the critical value, are damped much stronger for the increased viscosity.

The variation of the slip length has a similar effect on the dynamics. The results for $L/R = 2/5$ and $\eta = 0.01\,\mathrm{Pa \cdot s}$ are shown in Figure 12.24. The critical initial height increases due the reduced dissipation and lies within the interval

$$1.24 \leq \tilde{H}_c \leq 1.25.$$

In summary, the capillary rise problem for a structured surface shows an interesting dynamic behavior and shall be studied in more detail in future work.

Part IV.

Conclusion and Outlook

13. Concluding remarks

Finally, let us conclude this work with some final remarks. The aim is to put the present work into the context of the large body of research on the moving contact line problem and to give an outlook on future research directions. Please note that the following remarks reflect the author's personal perspective on the subject.

The kinematic evolution equation for the dynamic contact angle (4.12) is one of the main results of the present work. The application of (4.12) to the "standard model" (3.22) shows that regular solutions in the sense of (4.21) do not allow for a relaxation to the equilibrium state. To resolve this apparent paradox, there are two options in principle: One may either change the mathematical model or the solution concept, i.e. the desired regularity of the solution. There are many examples of both approaches present in the scientific literature on the topic.

There is a well-established mathematical theory of singularities in hydrodynamics; see, e.g., the monograph [EF15] and the references given therein. According to Eggers and Fontelos, "many key phenomena in physics and engineering can be understood as singularities in the solutions to the differential equations describing them" [EF15, Abstract]. Indeed, it has been shown that singular solutions to the standard model are able to describe wetting flows (and other hydrodynamic phenomena) in agreement with experimental data on the macroscopic scale [Dus76]. However, the presence of singularities may also lead to technical difficulties. For example, Sprittles and Shikhmurzaev found spurious multivaluedness and mesh-dependence of the pressure distribution in a finite element simulation of viscous flow in a wedge geometry for obtuse contact angles [SS11a, SS11b]. Specialized numerical methods are required to resolve this issue. The authors in [SS11a] developed a method that uses the knowledge about an eigensolution of the biharmonic equation to remove the artifacts in the pressure distribution. Another difficulty that arises from the presence of a singularity affects the well-posedness of the ordinary differential equation (4.6) defining the flow-map. If the well-posedness of the flow-map is lost, one cannot even define properly the concept of a co-moving control volume and it is not clear whether or not the transport of the interface and the contact line is still uniquely determined by the kinematic boundary conditions alone.

The second possible route to overcome the paradox is to change the mathematical model itself. The Interface Formation Model [Shi08] changes the kinematics fundamentally by relaxing the impermeability condition at the solid surface. The model proposed by Lukyanov and Pryer [LP17] is an interesting adaptation of the full interface formation model that might give rise to regular solutions. Indeed, we showed that, depending on the model parameters, the boundary conditions at the contact line are compatible for the later model. It would be interesting to see if the well-posedness of the model [LP17] can be proven mathematically and, if so, what the regularity of the solution happens to be. A further possibility in the framework of the standard model is to vary the slip length in such a way that it becomes infinite at the contact line (i.e. $L \to +\infty$). We have shown that, in this case, the contact angle is necessarily constant. An example of such a model is the one by Ruckenstein and Dunn [RD77], for which the slip length is inversely proportional to the height of the liquid film, i.e. $L \propto 1/h$, and, hence, infinite at the contact line. Another approach assumes that the solid is always covered by a so-called "precursor" film of finite thickness. In this case, no actual contact line is present and the problem is well-posed even with no-slip. According to Rednikov and Colinet [RC13, RC19], the moving contact line singularity can also be regularized completely by the incorporation of evaporation and condensation effects at the contact line (at least for volatile liquids). Moreover, rheological effects have been proposed as another regularization mechanism [AG02]. The kinematic evolution equation (4.12) might lead to interesting new insights into the qualitative properties of the model whenever the solution is indeed sufficiently regularized. Moreover, the kinematic evolution equation can also be used as a tool to derive new types of boundary conditions. The idea is to allow for a dynamic relaxation of the contact angle, in contrast to a strict geometric boundary condition for the interface orientation. The Generalized Navier boundary condition (GNBC) is an example of such a model but formulated in the diffuse interface context. A kinematic analysis of a formal approximation of the GNBC shows that, in this case, a functional relation between contact angle and contact line speed is obtained for quasi-stationary cases (i.e. for $\dot{\theta} = 0$).

The interface reconstruction methods developed in Chapter 8 allow for an accurate and kinematically consistent transport of the contact angle. In the next step, these methods will be generalized to three dimensions and to a geometrical VOF method on unstructured grids in openFoam [MMB18, MKB20]. In particular, the unstructured grid will allow for local adaptive mesh refinement, an important technique that is currently missing in FS3D. The increased accuracy in the contact angle transport will allow to implement new types of boundary conditions to model the wettability of the solid surface. For example, a GNBC type boundary condition could be realized with a contact angle evaluation based on the local interface reconstruction.

Part V.

Appendix

A. Proof of the entropy production theorem

Preliminaries: Transport theorems for moving hypersurfaces. In order to compute the entropy production, we need the following transport theorems reviewed in [BP16] (see also [PS16]). It is assumed that all fields are sufficiently regular on $\Omega^{\pm}(t)$ and admit continuous limits to the moving interface $\Sigma(t)$.

Lemma A.1 (Volume transport). *Let $V \subseteq \Omega$ be a* fixed *control volume and $\Sigma_V(t) := \Sigma(t) \cap V(t)$. Then the following transport theorem holds:*

$$\frac{d}{dt} \int_V \rho \phi \, dV = \int_{V \setminus \Sigma(t)} \rho \frac{D\phi}{Dt} \, dV + \int_{\Sigma_V(t)} [\![\dot{m}\phi]\!] \, dA - \int_{\partial V} \rho \phi \, v \cdot n_V \, dA. \tag{A.1}$$

Here n_V denotes the unit outer normal field to ∂V. In particular, for $V_\Sigma = v \cdot n_\Sigma$, i.e. $\dot{m} = 0$, we have

$$\frac{d}{dt} \int_V \rho \phi \, dV = \int_{V \setminus \Sigma(t)} \rho \frac{D\phi}{Dt} \, dV - \int_{\partial V} \rho \phi \, v \cdot n_V \, dA, \tag{A.2}$$

Lemma A.2 (Surface transport). *Let $V \subseteq \Omega$ be a* fixed *control volume and $\Sigma_V(t) := \Sigma(t) \cap V(t)$. Then the following transport theorem holds:*

$$\frac{d}{dt} \int_{\Sigma_V(t)} \phi^\Sigma \, dA = \int_{\Sigma_V(t)} \left(\frac{D^\Sigma \phi^\Sigma}{Dt} + \phi^\Sigma \operatorname{div}_\Sigma v_\Sigma \right) dA - \int_{\partial \Sigma_V(t)} \frac{\phi^\Sigma v_\Sigma \cdot n_V}{\sqrt{1 - (n_\Sigma \cdot n_V)^2}} \, dl. \tag{A.3}$$

Here n_V denotes the unit outer normal field to $\partial V(t)$.

Moreover, we need the following divergence theorems.

Lemma A.3 (Two-phase divergence theorem). *Let $V \subset \Omega \subset \mathbb{R}^3$ be open, bounded with ∂V piecewise $\mathscr{C}^1$ and unit outer normal field n. Let Σ be a $\mathscr{C}^1$-hypersurface. Then*

$$\int_{V \setminus \Sigma} \nabla \cdot f \, dV = \int_{\partial V} f \cdot n \, dA - \int_{\Sigma_V} [\![f]\!] \cdot n_\Sigma \, dA. \tag{A.4}$$

Lemma A.4 (Surface divergence theorem). *Let Σ be $\mathscr{C}^1$-surface with bounding curve $\partial \Sigma$ and conormal N. Let $f : \overline{\Sigma} \to \mathbb{R}^3$ be a vector field and assume that $\operatorname{div}_\Sigma f$ exists and is continuous. Then*

$$\int_{\partial \Sigma} f \cdot N \, dl = \int_\Sigma \operatorname{div}_\Sigma f \, dA + \int_\Sigma \kappa f \cdot n_\Sigma \, dA, \tag{A.5}$$

where κ denotes the mean curvature of Σ.

In the following, we consider the rate-of-change of the free energy defined as (see Definition 3.5)

$$\mathscr{E}(t) = \int_{\Omega \setminus \Sigma(t)} \frac{\rho v^2}{2} \, dV + \int_{\Sigma(t)} \sigma \, dA + \int_{W(t)} \sigma_w \, dA. \tag{A.6}$$

Theorem A.5. *Let σ be constant with $\sigma > 0$ and σ_w be a smooth function on $\partial\Omega$ such that $|\sigma_w(x)| < \sigma$ for all $x \in \partial\Omega$. Let $(v, p, \operatorname{gr}\overline{\Sigma})$ be a sufficiently regular (classical) solution of the system (3.9) - (3.12). Then, the rate-of-change of the free energy is given as*

$$\frac{d\mathscr{E}}{dt} = -2 \int_{\Omega \setminus \Sigma(t)} D : T^0 \, dV + \int_{\partial\Omega} \langle v, T n_{\partial\Omega} \rangle \, dA$$

$$- \int_{\Sigma(t)} ([\![T]\!] n_\Sigma + \sigma \kappa n_\Sigma) \cdot v \, dA + \sigma \int_{\Gamma(t)} (\cos\theta - \cos\theta_{\mathrm{eq}}) V_\Gamma \, dl, \tag{A.7}$$

where $\kappa = -\operatorname{div}_\Sigma n_\Sigma$ denotes the mean curvature of Σ, $D = \frac{1}{2}(\nabla v + \nabla v^\top)$ is the rate-of-deformation tensor and

$$T^0 = T - \frac{\operatorname{tr}(T)}{d}\,\mathbb{1}$$

is the traceless part of T (in dimension d).

Proof. We investigate the three contributions to the free energy separately, i.e.

$$\mathscr{E}(t) = \mathscr{E}_k(t) + \mathscr{E}_\Sigma(t) + \mathscr{E}_w(t).$$

(i) We start with the kinetic energy. Lemma A.1 yields for $V := \Omega$

$$\frac{d}{dt}\mathscr{E}_k := \frac{d}{dt}\int_{\Omega\setminus\Sigma(t)} \frac{\rho v^2}{2}\,dV = \int_{\Omega\setminus\Sigma(t)} \rho\frac{D}{Dt}\left(\frac{v^2}{2}\right)dV - \int_{\partial\Omega} \frac{\rho v^2}{2}\,\underbrace{v\cdot n_{\partial\Omega}}_{=0}\,dA$$

$$= \int_{\Omega\setminus\Sigma(t)} v\cdot\left(\rho\frac{Dv}{Dt}\right)dV.$$

Using (3.9), we get

$$\frac{d}{dt}\mathscr{E}_k = \int_{\Omega\setminus\Sigma(t)} \langle v, \nabla\cdot T\rangle\,dV,$$

where $T = -P\mathbb{1} + T^0$ is the Cauchy stress tensor. It follows from the identity

$$\nabla\cdot(Tv) = \langle v, \nabla\cdot T\rangle + \nabla v : T$$

and the two-phase divergence theorem (A.4) that

$$\int_{\Omega\setminus\Sigma(t)} \left(\langle v, \nabla\cdot T\rangle + \nabla v : T\right)dV = \int_{\Omega\setminus\Sigma(t)} \nabla\cdot Tv\,dV$$

$$= \int_{\partial\Omega} \langle Tv, n_{\partial\Omega}\rangle\,dA - \int_{\Sigma(t)} \langle[\![Tv]\!], n_\Sigma\rangle\,dA.$$

Hence, we obtain

$$\int_{\Omega\setminus\Sigma(t)} \langle v, \nabla\cdot T\rangle\,dV = \int_{\partial\Omega} \langle Tv, n_{\partial\Omega}\rangle\,dA - \int_{\Sigma(t)} \langle[\![Tv]\!], n_\Sigma\rangle\,dA - \int_{\Omega\setminus\Sigma(t)} \nabla v : T\,dV.$$

Making use of the symmetry of T and the continuity of v, we get

$$\frac{d}{dt}\mathscr{E}_k = \int_{\partial\Omega} \langle Tn_{\partial\Omega}, v\rangle\,dA - \int_{\Sigma(t)} \langle v, [\![T]\!]n_\Sigma\rangle\,dA - \int_{\Omega\setminus\Sigma(t)} \nabla v : T\,dV$$

Thanks to the incompressibility condition, the last term may be rewritten according to

$$\nabla v : T = -P\underbrace{\nabla v : \mathbb{1}}_{=\nabla\cdot v=0} + \nabla v : T^0 = D : T^0.$$

In total, we get for the rate-of-change of the kinetic energy

$$\frac{d}{dt}\mathscr{E}_k = \int_{\partial\Omega} \langle Tn_{\partial\Omega}, v\rangle\,dA - \int_{\Sigma(t)} \langle v, [\![T]\!]n_\Sigma\rangle\,dA - \int_{\Omega\setminus\Sigma(t)} D : T^0\,dV.$$

(ii) We compute the rate-of-change of the free surface surface using Lemma A.2 (for constant σ)

$$\frac{d}{dt}\mathscr{E}_\Sigma = \sigma\frac{d}{dt}\int_{\Sigma(t)} 1\,dA = \sigma\int_{\Sigma(t)} \operatorname{div}_\Sigma v\,dA. \tag{A.8}$$

(iii) For the case of variable wetting energy, i.e. $\sigma_w = \sigma_w(x)$, we show that

$$\frac{d}{dt}\mathscr{E}_w = \int_{\Gamma(t)} \sigma_w V_\Gamma \, dl.$$

It follows from Lemma A.2 that

$$\frac{d}{dt} \int_{W(t)} \sigma_w \, dA = \int_{W(t)} \left(\frac{D^W \sigma_w}{Dt} + \sigma_w \operatorname{div}_W v_W \right) dA,$$

where $v_W := \mathscr{P}_{\partial\Omega} v = v_\parallel$ is the velocity tangential to $\partial\Omega$ and D^W/Dt is the corresponding Lagrangian time-derivative. We make use of the identity

$$\operatorname{div}_W (\sigma_w v_\parallel) = \sigma_w \operatorname{div}_W v_W + v_\parallel \cdot \nabla_W \sigma_w$$

and arrive at

$$\frac{d}{dt} \int_{W(t)} \sigma_w \, dA = \int_{W(t)} \left(\frac{D^W \sigma_w}{Dt} - v_\parallel \cdot \nabla_W \sigma_w + \operatorname{div}_W (\sigma_w v_\parallel) \right) dA$$

$$= \int_{W(t)} \left(\underbrace{\frac{\partial \sigma_w}{\partial t}}_{=0} + \operatorname{div}_W (\sigma_w v_\parallel) \right) = \int_{\Gamma(t)} \sigma_w v_\parallel \cdot n_\Gamma \, dl.$$

(iv) To summarize, the time derivative of the total energy is given by

$$\frac{d}{dt}\mathscr{E} = \int_{\partial\Omega} \langle T n_{\partial\Omega}, v \rangle \, dA + \int_{\Sigma(t)} (\sigma \operatorname{div}_\Sigma v - \langle v, [\![T]\!] n_\Sigma \rangle) \, dA - \int_{\Omega\backslash\Sigma(t)} D : T^0 \, dV + \int_{\Gamma(t)} \sigma_w V_\Gamma \, dl.$$

To complete the proof, we use the surface divergence theorem (A.5) to compute

$$\int_{\Sigma(t)} \operatorname{div}_\Sigma v \, dA = \int_{\Gamma(t)} v \cdot N \, dl - \int_{\Sigma(t)} \kappa v \cdot n_\Sigma \, dA.$$

Note that $N = -\tau = \cos\theta n_\Gamma + \sin\theta n_{\partial\Omega}$ and, hence, it follows from (3.11) and (3.12) the identity

$$\int_{\Sigma(t)} \operatorname{div}_\Sigma v \, dA = \int_{\Gamma(t)} \cos\theta V_\Gamma \, dl - \int_{\Sigma(t)} \kappa v \cdot n_\Sigma \, dA.$$

Finally, we get

$$\frac{d}{dt}\mathscr{E} = \int_{\partial\Omega} \langle T n_{\partial\Omega}, v \rangle \, dA - \int_{\Sigma(t)} (\sigma \kappa n_\Sigma + [\![T]\!] n_\Sigma) \cdot v \, dA$$

$$- \int_{\Omega\backslash\Sigma(t)} D : T^0 \, dV + \int_{\Gamma(t)} (\sigma \cos\theta + \sigma_w) V_\Gamma \, dl.$$

The claim follows by rewriting the last term using (3.14), i.e.

$$\sigma \cos\theta + \sigma_w = \sigma \cos\theta - \sigma \cos\theta_{eq}.$$

$\square$

B. Kinematics of moving contact lines: Some mathematical details

This chapter (see also Appendix of [FKB19]) provides some technical details for the proofs given in Chapter 4.

Lemma B.1 (Separated local parametrization)**.** *Let* $\{\Sigma(t)\}_{t\in I}$ *be a* $\mathscr{C}^{1,2}$*-family of moving hypersurfaces and* (t_0,x_0) *be an inner point of* $\mathscr{M} = \mathrm{gr}\,\Sigma$. *Then there exists an open neighborhood* $U \subseteq \mathbb{R}^4$ *of* (t_0,x_0), $\delta, \varepsilon > 0$ *and a* $\mathscr{C}^1$*-parametrization*

$$\phi : \underbrace{(t_0 - \delta, t_0 + \delta)}_{=:I_\delta(t_0)} \times B_\varepsilon^2(0) \to \mathscr{M} \cap U$$

of $\mathscr{M}$ *such that* $\phi(t_0,0) = (t_0,x_0)$ *and*

$$\phi(t,\cdot) : B_\varepsilon^2(0) \to \{t\} \times \Sigma(t)$$

is a $\mathscr{C}^2$*-parametrization of* $\Sigma(t)$. *In particular*

$$\phi(t,u) = (t, \hat{\phi}(t,u)),$$

with a $\mathscr{C}^1$*-function* $\hat{\phi}$.

Proof. By definition of a $\mathscr{C}^{1,2}$-family of moving hypersurfaces, there is $\eta > 0$ and an open neighborhood of $(t_0,x_0) \in \mathbb{R}^4$ and a local $\mathscr{C}^1$-parametrization

$$\psi = (\psi_t, \psi_x) : \mathbb{R}^3 \subset B_\eta^3(0) \to \mathrm{gr}\Sigma \cap U \tag{B.1}$$

such that $\psi(0) = (t_0,x_0)$ and $\psi_x(u) \in \Sigma(\psi_t(u))$ for all $u \in B_\eta^3(0)$. The goal is to find a coordinate transformation

$$T : I_\delta(t_0) \times B_\varepsilon^2(0) \to B_\eta^3(0)$$

such that

$$\psi_t(T(s,y_1,y_2)) = s.$$

Since $\psi'(0,0,0)$ is injective, there is $i \in \{1,2,3\}$ such that

$$(\partial_{u_i} \psi_t)(0,0,0) \neq 0, \tag{B.2}$$

where we may assume $i = 1$. We now choose a special function T of the form

$$T(s,y_1,y_2) = (\varphi(s,y_1,y_2),y_1,y_2)$$

and look for a function φ satisfying

$$\psi_t(\varphi(s,y_1,y_2),y_1,y_2) = s \quad \Leftrightarrow \quad 0 = f(s,y_1,y_2;\varphi(s,y_1,y_2)).$$

The $\mathscr{C}^1$-function $f(s,y_1,y_2;\varphi) := \psi_t(\varphi,y_1,y_2) - s$ satisfies $f(t_0,0,0;0) = 0$ and (B.2) implies

$$\partial_\varphi f(t_0,0,0;0) \neq 0.$$

Now the claim follows by the Implicit Function Theorem. $\qquad\qquad\square$

Note that exactly the same procedure yields a $\mathscr{C}^1$-parametrization of the submanifold $\mathrm{gr}\,\Gamma$ of the form

$$\phi : (t_0 - \delta, t_0 + \delta) \times (-\varepsilon, \varepsilon) \to \mathrm{gr}\,\Gamma \cap U$$

such that $\phi(t_0, \cdot)$ is a $\mathscr{C}^1$-parametrization of $\Gamma(t_0)$. As a consequence of that, we can give an explicit characterization of the tangent spaces of $\mathrm{gr}\,\Sigma$ and $\mathrm{gr}\,\Gamma$.

Lemma B.2 (Tangent spaces). *The tangent space of* $\mathrm{gr}\,\Sigma$ *at the point* (t,x) *is given by*

$$T_{\mathrm{gr}\Sigma}(t,x) = \{\lambda\,(1, V_\Sigma n_\Sigma(t,x)) + (0, \tau) : \lambda \in \mathbb{R},\ \tau \in T_{\Sigma(t)}(x)\}.$$

Likewise, the tangent space of $\mathrm{gr}\,\Gamma$ *at the point* (t,x) *is given by*

$$T_{\mathrm{gr}\Gamma}(t,x) = \{\lambda\,(1, V_\Gamma n_\Gamma(t,x)) + (0, \tau) : \lambda \in \mathbb{R},\ \tau \in T_{\Gamma(t)}(t,x)\}.$$

Proof. We make use of the parametrization constructed in Lemma B.1.

For $(t_0, x_0) \in \mathrm{gr}\,\Sigma$ choose a $\mathscr{C}^1$-parametrization

$$\phi : (t_0 - \delta, t_0 + \delta) \times B_\varepsilon^2(0) \to \mathscr{M} \cap U, \quad \phi(t, u_1, u_2) = (t, \hat\phi(t, u_1, u_2))$$

such that $\phi(t_0, 0, 0) = (t_0, x_0)$. A basis for the tangent space $T_{\mathrm{gr}\Sigma}(t_0, x_0)$ is then given by

$$\{\partial_t \phi(t_0,0,0), \partial_{u_1}\phi(t_0,0,0), \partial_{u_2}\phi(t_0,0,0)\}$$
$$= \{(1, \partial_t\hat\phi(t_0,0,0)), (0, \partial_{u_1}\hat\phi(t_0,0,0)), (0, \partial_{u_2}\hat\phi(t_0,0,0))\},$$

where the vectors

$$v_1 := \partial_{u_1}\hat\phi(t_0,0,0) \quad \text{and} \quad v_2 := \partial_{u_2}\hat\phi(t_0,0,0)$$

constitute a basis of $T_{\Sigma(t_0)}(x_0)$. By definition of the normal velocity V_Σ, we have

$$\partial_t\hat\phi(t_0,0,0) = \langle \partial_t\hat\phi(t_0,0,0), n_\Sigma(t_0,x_0)\rangle\, n_\Sigma(t_0,x_0) + \mathscr{P}_\Sigma\,\partial_t\hat\phi(t_0,0,0)$$
$$= V_\Sigma(t_0,x_0)n_\Sigma(t_0,x_0) + \mathscr{P}_\Sigma\,\partial_t\hat\phi(t_0,0,0).$$

Since the second term can be expressed in terms of v_1 and v_2, we obtain a basis of the desired form

$$\{(1, V_\Sigma(t_0,x_0)n_\Sigma(t_0,x_0)), (0, \partial_{u_1}\hat\phi(t_0,0,0)), (0, \partial_{u_2}\hat\phi(t_0,0,0))\}.$$

For $(t_0, x_0) \in \mathrm{gr}\,\Gamma$ choose a $\mathscr{C}^1$-parametrization

$$\phi : (t_0 - \delta, t_0 + \delta) \times (-\varepsilon, \varepsilon) \to \mathrm{gr}\,\Gamma \cap U, \quad \phi(t, u) = (t, \hat\phi(t, u)),$$

such that $\phi(t_0, 0) = (t_0, x_0)$. The same procedure as above shows that the set

$$\{(1, V_\Gamma n_\Gamma(t_0,x_0)), (0, \partial_u\hat\phi(t_0,0))\}$$

is a basis of the Tangent space $T_{\mathrm{gr}\Gamma}(t_0, x_0)$, where $\partial_u\hat\phi(t_0,0)$ is a basis of $T_{\Gamma(t_0)}(x_0)$. $\qquad\square$

Lemma B.3 (Signed distance function). *Let* $\{\Sigma(t)\}_{t\in I}$ *be a* $\mathscr{C}^{1,2}$-*family of moving hypersurfaces and* (t_0, x_0) *be an inner point of* $\mathscr{M} = \mathrm{gr}\,\Sigma$. *Then there exists an open neighborhood* $U \subset \mathbb{R}^4$ *of* (t_0, x_0) *and* $\varepsilon > 0$ *such that the map*

$$X : (\mathscr{M} \cap U) \times (-\varepsilon, \varepsilon) \to \mathbb{R}^4,$$
$$X(t,x,h) := (t, x + h n_\Sigma(t,x))$$

is a diffeomorphism onto its image

$$\mathscr{N}^\varepsilon := X((\mathscr{M} \cap U) \times (-\varepsilon \times \varepsilon)) \subset \mathbb{R}^4,$$

i.e. X is invertible there and both X and X^{-1} *are* $\mathscr{C}^1$. *The inverse function has the form*

$$X^{-1}(t,x) = (\pi(t,x), d(t,x))$$

with $\mathscr{C}^1$-*functions* π *and* d *on* $\mathscr{N}^\varepsilon$.

Proof. According to Lemma B.1, we can choose a local $\mathscr{C}^1$-parametrization ϕ of $\mathscr{M}$ of the form (with $\delta, \varepsilon > 0$, $U_0 \subset \mathbb{R}^4$ open)

$$\phi : \underbrace{(t_0 - \delta, t_0 + \delta)}_{=:I_\delta(t_0)} \times B^2_\varepsilon(0) \to \mathscr{M} \cap U_0,$$

where ϕ has the following form

$$\phi(t,u) = (t, \hat{\phi}(t,u)), \quad \phi^{-1}(t,x) = (t, u(t,x)).$$

Then X can be expressed as

$$X(t,x,h) = X^0(\phi^{-1}(t,x), h)$$

with

$$X^0(t,u,h) := (t, \hat{\phi}(t,u) + h n_\Sigma(t, \hat{\phi}(t,u))).$$

The function

$$X^0 : I_\delta(t_0) \times B^2_\varepsilon(0) \times \mathbb{R} \to \mathbb{R}^4$$

is continuously differentiable (since $\hat{\phi} \in \mathscr{C}^1(I_\delta(t_0) \times B^2_\varepsilon(0))$ and $n_\Sigma \in \mathscr{C}^1(\mathscr{M})$) and the Jacobian of X^0 has the form

$$(DX^0)(t,u,h) = \begin{pmatrix} 1 & 0 & 0 & 0 \\ * & & & \\ * & & DX^0_t(u,h) & \\ * & & & \end{pmatrix},$$

where X^0_t corresponds to X^0 at fixed t, i.e.

$$X^0_t(u,h) := \hat{\phi}(t,u) + h n_\Sigma(t, \hat{\phi}(t,u)).$$

Obviously, DX^0 is invertible at (t,u,h) if and only if DX^0_t is invertible at (u,h). The invertibility of $DX^0_{t_0}$ at the point $(0,0)$ is a well-known result from the theory of $\mathscr{C}^2$-hypersurfaces. In particular, one can show by the Banach contraction principle that DX^0_t is invertible on $B_{\frac{\varepsilon}{2}}(0) \times (-\varepsilon(t), \varepsilon(t))$ if (see [PS16], chapter 2.3 for details)

$$\varepsilon(t) \|\nabla_\Sigma n_\Sigma(t, \hat{\phi}(t, \cdot))\|_{\mathscr{C}\left(\overline{B_{\frac{\varepsilon}{2}}(0)}\right)} < 1. \tag{B.3}$$

Since $n_\Sigma \in \mathscr{C}^1(\mathscr{M})$, we can choose for every compact subset $I \subset I_\delta(t_0)$ an $\hat{\varepsilon} > 0$ such that (B.3) holds for all $t \in I$ with $\varepsilon(t) := \hat{\varepsilon}$. In particular, DX^0 is invertible at the point $(t_0, 0, 0)$. Now it follows from the Implicit Function Theorem that there are open neighborhoods V of $(t_0, 0, 0)$ and $U \subseteq U_0$ of $(t_0, x_0) \in \mathbb{R}^4$ such that $X^0 : V \to U$ is a bijection and both X^0 and $(X^0)^{-1}$ are $\mathscr{C}^1$. Since the parametrization $\phi : I_\delta(t_0) \times B^2_\varepsilon(0) \to \mathscr{M} \cap U_0$ is a diffeomorphism between manifolds, the claim for X follows from the properties of X^0. $\qquad\square$

C. Some geometrical relations

Spherical cap in three dimensions: Let L and h be the base radius and the height of the spherical cap in three dimensional space and R be the radius of the corresponding sphere and θ be the contact angle. Then we have

$$h = R(1 - \cos\theta), \quad V = \frac{4}{3}\pi R^3 = \frac{\pi}{3}h^2 \underbrace{(3R - h)}_{\geq R}.$$

Since $L = R\sin\theta$, one can rewrite the equation for the height to find

$$h = \frac{L(1 - \cos\theta)}{\sin\theta} = L\tan(\theta/2).$$

Using the geometric relation (2.10), the formula for the height of a spherical cap as a function of the volume and the contact angle follows:

$$h_{\text{cap}}(\theta, V) = V^{1/3} g(\theta)\tan(\theta/2) =: V^{1/3}\tilde{g}(\theta). \tag{C.1}$$

Note that the function $\tilde{g}$ is monotonically increasing on $[0, \pi]$ with $\tilde{g}(0) = 0$ and $\tilde{g}(\pi) = (6/\pi)^{1/3}$. An equivalent formulation in terms of L and V is obtained from (2.10) according to

$$h_{\text{cap}}(L, V) = V^{1/3}\tilde{g}\left(g^{-1}\left(\frac{L}{V^{1/3}}\right)\right) = L\tan\left(\frac{1}{2}g^{-1}\left(\frac{L}{V^{1/3}}\right)\right). \tag{C.2}$$

D. On the implementation of the Boundary ELVIRA method

The aim of this chapter is to give some details on the implementation of the (Boundary) ELVIRA method in two dimensions. The complete source code in FORTRAN can be found in an open research data repository [FMB20b].

As discussed in Section 8.2, the implementation of the Boundary ELVIRA method requires the evaluation of the functional (for given data α_{ij})

$$\mathscr{F}_b = \sum_{k=-2}^{2} \sum_{l=0}^{2} [\tilde{\alpha}_{i+k,1+l}(n) - \alpha_{i+k,1+l}]^2, \tag{D.1}$$

where $\tilde{\alpha}_{i+k,1+l}(n)$ is the volume fraction in cell $(i+k, 1+l)$ which is induced by a straight line with orientation n satisfying $\tilde{\alpha}_{i,1}(n) = \alpha_{i,1}$. We present a simple and efficient method to compute the induced volume fractions on structured Cartesian grids with fixed mesh spacings Δx_1 and Δx_2.

Representation of the discrete volume fractions: The discrete volume fractions α_{ij} on a Cartesian mesh with fixed mesh spacings can be understood as the evaluation of the continuous function

$$f(x) = \frac{1}{|V_0|} \int_{V_0} \chi(x+x')\,dV(x') \tag{D.2}$$

at the cell centers. Here, V_0 denotes the control volume

$$V_0 = \left[-\frac{\Delta x_1}{2}, \frac{\Delta x_1}{2}\right] \times \left[-\frac{\Delta x_2}{2}, \frac{\Delta x_2}{2}\right].$$

So, in fact, the discrete volume fractions are obtained by a volume averaging of the characteristic function. Clearly, the indicator function χ is recovered in the limit $\Delta x_1, \Delta x_2 \to 0$.

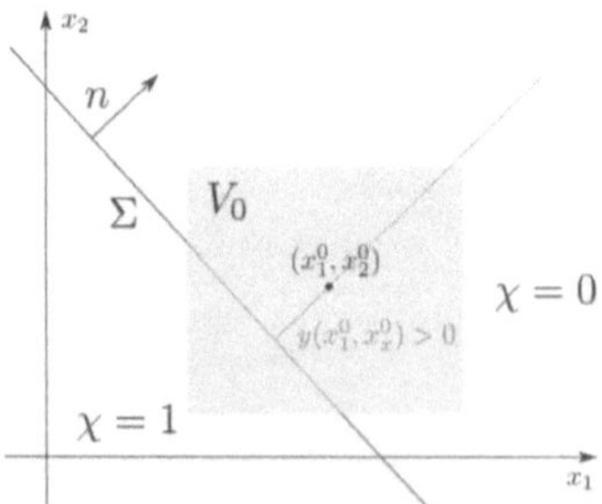

Figure D.1.: Illustration of the setup and the coordinate transformation.

The main observation, which allows to greatly simplify the formulation, is the *symmetry* of f if Σ is a straight line in two dimensions (or a plane plane in three dimensions). Obviously, the function $f(x)$ depends only on the signed distance of x relative to the planar interface Σ. Let us assume that the planar interface is described by the equation

$$n_1 x_1 + n_2 x_2 = \lambda,$$

where the vector $n = (n_1, n_2)$ with $|n| = 1$ describes the interface orientation (pointing outwards with respect to $\chi = 1$; see Fig. D.1). Then, the signed distance is given by the expression

$$\mathrm{dist}(x, \Sigma) = (x_1, x_2) \cdot (n_1, n_2) - \lambda.$$

Coordinate transformation: In order to obtain simpler formulas in the following, we rescale the signed distance and define the new variable (see Fig. D.1)

$$y(x_1, x_2) := 2 \frac{(x_1, x_2) \cdot (n_1, n_2) - \lambda}{|n_1| \Delta x_1 + |n_2| \Delta x_2}. \tag{D.3}$$

Now, we can express the function f as

$$\boxed{f(x_1, x_2) = \psi(y(x_1, x_2)) + \frac{1}{2}.} \tag{D.4}$$

In particular, the whole information about the volume fraction field for the planar interface is encoded in a one-dimensional function[1]. Here, the offset $1/2$ has been chosen in order to make the function ψ defined by the relation (D.4) *antisymmetric*. The gradient of f is given as

$$\nabla f(x) = \psi'(y(x)) \nabla y(x) = \psi'(y(x)) \frac{2n}{|n_1| \Delta x_1 + |n_2| \Delta x_2}. \tag{D.5}$$

Hence, we indeed have $\nabla f \propto n$. The Youngs reconstruction method (7.18) is nothing but a finite differences approximation of ∇f. But the problem is the lack of regularity of the function f (see below). As a consequence, the Youngs method fails to reconstruct an arbitrary straight line exactly.

Properties of the function ψ: An explicit expression for ψ can be found using the formula for the volume fraction given in [GLN$^+$99], [SZ00]. Following [GLN$^+$99], we have the relations

$$f = 0 \Leftrightarrow \psi = -\frac{1}{2} \quad \text{if } y \geq 1 \quad \text{and} \quad f = 1 \Leftrightarrow \psi = \frac{1}{2} \quad \text{if } y \leq -1. \tag{D.6}$$

The function ψ for $y \in [-1, 1]$ is given as

$$\psi = \psi(y; \beta) = \frac{(1-y)^2 - F_2(\beta - y) - F_2(-\beta - y)}{2(1 - \beta^2)} - \frac{1}{2}, \quad -1 \leq y \leq 1 \tag{D.7}$$

and has only one scalar parameter (reflecting the orientation of the plane) given as

$$\beta = \frac{||n_1| \Delta x_1 - |n_2| \Delta x_2|}{|n_1| \Delta x_1 + |n_2| \Delta x_2} \in [0, 1]. \tag{D.8}$$

For a fixed value of β, we write $\psi(y) = \psi(y; \beta)$ for short. Here, the functions $F_n : \mathbb{R} \to \mathbb{R}$ are defined as

$$F_n(x) := \begin{cases} x^n & \text{if } x \geq 0 \\ 0 & \text{otherwise} \end{cases}.$$

Lemma D.1 (Properties of ψ). *It is easy to verify the following properties of the function $\psi : \mathbb{R} \to \mathbb{R}$ (see Fig. D.2):*

---

[1]Note that this is true for planar interfaces in any dimension.

(i) ψ is antisymmetric, *i.e. it holds that* $\psi(-y) = -\psi(y) \ \forall y \in \mathbb{R}$. *It is, therefore, sufficient to consider the case* $y \geq 0$. *Since* $0 \leq \beta \leq 1$, *we have*

$$\psi(y) = \frac{(1-y)^2 - F_2(\beta - y)}{2(1-\beta^2)} - \frac{1}{2} \tag{D.9}$$

for $0 \leq y \leq 1$.

(ii) For $\beta < 1$, *the function* ψ *is* globally *continuously differentiable with (symmetric) derivative*

$$\psi'(y) = \frac{y - 1 + F_1(\beta - y)}{1 - \beta^2}$$

for $0 \leq y \leq 1$ *and* $\psi'(y) = 0$ *for* $y \geq 1$. *In particular,* ψ *is a* linear *function on* $[0, \beta]$ *which can be expressed as*

$$\psi(y) = -\frac{y}{1+\beta}, \quad 0 \leq y \leq \beta. \tag{D.10}$$

(iii) ψ *is* not *globally* $\mathscr{C}^2$ *since* ψ'' *exhibits jump discontinuities at* $\pm\beta$ *and* ± 1. *More precisely, the (antisymmetric) second derivative is given by the expression*

$$\psi''(y) = \begin{cases} 0 & \text{if } 0 \leq y \leq \beta \\ \frac{1}{1-\beta^2} & \text{if } \beta \leq y \leq 1 \\ 0 & \text{if } 1 \leq y \end{cases}. \tag{D.11}$$

(iv) ψ *is monotonically decreasing on* $[-1, 1]$ *and, hence, invertible there with (antisymmetric) inverse* $\Psi :$ $[-1/2, 1/2] \to [-1, 1]$. *For* $\beta < 1$ *the inverse is given as*

$$\Psi(\psi; \beta) = \begin{cases} -(1+\beta)\,\psi & \text{for } \psi \in [-\psi_\beta, 0] \\ 1 - \sqrt{2(1-\beta^2)(\psi + 1/2)} & \text{for } \psi \in [-\frac{1}{2}, -\psi_\beta] \end{cases}, \tag{D.12}$$

where

$$\psi_\beta = \frac{\beta}{1+\beta} \in \left[0, \frac{1}{2}\right].$$

(v) Note that in the special case $\beta = 1$, *i.e.* $\vec{n} = e_i$, *the function* ψ *is linear within* $[-1, 1]$ *with*

$$\psi(y; \beta = 1) = -\frac{y}{2}. \tag{D.13}$$

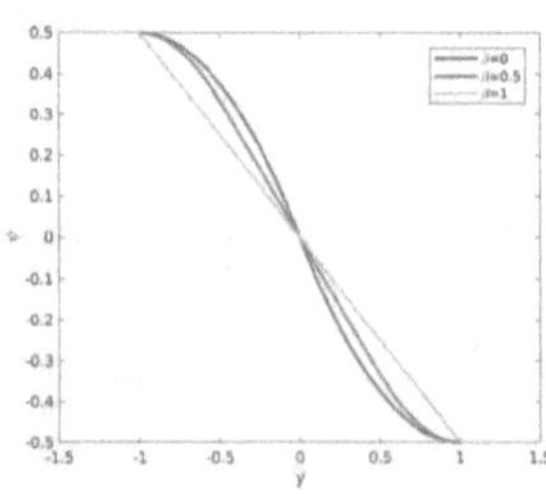

Figure D.2.: The function ψ for different values of β.

Evaluation of the (Boundary) ELVIRA functional: Thanks to the definitions and properties given above, we can now evaluate the Boundary ELVIRA functional (D.1) (and, similarly, the ELVIRA functional) quite efficiently. Consider a cell adjacent to the boundary with index $(i,1)$; see Fig. D.3 for an example.

Then, the algorithm to calculate the induced volume fraction $\tilde{\alpha}_{i+k,1+l}(\hat{n})$ in the cell with index $(i+k,1+l)$ for an candidate normal vector $\hat{n} = (\hat{n}_1, \hat{n}_2)$ proceeds as follows:

(1) Compute the parameter β according to (D.8), i.e.

$$\beta(\hat{n}) = \frac{||\hat{n}_1|\Delta x_1 - |\hat{n}_2|\Delta x_2|}{|\hat{n}_1|\Delta x_1 + |\hat{n}_2|\Delta x_2} \in [0,1].$$

(2) Compute the y-coordinate of the cell $(i,1)$ using the inverse of ψ, i.e.

$$y_{i,1} = \Psi(\alpha_{i,1} - 1/2; \beta(\hat{n})).$$

(3) Compute the y-coordinate of the cell $(i+k,1+l)$ using the identity

$$\nabla_{x}y(x) = \frac{2\,\hat{n}}{|\hat{n}_1|\Delta x_1 + |\hat{n}_2|\Delta x_2}.$$

for the (constant) gradient of y, i.e.

$$y_{i+k,1+l} = y_{i,1} + 2\frac{k\Delta x_1\,\hat{n}_1 + j\Delta x_2\,\hat{n}_2}{|\hat{n}_1|\Delta x_1 + |\hat{n}_2|\Delta x_2}.$$

(4) Finally compute the volume fraction according to

$$\tilde{\alpha}_{i+k,1+l}(\hat{n}) = \psi\left(y_{i+k,1+l}, \beta(\hat{n})\right) + \frac{1}{2}.$$

Note that the candidate orientations $\hat{n}$ are obtained from central-, forward- and backward-finite-differences of column or row sum as described in Section 7.3 and 8.2, respectively.

0.955	0.144	0.000	0.000	0.000
1.000	0.784	0.002	0.000	0.000
1.000	1.000	0.500	0.000	0.000

Figure D.3.: Setup for the Boundary ELVIRA method on a 5×3-stencil in 2D.